Studies in the Theory of Ideology

John B. Thompson

University of California Press
Berkeley   Los Angeles

First published in the United States in 1984
by the University of California Press
Reprinted 1985

Library of Congress Cataloging in Publication Data
Thompson, John B.
  Studies in the theory of ideology.
  Bibliography: p.
  Includes index.
  B 823.3.T54   1985   84–16129

  ISBN 0–520–05411–3 [clothbound]
  ISBN 0–520–05412–1 [paper]

Printed in Great Britain

Contents

Preface and Acknowledgements

The essays which comprise this volume were written between 1979 and 1984. They are the outcome of an attempt to assess some of the outstanding contemporary contributions to the theory of ideology. I have tried to bring out the value of these contributions as well as their limitations, their innovations as well as their faults. I have also tried, in the course of these critical appraisals, to formulate the elements of a positive account of ideology. This account draws upon ideas initially sketched in my *Critical Hermeneutics* and defines an approach which will be developed in my forthcoming book, *The Interpretation of Ideology*.

Most of the essays were written during the tenure of a Research Fellowship at Jesus College, Cambridge. I wish to thank the Fellows of the College for their generous and extended support.

I also wish to thank the individuals, too numerous to cite here, who have provided me with comments and criticisms during the past five years. Some of these individuals are identified in the notes to the essays; but Anthony Giddens and David Held deserve to be mentioned in a more prominent place. They have read and re-read these essays, pointing out difficulties, offering suggestions and encouraging me to develop my ideas. Their sympathetic criticism and constant support have been an invaluable aid.

Some of the essays have been published in journals or anthologies; they are reprinted here with permission. Details of original publication are as follows:

'Ideology and the social imaginary: an appraisal of Castoriadis and Lefort', *Theory and Society*, 11 (1982), pp. 659–81. The essay printed here is a modified and expanded version of the original article.

'Theories of ideology and methods of discourse analysis: towards a framework for the analysis of ideology' was published in a reduced and altered form in the *Canadian Journal of Political and Social Theory*. Part I of the essay was published under the title of 'Ideology and the critique of domination, I', in vol. 7, nos. 1–2 (1983), pp. 163–83; part III of the essay appeared under the title of 'Ideology and the critique of domination, II', in vol. 8, nos. 1–2 (1984), pp. 179–96; part II of the essay is published here for the first time.

'The theory of structuration: an assessment of the contribution of Anthony Giddens' will be published in a volume provisionally entitled *Critical Theory of the Industrial Societies*, ed. David Held and John B. Thompson (Cambridge: Cambridge University Press, forthcoming).

'Ideology and the analysis of discourse: a critical introduction to the work of Michel Pêcheux', *Sociological Review*, 31 (1983), pp. 211–35.

'Universal pragmatics: Habermas's proposals for the analysis of language and truth' is a slightly modified version of my article in *Habermas: Critical Debates*, ed. John B. Thompson and David Held (London: Macmillan, 1982), pp. 116–33.

'Rationality and social rationalization: an assessment of Habermas's theory of communicative action', *Sociology*, 17 (1983), pp. 278–94.

J.B.T., Cambridge, April 1984

Introduction

Few areas of social inquiry are more exciting and important, and yet at the same time more marked by controversy and dispute, than the area staked out by the theory of ideology. To some extent the controversial character of the study of ideology is a product of the history of the term 'ideology'. Derived from the so-called *'idéologues'* of post-Revolutionary France, the term quickly acquired a negative sense, as the *idéologues* were accused by Napoleon of perpetrating doctrines which were responsible for the country's misfortune. The negative connotation of the term 'ideology' was preserved by Marx and Engels in their swingeing attack on *Die deutsche Ideologie*. This ideology of the Germanic world, by which they meant the views expressed by 'Young Hegelians' such as Ludwig Feuerbach and Max Stirner, was too preoccupied with ideas and the critique of ideas; it thus failed to see that ideas and other 'products of consciousness' are rooted in the material conditions of social life. Since its early appearances in France and in the writings of Marx and Engels, the term 'ideology' has been taken up by other authors and other disciplines. It has been appropriated by sociologists, by anthropologists, by political analysts; it has been integrated into the corpus of concepts employed by the social sciences. Yet however much these disciplines would like to domesticate the concept of ideology, the term cannot be easily stripped of its negative sense. Few people today would proudly proclaim themselves to be 'ideologists', whereas many would not hesitate to declare that they were conservatives, socialists or revolutionaries. Ideology is the thought of the *other*, the thought of someone other than oneself. To characterize a view as 'ideological' is *already* to criticize it, for 'ideology' is not a neutral term. Hence the study of ideology is a controversial, conflict-laden activity. It is an activity which plunges the analyst into a realm of claim and counter-claim, of allegation, accusation and riposte. It is also an activity which presses to the heart of issues concerning the nature of social inquiry and its relation to the conduct of critique.

If the theory of ideology has been marked since its origins by controversy and dispute, it is only in recent years that this theory has been enriched and elaborated through a reflection on *language*. For increasingly it has been realized that 'ideas' do not drift through the social world like clouds in a summer sky, occasionally divulging their contents with a clap of thunder and a flash of light. Rather, ideas circulate in the social world as utterances, as expressions, as words which are spoken or inscribed. Hence to study ideology is, in some part and in some way, to study language in the social world. It is to study the ways in which language is used in everyday social life, from the most mundane encounter between friends and family members to the most privileged forums of political debate. It is to study the ways in which the multifarious uses of language intersect with power, nourishing it, sustaining it, enacting it. The theory of ideology, thus enriched and elaborated through a reflection on language, enriches in turn our view of language. For it directs our attention towards aspects of language use which have been neglected or suppressed by some perspectives in linguistics and the philosophy of language. To explore the interrelations between language and ideology is to turn away from the analysis of well-formed sentences or systems of signs, focusing instead on the ways in which expressions serve as a means of action and interaction, a medium through which history is produced and society reproduced. The theory of ideology invites us to see that language is not simply a structure which can be employed for communication or entertainment, but a social-historical phenomenon which is embroiled in human conflict.

The studies which comprise this volume may be regarded as a series of attempts to explore the relation between the theory of ideology and the analysis of language. The studies focus on contemporary thinkers whose work contributes to our understanding of this relation. In many cases these thinkers are authors who write in French or German and whose writings are not (or not yet) available in English. My decision to concentrate on their work is not the outcome of some penchant for the obscure; it stems from the conviction that these thinkers have made, and continue to make, contributions which are of great value and which deserve to be more widely discussed in the English-speaking world. I have sought to facilitate this discussion by providing critical introductions to their work. I have not tried to offer a comprehensive survey of contemporary debates, nor have I tried to tell a progressive story of theoretical enlightenment. What follows is a series of studies, a series of *ballons d'essai*, each of which engages with a particular thinker (or thinkers) and each of which stands on its own. These essays do not form a systematic treatise on the theory of ideology but rather a systematic reflection on contemporary theories of ideology, on ways of thinking about ideology and its relation to language, action and social life. The following studies are not an alternative to a systematic account of ideology, even less a candidate for such an account. They are a prelude to the development of a framework for the interpretation and critique of ideology, a framework which I shall develop in a subsequent volume.

The elements of a positive account are nevertheless evident in each of the essays. These elements are introduced in the context of my critical discussions of contemporary thinkers, in an attempt to move beyond the limitations of their work. These critical discussions and constructive proposals are developed along certain lines which run throughout the essays, lines which form, in my view, the central contours of the theory of ideology. In this introduction I want to sketch these central contours. In so doing I shall provide an overview of the essays and shall highlight some of the ways in which the material discussed therein contributes to the theory of ideology. I shall also present some of the elements which form the basis of my own account.

CONCEPTUALIZATION OF IDEOLOGY

The term 'ideology', as noted above, has a long and complex history, appearing in the writings of many authors and infiltrating nearly every modern discipline in the social sciences and humanities. A survey of its occurrences in the literature today would show that the term is used in two fundamentally differing ways. On the one hand, 'ideology' is employed by many authors as if it were a purely descriptive term: one speaks of 'systems of thought', of 'systems of belief' of 'symbolic practices' which pertain to social action or political projects. This use of the term gives rise to what may be called a *neutral conception* of ideology. No attempt is made, on the basis of this conception, to distinguish between the kinds of action or projects which ideology animates; ideology is present in every political programme, irrespective of whether the programme is directed towards the preservation or transformation of the social order. There is, however, another sense of 'ideology' which is evident in the current literature. In the writings of some authors, ideology is essentially linked to the process of sustaining asymmetrical relations of power – that is, to the process of maintaining domination. This use of the term expresses what may be called a *critical conception* of ideology. It preserves the negative connotation which has been conveyed by the term throughout most of its history and it binds the analysis of ideology to the question of critique.

The essays in this volume offer a plea for, as well as a reformulation and defence of, a critical conception of ideology. In my survey of recent work in English on the theory of ideology (essay 3), I criticize the ways in which authors such as Martin Seliger and Alvin Gouldner conceive of ideology, for their accounts effectively strip the term of its negative sense. I then attempt, in the final part of essay 3 and elsewhere, to formulate the key features of a critical conception. To study ideology, I propose, is to study the ways in which meaning (or signification) serves to sustain relations of domination. I argue that, in order to clarify the nature of such a study, we must provide a cogent analysis of power and domination within the context of an account of the relations between action, institutions and social structure. Here I do not claim to provide this analysis, nor do I develop a thorough and detailed account of the latter relations. However, I do offer the beginnings of such an analysis in the final part of essay 3; and in my study of 'the theory of structuration' (essay 4), I assess one of the leading attempts to explicate the relations between action and structure. In these various ways I seek to substantiate the view that the study of ideology can be satisfactorily pursued only in the context of a more general *social theory*.

By situating the study of ideology within the context of social theory, we can illuminate some of the misleading assumptions which have often been associated with the notion of ideology. For it has often been assumed that ideology operates like a sort of social cement, binding the members of a society together by providing them with collectively shared values and norms. The pervasiveness of this assumption is attested to by the number of times that I return to it in the essays that follow. Yet however pervasive it may be, this assumption is highly questionable. There is little evidence to suggest that certain values or beliefs are shared by all (or even most) members of modern industrial societies. On the contrary, it seems more likely that our societies, in so far as they are 'stable' social orders, are stabilized by virtue of the diversity of values and beliefs and the proliferation of divisions between individuals and groups. The stability of our societies may depend, not so much upon a consensus concerning particular values or norms, but upon a lack of consensus at the very point where oppositional attitudes could be translated into political action. In emphasizing this point I concur with some of the arguments which have been developed by sociologists and social theorists in recent years. However, to endorse these arguments is not necessarily to abandon the theory of ideology. Rather, it is to redirect this theory away from the search for collectively shared values and towards the study of the complex ways in which meaning is mobilized for the maintenance of relations of domination. In the final part of essay 3 I distinguish some of the ways in which this mobilization of meaning may occur.

If we must be sceptical of the assumption that our societies are stabilized by a consensus concerning values and norms, we must also resist the view that ideology is pure *illusion*, an inverted or distorted image of what is 'real'. This view draws support from a famous and oft-quoted passage in which Marx and Engels compare the operation of ideology to the workings of a *camera obscura*, which represents the world by means of an image turned upside-down. We must resist this view because, once we recognize that ideology operates through language and that language is a medium of social action, we must also acknowledge that ideology is partially constitutive of what, in our societies, 'is real'. Ideology is not a pale image of the social world but is part of that world, a creative and constitutive element of our social lives. This fundamental feature of ideology is brought out well by Cornelius Castoriadis and Claude Lefort, whose work I discuss in the first essay. These authors explore the links between ideology and 'the social imaginary', by which they understand primarily the creative and symbolic dimension of the social world, the dimension through which human beings create their ways of living together and their ways of representing their collective life. Whatever difficulties there may be in the writings of Castoriadis and Lefort, I believe that this notion of the social imaginary is of great interest for the attempt to explore the relation between language and ideology. For in using language we are constantly engaged in a creative, imaginary activity. We are constantly involved in extending the meaning of words, in producing new meanings through metaphor, word-play and interpretation; and we are thereby also involved, knowingly or not, in altering, undermining or reinforcing our relations with others and with the world. To study ideology is to study, in part, the ways in which these creative, imaginary activities serve to sustain social relations which are asymmetrical with regard to the organization of power.

LANGUAGE AND THE ANALYSIS OF DISCOURSE

In proposing to explore the relation between language and ideology, I am recommending a course of research which has been neglected by many philosophers and linguists. This neglect may seem somewhat surprising, in view of the emphasis of the later Wittgenstein, Austin and others on the *social* character of language and on the *active* character of language use. Did not Wittgenstein stress that expressions function only in the context of language-games which are played (and must be playable) by more than one individual, and which are therefore, in some sense, forms of social life? Did not Austin remind us that speaking is a way of acting and not simply a way of reporting or describing what is done, so that an adequate account of language must take into consideration the various kinds of things we do, and the various conditions which render these doings possible and appropriate, when we utter speech-acts? The contributions of Wittgenstein and Austin are

profoundly insightful and I do not wish to impugn their importance. However, their emphasis on the social character of language
and the active character of language use has tended to remain
abstract. Few attempts have been made to examine just what is
involved in regarding language as a social phenomenon, that is, as a
phenomenon which is enmeshed in relations of power, in situations of conflict, in processes of social change. Few attempts have
been made to explore the institutional aspects of the conditions
which render speech-acts possible and appropriate, aspects which
are related to specific social-historical circumstances and which
could not be derived by attending to the utterances alone. To
explore the relation between language and ideology requires an
analysis which is more concrete. It requires, therefore, that we
develop an approach which differs somewhat from the perspectives
adopted by many English-speaking philosophers.

The development of such an approach also requires that we
break with some of the presuppositions of modern linguistic
theories. The ways in which these presuppositions have restricted
our view of language, highlighting some features at the expense of
others, are analysed by Pierre Bourdieu, whose work I discuss in
the second essay. Bourdieu forcefully argues that any attempt to
construct an autonomous and homogeneous object of linguistic
analysis – whether Saussure's *langue* or Chomsky's 'competence' –
is bound to lead astray, for it conjures away the social-historical
conditions under which a particular language or competence is
constituted as legitimate, is acquired by some speakers, imposed on
others, and reproduced as the dominant form of language use.
Moreover, the Chomskyan notion of competence is deceptively
abstract. For what we possess as competent speakers is not the
capacity to produce an unlimited sequence of grammatically well-
formed sentences, but rather the capacity to produce sentences *à
propos*, that is, expressions which are relevant to specific situations
and tacitly adjusted to the relations of power which characterize
those situations. Our competence lies not in our capacity to produce an utterance like 'I name this ship the Queen Elizabeth'
anytime and anywhere, but rather in our capacity to produce such
a sentence when it is appropriate to do so and when we are
endowed with the requisite authority to carry out the act. Our
competence to speak is a *practical* competence. It is also a com-

petence which is differentiated socially and which is always manifested in actual instances of discourse.

To introduce the concept of *discourse* is to open an avenue for the investigation of the relation between language and ideology. This is a concept which has been widely used, and much abused, in recent discussions, partly because it derives from many different sources and debates. Here I shall not attempt to enumerate these sources or to review these debates; some of the relevant literature is discussed in essays 3, 5 and 7. I shall try instead to indicate, in a brief and very general way, some of the characteristics which are common to much of the work that is done under the label of 'discourse analysis'. In the first place, to study discourse is to study actually occurring instances of expression. The object of analysis is not a well-honed example designed to test our linguistic intuitions, but rather actual instances of everyday communication: a conversation between friends, a classroom interaction, a newspaper editorial. A second characteristic which is common to many forms of discourse analysis is a concern with linguistic units that exceed the limits of a single sentence; hence the focus on extended sequences of expression in a conversation or a text. A third feature shared by most forms of discourse analysis is an interest in the relations between linguistic and non-linguistic activity. It is this interest – expressed in a variety of ways and with varying degrees of sophistication – which makes discourse analysis particularly relevant to the attempt to explore the relation between language and ideology.

While the analysis of discourse may offer a promising approach for the study of language and ideology, the various forms of discourse analysis have yielded results which are disappointing in many ways. In essays 3 and 7 I argue that the principal shortcomings of this material can be traced back to certain methodological limitations. There are two limitations which are most prominent in this regard. First, by focusing on extended sequences of expression, the discourse analysts have tended to emphasize form and structure at the expense of content. These analysts have examined exchange structure, conversational structure and the structure of 'semantic domains'; but they have tended to neglect the question of *what is said* in discourse, that is, the question of *meaning* and of the interpretation of meaning. To raise this question is to prepare the way for a constructive appropriation of the methods of discourse analysis within the framework of a more comprehensive interpretative theory. The second limitation of these methods is that, while they are rightly concerned with the relations between linguistic and non-linguistic activity, they fail to provide a satisfactory account of the non-linguistic sphere and of the relations between linguistic and non-linguistic activity. This failure is especially evident in the English-speaking literature, which seldom explores the social relations within which discursive sequences are embedded. But a similar shortcoming can be discerned in the rigorous and original methods developed by Michel Pêcheux and his associates in France (essay 7), in so far as the implementation of their methods depends upon a series of assumptions about social structure which are not provided with an explicit and convincing defence.

METHODOLOGY OF INTERPRETATION

As the above remarks indicate, many of the essays in this volume are concerned with issues of a properly *methodological* kind. These issues are of the utmost importance, for in addressing the theme of ideology we must ask, not only how ideology is to be conceptualized and how its links with language are in general to be understood, but also how ideology can be analysed, specifically and concretely, in the expressions which are uttered in the course of our everyday lives. It is in an attempt to respond to this methodological demand that I have outlined a theory for the interpretation of ideology. The word 'interpretation' is used advisedly: it bears the weight of a tradition of thought which, for many centuries, has been concerned with problems of meaning and interpretation. The tradition of hermeneutics reminds us that the object of our investigations – utterances, expressions, texts – is a *pre-interpreted domain*. It reminds us, that is, that the forms of discourse which we seek to analyse are already an interpretation, so that to undertake an analysis of discourse is to produce an interpretation of an interpretation, to re-interpret a pre-interpreted domain. The tradition of hermeneutics also reminds us that the discourse which forms the object of investigation is the discourse *of a subject*. To analyse discourse is to investigate an object which is produced by a subject and received – read, listened to, understood – by other subjects; and the understanding of discourse by the subjects who produce and receive it is an element, although by no means the only element, of our investigation. These hermeneutical conditions of social-historical inquiry have consequences not only for the nature of the methodology appropriate to the study of ideology, but also for the status of the results of such a study.

While the tradition of hermeneutics reminds us of some of the conditions of our inquiry, it is not immediately clear that this tradition provides the most suitable resources for the study of ideology. For the tradition of hermeneutics, it might be remarked, has emphasized the symbolic constitution of the social-historical world, the way in which this world is created by speaking and acting individuals whose creations can be understood by others who partake of this world; but authors within this tradition have given less attention to the ways in which the social-historical world is *also* a field of force, a realm of conflict and coercion in which 'meaning' may be a mask for repression. How can we elaborate a methodology which takes account of the latter phenomena, without losing sight of the meaningful character of the discourse which is the object of investigation? I believe that a valuable key to this task may be found in the theory of interpretation developed by Paul Ricoeur. In numerous studies of language, of literature and of psychoanalysis, Ricoeur has sought to develop a 'depth hermeneutics' which would integrate explanation and understanding into a comprehensive interpretative theory. In essay 5 I assess the strengths and weaknesses of this imaginative project. I argue that, while there is much to be praised in Ricoeur's approach, nevertheless he tends to abstract too readily from the social-historical conditions in which texts (or analogues of texts) are produced and received, an abstraction which limits the usefulness of his approach for the study of ideology.

In an attempt to unfold the potential of Ricoeur's account without succumbing to its limitations, I sketch (in essay 5 and in the final part of essay 3) a procedure for the interpretation of ideology. The procedure consists of three principal phases which together constitute a form of depth hermeneutics. The first phase, which may be described as 'social analysis', is concerned with the social-historical conditions within which agents act and interact. It is essential to analyse these conditions – both in terms of their institutional features and in terms of their historical specificity – because we cannot study ideology without studying relations of domination and the ways in which these relations are sustained by meaningful expressions. The second phase of the depth-hermeneutical procedure may be described as 'discursive analysis'. To undertake a discursive analysis is to study a sequence of expressions, not only as a socially and historically situated occurrence, but also as a linguistic construction which displays an articulated structure. This structure can be studied in various ways, with a view towards explicating the role of discourse in the operation of ideology. In essays 3, 6 and 7 I discuss some of these methods of study and indicate what seem to me to be the most promising forms. However – and here I rejoin my earlier remarks about the limitations of discourse analysis – I do not believe that a study of the *structure* of discourse can be treated as an autonomous and exhaustive concern, let alone as a sufficient method for the investigation of ideology. Such a study must be complemented and completed by a third phase of analysis, a phase which may properly be described as 'interpretation'. In interpreting a form of discourse we may seek to move beyond the study of discursive structure and to *construct* a meaning which shows how discourse serves to sustain relations of domination. The interpretation of ideology may thus be conceived as a form of depth hermeneutics which is mediated by a discursive analysis of linguistic constructions and a social analysis of the conditions in which discourse is produced and received.

One of the kinds of discursive analysis which is particularly interesting for the investigation of ideology is the analysis of *narratives*. For ideology, in so far as it seeks to sustain relations of domination by representing them as 'legitimate', tends to assume a narrative form. Stories are told which justify the exercise of power by those who possess it, situating these individuals within a tissue of tales that recapitulate the past and anticipate the future. Various methods have been developed for the analysis of narratives, from Propp to Greimas and Barthes; in essay 6 I focus on one approach which I regard as exemplary. In his extensive study of the narratives produced by political groups in Germany during the Weimar period, Jean Pierre Faye shows how these narratives circulated in a structured space which circumscribed their sphere of operation and endowed them with efficacy. And there can be no doubt that these narratives *were* efficacious. Hitler and the Nazi Party did not rise to power in a vacuum. Their accession was rendered possible, not only by a series of traumatic economic events, but also by a battle that took place in words, a battle which drew upon the languages of German nationalism, of anti-Semitism, of revolution and restoration. In the course of this battle old words acquired new meanings and fresh alliances were formed, creating a field within which Hitler and his associates could exploit the accumulated reservoirs of sense. One may have doubts about Faye's preoccupation with the narrative field and his relative neglect of certain social and political considerations; but his insightful study attests to the interest and importance of exploring the ways in which expressions circulate in the social world.

IDEOLOGY, JUSTIFICATION AND CRITIQUE

One of the reasons why the study of ideology has been treated with suspicion by many thinkers is that it seems to give rise to intractable problems of justification. If 'ideology' is an evaluative term, if its very use conveys a critical note and calls for a process of critique, then how are we to justify the characterization of some discourse as ideological? How can we pretend to stand above the fray, aloofly assessing the discourse of others, when our interpretation is but another interpretation, no different in principle from the interpretations of those whose discourse we seek to assess? Questions such as these give rise to complex problems which must, in my opinion, be confronted in a direct and systematic way. I therefore wish to put aside two types of response which I regard as unsatisfactory. In the first place, it will not suffice to suppose that these problems can be resolved by discarding the critical conception of ideology and adopting a more neutral notion, as some authors seem to think. This will not suffice because the term 'ideology' cannot be so readily stripped of its negative sense and because problems of justification are not thereby resolved but only displaced, pushed into a murky background where they are conveniently lost from sight. The second type of response which I regard as unsatisfactory is the appeal to some form of 'science' which allegedly provides the counter-pole to ideology and the standpoint from which the illusions of the latter can be grasped. This type of response establishes too close a connection between ideology and illusion and commonly takes for granted a conception of science which is by no means self-evident.

In attempting to formulate a different response to the epistemological problems raised by the study of ideology, we can learn a great deal from the work of Jürgen Habermas. More rigorously than any other contemporary thinker, Habermas has examined the conditions of possibility of a critical theory of modern societies. He has sought to do so in a way which renounces a dogmatic appeal to 'science' and a confident anticipation of the future, without abandoning either systematic analysis or a concern for developmental trends. Through an investigation of various aspects of language use, he has tried to show that participants in linguistic interaction make certain assumptions which are relevant to questions of knowledge and critique. In uttering a speech-act we necessarily assume, for example, that the statement made is *true* and that the speech-act is *correct* in terms of the prevailing normative context. We also assume that, if challenged, these presupposed claims of truth and correctness could be defended or 'redeemed' by being supported with *reasons* which would be capable of eliciting the agreement of others. Hence there is an internal connection between the 'validity-claims' raised by speech-acts and the notion of reason or rationality. In his most recent work, a two-volume treatise entitled *Theorie des kommunikativen Handelns*, Habermas attempts to link this notion of communicative rationality to an account of social rationalization, itself couched within the framework of a theory of social evolution.

In essays 8 and 9 I offer an assessment of Habermas's novel and far-reaching proposals. The first of these essays was written in 1979 and focuses on the programme of universal pragmatics, as it had been developed up to that time. By 'universal pragmatics' Habermas understands the attempt to elucidate the general competencies required for the successful exchange of speech-acts and thereby to reconstruct the 'universal validity basis' of speech. I try to unravel the basic theses of this programme, explicating and criticizing the arguments upon which they rest. Among other things I maintain that Habermas does not satisfactorily justify the restriction of his analysis to speech-acts in the 'standard form', so that the exclusion of counter-examples to his theses is somewhat arbitrary. I also call into question Habermas's analysis of truth and try to show that his characterization of the conditions under which a truth-claim can be redeemed – the so-called 'ideal speech situation' – is problematic in several respects. Some of these issues are re-addressed in the second essay, which examines the central arguments of the two-volume treatise that appeared in 1981. By situating Habermas's views on language within the context of his account of social rationalization, this essay provides a more general perspective on Habermas's recent work. Once again, however, I express certain reservations about Habermas's analyses. Not only does his notion of communicative rationality remain abstract, largely unrelated to the specific issues which confront the conduct of critique, but also his account of social rationalization is linked to a theory of evolution which is as sweeping as it is unsubstantiated. Moreover, the problem of ideology and the critique of ideology, far from being the focal point of Habermas's current concerns, seems to have faded into the background of his work.

While I have reservations about some of Habermas's views, I nevertheless believe that he has proposed a line of reflection which is worthy of being pursued. In various parts of this volume – especially in the final part of essay 3 – I take up this line of reflection and indicate how it could be rendered relevant to a critique of ideology. For an interpretation of ideology, as a construction of meaning and a formulation of what is said in discourse, raises a claim to truth which calls for recognition. That is, an interpretation raises a claim to be acceptable or *justifiable* in some way; and we seem to presuppose, as Habermas suggests, that an interpretation could not be justified by being *imposed*. Hence we could say that an interpretation of ideology raises a claim to truth which could be justified only under certain conditions. An adequate characterization of these conditions would have to take account both of the formal requirement of non-imposition and of the specific procedures by means of which particular claims may be defeated or sustained. But it is important to stress that, in the case of interpreting ideology, there is an additional consideration which comes into play. For the interpretations generated by the depth-hermeneutical method are about an object domain which consists, among other things, of subjects capable of reflection; and if their claim to truth is to be sustained, then these interpretations would have to be justifi*able* in the eyes of the subjects about whom they are made. Such interpretations thus provide a potential basis for the *self*-criticism of the subjects whose discourse is the object of interpretation, as well as a relevant resource for a critique of the relations of domination which meaning serves to sustain.

The following essays contain the elements of a positive account of ideology and the critique of ideology, but they do not purport to develop this account in the detail that it demands. The essays seek primarily to introduce the reader to a rich and varied field of research. And if in the present volume my own contributions are more critical than constructive, more concerned to identify short-comings than to elaborate alternatives, they are nevertheless offered with a constructive aim. For the theory of ideology cannot be advanced unless we are fully aware of the difficulties to be overcome.

1

Ideology and the Social Imaginary

An Appraisal of Castoriadis and Lefort

Since its earliest formulations, the concept of ideology has been linked to the dimension of the imaginary. In *The German Ideology* Marx and Engels compare the operation of ideology to the workings of a *camera obscura*, which represents reality by means of an inverted image of life. Even later, in *Capital*, it is the phantasmagorical character of the commodity form which underlies the fetishism of commodities and thereby occludes the origin of their value. The link between ideology and the imaginary has generally been subsumed, however, to an overall opposition between reality and ideas; ideology and the imaginary stand together on the side of ideas, constituting a sort of ethereal medium which veils the hard reality of material production. There can be no doubt that some of Marx's writings, with their positivistic and naturalistic overtones, have contributed to the latter tendency. In recent years a number of authors have attempted to rethink the problematic of ideology and the imaginary and to free it from the confines of a crude materialism. Outstanding among these authors are Cornelius Castoriadis and Claude Lefort. Their far-reaching investigations have raised afresh the question of historical creativity, the question of social division and dissimulation, the question of the symbolic constitution of the social-historical world. In so doing they have rethought the very nature of politics in modern societies and have helped to redefine the tasks of contemporary social and political theory.

In this essay I wish to discuss the contributions of Castoriadis and Lefort to the theme of ideology and the imaginary.[1] By focusing on their contributions to this specific theme, I shall necessarily disregard many aspects of their work. As co-editors during the

1950s of the journal *Socialisme ou Barbarie*, they published numerous studies of capitalism, socialism and bureaucracy as well as detailed analyses of events and developments in Eastern and Western Europe; and in more recent years they have written extensively on authors such as Machiavelli, Merleau-Ponty and Freud.[2] These diverse and important writings will, in what follows, largely be left aside. Moreover, to discuss both Castoriadis and Lefort within the limits of a single essay is to run the risk of over-emphasizing their proximity. While they worked together for many years and often acknowledged their mutual indebtedness, the final split in 1958 pointed to deep differences in their views.[3] Here I shall not be concerned to analyse these differences in any detail. I shall try, instead, to bring out a certain coherence and consensus in their work, to show that in certain respects their views are complementary. I shall begin with Castoriadis's critique of Marx and his reformulation of the dimension of the social-historical and the concept of the social imaginary. The second section will present Lefort's account of the relation between ideology and the imaginary and his analysis of ideology in modern societies. In the third section I shall offer some critical and constructive remarks on the contributions of Castoriadis and Lefort. Finally, I should like to stress that, in adopting this mode of presentation, I do not wish to imply any sort of priority with regard to the origins or originality of the ideas concerned.

I

Critique of Marx

Castoriadis develops his account of the social-historical world against the backcloth of his critique of Marx and Marxism. This critical stance towards Marx emerged gradually in the course of his career. In his early writings Castoriadis remained roughly within the framework elaborated by Marx, using some of the latter's ideas to formulate an original analysis of exploitative relations and bureaucratic tendencies in Russia and Eastern Europe. Serious reservations about Marx's economic analysis of capitalism began to appear, however, in 1953–4; and the decisive break finally came in

1964–5, with the publication of an essay entitled 'Marxisme et théorie révolutionnaire'.[4] In this essay Castoriadis argues that the difficulties in Marx's work are not of a local and corrigible character, minor oversights which could be amended and brought up to date. Rather, the whole approach of Marx is misguided, for it rests upon a conception of history and historical change which is fundamentally unsound. The evolutionary schema which Marx sketches in the 1859 'Preface to *A Contribution to the Critique of Political Economy*' and elsewhere involves, in Castoriadis's view, 'an unjustified extrapolation to the whole of history of a process which only occurred during a single phase of this history, the phase of the bourgeois revolution'.[5] This schema is inapplicable to pre-feudal societies and to non-industrialized societies outside Europe. Moreover, the attempt to endow a single factor – the development of *technique* in the broadest sense – with a determining role in history is mistaken. Technique is not autonomous. The whole idea of applying knowledge for technical development, of regarding nature as a domain to be exploited, requires a certain attitude which is by no means universal; and the systematic planning of research and development which characterizes contemporary capitalist societies deprives the supposed 'autonomy of technique' of all sense.

The source of these difficulties in Marx's work lies at a deeper level still. Underlying Marx's evolutionary schema is a philosophy of history which bears the unmistakable imprint of 'Western rationalism'. History conforms to Reason, for historical events are governed by laws which can be elucidated through scientific inquiry. Castoriadis contends that this deterministic and scientistic tendency stands in radical opposition to Marx's own emphasis on revolution and class struggle. If classes are to be real elements in history, capable of actively transforming society, then they must be able *to make a difference* in social development; and hence the latter cannot be subsumed to the rigid and preconceived categories of evolutionary theory. That these two tendencies are radically opposed is amply attested to by the history of Marxism. With the October Revolution and its subsequent degeneration into an ossified bureaucratic state, the rationalistic tendency firmly eclipsed the theme of autonomous and revolutionary action. Marxism was moulded by Soviet theoreticians into a closed system describing a reality which is essentially fixed; whence the exclusion of the idea of revolution, which presupposes that the future is open and that its realization is something *to be done*. The implication of this argument for someone who, like Castoriadis, wishes to remain faithful to the revolutionary impetus of Marx's work seems clear:

> Having begun from revolutionary Marxism, we reached the point where it was necessary to choose between remaining Marxists and remaining revolutionaries; between fidelity to a doctrine which for a long time has no longer animated either reflection or action, and fidelity to a project of a radical transformation of society.[6]

Yet if no objective analysis can demonstrate the necessity of the crisis of capitalist society and its transcendence by socialism, then upon what basis can the revolutionary project be pursued? To answer this question requires a fundamental re-examination of human action and the constitution of the social-historical world.

Revolutionary project

The social-historical world, according to Castoriadis, is the world of human action or 'doing' (*faire*). While action always stands in some relation with knowledge (*savoir*), that knowledge is never exhaustive or absolute. For action is neither an unconscious reflex nor the implementation of some project whose conditions and consequences are fully known in advance. Rather, it is a process which is undertaken more or less consciously and with more or less clarity, depending on the nature of the task and the competence of the agents involved. Writing theory is itself an action which seeks – always tentatively and without guarantees – to realize the project of clarifying the world. Theory may help to guide a specific type of action which can be called *praxis* and which is the proper domain of politics. *Praxis* is a type of action which involves taking others into account and regarding them as autonomous beings capable of developing their own autonomy. *Praxis* draws upon knowledge, but the latter is always fragmentary and provisional; nor is this merely a negative limitation, for it is the condition of possibility of bringing about something which is *new*.

The revolutionary project builds upon the creativity and autonomous aim of *praxis*. It is, in essence, the project of a radical transformation of society with a view to the autonomy of all, 'the reorganization and reorientation of society by the autonomous action of men'.[7] This transformation cannot be limited to the domains traditionally and narrowly defined as 'politics' or 'the economy', but must pertain to all levels and spheres of social life. The proletariat no longer remains the privileged bearer of the revolutionary project; more than ever, this project is the concern of everyone – a theoretical premonition which was dramatically confirmed by the events of May 1968.

Although the revolutionary project is in no way necessitated by the development of capitalism, it nevertheless finds 'points of support' in certain features of capitalist society. In the sphere of production, capitalist organization is dominated by a central conflict: workers cannot participate in production, and yet they cannot not participate in it. They cannot not participate in it because, if they were reduced to mere cogs in the productive machine, capitalism would collapse immediately. The fact that they are constantly called upon to be active participants in production while simultaneously being excluded from its control is the conflict which gives rise to workers' demands for self-management. The revolutionary project is thus 'rooted' in the crisis of the capitalist enterprise in the specific sense that

> the social organization can realize the ends which it gives itself only by putting forward means which contradict them, by giving birth to demands which it cannot satisfy, by positing criteria which it is incapable of applying, norms which it is obliged to violate.[8]

Capitalist enterprises are torn apart by the contradiction which inheres in them and which provides a point of support for the revolutionary project. However, just as the revolutionary project cannot be restricted to the level of the economy, so too the conception of an autonomous society must go beyond the notion of workers' control. The full sense of this conception can only be grasped by rethinking the dimension of the social and its inseparable link with history.

Institution of the social-historical

It is Castoriadis's view that the nature of society and history has been obscured by certain emphases which run throughout the whole tradition of Western thought. For this tradition, to which Marx belongs, has always situated reflection on the social-historical within an ontology of determinacy; it has always assumed that 'to be' has one sense: 'to be determined'. Traditional thought thus misses the essential feature of the social-historical world, namely that this world is not articulated once and for all but is in each case the creation of the society concerned. In instituting itself society *creates* in the fullest sense of the term; it posits a new *eidos* which could not be deduced from or produced by a prior state of affairs. Just as the social cannot be conceived within traditional schemata of the coexistence of elements, so too the historical cannot be subsumed to traditional schemata of succession. 'For what is given in and by history is not a determinate sequence of the determined, but the emergence of radical alterity, immanent creation, non-trivial novelty.'[9] To conceptualize time and history one must reject the traditional ontology of determinacy. Genuine time is not merely in-determination but the emergence of *new* and *other* determinations. Time is the auto-alteration of what is; time 'is', as Castoriadis says, only in so far as it is 'being towards' (*à-être*).

Each society institutes a specific type of temporality which defines its specific mode of auto-alteration. What we call 'capitalism', for instance, would have been impossible outside the specific mode of auto-alteration which, in a sense, *is* capitalism. More precisely, Castoriadis distinguishes between two layers in the capitalist institution of temporality. There is the layer of homogeneous uniform, measurable time, the time of accumulation, rationalization and the conquest of nature. This is the temporality *explicitly* instituted by capitalism, but it is not its *effective* temporality. The effective temporality of capitalism is the time of incessant rupture, of recurrent crises, of the perpetual tearing up of what is. It is this effective temporality which, as Marx perceived, distinguishes capitalism from most archaic and traditional societies. In the latter societies, the explicitly instituted temporality is much closer to the effective temporality, which appears more like regular pulsations than radical ruptures. There is, nonetheless, a striking feature which is common to all hitherto existing societies, irrespective of their particular differences. For in all hitherto existing societies, the effective temporality of alterity and auto-alteration seems to get covered over and excluded from view. Castoriadis's account of this remarkable process is worthy of extended quotation:

> Thus everything happens as if the time of social doing, essentially irregular, accidental, altering, must always be imaginarily reabsorbed through a denial of time by means of the eternal return of the same, its representation as pure usury and corruption, its levelling out in the indifference of the merely quantitative difference, its annulment before Eternity. Everything happens as if the terrain where the creativity of society is manifested in the most trangible manner, the terrain where it makes, makes be and makes itself be in making be, must be covered over by an imaginary creation ordered in such a way that the society can conceal from itself what it is. Everything happens as if the society must negate itself as society, hide its social being in negating the temporality which is first and above all its own temporality, the time of alteration-alterity which it makes be and which makes it be as society. Another way of saying the same thing: everything happens as if society could not recognize itself as making itself, as institution of itself, as self-institution.[10]

The misrecognition by society of its own social-historical being corresponds to a certain necessity of the social institution such as we know it, that is, such as it has been instituted hitherto. Obliging its subjects to integrate themselves into the time which is explicitly instituted, society also provides them with the means to compensate for this negation of effective temporality, endowing them with the comfort of the unchanging and the routine. Castoriadis insists, however, that this misrecognition is not an 'ontological necessity'; it must not be assumed a priori that society could not recognize itself as instituting, as the source of its own alterity and alteration. For *that* is the question of revolution: the setting up of a society which makes and remakes itself as an explicitly self-instituting collectivity.

Social imaginary

To acknowledge the fundamental and irreducible creativity in the institution of the social-historical is to encounter what Castoriadis calls the 'social imaginary' (*l'imaginaire social*). The imaginary element of the social-historical world has, like the social-historical itself, been persistently misunderstood by traditional thought. For it has always been assumed that the imaginary is a mere reflection, a specular image of what is already there. Rejecting this assumption and the classical ontology upon which it rests, Castoriadis contends that the imaginary is what renders possible any relation of object and image; it is the creation *ex nihilo* of figures and forms, without which there could be no reflection *of* anything. On the level of the social-historical,[11] it is the imaginary which accounts for the orientation of social institutions, for the constitution of motives and needs, for the existence of symbolism, tradition and myth. Here, once again, it is worth quoting Castoriadis:

> This element, which endows the functionality of each institutional system with its specific orientation, which overdetermines the choice and connections of symbolic networks, which creates for each historical period its singular way of living, seeing and making its own existence, its world and its relations to it, this originary structuring, this central signifier-signified, source of what is each time given as indisputable and indisputed sense, support of the articulations and distinctions of what matters and of what does not, origin of the augmented being (*surcroît d'être*) of the individual or collective objects of practical, affective and intellectual investment – this element is nothing other than the *imaginary* of the society or period concerned.[12]

No society could exist without organizing the production of material goods and the reproduction of its members; but neither of these forms of organization is dictated by natural laws or by purely technical considerations. What is important in the dimension of the social-historical is not that human beings always eat and have children, but that they do so in an infinite variety of ways. It is precisely this infinite variety, this indeterminate range of possibilities which builds upon but always exceeds the material conditions of human life, which is the domain of the social imaginary.

The social imaginary is expressed primarily through the constitution of a world of significations. By means of these significations – these symbols and myths in which a society represents its present and its past – a society is endowed with an identity and distinguished both from other societies and from an undifferentiated chaos. The creative and constitutive character of significations can be seen in the operation of language, which Castoriadis regards as a particular sphere of the symbolic. Here signification is the co-belonging of a term and that to which it 'refers', both in the Saussurian sense of *signifié* and in the broader sense of 'referent'. In both senses the cluster of references is necessarily open, for the referent itself is an indeterminate being. Hence 'a signification is indefinitely determin*able* (and this "indefinitely" is evidently essential), although that does not mean that it is determin*ed*'.[13] It follows that no rigorous and ultimately valid distinction can be made between the proper and the figurative sense of a word, since all language is essentially 'tropical'. It also follows that any attempt to treat language as a self-enclosed system of interrelating terms, in the manner of structuralism, is at best a partial approach. Such an attempt draws upon a logic which is implicit in all social activity, *la logique ensembliste-identitaire*, but it can never grasp the open and creative character of language. Social imaginary significations necessarily escape from the confines of a self-enclosed system, comprising a *magma* of meanings which cannot be organized into a logically structured whole. When one considers, moreover, the central imaginary significations of a society, one sees that they cannot be thought of in terms of their relations to referents, however open this relation may be; for these significations are what renders 'referents', and hence the relation to them, possible. What is the referent of the word 'God', asks Castoriadis, if not the individual representations of God which are created by means of the institution of the central imaginary signification which is God? The central imaginary significations of a society, far from being mere epiphenomena of 'real' forces and relations of production, are the laces which tie a society together and the forms which define what, for a given society, is 'real'.

II

Ideology and the imaginary

The relations between the notion of the social imaginary and the phenomenon of ideology are explored in an important essay by Lefort.[14] Like Castoriadis, Lefort adopts a critical approach to the work of Marx, seeing it as both a source of invaluable insights and an expression of naturalistic illusions. Marx formulated, rightly in Lefort's view, the problem of ideology in terms which precluded the reduction of ideology to the discourse of the bourgeoisie. Ideology is linked, not to a particular class, but to the fundamental feature of 'social division' – the division, that is, between the dominant and the dominated, whether this division assumes the form of kinship relations, class relations or the relation between state and civil society. A society cannot exist, suggested Marx, without forging a representation of its unity. While this unity is attested to by the reciprocal interdependence of social agents, it is constantly threatened by the separation of their activities and the temporal mutability of social relations. The representation of unity in the context of restricted and mutable social relations thus implies the projection of an 'imaginary community' by means of which 'real' distinctions are portrayed as 'natural', the particular is disguised in the universal, the historical is effaced in the atemporality of essence. 'The discourse inscribed in the institution', observes Lefort,

> maintains the illusion of an essence of society, staves off the double threat which weighs upon the established order by virtue of the fact that it is divided and the fact that it is historical; it imposes itself as a discourse rational in itself, a closed discourse which, masking the conditions of its own engendering, claims to reveal that of the empirical social reality.[15]

If the role of the imaginary was glimpsed by Marx, it was nevertheless distorted by his claim to determine, through the procedures of positive science, the nature of social reality. Marx traced social division back to the brute facts of evolution, thus failing to see that the division is essentially interwoven with the 'thought' of the division, that is, with the order of the symbolic. Social division must not be confused with the empirical distribution of human beings in the process of production, for to do so is to succumb to the naturalistic fiction. Rather, social division must be seen as part of the 'social space' which is instituted only in so far as it is articulated in discourse, that is, only in so far as it is constituted by the discourse of the social.

The phenomenon of ideology appears, in the view of Lefort, as a certain type of discourse subsumed to a specific order of the imaginary. Ideology is a type of discourse which no longer sustains legitimacy by referring to a transcendent realm, a realm of gods, spirits or mythical figures. Ideological discourse is inscribed in the social itself; it seeks to conceal the social division and temporality without appealing to 'another world'. There is thus a singular relation between ideology and 'historical society': 'ideology is the linking together of representations which have the function of re-establishing the dimension of society "without history" at the very heart of historical society'.[16] Marx implicitly recognized this relation when he contrasted capitalism with all previous modes of production. He perceived that, unlike earlier forms of social organization, the capitalist mode of production is 'revolutionary' in the sense that it is prone to incessant expansion and change; and yet, precisely because of this continuous upheaval, the divisions inherent in capitalist society cannot be concealed by an imaginary flight into transcendent realms. The task of ideology is to conceal, within the social space itself, the divisions and mutations entailed by the development of capitalism. But if Marx perceived the singular relation between ideology and historical society, once again he misconstrued this relation by assuming that ideology is a dissimulation, more or less effective, of something 'real'. Lefort argues that the analysis of ideology can be freed from this naturalistic assumption only if ideology is conceived as a fold or crease (*repli*) of the social discourse upon itself, a kind of second discourse which follows the lines of the instituting discourse and seeks to cover over the divisions instituted therein. Ideology takes hold of the signs of novelty and conflict and moulds them into a discourse of dissimulation. It must constantly diversify and displace its references – to past and future, to science and ethics – in order to sustain its attempt to seal every crack and thereby to justify the established order. This attempt cannot, however, succeed; the process of dissimulation is bound to fail, for ideology cannot accomplish its task without revealing itself as a discourse, and hence without disclosing the gap which separates it from that about which it speaks. It is the ineluctable failure of the process of dissimulation which determines, in part, the necessity of its internal transformation.

Bourgeois ideology

The general properties of ideological discourse apply to the bourgeois ideology which matured in nineteenth-century Europe. This ideology presents itself as an anonymous discourse on the social, a discourse in which the universal speaks of itself. Whatever support it may draw from religion and traditional world-views, bourgeois ideology is governed by the ideal of positive knowledge and calls into question the reference to 'another world'. Bourgeois ideology is structured by a division between 'ideas' and a supposed 'real'; the 'other place' of religious and mythical conceptions is effaced, but the ideology refers to itself only via the transcendence of ideas. The text of bourgeois ideology, remarks Lefort, is written in capital letters: Humanity, Progress, Science, Property, the Family. These ideas imply an opposition between the subject who speaks and establishes itself in accordance with the rule laid down by the idea, and the 'other' (*autre*) who has no access to the rule and is thereby deprived of the dignity of the subject. The opposition is expressed in a series of dichotomies: worker/bourgeois, savage/civilized, mad/normal, child/adult. Across these dichotomies emerges a 'natural being' whose image underpins the affirmation of a society above nature:

> Such is the artifice by which the social division is dissimulated: the positing of reference points which enable a difference to be fixed between the social and the sub-social, order and disorder, the world and the underworld (a difference which has no status in 'precapitalism', where the social is conceived from another place, from an order which exceeds it), in such a way that what reality withholds (*dérobe*) from discourse is identified and mastered.[17]

What gives strength to bourgeois ideology is the fact that its discourses remain disjoint. It does not 'speak' from a single place, but multiplies and divides itself in accordance with the differentiation of social institutions (the state, the law, the business firm, the school). There is a continuous interplay of procedures of legitimation and dissimulation, brought into play here and there, so that a gap is preserved between discourse and power.

The conditions which secure the efficacy of bourgeois ideology contain, however, the seeds of its failure. The ideology is undermined by an inescapable contradiction: it relies upon ideas which seek to present themselves as transcendent and beyond the social, but it is precisely the loss of such a 'beyond' which is at the origin of ideology. Bourgeois ideology is thus obliged to take hold of signs in the supposed real which attest to and support it. Claiming to provide a point of certainty from which the social can be conceived, it must nevertheless appeal to the social and hence reveal itself as contingent. What renders bourgeois ideology vulnerable is its incapacity to fix the social order 'without letting its contingency appear, without condemning itself to slide from one position to another, without thus exposing the instability of an order which it is designed to raise to the dignity of essence'.[18] Whence the dispersion of the discourses that comprise bourgeois ideology, a dispersion which is governed by the impossible quest for origins, a dispersion which is, in principle, deprived of any 'safety catch' (*cran d'arrêt*).

Totalitarian ideology

The contradiction which inhabits bourgeois ideology is reflected in the phenomenon of totalitarianism. Lefort uses 'totalitarianism' as a generic term to encompass fascist regimes as well as those which are called 'communist'. He does not deny that there are important differences between fascism and communism; but he contends that, for the purpose of analysing the genesis of ideology, these types of regime can be considered together. For both types are characterized by a discourse which claims to express universal knowledge and to secure thereby the unity and homogeneity of the social field. Totalitarian discourse effaces the oppositions that bourgeois ideology employed in order to dissimulate the social division; the explicit quest for totalization supplants the implicit and interminable labour of occultation. In particular, totalitarian discourse obliterates the distinction between state and civil society, seeking to diffuse, by means of the mass party, the presence of the state throughout the social space. This attempt to fuse the political and the non-political presupposes the unfolding of a system of articulations by means of which power can be exercised without being divided. This system, appearing as a manifestation of human logos and drawing support only from itself, nevertheless forms itself around a centre which possesses knowledge and power and from which social life is organized. So while the discourse of totalitarianism is structured in such a way that anonymous knowledge governs the thought and activities of social agents, it 'supports itself only by a constant reference to the authority in which the decision is concentrated. It is on this double condition that the contradiction of bourgeois ideology is "overcome" in the concept of the total State.'[19]

In overcoming the contradiction of bourgeois ideology, the discourse of totalitarianism engenders a contradiction of its own. The two elements of anonymous knowledge and authoritative centre hold together only in so far as oppositions of power within the bureaucracy are ignored and the masses are excluded from the power apparatus. While bourgeois ideology preserved a gap between discourse and power and could therefore oppose itself without destroying itself, totalitarian discourse must identify itself with power and with those who hold it. Hence oppositions cannot be tolerated: they must be absolutely rejected or, if not, discourse gives way to terror. 'In a general way', explains Lefort,

> the contradiction of totalitarianism stems from the fact that power doubly masks itself therein, as the representative of the society without divisions and as the agent of the rationality of the organization, while on the other hand it appears there, as in no other society, as an apparatus of coercion, the bearer of naked violence.[20]

The bureaucratic organization is governed by a principle of instability which constantly threatens to expose this contradiction, and with it the mechanism of domination. All kinds of events occur, economic as well as cultural, which escape the prediction of the leaders and are capable of displaying an organizational failure. One way of defusing these potentially disruptive events is to *exclude* them, to treat them as representatives of the 'outside' (*dehors*) of a society claimed to be homogeneous. But this exclusion cannot succeed; the event or agent returns, haunting the bureaucratic world with insecurity and threatening to betray totalitarian discourse as the mere mask of oppression.

Invisible ideology

The key features of bourgeois and totalitarian ideologies are integrated and transformed in the new ideology which, according to Lefort, prevails in contemporary Western societies. As in totalitarianism, this new ideology seeks to secure the homogenization and unification of the social; but this project is severed from the affirmation of totality, is rendered latent, implicit, 'invisible'. In this way, the project of homogenization is reconnected to the key principle of bourgeois ideology, which required the displacement of imaginary formations, which tolerated their conflict and constantly worked out compromises.

> Cover over the distance between the representation and the real, which endangers bourgeois ideology, renounce the fulfilling of the representation in the form of the totalization of the real, which endangers totalitarian ideology: such is, in our view, the double principle which organizes a new logic of dissimulation.[21]

The new ideology depends crucially on the mass media, by means of which the implicit homogenization of the social field is achieved. The broadcasting of debates and discussions dealing with all aspects of life, from science and politics to art, cookery and sex, creates the impression that the social relation is fully reciprocal, that speech circulates without internal obstacles and constraints. The word of the expert appears as anonymous and neutral, expressing and diffusing objective knowledge; but at the same time it singularizes itself, assumes the attributes of the person in order to reach an audience which, in spite of its mass and dispersion, is brought together by the very proximity and familiarity of the one who speaks. The most banal programmes on radio and television, the chat shows and question times, become inner sanctums in a mass society, intimate worlds where the sense of distance and adversity has been abolished. Therein lies the imaginary dimension of communication: it provides the constant assurance of the social bond, attests to the permanent presence of the 'between-us' (*entre-nous*), and thereby effaces the intolerable fact of social division.

The efficacy of the new ideology presupposes the 'scientificity' and 'objectivity' of discourse. In this regard, it is similar to bourgeois ideology; but whereas the latter exploits a discourse on science in order to discuss the social, the new ideology is not an application of science but an embodiment of it. The modern organization appears as a perfectly rational structure which functions by itself, independently of the desires and decisions of human beings, who are themselves transformed into 'organization men'.[22] The cult of scientificity and objectivity also marks a point of comparison with totalitarian ideology; but unlike the latter, the new ideology does not and need not represent knowledge as closed. Rather, it takes hold of the signs of novelty, incorporates and cultivates them in order to discharge the threat of history. 'Invisible once again is the operation which defuses the effects of the institution of the social, which tries to preclude the question concerning the sense of the established order the question concerning the *possible*.'[23] It is in this perspective that Lefort interprets Baudrillard's provocative analysis of consumer society.[24] What is consumed is always 'new', but this novelty is a mere difference which marks the eternal return of the same, the eternal return of the object of consumptive desire. The consumer is presented with a world in which everything can be grasped, like the house of our dreams which is simply waiting, door slightly ajar, to be entered. The new ideology thus establishes a closed universe, repetitive and pre-arranged, but renders this closure invisible by the very absence of a totalizing discourse. This does not mean, however, that the contradictions which disrupt the bourgeois and totalitarian ideologies are comfortably resolved in the new ideology. On the contrary, insists Lefort, the more this ideology seeks to coincide with the social itself – the more 'invisible' it seeks to become – the more it runs the risk of losing the function which ideology has assumed hitherto: the legitimation of the established order. It creates the conditions for a contestation which, in the East as well as the West, may lead beyond particular forms of power and domination and may bring to reflection the general question of the social and of being.

III

In the foregoing sections I have attempted to sketch some central themes in the recent writings of Castoriadis and Lefort; I should now like to offer a few critical and constructive comments on their work. There are, I believe, many aspects of their work which are largely justified and highly suggestive: their critical analyses of Marx and Marxism, their emphasis on the spatial and temporal constitution of the social-historical world, their concern with the interconnections between signification, ideology and the imaginary. In these and other respects, the work of Castoriadis and Lefort deserves to be more widely read outside France and to be compared with the major contributions of contemporary social thought. It is by means of such comparison that one can begin to see, however, that the writings of Castoriadis and Lefort are unsatisfactory and incomplete at a number of crucial points. I cannot, within the confines of this essay, pursue all of the reservations to which this comparative and critical reflection has given rise. For the sake of clarity, I shall therefore focus my comments around the following four themes: cohesion and fragmentation; discourse and domination; ideology and the imaginary; rationality and the revolutionary project.

Cohesion and fragmentation

Let me begin with Lefort's discussion of the 'invisible ideology' which, according to him, currently prevails in the Western societies. This ideology effectively integrates the key principles of bourgeois and totalitarian ideologies while defusing their contradictions; it realizes the totalitarian project of unifying the social field by the bourgeois method of tolerating conflicts and working out compromises. Social division and temporality are dissimulated by the incantation of familiarity and the management of novelty. The proximity of this analysis to the well-known work of Marcuse, to his swingeing critique of 'one dimensional society',[25] is evident and is acknowledged by Lefort himself. Moreover, Lefort's contention that the new ideology does not succeed in resolving all contradictions but that, on the contrary, it runs the risk of failing in its task of legitimating the established order – this contention bears a certain resemblance to the recent work of Habermas and Offe.[26] It is by comparison with the work of Habermas and Offe, however, that the account offered by Lefort begins to appear inadequate. For Habermas attempts to elucidate, with more theoretical rigour and empirical detail than can be found in the writings of Lefort, the mechanisms by which the ideological defence of the contemporary capitalist order is constantly threatened and potentially undermined. Habermas argues that crises stemming from the process of production are displaced into the political sphere, placing severe strains on the state apparatus. The state is called upon to meet contradictory demands, to stabilize the conditions for private accumulation while responding to calls for social welfare and political participation; and in so far as the state fails in this practically impossible task, the conditions are created for a breakdown of legitimation and a withdrawal of motivation. I do not wish to endorse every aspect of this provocative account, an account which can be questioned in numerous respects.[27] In this context I refer to Habermas's work only in order to highlight the fact that Lefort's cursory treatment of the 'contradiction' inherent in the new ideology is, by contrast, rather thin.

The criticism must be pressed further. Not only is Lefort's treatment of the 'contradiction' inadequate, but his whole analysis of the new ideology seems to over-emphasize the phenomena of homogeneity and unification. This over-emphasis follows directly from his methodological assumption that the new ideology incorporates, albeit in a different form, the totalizing project of totalitarian discourse. It seems to me, however, that this assumption may be misleading, for it may rest upon a mistaken view of the factors involved in the sustaining of stability in contemporary capitalist societies. Recent research suggests that such stability is based, not so much on an underlying consensus concerning values and an apparent absence of social barriers, but rather on the *lack* of consistent commitment and the propagation of social divisions.[28] It is not so much unification and homogenization, but rather fragmentation and differentiation, which may be responsible for the social cohesion that exists in Western liberal democracies. Perhaps the principal division in this regard is the insulation of the economy and the polity, which prevents questions of industrial organization from appearing as political issues. The division is ramified by a differentiation in levels of skill and qualification, as well as by deep divisions concerning gender and race. The overall effect of this fragmentation is the canalization of class conflict into localized struggles for the redistribution of scarce economic rewards; wider issues pertaining to the control of the enterprise and of society as a whole are excluded from view, obscured by the very multiplicity of apparently divergent interests and groups. There seems little reason to suppose that the fragmentation of the social order is being steadily effaced by the mass media, which may serve to reinforce rather than eradicate the existing forms of differentiation. In emphasizing the phenomena of unification and homogenization, Lefort gives insufficient attention to these considerations and fails to appreciate their significance for the analysis of ideology.[29] Lefort's emphasis also results in a neglect of the continuing importance of classes and class conflict, which are hardly mentioned in his discussion of the 'invisible ideology'. The attempt to analyse the nature of ideology in contemporary capitalist societies cannot disregard, I believe, the question of class. An analysis which confronted this question more directly would prepare the ground for a study of the ways in which ideological expressions are essentially contested, their universe of meaning essentially disrupted, their claim of legitimacy incessantly challenged, by the actions of agents enmeshed in the existing system of domination.

Discourse and domination

I now wish to consider Lefort's account of ideology at a more general and abstract level. According to Lefort, the concept of ideology is inapplicable to 'precapitalist societies', in which the social division is dissimulated beneath the representation of 'another world'. It is the emergence of capitalism which undermines this transcendent reference and creates the conditions for the formation of ideology. The distinctive characteristic of ideology, in Lefort's view, is that it is implicated in the social division which it serves to dissimulate; that is, the division is both represented and concealed *within* the social world, and no longer with reference to an imaginary 'beyond'. The formation of ideology is thus coeval with the appearance of a discourse *on* the social, a properly *political* discourse whose origins may be traced back to the Italian Renaissance.[30] Lefort may well be right to emphasize the radical break effected by the emergence of capitalism; no doubt he is also right to underline the importance of the Italian Renaissance for the formation of modern political thought. Nevertheless, Lefort's restriction of the concept of ideology to the types of society ushered in by these developments seems questionable. For, on the one hand, it seems misleading to maintain that social division in 'precapitalist societies' is dissimulated by reference to another world, as if this dissimulation were not also implicated in 'effective social relations'. The work of Bourdieu and Godelier, among others, has shown that relations of domination in what might be called 'precapitalist societies' are sustained by everyday social practices which are permeated by power.[31] Nourished by kinship relations and tradition, these everyday social practices play a vital role in the stabilization of the social order; explicit discourses of legitimation, in 'precapitalist' as well as capitalist societies, are probably of greater significance for integrating the ruling élite than for stabilizing the society as a whole.[32] On the other hand, it seems equally misleading to contend that social division in capitalist societies is dissimulated within the social world, as if this dissimulation were entirely freed of 'transcendent reference'. With the differentiation of the economy and the polity which characterizes the development of capitalism, the task of dissimulating relations of domination within the economy may be borne, at least in part, by the projection of an 'imaginary unity' within the political sphere. This imaginary unity, linked to the pervasive if ill-understood phenomenon of nationalism, could be seen as a 'transcendent essence' by reference to which the divisions and transformations of the present are effaced.[33] If these considerations are sound, then it seems that Lefort has failed to provide a convincing case for restricting the application of the concept of ideology to the types of society introduced by capitalism.

The concept of ideology cannot be extended in its application without broadening the way in which ideology is understood. Lefort tends to regard ideology as a specific type of discourse which was instituted at a particular point in time; and while ideological discourse, or ideological discourses, have undergone complex transformations since their time of institution, nevertheless their identity as a type can be discerned. I wish to propose a different and more general view of the nature of ideology.[34] According to this view, to study ideology is primarily to investigate, not a particular type of discourse linked to a particular type of society, but rather the ways in which meaning (signification) serves to sustain relations of domination. The study of ideology is fundamentally concerned with language, for it is largely within language that meaning is mobilized in the defence of domination.

In so far as the use of language is a form of action interwoven with other activities, ideology is always 'immanent' in 'effective social relations'. Ideology is not only, nor even primarily, to be found in the discourses of the ideologues; its principal *locus* is the language of everyday life, the communication in which and through which we live out our daily lives. This does not imply, however, that the ideological use of language involves no reference to 'another world'. As Marx so perceptively remarked, it is just when human beings seem engaged in revolutionizing themselves and their social order, in creating something that has never existed, that 'they anxiously conjure up the spirits of the past to their service and borrow from them names, battle cries and costumes in order to present the new scene of world history in this time-honoured disguise and this borrowed language'.[35] Of course, this reference to another world, this 'conjuring up of the dead of world history', may not always invoke an ethereal realm of gods and spirits; but then again it *may*, as is amply attested to by the political rhetoric of some modern would-be saints.[36] Moreover, the reference to another world, or to this world *via* another world, may not always be direct. For ideology often operates, I want to suggest, by way of a 'splitting' of the referential domain, such that expressions explicitly referring to one thing may implicitly refer to another.[37] It is often by means of this splitting of the referential domain that ideology is able to dissimulate relations of domination and to endow the mark of legitimacy upon that which it conceals.

Ideology and the imaginary

To speak of dissimulation and concealment is to raise once again the key question of the imaginary. Castoriadis and Lefort have returned this question to the centre of social and political thought; and while the role of the imaginary has been discussed in other domains,[38] such discussions do nothing to diminish the originality with which it is treated in their work. Even in the writings of Castoriadis and Lefort, however, the concept of the imaginary has a plurality of meanings which must be carefully distinguished. For Castoriadis the imaginary is to be conceived of primarily as the *creative core* of the social-historical and psychic worlds, as the element which creates *ex nihilo* the figures and forms that render 'this world' and 'what is' possible. While Lefort appears to accept some such conception, nevertheless he tends to emphasize the *dissimulatory dimension* of the imaginary. It is by means of a specific form of the imaginary that ideology carries out its task of dissimulating the social division, a task that was accomplished in 'precapitalist societies' by other forms of the imaginary. There are passages in which Castoriadis also speaks of dissimulation; but what is imaginarily dissimulated in Castoriadis's sense is not the social division, but rather the creative imaginary itself.[39] The concept of the social imaginary thus has at least three distinct meanings in the writings of Castoriadis and Lefort: creative core, dissimulation of the social division, and dissimulation of the creative imaginary.

The question which I now want to ask is whether, and if so at what price, these basic senses of the imaginary can be reconciled. The conception of the social imaginary as the creative core of the social-historical world is formulated in opposition to the reductionistic and deterministic tendencies of Western metaphysics, of which Marx's materialism is a particular form. Just as Marx treats social change as the unfolding of 'real contradictions' and thereby fails to grasp the role of social imaginary significations which constitute what 'is real', so too Western metaphysics defines being in terms of determinacy and thereby precludes the possibility of creation, the undetermined emergence of something new. Without wishing to contest the interest and importance of this radical conception of the imaginary, it must nevertheless be asked how, on the basis of this conception, one can continue to speak of dissimulation. Does not the notion of dissimulation used by Lefort reintroduce a conception of 'social division' as a definite and definable 'being'? For *what* is being dissimulated, if not a relation which can be specified in some sense 'independently' of that which dissimulates? It may be thought that this problem can be resolved by distinguishing, along with Lefort, between the instituting discourse in which social reality is constituted, and the dissimulating discourse which, as it were, 'follows the lines' of the instituting discourse and seeks to cover over the social division instituted therein. But how can one draw this distinction, without presupposing some conception of what social reality *is*? How can one distinguish, that is, between the instituting discourse and the dissimulating discourse, without presupposing some criterion of 'the real' by reference to which the process of instituting can be circumscribed?[40] Perhaps these questions could be deflected by speaking of dissimulation in Castoriadis's sense; but *this* notion of dissimulation, it must be said, remains very abstract. Lost is the sense in which historically specific divisions between classes, races and sexes may be concealed or explained away; lost is the sense in which historically specific relations of domination may be sustained by the dissimulating interplay of meaning and power. A fuller and more concrete notion of dissimulation must be preserved; and it can be preserved, I believe, only by attenuating some of the claims associated with the radical conception of the imaginary. The question is whether and how this can be done without falling back on a reductionistic form of Marx's materialism, to which Castoriadis and Lefort have rightly ruled out any return.

Rationality and the revolutionary project

In order to confront more directly the philosophical issues which have now been raised, it may be helpful to reconsider the revolutionary project outlined by Castoriadis. The author rejects Marx's philosophy of history as well as his analysis of capitalism, arguing that they leave no room for autonomous action. The choice, it seems, is between rationalism and revolution, and Castoriadis chooses revolution. Yet the revolutionary project, thus severed from a rationalist philosophy of history, runs the risk of appearing groundless. If one can no longer appeal to objective laws of social development, then how is one to justify the claim that human beings should struggle for the realization of another society, rather than acting to sustain the status quo? In response to this question, Castoriadis observes that the revolutionary project finds 'points of support' in the objective tendencies of capitalist society and in the subjective desires of individuals, tendencies and desires which suggest that the revolutionary project is merely formulating clearly what contemporary society is already expressing in a confused and convoluted way. It is difficult to escape the impression that Castoriadis is here returning to a justification by means of immanent tendencies, whose 'rationalist' character is thinly veiled by the claim, altogether dubious, that it is only articulating what 'society' is already saying about itself.[41] This is not, however, where Castoriadis leaves the matter. He acknowledges that his reading of the tendencies is a *choice* in relation to a project, but he insists that this choice is not arbitrary: 'If we affirm the tendency of contemporary society to move towards autonomy, if we wish to work towards its realization, it is because we affirm autonomy as the mode of being man.'[42] This ultimate recourse to philosophical anthropology reveals that Castoriadis's ontology does not dispense altogether with the notion of determinacy. Just as the possibility of dissimulating the creative imaginary presupposes that the social-historical world has a *determinate mode of being* defined by the capacity of an historical society to institute itself as a self-instituting collectivity, so too the attempt to justify the revolutionary project leads to the affirmation of autonomy as the *mode of being* of 'man'. Yet this very strategy of argument, whereby an epistemological question concerning justification seems to terminate in an ontological affirmation concerning 'man', leaves an uncomfortable residue of doubt. Why should this affirmation be granted a privileged status, more privileged, for example, than the 'anthropological' assumptions, rejected by Castoriadis, which underlie Marx's conception of history? And even if it were granted a privileged status, how could this affirmation support anything other than the most abstract notion of a revolutionary project and a post-revolutionary society, a notion stripped of all content concerning the conditions under which autonomous action would be possible?

Perhaps further light can be shed on these issues by re-examining Castoriadis's views on language. Signification in language is a principal medium through which the social imaginary is expressed. Hence significations cannot be subsumed to the demands of determinacy; a signification is, as Castoriadis says, 'indefinitely determin*able*'. In everyday life expressions do, of course, effectively function as univocal, that is, as sufficiently univocal for the purposes of usage (*suffisament quant à l'usage*). Even the simplest declarative sentence posits the *quant à* which is specific to it, indicating that its univocity is ephemeral, transitory, always open to disruption and change. The *quant à* provides a point of reference which enables speakers to locate themselves in what they say, 'to support themselves on the same in order to create the other'.[43] How are we to understand this 'same', upon which speakers rest in order to create the other? In Castoriadis's view, this 'same' is to be explicated in terms of *la logique ensembliste-identitaire*, a logic of distinct wholes and definite relations which is an ineliminable dimension of language and of every social activity, although it does not exhaust what language and social life are. The dimension of *la logique ensembliste-identitaire* is present in language in so far as the latter is in part a code, that is, a system of elements and relations which is presupposed by meaning (*signification*), but which meaning always exceeds. Language as code is closed, whereas meaning is everywhere open, resting upon but moving beyond *la logique ensembliste-identitaire*. Yet does this appeal to a logic already present and always in language fully account for that which is collectively presupposed by individuals engaged in communication? Does not the activity of uttering statements, of asserting that something is the case or of calling into question what another says, presuppose a broader conception of the 'same', a 'same' which is not so much within language but, as it were, in front of it, giving sense to the very activity of asserting and questioning? It is my view that asymmetrical relations of power are sustained by historically specific forms of meaning; that these forms of meaning can be, and constantly are, challenged and disrupted; and that the emergent conflicts of interpretation could be, and demand to be, resolved in a counterfactual situation where the asymmetrical relations of power were suspended or dissolved.[44] Such a situation might exemplify a broader conception of the 'same' upon which speakers rest, as well as introducing a wider conception of rationality which Castoriadis, for the most part,[45] seems reluctant to accept. And if this wider conception of rationality could allow for a certain determinacy without destroying creativity, could lend support to a political project without resurrecting laws of development, could give sense to the notion of truth without arrogating absolute knowledge, then the elucidation of this conception would not be in vain.

I should like, by way of conclusion, to draw together the various sections of this essay. I began by sketching some of the main themes of Castoriadis's recent work, in particular his reformulation of the revolutionary project and his conceptions of the social-historical and the social imaginary. This prepared the way for a discussion of Lefort's views on the relation between ideology and the imaginary and his analyses of ideology in modern societies. Lefort's account of ideology in contemporary Western societies provided the point of departure for my critical reflection on their work; for this account, it seems to me, over-emphasizes homogeneity and tends to misrepresent the sources of stability in capitalist societies. On a more general level, I questioned Lefort's theoretical analysis of ideology, which precludes the application of this concept to 'precapitalist societies'. I asked how the concept of ideology can be linked to the notion of the social imaginary, when the latter is regarded as both creative and dissimulatory. One can continue to speak of dissimulation, in the fullest sense of this term, only if one is prepared to attenuate some of the claims associated with the creative imaginary and to search for a justifiable way of distinguishing between the institution of social relations and their ideological dissimulation. These and similar considerations give rise to complex epistemological problems which could be illuminated, I believe, through further inquiry into the conditions of communication.

Between the lines of these critical reflections, I have offered some constructive remarks on the themes concerned. To study ideology, I proposed, is not to analyse a particular type of discourse to be found in a particular type of society, but primarily to examine the ways in which meaning serves to sustain relations of domination. Ideology is both 'immanent' in social relations, in so far as the use of language is a social activity interwoven with others, and 'transcendent' to them, in so far as expressions used to sustain domination may refer beyond what is immediately given. By stressing the creative character of language use and its constitutive role in social life, this approach would draw upon the creative sense of the social imaginary. It would also draw upon the dissimulatory sense, for it would acknowledge that language may be used to conceal and obscure the relations of domination in which human beings are enmeshed. Perhaps the attempt to integrate and elaborate these two senses of the social imaginary would lead to a philosophical standpoint somewhat different from those adopted by Castoriadis and Lefort; but their rich and insightful studies would remain at the heart of any such attempt.

2

Symbolic Violence

Language and Power in the
Writings of Pierre Bourdieu

As competent speakers we are aware of the many ways in which linguistic exchanges can express relations of power. We are sensitive to the variations in accent, vocabulary and syntax which reflect different positions in the social hierarchy. We are aware that individuals speak with differing degrees of authority, that words are loaded with unequal weights, depending on who utters them and how they are said, such that some words uttered in certain circumstances have a force and a conviction that they would not have elsewhere. We are experts in the innumerable and subtle strategies by which words can be used as instruments of coercion and constraint, as tools of intimidation and abuse, as signs of politeness, condescension and contempt. These and other aspects of the relation between language and power have been studied by sociologists and linguists interested in the social stratification of speech and in the contextualized use of linguistic expressions. Such studies have important implications, not only for the form and status of linguistic theories, but also for the nature of the problems posed both by philosophers of language and by theorists of society who recognize that language is a central – albeit not the only – medium of social reproduction.

In this essay I want to explore some of the issues which concern the relation between language and power by focusing on the work of Pierre Bourdieu.[1] An immensely productive and imaginative author whose writings range from ethnographic studies of Algerian peasant life to sociological investigations of education and culture, Bourdieu has recently turned his attention to a systematic reflection on language and its role in the reproduction of social life.[2] In a sharp and suggestive way he has highlighted the twin dangers of a linguistic 'formalism' which ignores the social and political conditions of the formation and use of language, and a sociological 'interactionism' which fails to see that there is no linguistic exchange, however insignificant or personal it may seem, which does not bear the traces of the social structure that it helps to reproduce. Bourdieu attempts to steer between these dangers by elaborating a series of interrelated concepts which bring language into the scope of that general *theory of practice* which he brilliantly sketched a decade ago.[3] This theoretical framework enables one to analyse the ways in which symbolic practices exercise their own type of violence, 'a gentle, invisible form of violence' which is never recognized as such, or which is recognized only by concealing the mechanisms upon which it depends. The concept of symbolic violence directs us towards a reflection on the forms in which relations of communication are interwoven with relations of power.

In the space of this essay I cannot attempt to provide a general introduction to the work of Bourdieu,[4] nor can I endeavour to pursue all of the issues which are raised by his provocative claims. Rather, I shall restrict myself to a short exposition of his approach to language, referring where appropriate to other aspects of his work. I shall then undertake to assess, in a very selective way, some of his key concepts and claims. I want to argue that the concept of symbolic violence, however fruitful it may be in practice, is unrefined at a theoretical level and is linked to questionable assumptions concerning social reproduction. I shall also suggest that Bourdieu's preoccupation with *style*, with the way things are said and with the profits obtained thereby, leads him to neglect the *content* of what is said. He thus fails to give sufficient attention to the question of *meaning* (or signification) and he strips away all too abruptly the *rational* features of linguistic communication.

I

Reproduction of legitimate language

Bourdieu develops his approach to language through a critique of the presuppositions of modern linguistic theories. For such theories remain marked, in his view, by the initial *coup de force* whereby Saussure separated *langue* from the social conditions of its production, reproduction and utilization. Linguistics was thereafter preoccupied with the internal structure of *langue*, which was treated as an autonomous and homogeneous object of intellectual apprehension. In this respect, Chomsky's theoretical orientation is no different from Saussure's; Chomsky alters the terminology, speaking of 'competence' and 'performance' instead of *'langue'* and *'parole'*, but his concern with an idealized linguistic competence conjures away the question of the social and political conditions in which a particular competence is constituted as legitimate, is acquired by some speakers, imposed on others, and reproduced as the dominant form of language. As Bourdieu remarks,

> To speak of 'language' without further precision, as linguists do, is tacitly to accept the official definition of the official language of a political unit: this language is that which, within the territorial limits of this unit, is imposed on all the citizens as the only legitimate one, and all the more so when the circumstance is more official or 'formal'.[5]

Linguists incorporate a pre-constructed object in their theories, taking as a 'collective treasure' what is in many case a linguistic norm that has been imposed in a process of political unification. This tacit acceptance of a linguistic norm helps in turn to reinforce the legitimacy of the official language. It helps to secure, between all members of a 'linguistic community', a minimum level of communication which is a prerequisite of economic and symbolic production. In order to break this 'amnesia of the genesis' and to counter its political effects, one must begin by reconstructing the historical process by which a unified and asymmetrically structured *linguistic market* was formed.

In the case of French, the groundwork for such a reconstruction has been carried out by Ferdinand Brunot in his monumental study, *Histoire de la langue française des origines à nos jours*.[6] Brunot shows how, until the French Revolution, the process of linguistic unification was bound up with the construction of a monarchic state. In the central provinces of the *pays d'oïl* (Champagne, Normandie, Anjou, Berry), the dialects and literary languages of the feudal period gradually gave way, from the fourteenth century on, to the dialect of the *Ile de France*, promoted to the status of official language and used in a written form. During the same period, popular and purely oral dialects were relegated to the status of *patois*, defined negatively and pejoratively by opposition to the official language. The situation was different in the *pays de langue d'oc*, where it was not until the sixteenth century that the Parisian dialect was imposed as the official language. The latter did not eliminate the widespread use of local dialects in the *pays de langue d'oc*; a situation of bilingualism thus developed, with members of the peasantry and lower class speaking local dialects only, while the aristocracy and bourgeoisie had access to the official language as well. Members of the bourgeois class had everything to gain from the policy of linguistic unification which accompanied the French Revolution. Promoting the official language to the status of the national language gave them a *de facto* monopoly of the political apparatus and a privileged path of communication with the central power. The subsequent normalization, inculcation and legitimation of the official language was effected primarily by the educational system and its relation to the labour market. With the establishment of a system of educational qualifications endowed with a standardized value independent of social and regional properties, and with the unification of the labour market in which administrative positions depended upon educational qualifications, the school came to be seen as a principal means of access to the labour market, especially in areas where industrialization was weak. Thus, by the combined effect of various institutions and institutional mechanisms, people speaking local dialects were encouraged, if not compelled, 'to collaborate in the destruction of their instruments of expression'.[7]

Encouraged, if not compelled: this equivocation is not imprecise, because all forms of 'symbolic domination' presuppose a kind of complicity which is neither a passive submission to external constraint nor a free adoption of dominant values. Recognition of the legitimacy of the official language is inscribed in *dispositions* – more precisely, in *habitus*, a concept to which we shall return – through a process of inculcation which is most often gradual, implicit, imperceptible. Through this process, dispositions are adjusted, independently of any explicit calculation by the speakers concerned, to a specific state of the linguistic market. Speakers who do not possess the competence to speak the official language, but who nevertheless recognize its legitimacy, are thereby condemned to recognition without knowledge, to *reconnaissance sans connaissance*. 'Symbolic domination really begins', write Bourdieu and Boltanski, 'when the misrecognition (*méconnaissance*), implied by recognition (*reconnaissance*), leads those who are dominated to apply the dominant criteria of evaluation to their own practices'.[8] The reproduction of symbolic domination presupposes that those speakers dispossessed of the official language collaborate in their own dispossession, adopting criteria unfavourable for them in order to evaluate the linguistic productions of themselves and others. Here one might refer to the illuminating investigations of Labov, who shows, for example, that stigmatized features of speech are judged most severely by the very individuals whose speech exhibits most often these features.[9] But the most striking manifestation of *reconnaissance sans connaissance* is the silence to which those dispossessed of the official language are condemned, and condemn themselves, on 'formal' occasions: lacking the means of legitimate expression, they do not speak but are spoken to.

Power and the performative utterance

If linguistic theories have taken for granted a conception of language which is the product of, and which in turn reproduces, certain historical and political processes, so too linguists have tended to analyse language in isolation from the social conditions in which it is used. Thus by 'competence' Chomsky understands the capacity of an ideal speaker to generate an unlimited sequence of grammatically well-formed sentences.[10] But this notion of competence is altogether abstract, argues Bourdieu, so long as it is not related to the capacity to employ expressions in specific situations, that is, to produce sentences *à propos*. Speakers do not acquire linguistic competence alone, but acquire also the *practical competence* to employ the possibilities offered by their mastery of grammar. This practical competence enables speakers to embed sentences in strategies which have numerous functions and which are tacitly adjusted to the relations of force between speakers. Hence competence is *also* the capacity to make oneself heard:

> Language is not only an instrument of communication or even of knowledge, but also an instrument of power. One seeks not only to

be understood but also to be believed, obeyed, respected, distinguished. Whence the complete definition of competence as *right to
speak*, that is, as right to the legitimate language, the authorized
language, the language of authority. Competence implies the power
to impose reception.[11]

The Chomskyan notion of competence is too abstract to take
account of the *social conditions* for the establishment of communication. It takes no account of the fact that those who speak
must reckon that those who listen are worthy of listening, and
those who listen must reckon that those who speak are worthy of
speaking. More importantly, it overlooks the fact that in certain
situations some individuals, or some groups of individuals, are
effectively excluded from communication. The relations of force
implicit in all communicative situations are simply ignored by the
linguist, who treats the linguistic exchange as an intellectual
operation of coding and decoding a grammatically well-formed
message.

One of the merits of the theory of speech-acts, in Bourdieu's
view, is that it calls attention to the social conditions of communication. In singling out a class of 'performative utterances',
such as 'I do' uttered in the course of a marriage ceremony or 'I
name this ship the Queen Elizabeth' uttered while smashing a
bottle against the stem, Austin stressed that such utterances are not
strictly true or false but rather felicitous or infelicitous; and that
for such utterances to be felicitous they must, among other things,
be uttered by an appropriate person in accordance with some
conventional procedure.[12] This implies, according to Bourdieu,
that the efficacy of performative utterances is inseparable from the
existence of an *institution* which defines the conditions (such as the
place, the time, the agent) that must be fulfilled in order for the
utterance to be effective. It is the institution which endows the
speaker with the authority to carry out the act which the utterance
pretends to perform. Not anyone can stand before a freshly
completed ship, utter the words 'I name you . . .' while flinging a
bottle at its stem, and thereby succeed in *naming* the vessel. For the
person must be *authorized* to do so, must be invested with the
requisite *authority* to carry out the act. 'The real principle of the
magic of performative utterances', concludes Bourdieu, 'lies in the
mystery of the minister, the delegation at the end of which an

individual agent – king, priest, *porte-parole* – is appointed to speak and to act in the name of the group, thus constituted in him and by him'.[13] The practical competence which speakers employ is thus linked to the distribution of 'symbolic capital'. Individuals possess more or less of this capital in so far as they are in a position to mobilize more or less of the authority delegated by an institution. There are numerous aspects of language use – erudite references, elegant style, distinguished accent – whose *raison d'être* is primarily to attest to the authority of the speaker or author.

Speech-act theorists rightly call attention to the social conditions of communication, but they hardly do justice to the *social* character of these conditions. Austin refers to 'conventional procedures' which must be followed for the felicitous utterance of a performative; and later, when he shifts to the terminology of locutionary, illocutionary and perlocutionary acts, he suggests that illocutionary acts (the act performed *in* saying something) may be distinguished from perlocutionary acts (the act performed *by* saying something) by the fact that illocutionary acts employ 'conventional means'. But never does Austin examine in detail the nature of these conventions and explore their relation to the social institutions of which they are part. Consequently there is a tendency among speech-act theorists to assume that the conventions upon which speech-acts depend are primarily *linguistic* in character, that the power or force which speech-acts possess stems from language itself. But to succumb to this tendency, contends Bourdieu, 'is to forget that authority comes to language from outside':

> If, as Austin observes, there are utterances which do not only 'describe a state of affairs or state some fact' but also 'perform an action', it is because the power of words consists in the fact that they are not uttered on the personal account of someone who is merely the 'bearer': the authorized *porte-parole* can act by words on other agents, and thereby on things themselves, only because his speech concentrates the symbolic capital accumulated by the group which has mandated him and which provides the *basis of power*.[14]

Hence to give an adequate analysis of the relations between language and power, of the relations of symbolic force which are implicit in speech-acts, one must broaden the scope of the inquiry and examine the structures and properties of the linguistic markets within which speakers exchange their expressions.

Linguistic markets

Whenever two or more speakers exchange expressions, they do so within a linguistic market or field that is structured in certain ways. A market or field may be seen synchronically as a structured space of positions, such that the properties of these positions depend upon their location within the space and not upon the personal attributes of their occupants. However different the fields may be – whether, for example, it is a pedagogical space in which teachers transmit a form of 'knowledge' or a cultural space in which literary works are offered for consumption – there are certain general laws which commonly obtain. Thus, in every field, one may find a struggle between the *nouveaux entrants* who try to jump over the rights of entry and to alter the structure in their favour, and those established agents or groups who try to defend their monopoly and to exclude competition. The 'structure' of the market or field is a certain state of the relation of force between the agents or groups engaged in struggle; or, more precisely, a certain state 'of the distribution of the specific capital which, accumulated in the course of previous struggles, orients subsequent strategies'.[15] Just as there are different kinds of market, so too there are different kinds of capital ('economic', 'cultural', 'symbolic'), and one of the most important properties of fields is the way that they allow one kind of capital to be converted into another (in the way, for example, that certain educational qualifications can be cashed in for lucrative jobs).[16] What is at stake in the struggles within particular fields is the structure of the field itself, that is, the distribution of the capital which is specific to it. Those who, in a given state of the distribution, possess the greatest capital are inclined towards strategies of conservation, towards preserving a state of *doxa* in which the established structure is not questioned. Those least endowed with capital (often the young and newly arrived) are inclined towards strategies of subversion, of heresy or *heterodoxy*. By bringing what is undiscussed into the universe of discourse and hence criticism, heterodoxy impels the dominant agents or groups to step out of their silence and to produce a defensive discourse of *orthodoxy*. The relation between the different strategies which can be adopted in the struggles characteristic of particular markets or fields – struggles which must always be analysed, of course, in their historical specificity – can be represented as in figure 1.[17] While those engaged in struggles may have antagonistic aims, nevertheless they generally share a basic interest in the preservation of the market or field. By participating in the struggle they help to reproduce the very game whose rules have become the object of dispute.

As in other kinds of market, linguistic markets are characterized by the distribution of a specific capital and by the existence of what may be called a 'law of price formation'. The specific capital is *linguistic capital*: not just the competence to produce grammatically well-formed expressions, but the capacity to produce expressions *à propos, for* a particular market. In producing an utterance the speaker invests linguistic capital, with the implicit aim of maximizing the material and symbolic profit that can be obtained. This aim is 'implicit' because it is not so much a conscious calculation as a tacit anticipation, based on a practical sense of the acceptability and probable value of one's own linguistic products on the market concerned. Hence the anticipated conditions of reception are part of the conditions of production of discourse. The *value* of a linguistic product is determined by its confrontation on the market with products presenting differences

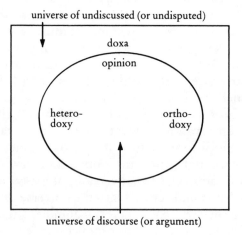

Figure 1

associated with social differences – this is what Bourdieu calls, continue the analogy, the 'law of price formation'. A language offers many different ways of saying things. These regulated differences and rules of variation form a system of linguistic oppositions in which a system of social differences is expressed. The initial task of a 'structural sociology of language', as Bourdieu conceives it, is thus *'to relate structured systems of sociologically pertinent linguistic differences to equally structured systems of social differences'.*[18] The very differences overlooked by linguistics are indices of the social positions of the speakers and reflections of the quantities of linguistic capital which they possess. In a society divided into classes, variations in accent, syntax and vocabulary are socially marked (as distinguished or vulgar) and mark the speakers who employ them. Even the most elementary or intimate exchange between two speakers bears the traces of the social structure of which they are part and which their utterances help to reproduce. The more linguistic capital that speakers possess, the more they are able to exploit the system of differences to their advantage and thereby to secure a *profit of distinction*. For the material and symbolic profits which accrue to linguistic capital do not correspond directly to the cost of formation of speakers: they depend in part upon the scarcity value that linguistic products have on various markets in virtue of their position in the structure of distribution. The modes of expression which receive the greatest value and secure the greatest profit are those which are most unequally distributed, both in the sense that the conditions for the acquisition of the capacity to produce them are restricted and in the sense that the expressions themselves are rare.

Consider an example. It is September 1974 in Béarn, a province in southern France where a local dialect, Béarnais, is spoken. The occasion is an official celebration of the centenary of the birth of a Béarnais poet, Simin Palay. A French newspaper published in the province reported an event that 'greatly moved the audience who applauded at length': the event was that the mayor of Pau addressed the audience in a 'Béarnais of quality'.[19] Why should a group of people whose tongue is Béarnais feel greatly moved by the fact that a Béarnais mayor addresses them in Béarnais on the occasion of honouring a Béarnais poet? Such a reaction is possible, argues Bourdieu, only in so far as they tacitly recognize the unwritten law which imposes French as the only acceptable language on official

ie mayor of Pau employs a *strategy of condescension*
the very act of symbolically negating the objective
orce between the two languages which confront one
draws *profit* from this relation. He draws profit from
hy between the languages because everyone knows that,
of a large town, he also has all of the qualifications which
his competence in the 'superior' language. And it is
precisely in virtue of this position that he is able to negate symbolically the hierarchy, to transgress the unwritten law and thereby to
exploit the hierarchy in the very process of reinforcing it. What is
praised as a 'Béarnais of quality' when issued from the mouth of
the mayor would have had a quite different (and no doubt much
less) value had it been uttered by a peasant who spoke mere
fragments of French. In language as in culture more generally,
strategies of subversion 'have a good chance of being *also* strategies
of condescension reserved for those who are sufficiently assured of
their position in the objective hierarchies to be able to negate them
without appearing to ignore them or to be incapable of satisfying
their demands'.[20]

Linguistic habitus and corporeal hexis

The anticipation of profit is based on a practical sense which is
seldom articulated as such, but which operates as a *generative
principle* for the production and appreciation of linguistic
expressions. The idea of a principle which generates action is part
of Bourdieu's more general concept of *habitus*. In *Outline of a
Theory of Practice* this concept is introduced in the context of a
remarkable discussion of the gift exchange in Kabyle society.
Bourdieu argues that the structuralist attempt to conceptualize the
exchange of gifts as a 'reversible' process is at best one-sided, for it
overlooks the fact that *time* is intrinsic to the exchange of gifts. To
offer a gift is to call for a response, and the inaugural act receives its
sense from the response that it calls forth. If it is not to be an insult,
the counter-gift must be both deferred and different; to reveal
one's haste to return a gift is to denounce the inaugural act as
motivated by the intention of obliging the recipient. By playing
with the tempo of the exchange each participant responds to the
challenge of the other and seeks to sustain a 'sense of honour'. The
latter is an inculcated disposition which provides certain para-

meters of action, enabling each agent to engender a whole range of practices, and only those practices, which are consistent with the logic of challenge and riposte. Such a disposition, or system of dispositions, is what Bourdieu calls 'habitus', the main features of which are summed up (rather densely) in the following passage:

> the structures constitutive of a particular type of environment . . . produce the habitus, systems of durable *dispositions*, structured structures predisposed to function as structuring structures, that is, as the principle of generation and structuration of practices and representations which can be objectively 'regulated' and 'regular' without in any way being the product of obedience to rules, objectively adapted to their goal without presupposing the conscious orientation towards ends and the express mastery of the operations necessary to attain them and, being all that, collectively orchestrated without being the product of the organizing action of a conductor.[21]

Let us unpack a few of these features. The habitus is a system of durable, transposable dispositions which mediates between structures and practices. It is a product of the structures constitutive of the conditions of existence within which it is acquired – for example, the conditions of existence of a particular class in a class-divided society. The dispositions are acquired through a gradual process of inculcation, the specific modes and characteristics of which depend upon the institutional arrangements of the society concerned. The dispositions are inculcated in a *durable* way: the body is literally moulded into certain forms, so that the habitus is reflected in the whole way that one carries oneself in the world, the way that one walks, speaks, acts, eats. The dispositions are 'transposable' in the sense that they are capable of generating practices in fields other than that in which they were originally acquired. As durably installed systems of dispositions, the habitus tends to generate practices and perceptions which concur with the conditions of existence of which they are the product, and which those practices and perceptions thereby reproduce. This does not mean, Bourdieu stresses, that actors are to be regarded as mere dupes of the social structures which determine their every action. On the contrary, actors have numerous strategies at their disposal and they often act in reflective and deliberative ways; but their action and reflection always takes place within a structured space of possibilities that defines a certain *style of life*.[22]

The *linguistic* habitus is a specific instance of the system of dispositions which govern practice. Acquired in the course of learning to speak in particular markets (most importantly, in a family occupying a determinate position in the social space), the linguistic habitus governs both our subsequent linguistic practices and our anticipation of the value that our linguistic products will receive on other markets, such as the school or the labour market. 'The system of successive reinforcements or refutations thus constitutes in each of us', observes Bourdieu, 'a sense of the social value of linguistic usages and of the relation between different usages and different markets which organizes all subsequent perceptions of linguistic products, tending to give them a high degree of stability.'[23] The sense of the value of one's own linguistic products is a fundamental dimension of the sense of one's position in the social space; it governs not only the expressions one produces, but also the very relation one adopts to different markets. For members of the dominant class, whose linguistic habitus incorporates the dominant norm, there is a concordance between the necessities of most markets and the dispositions of the habitus; whence the confident if circumspect ease with which they speak, the *relaxation within tension* which underlies all the distinctive traits of the dominant mode of expression. The hyper-correction of the *petits-bourgeois*, on the other hand, is the consequence of a class divided against itself, seeking to produce, at the cost of a constant anxiety and tension, linguistic expressions which bear the mark of a habitus other than their own. For members of the lower class, whose conditions of existence are least conducive to the acquisition of the dominant norm, there are many markets in which their linguistic products are assigned, by others as well as by themselves, a limited value. Hence the tendency of lower-class children to eliminate themselves from the educational system, or to resign themselves to devalorized courses of training.[24] Hence also the unease, the hesitation leading to silence, which, as previously noted, overcomes many members of the lower class on occasions defined as official.

As a durably installed system of dispositions, the linguistic habitus is inscribed in the body, forming 'one dimension of the corporeal hexis where the whole relation to the social world, and the socially inculcated relation to the world, is expressed'.[25] The inculcation of habitus is the incorporation of habitus: through countless forms of linguistic-corporeal discipline ('sit up straight', 'don't talk with your mouth full', etc.), social structures are transformed into patterns of behaviour which are withdrawn from consciousness and which define our way of being in the world. Thus a particular accent is an aspect of what Bourdieu calls, following Pierre Guiraud, an 'articulatory style'.[26] Different classes have different articulatory styles which concern above all the use of the *mouth*. The relation of class and articulatory style is recognized not only in the perception of class accents mediated by the mouth, but also in the association of different conceptions of the mouth with different classes and sexes. Members of the lower class, for example, tend to draw a sexually overdetermined opposition between a closed and pinched mouth (*bouche*), tense and heavily censured, bourgeois and feminine, on the one hand; and a large and open mouth (*gueule*),[77] relaxed and unconstrained, popular and masculine, on the other. The large and open mouth is associated with a spontaneity and expression that excludes mannerisms, with a virility that manifests itself in verbal violence (*fort en gueule*, 'loud mouth') or physical violence (*casser la gueule*, 'smash somebody's mouth in'). One can see that, from this viewpoint, the adoption of the articulatory style of the dominant class may appear to some members of the lower class as a negation not only of their social identity, but also of their sexual identity. Lower-class male speakers can adopt the dominant articulatory style only at the cost of a double negation, involving both the acceptance of docility (already imposed on women by the sexual division of labour and the division of sexual labour) and the acquisition of dispositions which are perceived as effeminate. Perhaps this helps to explain the fact, recorded by Labov and others,[28] that lower-class women show a greater shift towards prestigious forms of speech than lower-class men, while the latter tend to take the lead in the use of new vernacular forms of expression.

Symbolic violence

Many of the features highlighted by Bourdieu's approach to language are instances of what he calls, poignantly and provocatively, 'symbolic violence'. This notion appears throughout his writings and is used in different ways in different contexts, depending upon the social phenomena under consideration. Let me introduce the notion by returning to Bourdieu's discussion of the gift exchange in Kabyle society. According to Bourdieu, one must distinguish between types of society like Kabylia in which there are no objectified institutions for sustaining relations of domination, and those types of society (such as our own) in which objectified institutions exist. In the former types of society, relations of domination can be established and sustained only by means of strategies which must be continuously renewed, because the conditions do not exist for a stable and mediated appropriation of other agents' labour or homage. When domination can only be exercised in this 'elementary' form – that is, between persons rather than via institutions – it must be disguised beneath the veil of an enchanted relationship, lest it destroy itself by revealing its true nature and provoking a violent response from the victims or forcing them to flee. Hence the mode of domination which may be found most pervasively in Kabyle society is not overt violence but 'symbolic violence', 'the gentle, invisible form of violence, misrecognized as such, chosen as much as it is submitted to, the violence of confidence, of personal loyalty, of hospitality, of the gift, of the debt, of recognition, of piety – of all the virtues, in a word, which are honoured by the ethics of honour'.[29] The exchange of gifts is a form of symbolic violence through which an interested relationship is transmuted into a disinterested, gratuitous relationship. For giving is also a way of possessing; a gift which is not met by a counter-gift, or which cannot be met by a counter-gift of comparable quality, creates a lasting bond and obliges the debtor to adopt a peaceful, co-operative attitude. This way of sustaining domination could not work, however, without the complicity of everyone involved. The misrecognition of the economic reality of the gift exchange is a collective deception without a deceiver, for it is a misrecognition embodied in the habitus of the group.

Symbolic violence assumes different forms in those types of society in which relations of domination are sustained by objectified institutions, such as a self-regulating market, an educational system or a state. The development of institutions renders possible both a continuous accumulation of material and symbolic goods and their differential allocation. In virtue of the objectivity and relative autonomy of the institutions, the individuals who are placed in dominant positions can dispense with strategies aimed directly at the domination of others: violence is built into the institution itself. Thus, in *Reproduction*, Bourdieu and Passeron conceive of the educational system as an institutionalized agency for the exercise of symbolic violence, where the latter is understood as the imposition of a 'cultural arbitrary'. That which is imposed by the educational system is 'arbitrary' in the sense that it cannot be deduced from any 'universal principle' of a physical, biological or spiritual kind; and yet the cultural arbitrary is embedded in the system of power relations between groups or classes, so that its imposition serves to sustain the existing relations of domination. The educational system can succeed in imposing the cultural arbitrary only in so far as the arbitrariness is misrecognized as such, that is, is recognized as legitimate. In reproducing the cultural arbitrary, the educational system both reproduces the relations of domination between groups or classes and legitimates those relations – for example, by presenting itself as autonomous and thereby concealing the fact that scholastic hierarchies reproduce social hierarchies. In the words of Bourdieu and Passeron,

> The educational system succeeds so perfectly in fulfilling its ideological function of legitimating the established order only because this masterpiece of social mechanics succeeds in concealing, as if by the interlocking of false-bottomed boxes, the relations which, in a class-divided society, unite the function of inculcation, that is, the function of intellectual and moral integration with the function of conserving the structure of class relations characteristic of that society.[30]

If symbolic violence is the imposition of a cultural arbitrary, then such violence is also implicit in the hierarchies of language and ways of using language. Every utterance, on Bourdieu's account, is the product of a compromise between an 'expressive interest' (what is to be said) and the *censorship* inherent in the structure of the market for which the utterance is produced. The 'law of price formation' which obtains in a given market functions as a structural censor on the nature and form of the expressions produced therein. By means of the practical anticipation of profit, this censor is exercised as a kind of self-censorship which inclines speakers to adopt a certain form, to *euphemize* their expressions by putting them into forms which are positively sanctioned by the market. Variations in the form of expressions depend both upon the objective tension of the market – that is, upon the formality of the

occasion and the social distance between the speaker and receiver –
and upon the capacity of the speaker to respond to this tension
with a suitably euphemized expression. The more 'formal' the
occasion, the more manifest the violence exercised on those speakers who are not endowed with the dominant language or the
dominant mode of language use. Hence this gentle, surreptitious
violence

> is never so manifest as in all the corrections, momentary or long-
> lasting, to which dominated speakers, in a desperate effort towards
> correction, consciously or unconsciously subject the stigmatized
> aspects of their pronunciation, their vocabulary (with all the forms
> of euphemism) and their syntax; or in the confusion which makes
> them 'lose their means', rendering them incapable of 'finding their
> words', as if they had been suddenly dispossessed of their own
> language.[31]

The tendency towards self-correction on formal occasions presupposes a *recognition* of the legitimacy of the dominant language
or dominant mode of language use, and hence a *misrecognition* of
the fact that this language or mode of language use is imposed *as*
dominant. The exercise of symbolic violence is so invisible to social
actors precisely because it presupposes the complicity of those
who suffer most from its effects.

II

Recognition, misrecognition, legitimacy

So far I have been concerned to present Bourdieu's views in a
systematic and sympathetic way, refraining from critical comment.
At this point I wish to change tack and to engage in a more critical
and constructive reflection on his work. I shall begin with the
concept of symbolic violence, for this concept crystallizes some
of the key aspects of Bourdieu's approach to language. Premised
upon a rejection of the distinction between relations of communication and relations of power, symbolic violence is that form
of domination which is exercised through the communication in
which it is concealed. Gentle because accepted, invisible because
unseen for what it is, symbolic violence is characterized by a

distinctive *mélange* of recognition (*reconnaissance*) and misrecognition (*méconnaissance*); and it is in virtue of this *mélange* that symbolic violence is an effective medium of social reproduction. Much of the interest of Bourdieu's concept lies in the highly suggestive analyses which it facilitates and from which it stems. The discussion of the gift exchange in Kabylia, the study of the educational system in capitalist societies, the investigation of censorship and self-censorship in language: all of these analyses are worthy of detailed consideration. However, the issues I want to raise here are of a more general character. I want to begin by probing, in an initial and analytical way, the notions of recognition and misrecognition which are so central to Bourdieu's account. I then want to argue that these notions incline Bourdieu to rely too heavily on a consensual model of social reproduction. At a later stage I shall return to the question of language and power, with the aim of indicating some ways in which Bourdieu's provocative insights could be pursued.

Symbolic violence is not any form of domination exercised through communication: it is the exercise of domination through communication in such a way that the domination is *misrecognized* as such and thereby *recognized* as legitimate. The difficulty with this conception is that it relies upon notions which are themselves vague and ambiguous, and which are never rigorously analysed by Bourdieu. Consider for a moment the notion of recognition. There are several senses in which it could be said that a certain agent A from the lower class recognizes a particular mode M of language use as dominant and legitimate:

1 A recognizes M as the mode characteristic of a group or class which occupies a privileged position in the society concerned.
2 A recognizes M as the mode characteristic of a group or class which occupies a privileged position in the society concerned *and* regards M as the appropriate or necessary way to speak in certain circumstances (for example, on 'official' occasions).
3 A recognizes M as the mode characteristic of a group or class which occupies a privileged position in the society concerned *and* regards M as the correct or proper way to speak *as such*.
4 A regards M as the correct or proper way to speak *as such*.

Each form of recognition could be correlated with specific kinds of misrecognition. In 1, for example, A may have a very partial or limited grasp of the social structure of the society concerned, even though A recognizes the privileged position of the group or class which employs M. The same could be said of A in case 2; here it could be added, however, that A mistakenly regards M as the appropriate or necessary way to speak in certain circumstances; or that in so doing A grants M a privileged status which it has only in virtue of its link with the group or class which employs M, although A does not fully grasp this link. In cases 3 and 4 the possibilities are even more numerous: A may have a very partial or limited grasp of the social structure of the society concerned; or A may fail to see that, in regarding M as the correct or proper way to speak *as such*, A is granting M a privileged status which it has only in virtue of its link with the group or class which employs M, even though A may recognize that M is characteristic of that group or class; or A may simply fail to see any connection between M and the social structure of the society concerned.

My purpose in delineating these various possibilities (to which others could easily be added) is not to engage in some analytical exercise for its own sake. For the time being I want to bracket, moreover, the question of how any imputation of misrecognition can be justified. My concern at this stage is to stress that Bourdieu's concept of symbolic violence, however suggestive it may be, is at best a signpost which points to social phenomena worthy of attention, but which obscures as many issues as it illuminates. Let me offer an example to support this contention. A working-class student who, in the course of an interview for admission to university, strives to eliminate the more prominent aspects of a class and regional accent and to speak a more 'scholarly' English: this, it would seem, is a prime instance of symbolic violence. Yet such action may involve different forms and different degrees of 'recognition' and 'misrecognition'. At one extreme, the student may assume that 'scholarly' English is correct or proper English and is therefore the English to be emulated, acquired and spoken; at the other extreme, the student may recognize 'scholarly' English to be a particular form of English employed by certain groups in certain places, may reckon that the use of this form will improve his or her chances of obtaining a university place, but may despise this form of language and have no wish to acquire it. No doubt there could be senses in which recognition and misrecognition entered into both extremes, but the senses are evidently very different. No doubt it could even be said that symbolic violence is possible in both cases only in so far as the student collaborates in the process, abandoning his or her own means of expression for another; but the nature of the collaboration is hardly comparable in the two cases. If complicity can be a sign of assimilation to the social order, it can also be a way of circumventing or even disrupting that order by employing the means which are proper to it. Lacking a rigorous analysis of the notions of recognition, misrecognition and legitimacy, Bourdieu's concept of symbolic violence fails to do justice to the different strategies which may be implicit in, and the different consequences which may follow from, the practices which appear to fall within its scope.

Consensus, fragmentation, social reproduction

The ambiguities in the concept of symbolic violence are connected to a fundamental assumption of Bourdieu's theory of social reproduction. This is the assumption – not so much an explicit thesis as an implicit, underlying theme – that social reproduction presupposes a certain kind of *consensus* with regard to the values or norms which are dominant in the society concerned. This is, of course, a very special kind of consensus; Bourdieu is too sensitive to the diversity of culture and the subtleties of power to suggest that our societies are populated by individuals who generally and openly agree with one another. Nevertheless, the concept of symbolic violence presupposes a form of complicity, a form of *reconnaissance sans connaissance*, through which and by means of which domination is sustained. Thus the educational system can reproduce relations of domination only in so far as pedagogic action is recognized, both by those who exercise it and by those who submit to it, as 'legitimate authority'. Similarly, the reproduction of symbolic domination (and therewith the broader relations of domination of which symbolic domination is part) presupposes that speakers dispossessed of the dominant language collaborate in their dispossession, accepting that the dominant language is the 'legitimate' one. Bourdieu is concerned to stress that the recognition or acceptance of dominant values or norms as legitimate is rarely a free and fully conscious act on the part of the agent.

Rather, agents accept or recognize these values or norms as legitimate in so far as the latter operate as practically effective schemes
of perception or evaluation, that is, in so far as they are constitutive
of the habitus. The consensus which exists with regard to dominant values or norms is a *practical* consensus, a collective orches-
tration which has no need of conscious orientation or explicit co-
ordination. Such is the core, on Bourdieu's account, of that
complex and bewildering phenomenon of social reproduction.

I do not wish to underrate the importance of Bourdieu's contribution to the problem of reproduction. While I think that all of
the key concepts in his theoretical framework – including the
concepts of disposition, habitus, structure and class – are in need
of more clarification and defence, nevertheless I believe that his
approach to the problem of reproduction is sound in many respects. The question that I wish to raise here is more a matter of
emphasis than a matter of principle: must we assume, as Bourdieu
appears to do, that social reproduction presupposes some sort of
consensus with regard to dominant values or norms? It seems to
me that there are good reasons to reject this assumption, for it may
well present a misleading view of the conditions underlying the
stabilization of, in particular, contemporary capitalist societies.
Such stabilization may depend, it can plausibly be argued,[32] not so
much upon an implicit consensus among social members, but
rather upon a pervasive *fragmentation* of the social order and a
proliferation of divisions between its members. Social theory can
relinquish the need to find a conductor for the concert of social
reproduction, not so much because this is a concert performed
without a conductor by the harmonizing effects of the habitus, but
because social reproduction is less a concert than a cacophony of
discordant and divergent notes. Many working-class youths are
sharply critical, for example, of the authority structure of the
school and of the values transmitted by it, distancing themselves
aggressively from the 'ear'oles' who, in their eyes, have gone over
to the enemy camp.[33] Numerous studies of political attitudes have
also indicated that the degree of allegiance to the liberal democratic
system is linked to the socio-economic status of the respondents:
white-collar and professional workers are more supportive of the
system, and have greater faith in its efficacy, than manual and
factory workers, who are more likely to be hostile to, and sceptical
of, the political apparatus.[34] Yet the hostility and scepticism of

particular groups or classes does not necessarily threaten the stability of the social order. For oppositional attitudes do not necessarily generate a coherent alternative view which would provide a basis for political action. Hostility and scepticism are often interfused with traditional and conservative values and are commonly tempered by a sense of resignation. Divisions are ramified along the lines of gender, race, qualifications and so on, forming barriers which obstruct the development of movements which could threaten the *status quo*. The reproduction of the social order may depend less upon a consensus with regard to dominant values or norms than upon a *lack of consensus* at the very point where oppositional attitudes could be translated into political action.

To call into question the consensual model of social reproduction is not to dismiss altogether the need for a concept of legitimacy and a theory of ideology; it is rather to suggest that the role of this concept and the task of this theory may be in need of reconsideration. The *legitimacy* of a social order may be conceived, not as a factual recognition conferred upon dominant values or norms and presupposed by social reproduction, but as a counterfactual claim raised by those members of a society who wish to maintain the existing system of social relations.[35] This claim is 'counterfactual' in the sense that it implies a normative ideal; it asserts that existing institutional arrangements are 'just', which implies that they *could be justified*, although the efficacy of this claim as a means of maintaining existing arrangements may require this counterfactual implication to be suppressed. To study the ways in which legitimacy is claimed for institutional arrangements which embody systematically asymmetrical relations of power – that is, which embody relations of domination – is one of the tasks of a theory of *ideology*. For the study of ideology may be conceived as the study of the ways in which meaning (signification) serves to sustain relations of domination. Just as it cannot be assumed that dominant values or norms are shared by all members of a society, so too it would be misguided to approach a society on the assumption that its unity and stability were secured by a 'dominant ideology'.[36] For ideology operates, not so much as a coherent system of statements imposed on a population from above, but rather through a complex series of mechanisms whereby meaning is mobilized, in the discursive practices of everyday life, for the maintenance of relations of domination. It is of the utmost importance, therefore, to search for ways in which the theory of ideology can be linked with methods for the analysis of the discursive forms in which ideology is expressed.[37]

Style and content

In developing his critique of linguistic theories, Bourdieu provides some valuable indicators for anyone who wishes to study the socially situated realization of a particular language. Such a realization cannot be seen, he plausibly argues, as the mere implementation of a capacity to produce grammatically well-formed sentences; for it is also inseparably the actualization of a capacity, possessed to a greater or lesser extent depending upon one's position in the social space, to produce expressions *à propos*. Hence Bourdieu urges the analyst to steer between the *formalism* of linguistic theories which ignore the practical competence of the agent and the *narrowness* of sociolinguistic studies which focus on the details of social interaction, in isolation from the structural features which interactions reproduce. While one may have doubts about Bourdieu's apparent extrapolation from certain features of a capitalistic market-place, nevertheless the concept of a linguistic market or field provides a potentially fruitful way to pursue this intermediate course.[38] It provides a way of linking the characteristics of linguistic products with the social and historical conditions of their production and reception, as well as with those properties of the producers and receivers which constitute their linguistic habitus.

However fruitful Bourdieu's approach may be, it results, I believe, in an over-emphasis on form or *style* at the expense of any consideration of *content*. This over-emphasis follows directly from his conception of the 'value' of a linguistic product. In spite of his forceful criticism of Saussure, Bourdieu takes over the latter's idea that the value of a term is determined by its *difference* with regard to the other terms which compose the system of which it is part. This idea is translated by Bourdieu into a sociological framework, whereby the differences expressed in language are related to a hierarchical system of social differences. Hence the value of a linguistic product is determined by its *social distinction*, that is, by its relation to other products on a market which is structured in specific ways. Agents seek to maximize their material and symbolic profit by adopting a particular style of expression or by realizing their expressions in a particular form. 'To speak', on Bourdieu's account, 'is to appropriate one or another of the expressive styles already constituted in and by usage and objectively marked by their position in a hierarchy of styles which expresses the hierarchy of corresponding groups.'[39] And yet that is not *all*, of course, that is involved in speaking. For to speak is *also* to say something, or to claim to say something, about something. I may express myself in an elegant or clumsy way, in a refined or vulgar way, in a circuitous or straightforward way, in a convoluted or perspicuous way, in a modest or pretentious way; but in any case I *express myself*, or try to express myself, and in many cases try *to say something about something*. My reservation concerning Bourdieu's approach is that, by conceptualizing the value of a linguistic product in terms of its social distinction, he tends to neglect the content of what is said or to treat the content as in some sense 'exhausted' by the style. One can readily admit that there is a close and vital connection between the content of a linguistic product and its form, between what is said and the way of saying it. But it is quite unjustified to proceed to analyse a linguistic product – as Bourdieu analyses the texts of Heidegger and Althusser – as if the *only* thing of interest in the product were its form, the particular way in which it plays with oppositions and distinctions and their relation to the system of social differences.[40] If this were the only issue of interest, then Bourdieu's own texts could have been abandoned long ago to an inconsequential appraisal of sociological style.

In raising the question of content, I wish to defend the dimension of meaning or *signification* and to claim that this dimension is not reducible to the level of *sens*, where the latter is understood as the differential value of a term in relation to the other terms of a system. This is not the place for me to embark upon an analysis of the concept of meaning, a concept of which there are almost as many formulations as there are authors who have treated it in their work. I shall limit myself to proposing three interrelated theses which define, in a rough and general way, the elements of a positive account. First thesis: 'meaning' is not a stable or invariant property of a linguistic product, but rather a multi-layered and fluctuating phenomenon which is constituted as much by the conditions of production as by the conditions of reception. Hence one cannot 'understand the meaning of an expression' without investigating the social-historical conditions in which it is produced as well as the conditions – historically specific and socially differentiated according to group, class, sex, region and so on – in which it is received. In this respect we may agree with Bourdieu's remark that 'the linguistic product is fully realized as message only if it is treated as such, that is, deciphered, and the schemes of interpretation which receivers employ in their creative appropriation of the product can be more or less distant from those which oriented the production'.[41] My second thesis is this: while meaning is not reducible to *sens*, nevertheless it is mediated by certain structural features of the linguistic product. In the case of linguistic products which exceed the length of individual utterances or sentences, such features include narrative and argumentative patterns as well as various aspects of grammar, syntax and style. The meaning of an expression is not wholly constituted by these features but is commonly constructed *with* them, so that an understanding of meaning may be facilitated by a reconstruction of the features which structure the linguistic product. It is my view, however, that such a reconstruction can never dispense with the need for a creative *interpretation* of meaning: this is my third thesis. A linguistic product is not only a socially and historically situated construction which displays an articulated structure, but is also an expression which claims to say something about something; and it is this claim, understood in terms of what is *asserted* by an expression and what that expression is *about*, which must be grasped by interpretation. It is at this point that I would rejoin my earlier remarks concerning the theory of ideology. For if ideology operates by the mobilization of meaning for the maintenance of relations of domination, then the analysis of ideology must seek to interpret the meaning of linguistic expressions in relation to the social and historical conditions in which they are produced and received. To the extent that such an analysis generates interpretations which diverge from the accounts of agents in the social world, it offers the possibility of a critique of ideology and a critique of the relations of domination which ideology serves to sustain.

Language and power

At this stage let us return to Bourdieu's texts and take up again the question of language and power. I believe that Bourdieu is right to emphasize the importance of this question and to call attention to its occlusion (or its repression) in many linguistic theories and philosophies of language. As soon as language or linguistic competence is constituted as an autonomous object, distinct from and independent of its realization in actual circumstances, one loses sight of the specific social conditions in virtue of which an agent is able to say something and thereby to have some effect on others and on the world. While some philosophers of language have attempted to take these conditions into account and have underlined their conventional character, they have not pursued their investigations far enough. For they have tended to take for granted, as a sort of undifferentiated backcloth of philosophical analysis, what is in fact a highly differentiated and stratified phenomenon: namely, the society or social 'form of life' which is the condition of meaningful speech. Philosophers have taken for granted something which calls for further reflection, a reflection which would show, as Bourdieu rightly suggests, that the utterance of speech-acts involves the implementation of institutionally established relations of power.

So far I concur with the thrust of Bourdieu's thought. Where he goes astray is in his contention that 'the power of words' is, exclusively and *in toto*, the power to mobilize the authority conferred on the agent by the group which he or she represents: 'the power of words', as Bourdieu puts it, 'is nothing other than the *delegated power* of the *porte-parole* and his words – that is, indissociably, the substance of his discourse and his way of speaking – are at the very most a testimony, and one testimony among others, of the warranty of delegation which is invested in him'.[42] I do not wish to deny that in many cases there is a close connection between the power or force that words may have, on the one hand, and the institutional position of the person who speaks, on the other. In many cases a speech-act *is* an 'institutional act' which is listened to, believed, obeyed, answered precisely because it is 'authorized' by the institution concerned – one need only think of the institutional arrangements in virtue of which the mayor of Pau was able to 'move' his Béarnais audience. But it seems to me quite misleading to take this sort of case as the *paradigm* of the way in which language and power intersect. For there are countless instances of everyday speech which are not 'authorized' by any 'institution' (a term used without precision by Bourdieu), and yet which could be said, I think, to be acts of power. Consider the case of a person who, in the course of a conversation among friends, seeks to embarrass or humiliate another, to silence or subordinate him or her, by commenting on some aspect of that person's appearance or past; or consider the case of a person who tries to probe into the life of another, like a special kind of surgeon who, 'instead of anaesthetizing, deliberately stimulates pain in certain organs in order to find out what he wants to know about the rest of the body';[43] or consider the case of a person who, when faced with the prospect of being left by a lover, threatens to commit suicide or to carry out some other act of self-mutilation. So many cases, it seems to me, in which to speak is to perform an act of power, but in which it could hardly be said that the latter was the delegated power of a *porte-parole*.

A more satisfactory account of the link between language and power would require a more systematic analysis of the concept of action and its relation to the institutional and structural dimensions of the social world. This is not the place for me to undertake such an analysis;[44] suffice it to indicate a few of the ways in which the notion of power and its link with language could be reappraised. Power can be loosely conceptualized as the capacity of an agent or agents to secure specific outcomes through their intervention (or non-intervention) in the course of events. As in all forms of action, it makes sense to describe what an agent does as an 'act of power' only in so far as it makes sense to say that the agent 'could have done otherwise', for only then is what the agent does an *act* at all. In exercising this capacity the agent implements various kinds of *resources*. The latter are often institutionally sustained and institutionally endowed resources, such as the 'economic capital' (fixed or variable) accumulated by an enterprise, the 'symbolic capital' (authority, prestige, respect) associated with an institutional position, or the 'cultural capital' (knowledge, rhetorical skills, titles, academic qualifications) transmitted through the family and the educational system. But there are other kinds of resources which are not necessarily linked to particular institutions: in interpersonal relationships, for example, it is the *affection of the other* which is often employed as a resource by agents in pursuit of divergent aims. The complexity of the relation between power and language stems in part from the ambiguous, indeed ubiquitous, role of language itself. For not only is language, in the form of 'linguistic capital', a resource employed by agents in pursuit of their aims, but it is also, *qua* speech-action, a principal medium through which their aims are pursued. To examine the relations between language and power is to study the ways in which agents implement in their speech-acts various kinds of resources – not only the competence to speak *à propos* but also and simultaneously the capital of an enterprise, the authority of an institution, the affection of another – in order to secure specific outcomes. That such an implementation often results in resistance, conflict and social struggle is not a consequence of the concept of power as such, but is partially a consequence of the fact that, in a society divided into groups and classes with differential privileges and opportunities, the outcomes sought by some agents seldom coincide with the aims and interests of those affected by the exercise of power.

Language and rationality

The final issue which I want to discuss concerns the connection between language and the notion of reason or rationality. This is an issue which is broached by Bourdieu in a negative way only. For it follows from his approach that the power of words is injected into language from outside, that is, from the institutions which delegate authority to the speaker. Hence it is senseless to suggest that linguistic expressions might have a 'rational force' of their own, that they might have a force of conviction which is anything other than the authority bestowed upon them by the institution in whose name they are uttered. 'To try to understand linguistically the power of linguistic manifestations, to search within language for the principle of the logic and efficacy of the *language of institution*, is to forget', stresses Bourdieu, 'that authority comes to language from outside'.[45] Hence Bourdieu's reservations about the term 'illocutionary force', introduced by Austin in an attempt to give a systematic account of the sense in which to say something is to do something. Bourdieu has reservations about this term precisely because it fails to identify the extra-linguistic source of the power which speech-acts have, clouding this source in so much philosophical speculation about quasi-linguistic forces.

I shall leave aside the question of the accuracy and adequacy of Bourdieu's reading of Austin's work, a reading which could be shown, I think, to be somewhat one-sided and incomplete.[46] The issue on which I want to focus here concerns the interrelation between language, power and rationality. Just as Bourdieu is mistaken, in my view, to conceptualize the relation between language and power exclusively in terms of the authority bestowed on words by an institution, so too he dismisses far too abruptly the idea that linguistic expressions might have a 'rational force', or a force of conviction, which is not reducible to their institutionally bestowed authority. No doubt many expressions derive a great deal of support from institutions and would be altogether ineffective without them. But surely it is implausible to suggest, as Bourdieu is inclined to do, that such support *exhausts* whatever force any expressions may have. Consider the statement of Bourdieu and Passeron that the educational system in capitalist societies contributes to the reproduction of class relations by ensuring the class distribution of cultural capital and by concealing this effect through the appearance of autonomy. Perhaps this statement derives some support from the fact that Bourdieu and Passeron are both associates of the *Centre de sociologie européenne* (among other things); perhaps it derives additional support from the fact that it is advanced in a volume which is written in a very distinctive (if not laboured) style, evoking the impression of rigour and scientificity. But whatever support the statement derives from such considerations, *it is also an assertion which claims to say something that is true* and it has a 'rational force' in so far as this claim has been, or could be, sustained. In uttering an assertion one raises the claim, implicitly or explicitly, that the statement uttered is true. This is a claim which can be criticized, which can be doubted or disputed by others, and which can withstand such criticism to the extent that it can be *supported by reasons*. While what counts as 'reasons' may vary from one context to another and may even depend upon certain institutional factors, nevertheless the claim which calls for support by reasons is not reducible to the authority bestowed by an institution.

To speak of a claim which calls for support by reasons is to suggest that there is a close connection between language or communication, on the one hand, and the notion of reason or rationality, on the other. This is a suggestion which has been developed in detail by Habermas, whose contributions are not really impugned by the critical remarks of Bourdieu.[47] Since I have examined Habermas's contributions elsewhere,[48] I shall restrict myself here to commenting on some aspects of the distinction between support by reasons and institutional authority. When we raise a claim that a statement is true, we presuppose that the claim could be justified if need be; we also presuppose that its justification is different from its *imposition*. I would express these presuppositions as follows: to say that a statement is true is to say that it could be justified under conditions which included the suspension of asymmetrical relations of power. These conditions are 'ideal' in the sense that they seldom (if ever) correspond to the circumstances of actual debate: truth, it could be said, is a *limiting notion*. However, the conditions are not ideal in the sense of being impossibly idealistic, as if one could conjure away, by some sort of conceptual hocus-pocus, the resources in virtue of which speechacts are also acts of power. The justification of a claim to truth presupposes, not the suspension of power as such, but rather the suspension of systematically asymmetrical relations of power, that is, relations of *domination*. For it is the power to dominate others and to impose one's will on them that stands opposed to the demand for justification. Since relations of domination are generally sustained by institutions which are structured in certain ways, it follows that the demand for justification, and the attempt to meet this demand by supporting the original claim with reasons, represents a form of discourse which diverges from the kinds of speech 'authorized' by existing institutions. Indeed it could be said that it is this very demand which renders possible a *rational* critique of existing institutions and of the ideological forms of expression by means of which they are sustained.

Let me draw this essay to a close by summarizing some of the central themes and theses. I have tried to present the key aspects of Bourdieu's approach to language and to identify some of its strengths and weaknesses. Bourdieu is right, I think, to be critical of many linguistic theories for failing to take into account the historical and political conditions of the constitution of the language which they take as their object and for neglecting the social conditions under which a language is actualized by competent speakers. Bourdieu is also right to criticize those philosophers of language who, while interesting themselves in the social conditions of speech, hardly do justice to the social character of these conditions. In his attempt to avoid the shortcomings of linguistic theories, philosophies of language and sociolinguistics, Bourdieu has elaborated a cluster of concepts which are of great interest in themselves and which he and others have employed in illuminating ways. The concepts of linguistic market, linguistic habitus and symbolic violence, all couched within the framework of a general theory of practice, are original and provocative ideas which are worthy of elaboration and appraisal.

As a contribution to such an appraisal, I have criticized the concept of symbolic violence for its dependence upon unclarified notions of recognition, misrecognition and legitimacy and for its connection with a consensual model of social reproduction. While Bourdieu is right to emphasize the link between language and power, he develops this link in a way which must be questioned, for it presupposes a consensus which may not exist. I have tried to suggest other ways in which this link could be developed in connection with a notion of meaning, a theory of ideology and an analysis of truth. My proposals are based upon criticisms of what I regard as conceptual lacunas or unjustified reductions in Bourdieu's account: his preoccupation with style at the expense of content, his identification of the power of words with the delegated power of the *porte-parole*, his dismissal of the idea that linguistic expressions might have any force other than the power they derive from the authority of the institution. If these criticisms and proposals are sound, then they may further the development of a project for which Bourdieu's account, whatever its limitations, has helped to open the way.

3

Theories of Ideology and Methods of Discourse Analysis

Towards a Framework for the Analysis of Ideology

The theory of ideology and the study of language are two concerns which bear a close connection. For the theory of ideology has commonly sought to examine the ways in which 'meaning' or 'ideas' affect the conceptions or activities of the individuals and groups which make up the social world. While the nature and modalities of ideology have been analysed in differing ways, it seems increasingly clear that the study of language must occupy a privileged position in any such analysis. The analysis of ideology *is*, in a fundamental respect, the study of language in the social world, since it is primarily within language that meaning is mobilized in the interests of particular individuals and groups. The recognition of this close connection between the theory of ideology and the study of language has offered the possibility of linking the analysis of ideology to forms of philosophy which have focused on the nature of language and meaning, on the one hand, and to forms of linguistics which have been applied to literary texts and social interaction, on the other. The task of accounting for the phenomenon of ideology has called for, and seems to require, an integrated approach to the nature and analysis of language in the social world.

While the desiderata seem clear, the results have so far been disappointing. The gap between what is required and what has been achieved can be discerned in the recent literature of the English-speaking world. Numerous books on ideology have appeared in English during the last few years; but these books, however insightful, are flawed in many ways. While often expressing an interest in language, the theorists of ideology have done little to link the study of linguistic expressions to the analysis of ideology. In the field of linguistics, there is a rapidly expanding body of material which is concerned with the study of socially situated speech. This diverse material, which may be roughly subsumed under the label of 'discourse analysis', is united by an interest in extended sequences of speech and a sensitivity to social context. However, this sensitivity has not been coupled with a clear formulation of the institutional and structural features of the social world; and the connection between discourse and ideology – a connection occasionally alluded to – is seldom pursued. English-speaking philosophers, for their part, have tended to remain aloof. Wittgenstein emphasized long ago that language is essentially social, but philosophers have rested content with a curiously non-social concept of the social. They have thus failed to appreciate the extent to which power and ideology are not mere sidetracks for the distraction of sociologists, but rather phenomena which lie at the heart of their own concerns.

In view of the unsatisfactory character of much current research, there remains an urgent need for an integrated approach to the study of language and ideology. This essay was conceived as a partial contribution to such a task.[1] My aim is to offer a critical survey of recent work in English which is concerned, in various ways, with the theory of ideology and the analysis of discourse. The essay falls into three parts. In the first part I examine some of the theoretical perspectives on ideology which have been propounded during the last decade and which have had some impact on social scientists. The second part of the essay is concerned with some of the methods of discourse analysis which are currently being developed by linguists and others; I present the main features of these methods and offer an appraisal of their adequacy and scope. These two critical sections prepare the way for a third, more constructive part. In the latter I attempt to sketch an alternative account of ideology, drawing together theoretical and methodological considerations with the aim of elaborating a unified approach.

A few preliminary remarks should be made concerning the selection of material. I do not provide a history of the concept of ideology, nor do I offer an introduction to the classical theoretical positions, such as those of Marx or Mannheim, with which the notion of ideology is commonly associated.[2] My focus is on the contemporary debates and, within that domain, I select material which seems to me to represent distinctive and relatively developed positions. Thus I have considered it justifiable to put aside the work of Geertz, for example, since his oft-quoted essay was published in the early 1960s and presents a perspective which shares many features with the theories examined below.[3] As regards the literature on discourse analysis, I similarly concentrate on writings which have appeared recently and which define specific orientations. While recognizing that the materials discussed belong to research projects with differing aims, I do not consider it satisfactory simply to distinguish these projects and differentiate these aims; for the projects employ concepts and methods which overlap to some extent and which are limited in ways that can be compared and assessed as a whole. Throughout the first two parts of the essay I restrict myself to material written in English. In imposing this restriction I do not wish to suggest that contributions which have appeared in other languages are of no interest. On the contrary, the work which is currently being done in France and Germany, for instance, is of the greatest interest and merits detailed discussion in its own right.[4] There is, moreover, a certain artificiality in restricting myself to English-speaking material, since some of this material has been influenced by contributions which have originated elsewhere. The initial restriction to material in English will nevertheless help to narrow down the domain of inquiry and will enable me to begin a critical and constructive discussion on what is, for English-speaking readers, readily accessible ground.

I   THEORIES OF IDEOLOGY

The last decade has witnessed the formulation of several different 'theories' of ideology in the English-speaking world. One such theory, that presented by Martin Seliger, is advanced against the backcloth of the 'end of ideology' debate and is cast within the framework of orthodox political science. A second account of ideology is developed by Alvin Gouldner. Strongly influenced by Habermas, this account views ideology as an historical phenomenon which emerged with the Enlightenment and which is interlaced with the technology of communication. A third perspective on ideology is one which stems from Althusser, whose views have been forcefully advocated by a number of authors writing in English. Prominent among these authors is Paul Hirst; he has written extensively on Althusser's theory of ideology and has attempted to incorporate many of its features in a somewhat revised account. In this part of the essay I wish to examine the three positions represented by Seliger, Gouldner and Hirst. I shall provide a short exposition of their views and then subject these views to a brief critique. In the course of these analyses I shall highlight a point which may be succinctly stated as follows: *the concept of ideology has lost its critical edge.* The three authors discussed below – and in this regard they are by no means exceptional – conceive of ideology as a system of symbols or beliefs which pertain, in some way, to social action or political practice; these authors thus dissolve the connection between the *concept of ideology* and the *critique of domination*, a connection which was certainly part (if not all) of Marx's notion of ideology and which should, I believe, be preserved. Just how such a connection could be re-established and developed is a question to which I shall return in the final part of the essay.

IDEOLOGY AS BELIEF SYSTEM: MARTIN SELIGER

In a substantial volume published in 1976, Martin Seliger develops an approach which is premised upon a distinction between two conceptions of ideology.[5] On the one hand, there is the 'restrictive conception' which confines the term 'ideology' to specific political belief systems; on the other hand, there is the 'inclusive conception' which applies the term to all political belief systems, irrespective of whether the beliefs guide action oriented towards preserving, destroying or rebuilding the social order. Seliger's aim is to defend the inclusive conception of ideology and to show how this conception can be linked to the processes of political debate. The first stage of his defence is to offer an 'immanent critique' of those authors who have advocated some form of the restrictive conception, from Marx and Engels to the theorists of the 'end of ideology'. In a separate study devoted to *The Marxist Conception of Ideology*, Seliger maintains that Marx and Engels conceived of ideology in a wholly negative and pejorative way, contrasting ideology with a 'true' or 'correct' perception of reality. Yet this conception cannot be consistently combined, according to Seliger, with the Marxist emphasis on free and purposive action; for ideology can animate such action only if it concurs to some degree with how things actually are. With the appearance of this inconsistency it

> becomes necessary to admit that bourgeois ideology is not bare of factual insights or even entirely wrong about causal relationships and predictive evaluations. It is also conceded that the proletarian belief system is coloured by false consciousness. Consequently, the argument reaches the point where the original absolute juxtaposition of objective or total perception of reality and ideology, of objective and subjective class consciousness, breaks down.[6]

From here it is a short step to the view, advocated in one form by Lenin, of ideology as class consciousness oriented towards political action, a step which Seliger interprets as a transition to the inclusive conception of ideology.

The implicit adoption of the inclusive conception can also be discerned in the writings of those who espoused the 'end of ideology' thesis.[7] There is, Seliger observes, a peculiarly close connection between Marx's concept of ideology and the modern, non-Marxist notion presupposed by the theorists of the end of ideology. For the latter also use 'ideology' in a restricted and pejorative sense, but apply it, unlike Marx, to political belief systems which call for radical social change, and hence to Marxism itself. The thesis that ideology has come to an end was very much a product of the Western liberal democracies in the late 1950s and early 1960s, when politics was a matter of pragmatism and even radicals had seemingly reconciled themselves to moderation. But Seliger shows that the main proponents of the end of ideology thesis – Aron, Shils, Lipset, Bell and others – were not entirely consistent in their use of the term 'ideology', occasionally lapsing into the inclusive conception. He argues, moreover, that the thesis cannot be sustained in so far as it assumes that 'attitude towards change' will suffice as a criterion of ideology. It will not suffice because one cannot establish an unequivocal link between the content of a political belief system and its character as conservative, moderate or radical. Whether a belief system is conservative, moderate or radical obviously depends upon the prevailing political culture and upon the attitude adopted towards it – Marxism may be as radical in the West as it is conservative in the East. From this argument Seliger draws a conclusion which anticipates his version of the inclusive conception: 'As that which guides and defends political action, ideology must therefore be defined so as to refer to political belief systems, whether they are revolutionary, reformist or conservative (traditionalist) in outlook.'[8]

Ideologies, according to Seliger, are action-oriented sets of beliefs which are organized into coherent systems. These systems are composed of a number of elements which may be formally distinguished and represented as in figure 2.

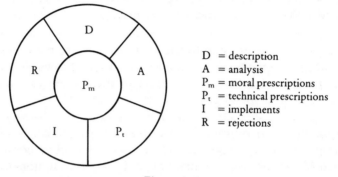

D   = description
A   = analysis
P_m = moral prescriptions
P_t = technical prescriptions
I   = implements
R   = rejections

Figure 2

As this diagram makes clear, all ideologies mix together factual description and the analysis of situations with moral prescriptions about what is right and good and technical considerations of prudence and efficiency. It is this peculiar mixture of factual content and moral commitment that gives ideology its appeal and enables it to guide political action. The action-guiding role of ideology is further attested to by the element which Seliger calls 'implements', that is, rules which provide ways and means of implementing commitments and adapting them to circumstantial requirements. The final element of ideologies, described as 'rejections', calls attention to the fact that ideologies are always defined in opposition to others and thus incorporate the denial or rejection of certain principles and beliefs; the separation of powers in constitutional democracy, for example, is premised upon the rejection of the divine right of kings. On the basis of this formal analysis of the elements of ideologies, Seliger offers a full definition of his inclusive conception:

An ideology is a group of beliefs and disbeliefs (rejections) expressed in value sentences, appeal sentences and explanatory statements. . . . [It is] designed to serve on a relatively permanent basis a group of people to justify in reliance on moral norms and a modicum of factual evidence and self-consciously rational coherence the legitimacy of the implements and technical prescriptions which are to ensure concerted action for the preservation, reform, destruction or reconstruction of a given order.[9]

From this definition it follows that politics and ideology are inseparable. All political action is ultimately oriented towards the preservation, reform, destruction or reconstruction of the social order, and hence all political action is necessarily guided by an ideological system of beliefs.

The actual implementation of ideology in concerted action has an effect on the formal structure of the belief system. In fulfilling its practical role, ideology is relied upon to devise and justify specific policies and to pronounce on issues of everyday politics. This endangers the purity and centrality of prescriptions which are essentially moral and leads to the 'bifurcation' of political argumentation into two dimensions: 'that of fundamental principles, which determine the final goals and the grand vistas on which they will be realized, and which are set above the second dimension, that of the principles which actually underlie policies and are invoked to justify them'.[10] Seliger calls this second dimension 'operative ideology' to distinguish it from the 'fundamental ideology' of the first. All the elements of ideology are realized in both dimensions, but with a different emphasis in each case. In justifying policies in the operative dimension, more consideration is given to norms of prudence and efficiency; whereas moral prescriptions are central in fundamental ideology, it is technical prescriptions which have priority in the operative dimension. Thus the elements of ideology are more accurately represented as in figure 3. The bifurcation of ideology generates a constant process of internal change. Tension and conflict arise between the principles of the operative ideology and those of the fundamental ideology, as well as between principles in the same dimension. So in order to maintain a minimum of coherence, ideologies must constantly adapt their elements and dimensions to one another, either re-aligning the operative principles to the original specifications of the funda-

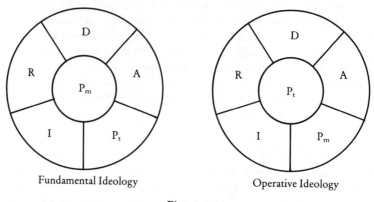

Fundamental Ideology   Operative Ideology

Figure 3

mental ideology or modifying these specifications in accordance with what is actually being done or what is possible.

Ideological change is also generated by conflicts between the principles of different fundamental ideologies. In this regard, Seliger observes a growing consensus concerning overall objectives within and between the various political systems; but, unlike the theorists of the end of ideology, he does not interpret this as the 'de-ideologization of politics':

> Relatively recent growth in America of 'the politics of consensus' signifies not a retreat from ideology but, as elsewhere in the West, the diminishing appeal and suitability of diametrically opposed social values and goals, following success in the battle for raising the standard of living among large sections of the working classes and the spread of social security.[11]

Moral absolutes have lost much of their appeal in the party politics of the West. In order to secure votes, however, parties must not dilute fundamentals beyond recognition, for there must be sufficient distinction between the parties in order for voters to choose. A conflict is produced between the rationality of maximizing votes and winning elections, on the one hand, and the rational defence of fundamental principles, on the other. Fundamental principles are generally protected from the changes in orientation to which policies attest; parties defend their fundamental principles in order to conceal a convergence in the operative dimension. The dynamics of party politics thus leads to a growing disparity between the two dimensions of each ideology and provides a constant source of ideological change.

Seliger's contribution to the theory of ideology provides a convenient point of departure for developing a critical discussion – 'convenient' not only because his views may be widely shared (if not widely known) among social scientists, but also because I wish to adopt a position which contrasts sharply with that which he defends. I wish to adopt, that is, a conception of ideology which Seliger would call 'restrictive' and which owes something to the work of Marx. It is therefore appropriate to begin my critical comments on Seliger's contribution by returning to his critique of the 'Marxist conception of ideology'. According to Seliger, the conception of ideology advanced by Marx and Engels is essentially a 'truth-excluding' notion: ideology is a distorted representation of reality, a 'false consciousness' in Engels's terms. At the same time, Marx and Engels tended to attribute ideology to the bourgeoisie alone, which seems inconsistent both with the realization that bourgeois ideas must have some factual content if they are to be efficacious, and with the recognition that the proletarian outlook is by no means free from distortion. These apparent inconsistencies lead Seliger to the conclusion that Marx's and Engels's restrictive, truth-excluding conception of ideology cannot be sustained. There is, however, a serious flaw in Seliger's argument. For he is mistaken to assume that ideology is conceived by Marx and Engels exclusively, or even primarily, in opposition to 'truth'.[12] What is equally or even more important in the work of Marx and Engels is the link between ideology and *class domination*. The truth or falsity of statements about the natural or social world is one matter; the ways in which such statements may serve to sustain class domination is another. I do not wish to suggest that Marx and Engels always drew a sharp distinction between those two sets of concerns, or that these two sets of concerns are the only elements which entered into their conception of ideology. In challenging Seliger's argument I do not want to imply, moreover, that the texts of Marx and Engels provide satisfactory answers to the key questions about ideology. I wish only to emphasize that Seliger's critique of Marx and Engels, in so far as it underplays the link between ideology and class domination, fails to demonstrate the untenability of a restrictive conception of ideology.

Seliger has, however, another argument against a restrictive conception. In criticizing the end of ideology theorists, he submits that the apparent demise of radical political doctrines does not indicate the end of ideology: radicalism cannot suffice as a criterion of ideology, for whether a doctrine is radical or not is a contingent matter which depends upon the prevailing political culture. It may now be asked whether such an argument could be used against a restrictive conception which established a link between ideology and class domination – or, more generally, between ideology and domination. Could it be argued that to conceive of ideology as ideas or utterances which serve to sustain a system of domination is unacceptable, because whether certain ideas or utterances serve to sustain a particular system or to undermine it will depend upon what that system is and the attitude adopted towards it? Such an argument would not show that this restrictive conception of ideology is unacceptable, but only that this conception does not provide a criterion for identifying certain ideas or utterances as ideological *as such*, independently of the particular conditions under which they are promulgated. Seliger's argument, in other words, does not show that a restrictive conception is unsound, but only that what counts as 'ideological' cannot be ascertained independently of the surrounding circumstances. For the advocate of a restrictive conception, it is harmless to acknowledge that a specific doctrine may be ideological in one context and non-ideological in another.

So far I have been concerned to cast doubt on Seliger's view that a restrictive conception of ideology is untenable. I now want to call attention to some features of Seliger's inclusive conception which seem to me misleading or mistaken. My first and most fundamental reservation stems directly from the preceding discussion: Seliger's inclusive conception is so general and indiscriminate that it breaks every connection between ideology and the critique of domination. For Seliger, the concept of ideology can be applied to any political belief system, whether revolutionary, reformist or reactionary; and thus the concept is stripped of the critical edge, the negative force, which it had in the writings of Marx. Having broken the connection between ideology and the critique of domination, it is no surprise to see that Seliger's conception of ideology is related in only the most diffuse way to the institutional and structural features of society and to the analysis of power. My second reservation pertains to the characterization of ideology as a belief *system*. In regarding ideology as a relatively coherent belief system which can be formally analysed into its constituent parts, Seliger exaggerates the unity and discreteness of ideologies. If one wishes to study ideologies one is invited to examine the articulated doctrines of organized political parties; one no longer sees that the most effective ground of ideology is not the domain officially defined as 'politics', but rather the domain of everyday life – the home, the workplace, the school, the media. Restricting the study of ideology to an examination of official politics is like confining a study of British culture to an excursion through the Tate. The third and final reservation which I want to express is concerned with the conceptualization of ideology as a system of *beliefs*. To conceptualize ideology in terms of beliefs is to divert attention away from the complex and crucial problem of the relation between ideology and *language*. Seliger speaks very loosely of ideology as a 'system of beliefs', a 'system of thought', a 'system of thought and speech'; he describes the ideological composite as comprising 'principles' and 'commitments', 'judgements of value and statements of fact', 'tested and testable empirical claims' and 'claims that are neither'; nowhere does he explore what might be involved in the connection, acknowledged partially and erratically in his work, between ideology and the language in which relevant 'beliefs', 'judgements' or 'commitments' are expressed. A greater sensitivity to the dimension of language is one of the features which characterizes the contribution of Alvin Gouldner.

IDEOLOGY AS RATIONAL PROJECT: ALVIN GOULDNER

In *The Dialectic of Ideology and Technology*, Alvin Gouldner elaborates a richly historical perspective on the concept of ideology. If Seliger examines the history of ideology in order to uncover the seeds of a conception which can no longer be sustained, Gouldner turns to history in order to recover a specificity which the concept of ideology is today in danger of losing. If Seliger regards ideology as a system of beliefs which can be studied by the methods of social science, Gouldner views ideology, not merely as a potential object of social science but as its alleged boundary, a boundary which stems from the simultaneous birth of ideology and social science in the Enlightenment. The rise of the social sciences and the new ideologies of the eighteenth and nineteenth centuries were both shaped by the growth of modern science and the decline of older traditions. When the notion of ideology is taken up by Marx, however, it is turned against its historical twin: Marx uses this notion to criticize the scientific pretensions of the new social science, to attack beliefs about society that make scientific claims which he holds to be unjustified. 'The modern interest in "ideology" thus emerges as a Marxist category whose underlying, latent paradigm is: *a belief system that makes pretentious and unjustified claims to scientificity.*'[13] This intrinsic, antagonistic relation between ideology and social science has, in Gouldner's view, fundamental implications for the way in which ideology can be studied. Ideology cannot be treated as a mere 'thing-out-there' to be observed and investigated empirically, for it necessarily points back to the problematic of *self*-understanding and calls for the sort of *reflexive* social theory which Gouldner is concerned to defend.

While ideology and social science have developed in opposition to one another, they nevertheless emerged together from the collapse of the 'old regimes' and their established system of authority. Ideology, like social science, is a modern symbol system premised upon the 'detraditionalization' of society and communication. Traditional society allowed only relatively fixed and limited claims to be made, and these claims were already known and established: the legitimate was the Old, the 'What-Has-Been'. Moreover, the way in which the claims could be justified was also limited, for speech was typically authorized by the authority or social position of the speaker. The emergence of ideology, according to Gouldner, both reflected and promoted the radical transformation of traditional society. New kinds of claims and legitimations became possible; traditional structures were called into question by new interpretations of social life and new projects of social change. Whereas religion focuses on the immediacies of everyday life and strives for transcendental reconciliation, ideologies are concerned with the organization of social life and advocate public, 'rationally grounded' projects of social reconstruction. Ideology is a call to action and a claim to justify that call by recourse to 'evidence' and 'reason'. 'Ideology thus entailed', writes Gouldner,

> the emergence of a new mode of political discourse; discourse that sought action but did not merely seek it by invoking authority or tradition, or by emotive rhetoric alone. It was discourse predicated

on the idea of grounding political action in secular and rational theory. . . . Ideology separated itself from the mythical and religious consciousness; it justified the course of action it proposed, by the logic and evidence it summoned on behalf of its views of the social world, rather than by invoking faith, tradition, revelation or the authority of the speaker.[14]

In breaking with authority and tradition, ideology submits to what Gouldner calls the 'grammar of modern rationality'. This is not a timelessly valid mode of cognition but an historically emergent set of rules for discourse which stipulate that claims should be justified by evoking the voluntary consent of those addressed on the basis of arguments alone. Although ideology is a 'rational' mode of discourse, it does not understand itself as such. Ideology claims to be autonomous from the social conditions on which it rests and the language in which it is expressed; the rationality of ideology is 'limited' by the pretension to be supra-historical and by the *hubris* of the disembodied word.

The *hubris* of the disembodied word: ideology does not float in some ethereal realm of ideas but is tied very closely to the medium of linguistic communication. Ideology pertains to that part of consciousness which can be *said*; it has a public objectivity which enables the projects it promotes to be discussed among strangers. While grounded in ordinary language, ideology restructures it and constructs itself 'as a sociolect of an "elaborated" sociolinguistic variant'.[15] Gouldner thus conceives of ideology as a 'language variant' which deviates from the common linguistic codes of everyday life. Incorporating a distinctive mode of justifying assertions, ideology is similar to what Bernstein calls 'elaborated codes', that is, codes which are relatively self-reflexive and independent of context.[16] The public and decontextualized character of ideology is reflected in the fact that *writing* was and still is its principal medium. 'A Socratic preference for the *spoken word*', remarks Gouldner, 'is inherently nonideological.'[17] Yet ideology allows only certain things to be communicated and discussed. It not only 'expresses' but also 'represses', excluding certain issues from discussion and creating a 'public unconsciousness'. Ideology is, as it were, the linguistic legislature which defines what is available for public discussion and what is not.

There is a profound historical connection between the emergence of ideologies and the revolution in communication associated with the development of printing. In unfolding this connection Gouldner leans heavily on Habermas's early study of the formation of the 'public sphere'.[18] The development of the mass media and the formation of a 'public' are, Gouldner explains, mutually supportive processes. A public is formed when the links between culture and social interaction are attenuated, so that people can share something without being in constant interaction. The development of the mass media facilitates this process by greatly increasing the exchange of information at a distance. But the proliferation of information created a need for interpretation, for the provision of publicly shareable *meaning*. It was in the cleared space of the 'public sphere' that the rational discourse of ideologies thus appeared, offering their interpretations 'openly' and without fear of sanctions. Ideologies serve to mobilize social movements through the mediation of newspapers and related media. Ideologies pertain to a news-reading public, and hence they may be further defined as

> symbol systems generated by, and intelligible to, persons whose relationship to everyday life is mediated by their reading – of newspapers, journals, or books – and by the developing general concept of 'news', as well as by the specific and concrete 'bits' of news now increasingly transmitted by the growing media, and is grounded in the experiencing of life as decontextualized events.[19]

Ideologies are not rooted directly in the experiential flux of everyday life but are *media*-ted by the news and the interpretation of news. Ideologies are second-order accounts, 'palimpsistic texts on texts', which interpret and integrate the information provided by the news-producing system. The modern period thus offers its own means of countering the special sense of groundlessness which accompanied its birth.

The emergence of ideologies is connected not only with the revolution in communication, but also with the industrial revolution and the rise of capitalism. As the ruling class in capitalist society becomes increasingly engaged in economic affairs, it is obliged to place the ultimate protection of its class position in the hands of others. The development of a relatively autonomous state thus accompanies economic growth and provides a basis for the expansion of administrative and political strata. The key political problem for the bourgeoisie is raised: how can it exercise influence over other sectors and ensure their loyalty? In response to this problem the bourgeoisie avails itself of ideology, which 'thus assumes a new historical role in the maintenance of social solidarities and class control'.[20] The bourgeoisie becomes more dependent than ruling classes in previous forms of society on a belief system which aims to win over other groups and define its dominance as legitimate. Gouldner argues, however, that this dependence is an increasingly fragile one, both because the bourgeoisie is separated from the cultural elite which produces ideologies, and because the hold of ideologies is being progressively undermined by the transformations in the communication media. The privileged link between ideology and the written word means that, with the growth of radio, cinema and television, ideology loses ground among the masses. A split appears between the 'cultural apparatus', centred on universities, which produces and consumes ideologies, and the 'consciousness industry' which takes over an ever greater role in shaping the opinions of the population. With this split between the cultural apparatus and the consciousness industry, 'ideology continues to ground an *elite* politics but loses effective influence over the masses';[21] a growing part of the population is placed beyond the reach of ideological discourse. But there will be no 'end of ideology' so long as government by oligarchic elites is bolstered up by a rational discourse which claims to represent the interests of all.

Gouldner's writings on ideology represent, in my opinion, one of the most interesting contributions in English which has appeared in recent years. No doubt this interest is due, in a very substantial part, to the debt which Gouldner owes to Habermas; but Gouldner has given a distinctive twist to certain Habermasian themes and has connected them up to other, more original ideas. One consequence of Gouldner's somewhat eclectic style is that the conception of ideology which he offers is not clear-cut and precise. Several definitions of ideology are offered, from 'a belief system that makes pretentious and unjustified claims to scientificity' to 'speech that seeks to reduce the dissonance between mutual dependence and differential allocation',[22] and it is not easy to see how these various definitions can be reconciled. Nevertheless, there are certain elements which emerge consistently from Gouldner's historical approach to ideology. Without wishing to dispute the value of such an approach, I want to argue that these elements form a concept of ideology which is unsatisfactory, for it is both too general and too specific. Too general: in conceiving of ideology in terms of public projects advocated by rational discourse, Gouldner dissolves the connection between ideology and *domination*. It makes no difference on Gouldner's account whether the public projects animated by ideology are directed towards reaction, reform or revolution; what is important, it seems, is that these projects are justified by evidence and reason, rather than by appeal to authority and tradition. This general use of 'ideology' demands the same riposte which I made to Seliger's inclusive conception: the concept is stripped of the critical edge, the negative force, which it had in the writings of Marx. Gouldner's discussion of Marx, like Seliger's, tends to accentuate the opposition between science and ideology, suggesting that Marx thought of ideology as essentially *failed science*. Gouldner is not unaware that Marx's concept of ideology is also linked to the problem of maintaining a system of class domination. This link is even drawn on by Gouldner himself, who observes at one point that ideologies 'help perpetuate the specific system within which the privileges and powers of the hegemonic class and its allied classes exist'.[23] But the link between ideology and domination seems, on Gouldner's account, to be no more than a contingent one, subsumed to the overall idea of ideology as rational discourse which mobilizes public projects.

If Gouldner's concept of ideology is too general, it is also too specific. The concept derives its specificity from two oppositions which Gouldner traces back to the Enlightenment and which define ideology as an essentially *modern* phenomenon. The first opposition is that between ideology and social science: ideologies are would-be social sciences, pretenders to a throne of relatively recent date. Whatever the historical accuracy of this observation, it seems to me mistaken to build such an opposition into the definition of ideology. For a symbol system to be ideological, it need not be dressed up in the guise of social science, as it attested to by Gouldner's own allusions to liberalism and nationalism as ideologies. Moreover, to oppose ideology and social science is to preclude the possibility that, under certain circumstances, the social sciences as well as the natural sciences may become ideological.

This is a point which is forcefully made by Habermas and which is in no way vitiated by Gouldner's unconvincing critique.[24] The second opposition which gives specificity to Gouldner's concept is that between ideology and tradition. Like social sciences, ideologies are 'rational belief-systems' which seek to justify their claims by referring to the world rather than by appealing to faith, authority or tradition. Ideology and social science thus fall on the same side of an historical fence that separates them from the pre-Enlightenment fields in which myth and religion flourished: ideology is a feature of the modern era. Here I do not wish to dispute this view as an account of the origins of the *concept* of ideology, an account which has been developed in a systematic way by other authors.[25] What I do want to question, however, is the advisability of employing this account for the purposes of *defining* ideology, which would imply that one could not even *speak* about ideology in societies which preceded the European Enlightenment or which have not been overturned by its effects. Why should the history of the *concept* of ideology – a history which has, after all, given rise to no single *conception* of ideology – be regarded as defining the parameters of *ideology as such*? How many thinkers would seriously maintain that one could not even *speak* about socialization processes or relations of domination and exploitation in societies which did not have a *concept* of socialization, domination or exploitation? When the curious assumption that underlies such a view is made explicit, the restriction of ideology to the modern era can be seen to rest on unsteady ground.

One of the commendable aspects of Gouldner's analysis is, as previously mentioned, his concern with the connection between ideology and language. Ideologies, he maintains, are 'symbol systems', 'language variants', 'elaborated codes'; they can carry out their task of mobilizing public projects only by being expressed in a language, primarily a written language, which is critical, rational and empirically plausible. It seems to me that Gouldner is right to emphasize the linguistic dimension of ideology, for language is the principal medium by which *meaning* is produced and transmitted in the social world. However, I believe that it is mistaken to maintain that the language of ideology is a discrete 'sociolect', a sort of meta-language which draws upon but remains distinct from the language of everyday life. I think that one must leave open the possibility that the language of everyday life is the very *locus* of ideology and the very *site* of the meaning which sustains relations of domination. Leaving open this possibility would prepare the way for an approach to ideology which is much more radical than that advanced by Gouldner and which avoids the paradoxical conclusion that he is obliged to draw. Having conceived of ideology as a discrete sociolect which is realized above all in *writing*, Gouldner is compelled to conclude that the growth of mass media such as radio and television marks a decline in the role of ideology, which is thereby displaced from society as a whole and increasingly confined to the university. Little do intellectuals know the power of their words! By an act of definition, Gouldner has excluded a vast arena of language and meaning – the arena *par excellence* in which attitudes and opinions are formed – from the object domain of ideological analysis. It is to the credit of Althusser and his followers, among others, to have redefined the terms of ideology in a way which brings such everyday phenomena as the family and the media, together with their subject-constituting effects, into focus.

IDEOLOGY AS SOCIAL RELATIONS: PAUL HIRST

During the 1960s Althusser published several essays on ideology which have received widespread attention in the English-speaking world. While writing from a Marxist perspective, Althusser's approach to ideology differs considerably from that adopted by Gouldner. For Althusser and his followers, ideology is not a specific creation of European culture but is a necessary feature of any society, in so far as any society must provide the means to form its members and transform them to their conditions of existence. 'Human societies secrete ideology as the very element and atmosphere indispensable to their historical respiration and life.'[26] It is a customary to view ideology as a form of consciousness or a realm of ideas; but this, Althusser argues, is a mistake. Ideology is not a distorted representation of real relations but rather a real relation itself, namely the relation *through which* human beings live the relation to their world. Ideological relations make up a specific instance of the social totality which, in a provocative essay, Althusser analysed under the label of 'ideological state apparatuses'.[27] This essay forms the focal point of a recent study in which Paul Hirst offers a critical and constructive commentary on

Althusser's work.[28] Hirst has been one of the major proponents of Althusser's views in the English-speaking world and, while he is not alone in seeking to elaborate Althusser's account of ideology,[29] his writings provide a suitable basis for an analysis of this orientation.

Althusser's account of ideology falls, according to Hirst, into two parts. The first part concerns the general notion of ideological state apparatuses. This notion is introduced by Althusser as a *response* to the question with which he begins, namely the question of reproduction. In order to produce in a society, it is necessary to reproduce the conditions of production, and so one must ask what is involved in the reproduction of the conditions of production. Such reproduction involves reproducing both the forces of production, such as buildings and machines, and the labour-power employed in production. To reproduce labour-power requires, among other things, that individuals are provided with a certain know-how and trained to perform certain jobs; it also requires that individuals are trained to submit to the rules of the established order – that is, it requires the reproduction of the relations of production. Althusser's view is that the reproduction of relations of production is secured essentially by the exercise of *state power* in the specific 'apparatuses' (or institutions) that make up the state. Two types of state apparatuses are distinguished by Althusser: the 'repressive state apparatus', comprising the government, army, police, courts, prisons and so on; and the 'ideological state apparatuses', which include the Church, schools, family, legal system, political parties, trade unions and communications network. Althusser then begins a more detailed discussion of ideology by observing that, whereas the repressive state apparatus functions primarily 'by violence', the ideological state apparatuses function primarily 'by ideology'. This way of setting up the problem of ideology is, however, very questionable in the eyes of Hirst. While Althusser's conception of society as a 'complex structured whole articulated in dominance' helped to counter the reductionist tendencies of Marxism, nevertheless his approach to the problem of ideology betrays, according to Hirst, a latent economism.

> Althusser's question – how is it that the relations of production are reproduced? – accepts the primacy of the 'economy'. The 'point of view of reproduction' amounts to asking the question, what is

necessary for existing class relations to be maintained? ... Class
society is unaffected by the forms in which its conditions of existence are provided. ISAs [ideological state apparatuses] become
agencies for the realisation of a functional task given by the
economy.[30]

Moreover, the very notion of ideological state apparatuses gives a
false unity to the ideological field. 'Ideological social relations' do
not fit into a single form. One must, Hirst stresses, attend to the
complexity and heterogeneity of such relations, just as, in political
practice, one must be concerned with struggles which cannot be
aligned in terms of capitalism and anti-capitalism.

Hirst is similarly critical of the second part of Althusser's
account. This is the part in which Althusser explores the nature
and *modus operandi* of ideology. Three theses are put forward in
Althusser's text. The first thesis asserts that ideology does not
represent reality but rather human beings' lived relation to their
conditions of existence. This relation is 'imaginary' in the sense
that it is the form in which the subject 'lives' its relation to the
world and to itself, living 'as if' it constituted itself as a subject.
The second thesis maintains that ideology has a material existence:
the representations which make up ideology are inscribed in social
practices and expressed in objective forms. If an individual
'believes' in God, for example, then he or she goes to church
regularly, prays, confesses and so on; 'beliefs' are realized in specific practices which are governed, in turn, by rituals relating to an
ideological apparatus. Althusser's third thesis is expressed in the
oft-quoted slogan, 'ideology interpellates individuals as subjects'.
As in the case of the police officer hailing an individual who
recognizes that the call was really addressed to him or her, so too
in ideology the individual is constituted as a subject by a process of
interpellation in which the subject recognizes itself *as* a subject,
although the subject does not recognize that its subjectivity is
thereby produced. It is with regard to this third thesis concerning
the ideological constitution of subjectivity that Hirst expresses a
serious reservation. For Althusser's account seems to assume that
subjects and individuals correspond, that the subject is the unitary
'identity' of the individual. But 'it is possible', writes Hirst, 'to
conceive the human individual not as the unitary terminal of an
"imaginary" subject, but as the support of a decentred complex of

practices and statuses which have distinct conditions of existence'.[31] Hirst points out that there are two ways in which the lack of correspondence between individuals and subjects can be shown. First, at a psychic level, it can be seen that the individual is the effect of multiple processes and cannot be equated with a subject conceived of in terms of 'conscious' functioning. Second, when we consider subjects as 'supports' of processes, we see that the subjects which perform this role may include non-human entities like joint-stock companies (or even animals in certain legal cases). Such subjects are not 'consciousnesses' and cannot be analysed in terms of an 'imaginary relation'.

The final major objection which Hirst makes against Althusser's account pertains to the concept of representation. While Althusser rejects the traditional view of ideology as a distorted representation of real relations, he nevertheless retains the concept of representation, for he proposes that ideology represents human beings' lived relation to their conditions of existence. This residual element of representation indicates, according to Hirst, that Althusser has not fully broken with the basic assumptions of 'empiricism'. The concept of representation presupposes the subject/object structure of knowledge: the represented (object) is the source or measure of representations (subject). The latent empiricism of Althusser's approach is closely connected to his well-known distinction between science and ideology.[32] Althusser renounced the claim to be able to differentiate between forms of consciousness as true or false representations of reality, but he did so by transforming Marxism into a science autonomous from the social formation and capable of producing knowledge which could be fed back into political practice. Althusser thus provided a philosophical underpinning for a traditional Marxist-Leninist conception of politics, a conception which has consigned Marxism to virtual irrelevance in the present conditions of political struggle. Hirst suggests that these theoretical and political weaknesses of Althusser's approach can be overcome by conceiving of Marxism, not as a science opposed to ideology, but as a political theory which provides a means of *calculating effects* in concrete political struggles.

> Socialism is nothing if it is not a political theory: a discourse which directs politics toward the construction of definite forms of social relations and in definite ways, a discourse which can construct and

evaluate political situations (relative to definite objectives). . . .
Political practice cannot dispense without [*sic*] calculation, and calculation, beyond the politics of preservation of established and
opportunist cliques, demands criteria of appropriateness: in a word,
'ideology'.[33]

It is Hirst's expectation that, by placing the issue of ideology in the
context of political calculation, a new set of theoretical questions
will be generated and Marxist theory will be rendered more atten-
tive to the many forms and changing circumstances of political
struggle.

In offering some critical remarks on views of Hirst, I do not
wish, by some curious alignment of theoretical forces, to defend
Althusser from attack. It does seem to me that there are certain
aspects of Althusser's work which are more plausible, and certain
aspects which are more intelligible, than the alternative formulations offered by critical commentators such as Hirst. Nonetheless,
the approach adopted by Althusser and his followers is not one
that I want to endorse. In recent years the prominence of this
approach, especially in the English-speaking world, has faded
considerably and it now seems to have begun a process of self-
destruction. Nowhere is this process more evident than in the
appropriation of Althusser's work on ideology. While Hirst expresses his desire 'to take up and extend certain of Althusser's
innovations in relation to Marxist theory' and praises Althusser's
'significant advances in trying to deal with the problem of what is
called "ideology" ',[34] nevertheless Hirst ends up with a concept of
ideology which – so far as it is discernible – bears little resemblance
to the view of Althusser. One of the merits of Althusser's account
is that it situates the problem of ideology within an institutional
and structural context: the problem of ideology is inseparably
linked to the issue of how societal arrangements are sustained. It is
my opinion that Althusser seriously misconstrues this link by
presenting it in functionalist terms and by neglecting the problem
of domination, so that ideology appears as a functional prerequisite
of any society. But Hirst, far from seeking to remedy these faults,
destroys the link between ideology and social reproduction. Precisely how Hirst conceives of ideology in the wake of his critique is
not altogether clear. At one point he seems to regard ideology as 'a

system of political ideas' which can be employed in 'political calculation'; at another point he offers this definition: 'We use the word "ideological" to refer to a non-unitary complex of social practices and systems of representations which have political significances and consequences.'[35] These loose and tentative definitions appear to promise a notion of ideology which is strikingly similar to Seliger's inclusive conception; Hirst may sketch a more heterogeneous and conflictual picture than Seliger, but the overall framework seems to be the same. What is lost by Hirst, no less than by Seliger and Gouldner, is the connection between ideology and *domination*. This is a connection which can only be explored through an investigation of the institutional and structural realization of asymmetrical relations of power and the ways in which these arrangements are sustained. I find no reason to believe that the theoretical questions generated by Hirst's proposals – questions which are self-confessedly 'cryptic in the extreme'[36] – would provide an avenue for approaching these issues.

Althusser and authors influenced by him have rightly emphasized the importance of the relation between ideology and the subject. The concept of ideology directs our attention towards processes whereby consciousness is constituted, both at an individual level and at the level of groups and classes. There can be little doubt that Althusser's analysis of these processes is oversimplified and excessively deterministic; his view that 'ideology interpellates individuals as subjects' leaves no room for the autonomous *action* of subjects who may decide to contravene the imperatives of reproduction. At first sight, Hirst appears to offer an alternative formulation which avoids the excessive determinism of Althusser's account. In discussing subjects as 'supports' of processes, Hirst distinguishes between two conceptions of the subject. On the one hand, the 'juridical conception' refers to the legal or political designation of entities which function as supports of processes; legal subjects, for example, are entities (of whatever kind) which are capable of initiating suits, appeals and so on. On the other hand, the 'operational conception' refers to agencies that have an 'effectivity' on the processes in which they are involved and where that effectivity is partially determined by the 'calculation' which the agencies undertake. By explicitly referring to agencies and their 'effectivity' and 'calculation', Hirst seems to break free from the deterministic framework of Althusser; but on closer inspection, this break is more apparent than real. To re-raise the question of the subject in the way that Hirst does is to assume from the outset that subjects can only 'support processes' which already exist in advance. The passively supportive role of subjects is in no way mitigated by Hirst's frequent appeal to 'calculation' – a notion which seems to have become a conceptual hold-all for the remains of Althusserianism. In the rare passages where Hirst attempts to clarify this concept, he suggests that calculation should be regarded as a practice depending on a body of technique which has its own history and conditions of existence. 'Calculations, account books, etc., are not the mere material auxiliaries of a perception; they designate the presence of a practice which cannot be reduced to *experience* and *intuition*.'[37] What Hirst calls 'calculation' seems to be nothing more than a process *dictated* by rules, methods and techniques which the agent is *trained* to employ. That rules, methods and techniques must always be *negotiated* by agents, that such negotiation is an inherently problematic process in which rules and methods are transformed in their very application, that agents can (and frequently do) act contrary to the rules and methods which allegedly guide their behaviour, that for many actions there simply are no relevant rules, methods or techniques – these are considerations that Hirst, in his vague appeal to the concept of calculation, appears to have overlooked.

Hirst's critique of Althusser's account of ideology is part of a more general attack on the possibility of 'epistemology'. As is evidenced by his retention of the notion of representation and his conception of Marxism as a science, Althusser is an 'epistemologist' who implicitly accepts the subject/object structure of knowledge. Althusser, in Hirst's eyes, has not remained true to his words; he has back-tracked on his own radicalism and left Marxism open to the twin dangers of rationalism and empiricism. The cure for this unfortunate relapse is to dispense with epistemology once and for all. Marxism must be regarded as a 'political theory' which facilitates the calculation of effects; and as Hindess and Hirst insist in a study dedicated to defending this view, '*there can be no "knowledge" in political practice*'.[38] Every epistemology, according to Hindess and Hirst, conceives of knowledge in terms of a relation between a realm of discourse and a realm of objects, where this relation is construed, in one way or another, in terms of 'correspondence' or 'representation'. Every epistemology must assume that there is a privileged level and form of discourse which provides a yardstick against which all claims to knowledge can be assessed; thus empiricist epistemology, for example, posits basic statements which purportedly reproduce what is given in experience. But the assumption of a privileged level and form of discourse merely betrays, in the view of Hindess and Hirst, that every epistemology is arbitrary and dogmatic, 'since there can be no demonstration that such-and-such forms of discourse are indeed privileged except by means of forms of discourse that are themselves held to be privileged'.[39] From such observations the authors infer that epistemology must be discarded and, along with it, the idea of knowledge as a representation, more or less adequate, of some independently existing reality. What we are offered instead is a vision of multiple 'theoretical discourses', in each of which numerous 'objects of discourse' are specified; neither within nor between these theoretical discourses is there any privileged level of discourse, so that the only way in which a theoretical discourse can be assessed is in terms of its own internal consistency. There is nothing particularly novel about this relativistic conclusion, although it is rare to find authors who embrace it so wholeheartedly.[40] It is my opinion, however, that this conclusion is untenable and that it is in no way established by the arguments of Hindess and Hirst. For their arguments are premised, it should be noted, upon very narrow and oversimplified conceptions of 'epistemology' and 'knowledge', conceptions which are difficult to pin on anyone other than the early logical positivists. When Hindess and Hirst maintain that every epistemology is dogmatic because it is incapable of providing a non-arbitrary justification of its privileged form of discourse, they overlook the possibility that epistemology may be, not so much a purported defence of a particular version of 'knowledge *qua* representation', but rather an attempt to elucidate what is presupposed by *claims to know*. And indeed Hindess and Hirst, despite their presumptuous dismissal of 'epistemology', proffer no shortage of claims to know. Thus Hirst, in discussing the nature of corporate enterprises today, argues that shares are increasingly held by financial institutions and other companies and adduces evidence from a Royal Commission: 'In 1973 financial institutions, companies and public bodies held over 52 per cent of quoted ordinary shares (5 per cent being held by overseas investors and 42 per cent by persons, executors and trustees), the total held by financial institutions was 38.3 per cent'; and these compare with considerably lower figures in previous years.[41] Why does Hirst offer us this information, if he does not assume that it is *evidence* which supports his *claim to know* that shares are increasingly held by financial institutions and other companies? And does he seriously believe that the only way of assessing this 'discourse' is to examine its internal consistency, as opposed, for example, to pointing out that the quoted percentages are inaccurate, misleading or out of date? Authors who, like Hindess and Hirst, work themselves into a theoretical cul-de-sac would do well to attend more carefully to the processes of argumentation by which claims to know are defeated or sustained. They would then see that some form of 'epistemology', far from being redundant, is vital for social theory in general and for the analysis of ideology in particular.

II   METHODS OF DISCOURSE ANALYSIS

Just as recent years have witnessed a proliferation of writings on the theory of ideology, so too there has been a growth of interest in methods of discourse analysis. Within linguistics the term 'discourse analysis' is often associated with authors such as Harris and Halliday, whose writings, for many years overshadowed by those of Chomsky, are becoming the object of renewed attention.[42] In the domain of sociology, the analysis of discourse or naturally occurring conversation has featured prominently in the work of authors influenced by Harold Garfinkel.[43] The concept of discourse is also employed, increasingly and rather erratically, by literary critics, political analysts and social theorists; in some cases this conceptual flourishing has been nourished by ideas from France, ideas which have not always had a wholly salutary effect.[44] In view of the diversity of approaches which the notion of discourse analysis has come to embrace, it may be helpful to emphasize three features which are common to most, if not all, of these approaches. In the first place, most forms of discourse analysis are concerned with naturally occurring instances of expression. Whether such instances are in the form of everyday conversation, recorded and transcribed, or in the form of written texts such as novels or newspapers, in any case it is the *actual organization* of the expressions which matters and not the extent to which they concur with some grammatical ideal. The second feature which is common to most forms of discourse analysis is their preoccupation with linguistic units that exceed the limits of a single sentence. This *supra-sentential concern* of discourse analysis – its concern, that is, with the interconnection of utterances in the flow of a conversation or a text – mark it off from dominant perspectives in linguistics, which have tended to focus on phonology and syntactic structure. A third feature is shared by most forms of discourse analysis: they are interested, in one way or another, in the relations between linguistic and *non-linguistic activity*. Traditionally such an interest was expressed in terms of the links between language and perception, language and thought, language and culture; but in recent years, discourse analysts have paid increasing attention to the ways in which language is used in specific social contexts and thereby serves as a medium of power and control. It is this increasingly sociological turn which has rendered discourse analysis relevant to, though by no means neatly integrated with, some of the principal tasks in the study of ideology. For if the language of everyday life is regarded as the very *locus* of ideology, then it is of the utmost importance to examine the methods which have been elaborated for the analysis of ordinary discourse.

In this part of the essay I want to examine three approaches to the analysis of discourse which have been developed in recent years. The first approach is centred on the work of John Sinclair and Malcolm Coulthard who, together with other members of the English Language Research Group at the University of Birmingham, have formulated a detailed model for the study of verbal interaction. A second approach may be found in the writings of Harvey Sacks, Emanuel Schegloff, Gail Jefferson and others. These sociologists of everyday life, strongly influenced by Harold Garfinkel, have investigated the mechanisms by means of which lay actors produce an ordered interaction while engaging in the most ordinary conversation. The third approach which I shall consider is one which has emerged from a group of linguists, sociologists and literary critics at the University of East Anglia. Roger Fowler, Robert Hodge, Gunther Kress and Tony Trew have sought to develop a 'critical linguistics' which is sensitive to the ways in which linguistic forms reflect and reproduce the social organization of power. I shall try to bring out the distinctive contributions of these various approaches and to identify some of their principal limitations. My critical appraisal of these approaches will be dominated by two over-arching themes. First, in concentrating on the organization of discourse at the supra-sentential level, *these authors have tended to emphasize form and structure at the expense of content.* Problems of meaning and interpretation are raised but rarely pursued by discourse analysts, whose 'structural' studies are at best a preliminary stage in a more comprehensive interpretative theory. The second theme which dominates the following discussion may be summarized by the claim that, while discourse analysts have been rightly concerned with the relations between linguistic and non-linguistic activity, *they have failed to provide a satisfactory account of the non-linguistic.* This failure is evident in the uses, as frequent as they are ill-defined, of key concepts such as power, ideology and control. My hope is that the following discussion will reaffirm the need – more urgent than ever – to explore the ways in which the analysis of language can be integrated with the study of the institutional and structural dimensions of the social world.

ANALYSIS OF EXCHANGE STRUCTURE: JOHN SINCLAIR ET AL.

The work of John Sinclair, Malcolm Coulthard and others associated with their Research Group at the University of Birmingham stems from a project concerned with the linguistic aspects of classroom interaction.[45] While their ultimate aim was to develop a model for the analysis of all forms of discourse, they saw distinct advantages in beginning with a situation that is more highly structured than the conversations of everyday life. In everyday conversation, observe Sinclair et al.,[46] topics change in unpredictable ways; participants are of equal status and have equal rights to determine the topic; and ambiguities lead to misunderstandings and confusions which are often exploited by participants. For these reasons the authors decided that it would be more productive to begin the analysis with a simpler type of spoken discourse, 'one which has much more overt structure, where one participant has acknowledged responsibility for the direction of the discourse, for deciding who shall speak when, and for introducing and ending topics'.[47] The authors found such a type in the classroom. In order

to make the situation as simple as possible, they chose circumstances in which the teacher was giving a lesson at the front of the
class, and was therefore likely to be exercising a high degree of
control over the discourse. The initial sample consisted of the tapes
of six lessons taught to groups of up to eight 10 to 11-year-old
children by their own class teacher. Once the analytical model had
been worked out, additional material was collected from other
teaching contexts and the model was revised accordingly.

The model of analysis developed by Sinclair et al. is essentially a
descriptive system, that is, a system which provides a comprehensive and finite means of classifying the constituent elements of the
discourse. The descriptive system is based on a 'rank scale' similar
to that outlined for grammatical models by Halliday.[48] The main
assumption of a rank scale is that a unit at a given rank (for
instance, 'word') is made up of one or more units of the rank below
('morpheme') and combines with other units of the same rank to
make up one unit at the rank above ('group'). Each rank has a
structure which can be expressed in terms of the units of the rank
below; the unit at the lowest rank has no structure, while the unit
at the highest rank does not form part of the structure
of any higher unit. Consider the following example of classroom
exchange:

Teacher: Can you tell me why you eat all that food?
        Yes.
Pupil: To keep you strong.
Teacher: To keep you strong. Yes. To keep you strong.
        Why do you want to be strong?

Sinclair et al. point out that a boundary occurs in the middle of the
teacher's second utterance, which suggests that 'utterance' is not
the smallest unit. Classroom exchanges are made up of what the
authors call 'moves'; and many moves, like the teacher's first
contribution in the above exchange, consist of smaller discrete
units or 'acts'. At the upper levels of the scale, exchanges combine
to form 'transactions', which combine in turn to form lessons.
Sinclair et al. thus propose a discourse scale which overlaps with
other scales at the lower and upper ends, 'lying between the level of
grammar and *non-linguistic organization*'.[49] These overlapping
scales may be represented as in table 1.

TABLE 1

Non-linguistic organization	Discourse	Grammar
course		
period	lesson	
topic	transaction	
	exchange	
	move	sentence
	act	clause
		group
		word
		morpheme

The distinctiveness of the discourse scale can be shown by examining the rank of *move*. Moves are made up of acts which correspond closely to the grammatical unit 'clause'; but whereas grammar is concerned with the formal properties of an item, discourse is concerned with functional characteristics, that is, with what the speaker is using the item *for*. Thus there is a disjunction between grammar and discourse. The grammatical types 'interrogative', 'imperative' and 'declarative' often realize the discourse acts of elicitation, directive and informative, but this is not always so.

> A native speaker who interpreted 'Is that the mint-sauce over there?' or 'Can you tell me the time?' as yes/no questions, 'Have a drink' as a command, or 'I wish you'd go away' as requiring just a murmur of agreement, would find the world a bewildering place full of irritable people.[50]

In order to deal with the disjunction between grammar and discourse, Sinclair et al. propose two factors which affect the discursive status of an item. The first factor is the *situation* of the discourse, which includes relevant aspects in the environment, social conventions and shared experience of the participants. In the classroom situation, knowledge about schools, teaching and so on is used to reclassify items already labelled by grammar; for example, the interrogative 'What are you laughing at?' can be interpreted either as a question or as a command to stop laughing, and in the classroom it is usually the latter. The second factor which affects the discursive status of an item is what Sinclair et al. call *tactics*. This factor concerns the syntagmatic patterns of discourse, that is, the way in which items precede, follow and connect with one another. Spoken discourse unfolds in time in such a way that speakers make mistakes, correct themselves or realize that they could have expressed themselves better. Thus a teacher often follows one potential informative, directive or elicitation with another, signalling by intonation, etc., that the first one was a 'starter' and that pupils were not supposed to respond:

> Teacher: What about this one? This I think is a super one.
> Isobel, can you think what it means?
> Pupil: Does it mean there's been an accident further along the road?
> Teacher: No.

The teacher begins with a question which appears to have been intended as an elicitation, but which is relegated to the status of a starter by the subsequent statement, followed in turn by a second question which does serve as an elicitation. Situation and tactics therefore play a crucial role in determining the discursive status of an item.

The level of analysis at which Sinclair et al. have produced some of the most original results is that of *exchange*. Unlike many everyday conversations in which a question–answer sequence can be repeated without interruption, in the classroom situation eliciting exchanges have a tripartite structure. An 'initiating move' by the teacher is followed by a 'responding move' by the pupil, which is followed in turn by a 'feedback' or 'follow-up move' by the teacher. The basic IRF exchange structure is evident in the example below, where the teacher asks a question, the pupil answers it and the teacher provides evaluative feedback before asking another question.

> Teacher: Those letters have special names. Do you know what it is? What is one name that we give to these letters?
> Pupil: Vowels.
> Teacher: They're vowels, aren't they?
> Teacher: Do you think you could say that sentence without having the vowels in it?

Reflection on the peculiar features of the classroom situation helps to explain why the eliciting exchange has a tripartite structure. The individuals in a classroom have been gathered together for the purpose of learning something; the teacher asks questions, not in order to know the answers, but in order to know whether the pupil knows the answers. In such circumstances the pupil needs to know whether the answers are right, and so some feedback or follow-up is essential. The tripartite structure is so powerful that if feedback does not occur 'it is', as one of the authors observes, 'often a covert clue that the answer is wrong'.[51]

Since the ultimate aim of Sinclair et al. is to develop a descriptive system that can deal with all forms of discourse, in subsequent research they have studied other kinds of situation. They focused on situations, such as doctor–patient interviews and chaired television discussions, which enabled them to vary situational features like the degree of control over the topic and over turn-taking which is invested in one person, the degree of status differentials and of familiarity between participants, the purpose of the interaction and so on. The authors add that,

> While these factors are quite obviously defined in sociological terms the investigation remained a linguistic one for, while initially it was essential to use concepts like 'status', and talk in terms of social roles like 'chairman', the hope was that eventually it would be possible to come full circle and define roles like 'chairman' as a set of linguistic options.[52]

In studying the new types of situation, Sinclair et al. adhered to the basic assumption that it would be possible to describe them in terms of a rank scale, while acknowledging that the ranks may have to be revised. Doctor–patient interviews, for instance, are bounded by greetings and farewells which demarcate the highest unit; this unit is not the lesson, as in classroom discourse, but rather the 'situation' during which a number of 'interactions' can occur. The exchanges which take place in doctor–patient interviews could not, moreover, be forced into a tripartite structure. Sometimes the doctor follows up the patient's response with a sequence of feedback components, giving an exchange structure of IRFFF. . . . In other cases, the doctor does not follow up the patient's response but makes instead a new initiating move. Such cases presented a specific analytic problem, since follow-up and initiating moves could be grammatically and lexically identical. To resolve this problem, the authors turned their attention increasingly to the role of *intonation*. Assuming that pitch-level contrasts between tone groups were significant, it was suggested that for each successive tone group the speaker must choose high, mid or low key. It seemed plausible to interpret the high-tone group as linking forward, with the implication 'there's more to follow'; the low-tone group could be interpreted as linking back, with the implication 'this is said in a particular situation created by what has gone before'. These phonological features provided a way of categorizing otherwise identical lexico-grammatical items, as may be seen in the following example:

Elicit	Doctor:	and how long have you had these for
Reply	Patient:	well I had 'em er a week last Wednesday
Follow-up	Doctor:	A WEEK LAST WEDNESDAY (low key)
Elicit	Doctor:	do you bring up sputum
Reply	Patient:	only when I get a bit of indigestion and I like bring the food up as well
Elicit	Doctor:	BRING THE FOOD UP AS WELL (high key)
Reply	Patient:	well if I get violent indigestion everything comes up as easy as wink you know got to get rid of it
Follow-up	Doctor:	yes

While the third move and the sixth move are formally identical in the sense that they simply repeat part of the previous reply, nevertheless there is a clear difference in tone which enables the third move to be classified as a follow-up and the sixth to be classified as an initiating or eliciting move. The analysis of discourse intonation, as undertaken especially by David Brazil,[53] thus promises to provide a way of developing and refining the original model of Sinclair et al.

It is worthwhile to begin my critical discussion of methods of discourse analysis with the work of Sinclair and his associates, if only because their work demonstrates how difficult it is to elaborate methods which are suitable for the study of everyday speech. Although their model for the analysis of discourse is still in a state of development, it is sufficiently clear that the primary concern of their approach is to provide an analysis of *exchange structure*. Much of their work on classroom interaction is concerned to identify and confirm the basic IRF exchange structure; and many of their subsequent studies seek to examine the ways in which this basic structure is ramified or revised. It is not difficult to see, however, that there are strict limits to the usefulness of this type of analysis. An initial indication of these limits can be discerned in the various attempts of Sinclair et al. to extend their model beyond the classroom situation. Unlike the doctor–patient interviews, which seemed simply to require a modification of the rank scale and a reformulation of the exchange structure, data from television discussions and committee meetings were much less tractable. For such data contained long stretches of monologue which were not interrupted by exchanges, 'embarrassingly long stretches for which we could offer no analysis'.[54] Uninterrupted monologue obviously presents a very serious problem for a method which places so much emphasis on exchange structure. It was partially in response to this problem that some of the associates of Sinclair began to study the structure of lectures. In a seemingly desperate attempt to preserve the key features of the original model, the authors argue that, although the discourse of a lecture suspends the turn-taking machinery, nevertheless 'the discourse is "shaped" or "structured" with interactive purposes in mind'.[55] The 'interactive work' within the monologic discourse can be discerned, it is proposed, by differentiating between a main discourse and a subsidiary discourse, so that categories like 'repeat', 'qualify' and 'comment' can be employed. Yet this proposal seems to offer a very partial and problematic solution. Not only would it be of little assistance in the case of monologues characterized by a minimum of repetition and qualification, but it is also difficult to see how one could employ categories like 'qualify' and 'comment' without attending in a more systematic way to the *content* of the monologue, that is, without attending to *what is being said*. The tendency to displace content by structure is a feature of the model of Sinclair et al. which deserves to be considered in more detail.

The rank scale of discourse is, the authors argue, situated between and distinguishable from the scales of grammar and non-linguistic organization. While there is some 'overlap' between these scales, nevertheless each is organized on different principles and is therefore irreducible to the other. At the lower end of the discourse scale, for example, the move overlaps with the grammatical category 'sentence' and the act overlaps with the 'clause'; but acts and moves are defined in 'functional' terms, whereas the sentence and the clause are defined 'formally' or 'syntactically'. Moreover, it is only by studying the functions of discursive items that one can fully specify what they 'mean', since a large part of what an item means depends upon how it is used in specific contexts. This is unquestionably so – a Wittgensteinian observation which, stated in a general way, could hardly be contested. However, the matter cannot be left there. One must ask just how the relations between the overlapping scales of grammar and discourse are to be specified; and one will see that, in response to such a question, the approach of Sinclair et al. has little to offer. For while their model enables the analyst to code items in so far as they are functional contributions to an interactional exchange, it provides no way of handling the internal features of the contributions themselves. The model presupposes, as Richardson aptly remarks, 'an essentially arbitrary view of who speaks, how much he or she says, and how these linguistic productions are put together'.[56] One might add: an essentially arbitrary view of what is said. To know that an utterance with the grammatical form of a question may, in certain circumstances, function as a request is so far to know nothing about what it is a request *for*. To know that an utterance occupies the position of responding move in a tripartite exchange structure is so far to know nothing about what it is a response *to*. Sinclair and his associates take for granted, but do not explicitly address, the issue of what the participants in an interactional exchange are *talking about*; and it is difficult to see how this issue, which is the issue of discursive *content*, could be addressed without moving beyond their formalistic framework and considering more carefully the discursive roles of grammatical structure, background knowledge and the topical coherence which underlies a sequence of intelligible utterances.

My final criticism concerns the relation between discourse and the dimension of 'non-linguistic organization'. In fact, Sinclair and his associates have very little of interest to say about the non-linguistic organization of discursive situations. They frequently appeal to the notion of control and occasionally allude to problems of power and domination, but these issues are never examined in a systematic way. In view of their reasons for choosing to focus on classroom interaction, this theoretical absence is somewhat surprising; it points, I believe, to deeper limitations of their work. In the first place, the authors appear to assume that relations of power and control can be fully explicated, and are fully disclosed, within the structure of discourse. Thus, in concluding their account of the original model, they remark that 'the domination of the teacher's language is fully displayed in the earlier chapters of this book. The basic IRF structure, giving the teacher the last word, allows him to recast in his own terms any pupil response.'[57] It seems to me, however, that this assumption is highly suspect. For if the teacher's language is 'dominant' in the classroom situation, it is not only because he or she has the last word, but also because that language is part of a broader organization of power within society as a whole. Language is a very important medium for the expression of relations of power; but it is not the only medium and it cannot be assumed that such relations are fully disclosed within discourse. When a teacher canes a pupil or police open fire on protesting students, power is expressed in a form which is not discursive. Moreover, it seems mistaken to assume that relations of power, even when they are expressed in discourse, are fully disclosed by the operation of the exchange structure. For there may be crucial divisions which cut across the general positions of, for example, 'teacher' and 'pupil', divisions which reflect and reproduce asymmetries within the whole of society. In an illuminating study which attests to this possibility, Stanworth argues that it matters very much *who* teachers speak to and *how* they speak to them, since their over-attention to male pupils contributes to the marginalization of girls.[58] It seems equally evident that *what* teachers and others say is of vital importance for sustaining and reproducing relations of domination which extend beyond the discursive situation. To explore such considerations – which are central to the study of ideology – would require a theoretical framework which is broader, and an attention to content which is greater, than that which can be found in the writings of Sinclair et al.

ANALYSIS OF CONVERSATIONAL STRUCTURE: HARVEY SACKS ET AL.

Some of the limitations which characterize the approach of Sinclair et al. are avoided by Harvey Sacks, Emanuel Schegloff, Gail

Jefferson and others. Since the mid-1960s these authors have been studying the systematic properties of various forms of linguistic interaction. Like Sinclair et al., Sacks and his colleagues have been particularly concerned with the *sequential organization* of communication; but their approach to this problem differs significantly from that of Sinclair et al. In the first place, Sacks and his colleagues do not begin with a situation which is highly structured in terms of control and highly restricted in terms of aim. Rather, they focus on occurrences of conversation which are altogether mundane: most commonly on telephone conversations, which have the advantage of excluding visual cues, but also on instances of storytelling among peers. A second major difference between the two approaches is that Sacks and his colleagues seek to describe, not some structure which the *analyst discerns* in the complex data of discourse, but rather the mechanisms by means of which the *participants produce* their interaction in an organized way. Here the influence of Garfinkel's 'ethnomethodology' – the investigation of the ordered properties and ongoing achievements of everyday social practices – is clear.[59] As Sacks and Schegloff explain, 'we have proceeded under the assumption . . . that in so far as the materials we worked with exhibited orderliness, they did so not only for us, but for the co-participants who had produced them'.[60] What Sacks et al. regard as *problems* are what they see as *problems for participants*, that is, as problems which lay actors must confront and resolve in order to sustain interaction. The solutions to such problems are not merely theoretical but 'practical', in the sense that they are practical devices which enable participants to carry out their interactional tasks. The approach of Sacks et al. thus promises to avoid the kinds of abstract and arbitrary categorization which characterize much of the work on discursive and linguistic structures.

In order to account for the sequential organization of communication, Sacks and his colleagues have elaborated a model of the *turn-taking system* employed in everyday speech.[61] This model must accommodate a variety of facts which characterize ordinary conversation: the fact that, for the most part, only one part speaks at a time; the fact that the role of speaker is transmitted from one party to the next; the fact that such transitions commonly occur with no gap or overlap; the fact that what parties say, and how long they speak, is not specified in advance; and so on. Sacks et al.

propose to accommodate these facts within a model which consists of two components and a set of rules. The first component, the 'turn-constructional component', comprises the various unit-types with which a speaker may set out to construct a turn. In English these unit-types include sentential, clausal, phrasal and lexical constructions; the use of a unit-type enables the parties to a conversation to project the point at which a speaker's contribution will come to an end, thus marking a 'transition-relevance place'. The second component, the 'turn-allocational component', comprises the various techniques by which the next turn is allocated. These techniques fall into two basic groups: those in which the next turn is allocated by the current speaker selecting the next speaker, and those in which the next turn is allocated by self-selection. The two components of the model are linked by a number of rules governing turn construction, allocation and transfer. For example, at the initial transition-relevance place of a turn-constructional unit, there are various possibilities which are ordered in a rule-governed way: (a) if the turn-so-far is constructed so as to involve the use of a 'current speaker selects next' technique, then the party so selected has the right and obligation to take the next turn to speak; (b) if the turn-so-far does not involve the use of a 'current speaker selects next' technique, then self-selection may (but need not) be instituted, in which case the first starter acquires the rights to a turn; (c) if the turn-so-far does not involve the use of a 'current speaker selects next' technique, and if another does not self-select, then the speaker may (but need not) continue, in which case rules a–c reapply at the next transition-relevance place. These rules eliminate gap and overlap from conversation by eliminating gap and overlap from most single turns. The rules and components comprise a 'local management system',

> in the sense that [the system] operates in such a way as to allow turn size and turn order to vary and to be under local management, across variations in other parameters, while still achieving both the aim of all turn-taking systems – the organization of '*n* at a time' – and the aim of all turn-taking organizations for speech-exchange systems – 'one at a time while speaker change recurs'.[62]

The turn-taking system provides a set of rules, collectively shared and recursively applied, which enables the participants in a conversation to transfer the right to speak from one party to the next with an astonishing degree of temporal precision. While abstracting from content and invariant across contexts, the system is nevertheless sensitive to the specific interactions which agents, with the aid of this system, sustain and produce.

One of the main techniques by means of which the current speaker selects next is what Sacks et al. call 'adjacency pair first parts'. *Adjacency pairs* are a class of utterance types which include sequences like greeting–greeting, question–answer, invitation–acceptance/decline. These sequences consist of an initial utterance, a 'first pair part', produced by one speaker and directly followed by another utterance, a 'second pair part', which is (a) produced by a different speaker and (b) from the same pair type as the first pair part. The use of a first pair part, in conjunction with an address term such as a personal pronoun or a name, is an important and effective technique for selecting the next speaker. The use of a first pair part also serves to secure the close ordering of utterances in conversation, thereby smoothly oiling the turn-taking machinery, and to produce a certain 'sequential implicativeness'. By the latter term Sacks et al. wish to call attention to the fact that many contributions to a conversation are 'other-directed', for they are designed to display an orientation to, or an understanding of, some co-participant in a conversation. Thus, by asking a question, a speaker S can get another to talk about some matter which S is about to talk about, or can check to see whether another has understood what S has been talking about; and by producing what is recognizable as an answer, a speaker can indicate a willingness to go along with the prior speaker's suggestion, or can show that what the prior speaker said has been understood. As Sacks and Schegloff remark,

> Wherever, then, there is reason to bring attention to the appreciation of some implicativeness, 'next utterance' is the proper place to do that, and a two-utterance sequence can be employed as a means for doing and checking some intendedly sequential implicative occurrence in a way that a one-utterance sequence can not.[63]

The notion of adjacency pair is of great assistance in analysing the opening and closing of telephone conversations.[64] As Schegloff shows, the ring of the telephone may be treated as the first pair part of an adjacency pair, a *summons* to which the initial 'hello' is an *answer*. The second turn – that is, the caller's first turn – is then the first pair part of a new adjacency pair; it frequently involves, not only a greeting, but also a claim to have recognized the answerer and a claim to have the answerer recognize the caller. If the answerer fails to recognize the caller from the initial greeting, the answerer can choose one of several second pair parts which, because they signal a breakdown, are 'dispreferred'. Thus the answerer may simply withhold the return greeting in order to allow the speaker of the first pair part to back down from the claim he or she has made, revise the initial utterance by upgrading the resources available for recognition, and thereby re-initiate the opening sequence.

As the example of failed recognition makes clear, a central feature of conversation is the mechanism which it provides for carrying out *repair*. The use of language in social interaction is an extremely complex process which, from time to time, is bound to go astray. But if language use has intrinsic sources of trouble, it also has 'a mechanism for dealing with them intrinsically'.[65] In order to investigate this mechanism, Sacks et al. distinguish, first, between the *initiation* of repair and the *outcome* of repair: the person who performs the repair is not necessarily the person who initiated the repair operation. One must then distinguish between the *self-initiation* and the *other-initiation* of repair. Self-initiations and other-initiations have regular and different *placements* with regard to the trouble source. Self-initiations can occur in any one of three positions: in the same turn as the trouble source, in the transition space following the troubled turn, or in the second turn subsequent to the troubled turn. Other-initiations occupy one main position: the turn just subsequent to the troubled turn. Moreover, other-initiations are often withheld a bit past the possible completion of the troubled turn, providing an expanded transition space for the speaker of the trouble source to initiate self-repair. Other-initiations are concerned primarily to *locate* the trouble source, as is evident in the following examples:

Ken: 'E likes the waider over there.
Al: Wait-*er*?
Ken: Waitress, sorry.
Al: 'At's bedder.

A: It's just about three o'clock, so she's probably free.
        I'll call her now.
B: *What* time is it?
A: Three, isn't it?
B: I thought it was earlier.
A: Oh, two. Sorry.

The other-initiations by Al in the first example, by B in the second, provide the speaker of the trouble source with another opportunity, in the next turn, to repair the trouble source. Thus, both the increased opportunity for the self-initiation of repair, and the fact that other-initiations generally result in self-correction, produce a preference for self-correction in the overall organization of conversation.

An interesting feature of much conversation is the way in which the turn-taking machinery is temporarily suspended by the telling of *stories*. Special techniques are employed to introduce a story and to show, upon completion of the story, that the story has been understood. Once a story has been introduced and the other participants have granted the right for it to be told, the speaker can tell the whole story without allowing any place for the talk of the recipients; if the recipients want to talk, they may have to interrupt. While the telling of the story temporarily suspends the turn-taking machinery, the story itself often has a complex constructional form. Some aspects of this form are brought out by Sacks in his insightful analysis of a dirty joke.[66] The joke, told by a seventeen-year-old boy to two male peers and one male adult, concerns three sisters who got married on the same day:

Ken: So, first of all, that night, they're – on their
        honeymoon the – uh mother-in-law, says – (to 'em)
        well why don'tcha all spend the night here an' then you
        cn go on yer honeymoon in the *morning*. First night,
        th'mother walks up t'the first door an' she hears
        this *uuuuuuuuuuhh*! hh Second door is
        HHOOOOHHH!
        Third door there's nothing. She stands there fer about
        *twu*nny-five minutes waiting fer sumpna happen, –
        nuthin.
                (1 second)
Ken: Next morning she talks t'the first daughter, and she

sz – uh how come ya – how com y'went
YEEEEEAAAAGGGHH
last night, 'n daughter sez well, it *tickled* mommy,
'n second girl, how come ya screamed. Oh mommy it
hurts. hh Third girl walks up t'her – why didn'
ya *say* anything last night. W'*you* told me it was
always impolite t'talk with my mouth full,
    (2 seconds)

Ken: hh hyok hyok,
    (1 second)

Ken: Hyok.
    (3 seconds)

Al: *HA-HA-HA-HA,*

Ken: ehh heh heh // hehhh

(Al):   hehhhehhheh hhh

Roger: Delayed reactio(h)n

Al: hehh I hadtuh think // about it awhile you know?

Roger: hhh heh
    (1 second)

Roger: hehh hh hehh hhh You mean the deep hidden mean-
    ing there doesn't hitcha right awa(hh)y heh heh //
    hehhhhhh hehhhhhh

Al: hh hhh // hhh

The joke is organized both temporally and sequentially. It proceeds in a simple temporal order, adopting a format which the
alleged events might have had; and it is sequentially structured in
such a way that an appreciation of some point in it depends upon
an appreciation of its position subsequent to some other point. The
joke consists of two interrelated sequences: the 'first night'
sequence and the 'next morning' sequence. The first night sequence
yields a puzzle in a way which is perfectly economical, for you
need at least three instances, but no more, to produce silence as
problematic. The next morning sequence is connected to the preceding sequence by means of a temporal reference and is sequentially structured in a parallel way. The sequence employs a pronoun, 'it', which has no prior-named referent but which permits of
a common interpretation. This common interpretation enables the
third answer to be interpreted, thereby solving the puzzle and
simultaneously providing the punch line to the joke. It is impor-

tant to stress that the solution is not asserted in the punch line but has to be *interpreted* out of it. The telling of a joke confronts the recipients with a task. They have to attend carefully to the sequence of events, suspending any doubt about their plausibility, in order to ensure that, when the punch line comes, they can get it. It is the function of jokes as *understanding tests* which accounts for the distinctive features of the response. The utterance of the punch line is followed by silence, laughter, silence. This tense and hesitant sequence is a product of what Sacks calls 'the recipient comparative wit assessment device': given that failure to get a joke can be treated as a sign of one's lack of sophistication, and given that recipient laughs can be differentiated in terms of their relative starts, the timing of laughs can provide a basis for comparatively assessing the wit of recipients. This device generates numerous possibilities: immediate laughter, erratic laughter, feigned laughter, as well as a collective silence which undercuts the device and amounts to a negative assessment of the joke or of its teller.

The work of Sacks and his colleagues, whose contributions I have sketched in the most schematic way, is of considerable interest and originality. In contrast to Sinclair et al., their approach to the analysis of discourse is concerned less with categorization and more with the procedures actually employed in the production and reception of discourse. With great insight they bring out the complexities of what are, apparently, the most trivial aspects of conversational practice; they thus help to show how the mechanisms which sustain social order are embedded in, and constitutive of, the multifarious details of everyday life. Nevertheless, as in the case of Sinclair et al., it is difficult to avoid the impression that some of the most interesting issues are those which the authors leave aside. Let me try to substantiate this impression by returning to the authors' account of the turn-taking system. In formulating this account, Sacks et al. seek to develop a model which is both 'context-free' and 'context-sensitive', that is, which is both invariant across situations and adaptable to the realities of specific contexts. It seems to me, however, that there are two features of specific contexts which are so important for the exchange of turns that any attempt to formulate a context-free model must be very partial at best. In the first place, the determination of what counts as a transition-relevance place depends entirely upon what is judged to be the turn-constructional unit. Participants in a conversation must engage in a constant process of interpretation; they must interpret what is being said and employ this interpretation in order to anticipate a point at which they may take a turn. Yet *which* interpretation is to count, and *which* participant is to succeed in holding or usurping the right to speak, depends upon *who* the participants are and how much *power* they respectively have in the situation concerned. The turn-taking system does not function in a vacuum; it presupposes, but does not itself address, an ongoing process of interpretation on the part of participants who are embedded in relations of power. While the analysis of turn-taking mechanisms may help to illuminate the social organization of conversation, it seems doubtful whether such mechanisms could be satisfactorily analysed in isolation from the interpretative and institutional aspects of conversation.

Similar reservations may be expressed with regard to the analysis of the organization of repair. Sacks et al. are able to show that, once a trouble source has been recognized by one or more of the parties to a conversation, there are specific procedures and priorities which may be implemented in the attempt to repair the trouble. However, by focusing on the ways in which these procedures and priorities are related to successive turns and thereby to the turn in which the trouble originally occurred, Sacks and his colleagues disregard the question of what *counts as* a 'trouble' and how the recognition of troubles is *differentiated* in social terms. An utterance can be treated as a 'trouble', by lay actors as well as by professional analysts, only in so far as the the individual so treating it has some conception of correct or 'untroubled' discourse; and *this* conception is not independent of relations of power and privilege in the society concerned. Tendencies towards correction or self-correction are not governed by procedures immanent in language alone, but are related to the social positions of the individuals whose utterances express these tendencies. Thus Labov has shown, for example, that the speech of middle-class women displays a strong tendency towards hyper-correction, while stigmatized features of speech are judged most severely by immigrants and other individuals whose speech most often exhibits these features.[67] In calling attention to what could be called the 'social differentiation of repair', I do not wish to claim that the conclusions of Sacks et al. are unfounded; but I do wish to suggest that these conclusions, in so far as they are based on analyses which abstract from certain social and contextual considerations, run the risk of occluding the most interesting issues.

The nature and importance of the issues at stake can be highlighted by reconsidering Sacks's analysis of a dirty joke. This analysis represents, in my opinion, one of the most valuable contributions to emerge from the approach of Sacks et al. By combining an interest in turn-taking with a sensitivity to the temporal and sequential organization of the joke, Sacks has provided some of the elements for an inquiry into the *narratives of everyday life*, an inquiry which could be of great interest from many points of view. Here I shall adopt one point of view, namely that which is concerned with the relations between language and power; and I shall assess the strength of Sacks's analysis by considering how he interprets the role and effect of his specimen joke. A dirty joke should be seen, he proposes, as an institution for packaging and transmitting information, where the transmission is restricted in some specific way. The joke under discussion, he goes on to argue, 'is a joke with information relevant for, and passage intendedly restricted to, 12-year-old girls'.[68] This argument is based on the fact that, while the joke is told by a seventeen-year-old boy to three male recipients, it is told by the boy as having been told to him by his twelve-year-old sister. The argument is also based on the claim that only twelve-year-old girls can understand the *squelch* effected by the punch line of the joke. For the punch line effects a squelch of the mother by the daughter: it says, effectively, 'if I violated a rule, I did so by reference to some other rule which *you* told me to follow'. The punch line sets up the daughter as victor, overturning the hierarchy of child–parent relations in a way that only daughters can understand. Be that as it may; the joke admits of another interpretation. A dirty joke, circulating among teenage boys, in which women are presented as objects of pleasure whose capacity to satisfy male desire is enhanced by their incapacity to distinguish between a dinner table and a bed: this is a construction of meaning which reproduces, and serves to sustain, a division and asymmetrical relation of power between the sexes. If Sacks had given more consideration to questions of power and social structure, perhaps he would not have been so naïvely oblivious to this dimension of his specimen joke. It is precisely this dimension, where the construction of meaning intersects with asymmetrical relations of power, which is the domain of ideology.

ANALYSIS OF GRAMMATICAL STRUCTURE: ROGER FOWLER ET AL.

If Sacks and his colleagues can be criticized for neglecting social and contextual considerations, this could not be so easily said of Roger Fowler, Robert Hodge, Gunther Kress and Tony Trew. These authors, all of whom have worked together at the University of East Anglia, have elaborated an approach to the analysis of discourse which aims to explore the links between grammatical structure and the social world.[69] The approach is premised upon a rejection of the dichotomy between 'linguistics' and 'sociolinguistic' patterning in utterances and texts, that is, the dichotomy between the grammatical structures of a language and the ways in which these are employed in actual instances of communication. This dichotomy, expressed most famously in Chomsky's distinction between competence and performance, has unduly restricted the scope of linguistic theory and has impeded the study of the interconnections between grammar and society. Like Sinclair and his associates, Fowler et al. find a helpful antidote in the work of Halliday. Fowler et al. are not so much interested in Halliday's formulation of a rank scale, but rather in his account of grammatical structure and linguistic function.[70] There are three general functions, according to Halliday, which all languages fulfil: they serve to communicate about events and objects in the world ('ideational function'), to establish and maintain social relations ('interpersonal function'), and to construct links with itself and with features of the situation in which it is used ('textual function'). These three functions form the basis of the grammatical structure of a language, for grammar provides the means whereby these functions can be transformed into intelligible communication. By studying the grammatical structure of a language, therefore, Fowler et al. hope to say something about the social relations and contexts in which the language is used, that is, about 'the nature of the society whose language it is'.[71]

Fowler and his associates view language as comprising a set of categories and processes. The fundamental categories are 'models' which describe the interrelation of objects and events. Deriving from perceptual processes, the models form schemata which serve to classify events in the world. The authors distinguish three basic models and several sub-models. In the first model, there are at least two entities related by a process; one entity is seen as causing the action, the other as affected by it, as in 'The player kicked the ball'. The authors call this first model the *transactive model*, since the action is seen as passing from the actor to the affected through the process indicated by the verb. The second model is the *non-transactive model*; here there is at least one entity related to a process, as in 'The player runs'. The first two models, which may be referred to jointly as 'actionals', must be distinguished from the *relational model*. The latter may involve a relation between two entities, as in 'The coach is an ex-football player', or between an entity and a quality, as in 'His footwork is superb'. Those relational models which establish relations between nouns are often 'equative', whereas those which establish relations between nouns and qualities are often 'attributive'. These distinctions yield the scheme of syntagmatic models for English found in figure 4.

syntagmatic models $\begin{cases} \text{actionals} & \begin{cases} \text{transactive} \\ \text{non-transactive} \end{cases} \\ \text{relationals} & \begin{cases} \text{equative} \\ \text{attributive} \end{cases} \end{cases}$

Figure 4

The syntagmatic models provide an initial classification of events and profoundly affect their causal interpretation. Whereas transactives commonly posit a clear causal relationship between two nominal entities, non-transactives have an immediacy and indeterminacy which helps to make what is happening seem extraordinary, magical and mysterious. This effect can be illustrated by an elementary example:

non-transactive: The ball moved.
transactive: The player kicked the ball.

Actual forms of language often present 'complex fields' which contain more than the two or three places of simple models. Within such fields there may be a *conflation* of two or more models, as in the following example discussed by Halliday.

The warder marched the prisoners.

This sentence, which apparently concurs with the transactive model, may be analysed into two non-transactives:

(A) The warder caused x.   (B) The prisoners marched.

(where x = B). In the conflation of the two non-transactive models, the actor/subject of B becomes the object of the verb, and the actor/subject of A becomes the subject of the verb. The resulting sentence is interpreted as a transactive with 'warder' as the actor and 'prisoners' as the affected. 'The effect of this linguistic process', argue Kress and Hodge,

> is to reassign the actor roles in the two conflated models. The real actor of the process is denied credit and responsibility for the action he performs, and this credit is assigned to the syntactic participant who is regarded as more powerful. It is a thing not lightly done. The ideological function is clear.[72]

The conflation of syntagmatic models in the surface form of a sentence is an instance of what Fowler et al. call *transformations*. This notion, borrowed from Chomsky, is used to refer to processes by which elements present in underlying structures are deleted, combined and reordered in surface forms, so that the latter must be interpreted by reconstructing their derivation. Two particularly common types of transformation are *nominalizations* and *passivizations*. Nominalizations occur when sentences or parts of sentences, descriptions of action and the participants involved in them, are turned into nouns; the effect is to attenuate the feeling of activity, to eliminate agency, modality and tense, to transform processes into objects. Passivization – the rendering of verbs in the passive form – also involves the deletion of actors and focuses the attention of the hearer or reader on certain themes at the expense of others. Kress and Hodge illustrate the operation of these and other forms of transformation by analysing an editorial from *The Guardian*. The editorial concerns the miners' overtime ban during the winter of 1972–3, in response to which the Conservative government introduced the three-day working week. While the editorial is purportedly about action, there are very few occurrences (five) of the transactive model. All of the transactives concern actions or events produced by, or seen as the responsibility of, the miners: the government is presented syntactically as unable to act. Moreover, with the exception of the miners, the actors in the editorial are nominalized. For example,

Picketing . . . curtailed coal deliveries.

The noun 'picketing' is formed by a process which could be represented as follows:

strikers picket a factory ⇒ picketing

(where ⇒ means 'is transformed into'). By means of this transformation, the identities of the actors are lost and the reader's attention is shifted away from actions and processes situated in time toward abstract nouns and concepts. The phrase 'Picketing . . . curtailed coal deliveries' is further complicated by the fact that 'coal deliveries' is another nominalization and 'curtail' is a comparative verb. A full version of this superficially simple phrase might be roughly as follows:

[miners] picket [mines and coal depots so that rail drivers do not] deliver as much coal as before [the start of the dispute to power stations]

(where square brackets indicate what has been deleted from the surface form). The use of nominalization and other devices helps to reduce complexity; but 'reducing the complexity of an argument and limiting the terms which it can contain is a drastic intervention. Showing less means someone else seeing less. And seeing less means thinking less.'[73] Transformations involve the suppression and distortion of material contained in the underlying linguistic structures. Transformations also involve, therefore, a mystification of the causal processes portrayed by underlying models, a mystification which can be countered, the authors contend, by reconstructing the ways in which the surface forms have been derived.

Language not only simplifies and mystifies: it also provides individuals with a system of classification. As a means of classification, language imposes order on the world, facilitating both the individual's control over the flux of experience and society's control over conceptions of reality. But classification systems are not shared by a society as a whole. Different groups have different systems, and these systems are strained by the contingencies of interaction and by conflicts of interest.

In this way classification becomes the site of tension and struggle – on one level between individuals, as each tries to impose his or her system on others or gives way to superior power. On another level, the struggle goes on between social, ethnic, national, or racial groupings.[74]

The importance of classification can be seen by attending to everyday examples of conflicting labels, such as the description of individuals as 'terrorists' or 'freedom fighters', as well as by studying cases of 'relexicalization' or relabelling. Kress and Trew point to many instances of relexicalization in their analysis of the *Sunday Times'* rewriting of a letter from the management of British Leyland.[75] While the authors of the rewritten letter claim that 'it says exactly the same thing' as the original letter, Kress and Trew argue that there are changes of wording, for example from 'commitment' to 'promise', which have important implications for the way in which the message is received. Yet classification is a question, not only of different conceptual frameworks, but of determinate grammatical processes. A simple sentence may be viewed as a set of places, each of which has additional slots which serve to classify further the main places. Consider the following phrase which headed a university information sheet circulated during a dispute about food prices:

The facts about catering prices.

Here 'prices' are classified as 'catering prices' – as opposed, for example, to 'food prices'; and 'catering prices' is used to delimit 'the facts', that is 'the real and relevant facts'. The strategy of classification implicit in 'The facts about catering prices' may thus be represented as in figure 5.

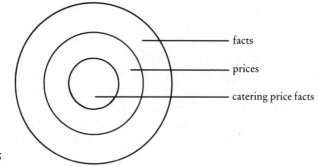

Figure 5

By limiting the area of concern, classification serves as an instrument for the control of information and experience. Moreover, the modifiers which are regarded as more important or essential will commonly be found closer to the noun, so that the order of words is revealing about the principles of classification used by speakers and cultures. By studying the patterns of inclusion and contiguity, one can, the authors suggest, discern some of the key features of classification and control.

One of the classification operations which must be performed on every utterance is the speaker's indication of generality, reliability and truth. This indication, which pertains to what is commonly called *modality*, may be provided in various ways. The use of modal adverbs ('possibly', 'certainly', 'necessarily') give a direct index of the speaker's attitude. Modal auxiliaries ('I should point out . . .'), verbs in the past tense ('I wondered whether . . .') and verbs referring to mental processes ('I think that would be difficult') can all be used to indicate the authority of an utterance or the relation of the speaker to an utterance. As Kress and Hodge remark, 'the speaker translates uncertainty about status in the power situation into uncertainty about the status of his utterances';[76] hence the many hesitations, the 'um's and 'sort of's, which characterize the speech of interviewees.[77] The interrelations of language, knowledge and power can also be discerned in the structure of speech-acts. Explicit directives are used to issue a command only when the power differential between the speaker and the hearer is large and can be openly acknowledged, as in the case of parent and child. Otherwise the command is issued in an indirect way, for example by means of an interrogative. Consider the situation described by Kress and Hodge in which a husband says to his wife, 'Can you get the meal ready?' This question provides an initial classification of the husband as someone who lacks knowledge (− knowledge) and wishes, by means of this question, to make up the deficit. However, since the relation between husbands and wives is commonly asymmetrical it may also be assumed that the speaker is in a position of superior power (+ power). If the wife immediately proceeds to prepare the meal, one can conclude that the classification (+ power) is dominant; if, on the other hand, she says 'yes' or 'no', one can infer that the classification (− knowledge) is relevant and dominant. Complexities can be introduced by intonation, context and the shifting nature of power relations themselves. But such complexities do not negate the fact that, through forms of modality and types of speech-act, asymmetrical relations of power and knowledge are expressed.

The writings of Fowler and his associates help, in a novel and suggestive way, to illuminate the overlapping area between linguistics and social analysis. Their studies of grammatical and syntactic processes, such as nominalization, passivization and classification, shed light on the ways in which our understanding of the world is affected by the language through which it is understood; and their analyses of modality and speech-acts call attention to the fact that language is not free from relations of power. Yet while Fowler et al. are right to search for links between language and social life, one may have doubts about the extent to which an understanding of social phenomena can be conveyed by this kind of linguistic approach. For their analyses frequently presuppose a specific account of relations between for example, different classes, races or sexes; but they provide no systematic discussion of these relations and no sustained justification of this account. Instead they tend to assume that by attending to linguistic processes one can discern, through the deceptive veil of surface forms, the underlying social reality. It is not difficult to appreciate that matters may be more complex. Consider the example of the question uttered by a husband to his wife, 'Can you get the meal ready?'. Kress and Hodge are undoubtedly correct to insist that such speech-acts are embedded in relations of power and that, in spite of its interrogative form, it may well be functioning as a command. But it seems quite misleading to suppose, as Kress and Hodge appear to do, that the role of this speech-act within the existing relations – its role *as* an act of power – can be ascertained by attending to the nature of the wife's response. It seems evident that, if she says 'yes' and proceeds to prepare the meal, this does not necessarily imply that considerations of knowledge have somehow overridden considerations of power. For complicity with the speech-acts of others, recognizing them as questions which are worthy of answers or as offers which are worthy of responses, may already be an affirmation of relations of power. Perhaps Fowler and his associates would not deny this; but I doubt whether such issues could be examined satisfactorily from within their perspective, a perspective which, however critical, remains largely linguistic.

A similar limitation in the work of Fowler et al. may be seen in their approach to questions of *meaning*. In principle the authors wish to adopt, following Halliday,[78] a social and contextual approach to these questions. They warn against an overly restrictive conception of linguistics as equivalent to the study of syntax, and of the latter as identical with transformational theory. They urge linguists to broaden their area of concern and to seek to integrate the study of syntax with an inquiry into 'the social uses of language'. Yet in spite of this sound advice, Fowler et al. remain curiously bound to syntactic analysis, assuming that 'meanings are carried and expressed in the syntactic forms and processes, that is, that the analyst can "read off" meaning from the syntax'.[79] This is, it seems to me, a questionable assumption that would be difficult to sustain in theory and in practice. In theory: for several years now, the idea that one could develop a theory of autonomous syntax from which meaning could be derived or 'read off', as Chomsky once believed, has been subjected to forceful criticism. Many linguists have argued that semantic and pragmatic information, far from being derivable from syntactic structure, must instead be *drawn upon* in order to determine whether a sentence is syntactically well formed.[80] Moreover, what an expression 'means' is not a fixed and invariant given, but is a fluctuating phenomenon which is determined as much by the contextual conditions of its production and reception as by the syntactic features of its construction. It is difficult to see how the assumption of Fowler et al. avoids these objections to a narrowly syntactic approach, an approach which they sharply criticize in other respects. And in practice, Fowler et al. often slip beyond the level of syntactic analysis. In a study of 'the ideology of middle management', for example, the authors elaborate on the implications of viewing the work-force of a factory in terms of a spatial metaphor, and of viewing management through the image of a 'figure-head'.[81] The link between this discussion and the analysis of syntax is very tenuous indeed, and it certainly could not be maintained that the implications drawn by the authors are simply 'read off' the syntax. What is needed, as Fowler et al. occasionally insist, is a method for the *critical interpretation* of linguistic expressions; but if the authors rightly recognize this need, their preoccupation with problems of syntax seriously limits their ability to fulfil it.

I now wish to consider briefly the principal dimension of the social world to which Fowler et al. seek to relate the study of language. The dimension concerned is that of *ideology*: 'Language as Ideology', Kress and Hodge boldly entitle their book. Yet in spite of its prominence, the concept of ideology is vaguely defined in the writings of Fowler et al. At one point 'ideology' is defined as 'a systematic body of ideas, organized from a particular point of view'; elsewhere ideologies are said to be 'sets of ideas involved in the ordering of experience, making sense of the world'.[82] It is easy to see how this conception of ideology, vaguely defined, concurs with the authors' emphasis on processes of classification. Just as different groups in society – social groups, racial groups, ethnic groups and so on – have different systems of classification, so too they have different ideologies, that is, different ways of 'making sense of the world'. This conception of ideology is, however, so loose and general that it is virtually useless. Different groups have different ideologies; but *which* groups are relevant, and how are they to be defined? Does the individual 'have' as many ideologies as there are groups to which he or she belongs? Is there a family ideology? a peer group ideology? a squash-and-tennis-player's ideology? Such questions indicate that what is missing from the writings of Fowler et al., as well as from the writings of many recent theorists of ideology, is a recognition of the link between *ideology and domination*. Such questions also indicate, once again, that the *theory of society* which animates the work of Fowler et al. remains in a largely implicit and unrefined state. Their writings are replete with terms like 'agency', 'power', 'control', 'domination', 'social structure'; but nowhere are these terms clearly defined and situated within a systematic social theory. While Fowler and his associates are surely right to search for connections between 'language and society', it seems evident that their study of society, in contrast to their analysis of language, has lagged well behind.

III   ANALYSIS OF IDEOLOGY: SOME OPEN ISSUES

The critical discussions of the previous two parts prepare the way for a more constructive contribution. Drawing upon the criticisms which I have made of other authors, I shall attempt to sketch the contours of an alternative approach to the analysis of ideology. I undertake this attempt with few pretensions: what follows is merely a sketch, rough and incomplete, of an approach which has yet to be filled out and put to use. My aim is not so much to resolve specific problems, but rather to identify some open issues. I shall locate these issues within three general areas of concern. First, there is the task of conceptualizing ideology. I shall pursue this task on the assumption that ideology must be conceptualized within the framework of a general social theory, a theory which explores, among other things, the relations between action, institutions, power and domination. The second general area of concern is that of methodology. Here my reflections will be guided by the desire to elaborate a systematic interpretative theory which incorporates the dimensions of social and discursive analysis. The third area in which relevant issues arise is the area of epistemology. The analysis of ideology cannot evade, I believe, questions of critique and justification. I shall confront these questions by seeking to clarify, in a tentative and exploratory way, the notion of truth and the conditions under which claims to truth can be sustained. In this final part of the essay I shall no longer restrict my discussion to material in English, but shall draw freely upon the contributions of French and German authors. Hopefully it will become clear that, while these authors have had an influence on recent work in English, their contributions may have more value than some of that work would suggest.

CONCEPTUALIZATION OF IDEOLOGY

The concept of ideology cannot be considered in isolation, but must be situated within the framework of a general social theory. That particular conceptions of ideology are affected by general theoretical assumptions is evident from the contributions discussed in the first part of the essay. Seliger's conception of ideologies as action-oriented sets of beliefs is closely connected to his pluralistic view of Western politics, a view which tends to play down the institutional and structural conditions of political action. The contribution of Hirst, on the other hand, preserves the deterministic emphasis of Althusser, in so far as he conceives of subjects as 'supports' of processes – including processes of calculation – which already exist in advance. What is missing from the theoretical frameworks of Seliger and Hirst is, among other things, a satisfactory account of the relation between action and social structure:

each author accentuates one aspect at the expense of the other, and each aspect is dealt with inadequately in the work of both. The importance of grasping the interplay of action and structure in the everyday reproduction of social life has been demonstrated most clearly by Anthony Giddens.[83] Rejecting the reductionist tendencies of 'interpretative sociologies', on the one hand, and of functionalism and structuralism on the other, Giddens elaborates a *theory of structuration* which seeks to integrate an account of action with an analysis of institutions and social structure. 'Structure', according to Giddens, may be conceived as the 'rules and resources' which are implicitly drawn upon by actors in their everyday activity and which are thereby reproduced, most often unintentionally. While this conception is highly provocative, it nevertheless suffers, in my opinion, from certain limitations. For 'structural properties' are apparently defined by each and every 'rule' which actors employ, and there would seem to be no grounds intrinsic to this conception for regarding some rules as more fundamental than others. Moreover, as soon as one turns to a more concrete analysis of the social world, Giddens's conception of structure as rules and resources appears to be inadequate, if not altogether irrelevant.[84] While wishing to sustain his attempt to develop a theory of structuration, it seems to me necessary to alter the specific terms of his account.

It is my view that the relation between action and structure must be conceived of by distinguishing three levels of abstraction.[85] On each of these levels I shall draw two further distinctions; and I shall allude to – although here I cannot pursue – the multiple ways in which these levels are linked. The first and most immediate level is that of *action*, whereby agents participate and intervene in the social world. Action as a flow of activity, monitored by agents capable of accounting for what they are doing, can be distinguished from particular actions, such as hitting, frowning, switching-on-the-light, which may be regarded as events describable in various ways. The second level of abstraction is that of *social institutions*. *Specific* institutions may be viewed as constellations of social relations, together with the reservoirs of material resources which are associated with them; *sedimented* institutions are those configurations which persist in various specific forms. Thus one is concerned with a specific institution when one inquires into the authority relations and capital resources which constitute, for example, the University of London, whereas one is concerned with a sedimented institution when one studies the university system as such. The third and most abstract level is that of *social structure*. I propose to conceive of social structure as a series of elements and their interrelations which conjointly define the conditions for the persistence of a social formation and the limits for the variation of its component institutions. Two categories of structural elements may be distinguished. On the one hand, there are those elements which must be present in any society, since they represent necessary conditions for the persistence of social life as such. On the other hand, there are those elements which are necessary conditions, not for the persistence of social life as such, but for the continuation of a particular *type* of society. So whereas production may be a necessary feature of any society, production by means of capital and wage-labour is not; and it is the interrelations between the latter elements which define the institutions of a society as capitalistic. Agents acting within an institutional context apply flexible 'schemata' which provide guidelines for coping with new and unanticipated situations. So long as agents do not flout such guidelines in a way which propels institutions beyond the limiting conditions, then their action may be said to reproduce social structure. However, one cannot preclude the possibility that these conditions may be exceeded by the cumulative consequences of collective action, a possibility which underlines the essentially creative and transformative character of action.

Each of the three levels in the relation between action and structure realizes an aspect of the phenomenon of *power*. At the level of action and in the most general sense, 'power' is the ability to act in pursuit of one's aims and interests: an agent has the *power to act*, the power to intervene in the sequence of events and to alter their course. In the sociologically relevant sense of 'power', however, the power to act must be related to the institutional site from which it derives. 'Power', at the institutional level, is a capacity which *enables* or *empowers* some agents to make decisions, pursue ends or realize interests; it empowers them in such a way that, without this institutionally endowed capacity, they would not have been able to carry out the relevant course. Power as an institutionally endowed capacity is *limited* by the structural conditions which circumscribe the range of institutional variation: thus the distribution of power in a capitalistic enterprise is 'structured by' the relation between wage-labour and capital. When the relations of power established at the institutional level are *systematically asymmetrical*, then the situation may be described as one of *domination*. Relations of power are 'systematically asymmetrical' when particular agents or groups of agents are institutionally endowed with power in a way which excludes, and to some significant degree remains inaccessible to, other agents or groups of agents, irrespective of the basis upon which such exclusion is carried out. Among the instances of domination which are of particular importance are those which are structured by the conditions which limit institutional variation. In capitalist societies the fundamental limiting conditions are specified by the capital/wage-labour relation, which secures systematically asymmetrical relations between classes at the level of the enterprise. It would be a serious mistake to assume, however, that the relation between the classes is the only important instance of domination in capitalist societies. As many authors have rightly emphasized, relations of domination subsist between nation-states, between ethnic groups and between the sexes which cannot be reduced to class domination.[86] A satisfactory analysis of domination and exploitation in contemporary societies would – without minimizing the importance of class – have to give considerable attention to the interrelated phenomena of racism, sexism and the system of nation-states.

The analysis of power and domination, situated within the context of an account of the relation between action and structure, provides the backcloth against which I want to reconsider the problem of ideology. Throughout the first part of this essay I emphasized the way in which contemporary theorists conceive of ideology in a *neutral* sense, regarding it as a system of symbols or beliefs which pertain, in some way, to social action or political practice. Whether Seliger's 'inclusive conception' of ideology as action-oriented sets of beliefs, or Gouldner's formulation of ideology in terms of public projects advocated by rational discourse, or Hirst's view of ideology as a system of ideas which can be employed in political calculation: in each case ideology bears no intrinsic connection to the problem of domination and the critique of domination. It is this aspect of many contemporary theories of ideology which I wish to reject. I wish to maintain, on the contrary, that *to study ideology is to study the ways in which meaning (signification) serves to sustain relations of domination.* Among the many ways in which ideology operates, three may be cited as central. In the first place, relations of domination may be sustained by being represented as *legitimate*. Every system of domination, observed Weber, seeks to cultivate a belief in its legitimacy, by appealing either to rational, traditional or charismatic grounds;[87] and such an appeal, it should be noted, is generally expressed in language. A second way in which ideology operates is by means of *dissimulation*. Relations of domination which serve the interests of some at the expense of others may be concealed, denied or 'blocked' in various ways; and these ways – often overlapping, seldom intentional – may conceal themselves by their very efficacy, presenting themselves as something other than what they are.[88] A third way in which ideology operates is by means of *reification*, that is, by representing a transitory, historical state of affairs as if it were permanent, natural, outside of time. 'To re-establish the dimension of society "without history" at the heart of historical society': that, argues Lefort in a remarkable essay, is the role of ideology.[89] These three modes by which ideology operates – legitimation, dissimulation and reification – should not be regarded as either exhaustive or mutually exclusive. There may be other *modus operandi* which are vitally important in certain circumstances and which would have to be elucidated through theoretical and empirical analysis; and in many cases the various modes intersect and overlap, such that reification legitimates and legitimation dissimulates. These qualifications do not, however, vitiate the importance of formulating a clear conception of ideology and of distinguishing the principal modalities through which it operates.

The analysis of ideology is fundamentally concerned with *language*, for language is the principal medium of the meaning (signification) which serves to sustain relations of domination. Speaking a language is a way of acting, emphasized Austin and others; what they forgot to add is that ways of acting are infused with forms of power. The utterance of the simplest expression is an intervention in the world, more or less effective, more or less endowed with institutional authority. 'Language is not only an instrument of communication or even of knowledge', writes Bourdieu, 'but also an instrument of power. One seeks not only to be understood but also to be believed, obeyed, respected, distinguished.'[90] It is important to stress, moreover, that forms of power infuse *the meaning of what is said* as well as the saying of it. 'The meaning of what is said', this cryptic, complex notion which seems everywhere to elude a satisfactory analysis: no claim can be made to offer such an analysis here. Suffice it to observe that the meaning of an expression is an essentially open, shifting, indeterminate phenomenon, often framed in rhetorical figures and always susceptible to change. Even a simple declarative sentence like 'The book is blue' is a metonymic construction, since it is not the book but its surface which is blue. As Castoriadis crisply remarks, '*tout langage est abus de langage*'.[91] Of course, expressions do have a use in everyday life, they function more or less univocally, that is, as univocal *suffisament quant à l'usage*. But the univocity secured by this *quant à* is limited and problematic; the closure is transitory and provisional, always open to disruption, contestation and change. Let me express this point in Wittgensteinian terms: if it is supposed that the meaning of an expression may be analysed, at least partially, in terms of the criteria of justified assertion, then it must be added that such criteria are subject to systematic differentiation and manipulation, so that what counts as 'justified assertion' is essentially open to dispute. What may have seemed like a sphere of effective *consensus* must in many cases be seen as a realm of actual or potential *conflict*. Hence the meaning of what is said – what is *asserted* in spoken or written discourse as well as that *about which* one speaks or writes – is infused with forms of power; different individuals or groups have a differential capacity *to make a meaning stick*. It is the infusion of meaning with power that lends language so freely to the operations of ideology. Relations of domination are sustained by a *mobilization of meaning* which legitimates, dissimulates or reifies an existing state of affairs; and meaning can be mobilized because it is an essentially open, shifting, indeterminate phenomenon. When we are told by Menachem Begin that the movement of thousands of troops and hundreds of tanks into Lebanon is not an 'invasion' because Israel has no plan to annex Lebanese territory,[92] or when the *Sun* reminds us that a proposed strike by the train drivers' union ASLEF may smash their own industry but will 'never break us', since, 'as the battle for the Falklands demonstrated so clearly, NOBODY can break this nation',[93] then it is not difficult to appreciate the ease with which, and the extent to which, meaning may be mobilized in the service of power and domination.

METHODOLOGY OF INTERPRETATION

The link between language and ideology provides the touchstone for the elaboration of a systematic methodology of interpretation. In characterizing this methodology as one of 'interpretation', I wish to call attention to two fundamental considerations. The first consideration has to do with the inescapable situation of that which forms the object of interpretation: *discourse* – that is, language realized in speech or in writing – *is already an interpretation.* Events, actions and expressions are constantly interpreted and understood by lay actors in everyday life, who routinely employ interpretative procedures in making sense of themselves and others. To undertake an analysis of discourse is to produce an interpretation of an interpretation, to re-interpret a pre-interpreted domain. This peculiar situation of the object of interpretation – a situation which reappears in all forms of social analysis – is a manifestation of what has been called the 'hermeneutical circle'; and here we may agree with Heidegger that 'what is decisive is not to get out of the circle but to come into it in the right way'.[94] The second consideration to which I want to call attention concerns *the creative character of the interpretative process.* The analysis of discourse can never be merely an analysis: it must also be a synthetic construction, a creative projection, of a possible meaning. This constructive, creative aspect of interpretation is often neglected or suppressed by those who practise some form of discourse analysis. The emptiness of so many of the analyses of Sinclair et al. is due to their preoccupation with exchange structure at the expense of all content, a preoccupation which gives their analytic methods a very limited applicability. While Fowler and his associates are more sensitive to the internal constitution of discourse, nevertheless their dubious assumption that meaning can be 'read off' from syntax obscures the creative character of interpretation. Without wishing to deny the importance of formal methods of analysis in the study of social phenomena, it is my view that such methods could never be more than a limited and preliminary stage of a more comprehensive interpretative theory.

I should like to propose, in a sketchy and provisional way, an interpretative methodology which is both tailored to the task of analysing ideology and capable of incorporating formal or 'explanatory' methods. To study ideology, I suggested above, is to study the ways in which meaning (signification) serves to sustain relations of domination. Meaning, domination: two concepts from different domains, from different orders of inquiry, uttered together in the same breath. How can the interrelation of meaning and domination be studied in a systematic way, without committing some sort of category mistake or falling into a facile eclecticism? I shall take as my model the provocative idea of a 'depth hermeneutics' elaborated by, among others, Paul Ricoeur.[95] While critical of the exhaustive claims of some forms of 'structuralist analysis', Ricoeur is not blind to their achievements. When dealing with a domain which is constituted as much by force as by meaning, or when analysing an artefact which displays a distinctive pattern through which something is said, it is both possible and advisable to mediate the process of interpretation by employing 'objectifying techniques'. 'Interpretation' and 'explanation' are not necessarily exclusive terms, but rather may be treated as complementary moments in a comprehensive interpretative theory, as mutually supportive steps along 'a unique *hermeneutical arc*'.[96] While concurring with the overall emphasis of Ricoeur's work, my specific proposals will diverge significantly from his account. For in his reaction against the excesses of 'historicism', Ricoeur tends to underplay the importance of social and historical circumstances in the interpretation of a work. The text and its analogues are autonomous, insists Ricoeur; but it seems to me that this autonomy is limited in important ways and that our interpretation of a work may be profoundly affected by an inquiry into the social-historical conditions of its production.[97] Nowhere is this counter-emphasis more important than in the attempt to elaborate a methodology for the analysis of ideology. To suppose that the study of the discursive forms in which ideology is expressed could be detached from the social-historical conditions of discursive production would be to lose sight of the relations of domination in virtue of which discourse is *ideological*.

The depth-interpretative procedure which I want to propose may be divided into three principal phases. It must be emphasized that this division is an analytic one; I am not suggesting that the phases must be regarded as discrete stages of a sequential method, but merely that they can be seen as thematically distinct dimensions of a complex interpretative process. The first phase of the process may be described as the dimension of *social analysis*. It is to Gouldner's credit that he has stressed the importance of situating ideology within a social-historical context, even if the details of his account are questionable in other respects. *The study of ideology is inseparable from the social-historical analysis of the forms of domination which meaning serves to sustain.* In accordance with my earlier discussion of the relation between action and structure, I should like to specify three levels at which such a social-historical analysis might proceed. First, at the level of action, an attempt must be made to identify the contexts of action and interaction within which agents pursue their aims. The realization of action (and speech-action) is situationally specific: actions are performed (or expressions are uttered) by particular agents at particular times in particular settings. As authors such as Goffman and Bourdieu have brought out so well, the spatio-temporal *location* of action and interaction is a vital part of social analysis.[98] A second level of social analysis is concerned with institutions. As constellations of social relations and reservoirs of material resources, specific institutions form a relatively stable framework for action and interaction; they do not determine action but *generate* it in the sense of establishing, loosely and tentatively, the parameters of permissible conduct. Institutions are the *loci* of power and the crystallization of relations of domination. A reconstruction of institutions – both in their specific and sedimented forms, both in their organizational aspects and their spatio-temporal features – is therefore an essential contribution to the analysis of ideology. Of particular interest in this regard is the reconstruction of the institutional *media* by which discourse is transmitted, a reconstruction for which Gouldner, among many others, has offered some insightful remarks.[99] At a third level of social analysis, one would be concerned, not with institutions as such, but with the structural elements which condition or *structurate* institutions. The relation between wage-labour and capital 'structurates' the institution of General Motors, for example, in the sense that it specifies certain conditions for the persistence of the institution, conditions which the institution cannot exceed without a change of structural type. The reconstruction of structural elements is an essential aspect of social analysis, for it is these elements which underpin some of the most important relations of domination at the institutional level.

The second phase of the depth-interpretative procedure may be described as the dimension of *discursive analysis*. The forms of discourse which express ideology must be viewed, not only as socially and historically situated practices, but also as *linguistic constructions which display an articulated structure*. Forms of discourse are situated practices *and* something more, precisely because they are linguistic constructions which claim to say something. To undertake a discursive analysis (in the sense here defined) is to study these linguistic constructions with a view towards explicating their role in the operation of ideology. I shall make no pretension to lay out in detail the appropriate method for such a study, as if methodological precepts could be specified a priori and in isolation from actual research. I shall limit myself to a series of suggestions which draw heavily upon the ongoing investigations of others. Let me distinguish, once again, three levels at which forms of discourse may be studied *qua* linguistic constructions and with a view towards explicating their ideological features. First, forms of discourse may be studied as *narratives* which display a certain logic or 'actantial structure'. The term 'actantial structure' is borrowed from Greimas, whose methods of structural analysis – so far largely unknown in the English-speaking world – have been applied in an imaginative way to political discourse.[100] Such an analysis may facilitate the explication of ideological features because ideology, in so far as it seeks to sustain relations of domination by representing them as legitimate, tends to assume a narrative form. Stories are told which glorify those in power and seek to justify the status quo: there is, as Barthes observed, a profound connection between ideology and myth.[101] Moreover, the stories which are relevant to the analysis of ideology are not only the myths of official political discourse. It is in the narratives of everyday life, the anecdotes and jokes which fill so much of the space of social interaction, that – as indicated in my discussion of Sacks et al. – the ideological features of discourse may be discerned. A second level of discursive analysis may be concerned with the *argumentative structure* of discourse. Forms of discourse, as supra-sentential linguistic constructions, comprise explanations and chains of reasoning which may be reconstructed and made explicit in various ways.[102] Such reconstructions may help to illuminate the ideological features of discourse by bringing out, not only their procedures of legitimation, but also their strategies of dissimulation. To conceal relations of domination and simultaneously to conceal the process of concealment is a risky, conflict-laden undertaking, prone to contradiction and contortion. The analysis of argumentative structure may highlight the dissimulating function of ideology by mapping out the contradictions and inconsistencies, the silences and *lapsus*, which characterize the texture of a discourse. At a third level, discursive analysis may focus on *syntactic structure*. Whatever the shortcomings of the work of Fowler et al., these authors have rightly called attention to a series of syntactic devices which play a vital role in discourse. In particular, the study of nominalization, passivization, the use of pronouns and the structure of tense may provide an initial access to processes of reification within language. Representing processes as things, deleting agency and constituting time as an eternal extension of the present tense: all of these are so many syntactic ways to re-establish the dimension of society 'without history' at the heart of historical society.

I now want to turn to the third and final phase of the depth-interpretative procedure, a phase that may properly be called *interpretation*. However rigorous and systematic the methods of discursive analysis may be, they can never abolish the need for a creative construction of meaning, that is for an interpretative explication of what is said. An interpretative explication may be mediated by the analytical methods, which may efface the superficial form of a discourse; but interpretative explication always goes beyond the methods of formal analysis, projecting a possible meaning which is always risky and open to dispute. In explicating what is said, the process of interpretation transcends the closure of discourse treated as a construction displaying an articulated structure. *Discourse says something about something*, and it is this transcending character which must be grasped. At this point it may be helpful to introduce the idea of *split reference*, employed with great imagination by Ricoeur.[103] The inscription of discourse in writing, observes Ricoeur, involves a suspension of ostensive denotation and the realization of a second order reference, that is, a reference to other aspects of experience or being which cannot be disclosed in a directly ostensive way. Let me adapt this intriguing idea to the specific task of studying ideology through an analysis of the forms of discourse in which it is expressed. The mobilization of meaning in order to sustain relations of domination commonly involves, I want to suggest, a splitting of the referential domain. The terms of a discourse carry out their ideological role by explicitly referring to one thing and implicitly referring to another, by entangling these multiple referents in a way which serves to sustain relations of domination. Recall the vivid image described by Barthes of a saluting black soldier on the cover of *Paris-Match*, an image which signifies not merely a particular individual but also the general context of French imperialism.[104] To interpret discourse *qua* ideology is to *construct* a meaning which unfolds the referential dimension of discourse, which specifies the multiple referents and shows how their entanglement serves to sustain relations of domination. Reconnecting discourse to the relations of domination which it serves to sustain: such is the task of interpretation. Mediated by the discursive analysis of linguistic constructions and the social analysis of the conditions of discursive production, the interpretation of ideology is necessarily a form of depth hermeneutics. How such a form of depth hermeneutics may be linked to a moment of critique, and how such a critique may facilitate the *self*-understanding of the subjects whose interpretations are the object of interpretation, are questions which I shall broach below.

Before turning to the final cluster of questions, however, I should like to render these abstract methodological remarks more concrete by focusing on a specific example. In an important study conducted during the 1970s, Michel Pêcheux and his associates examined the ambiguities contained in a report by the socialist Sicco Mansholt.[105] The Report, published at a time when French political life was animated by the possibility of radical social change through an alliance between the Socialist and Communist Parties, advocated rigorous economic planning and a reorientation of economic goals in order to overcome the current crises in capitalist societies. Pêcheux et al. propose to study the ambiguous political character of the Mansholt Report by analysing, not the Report itself, but rather two corpora which were generated in the following way. An extract from the Report was presented to two groups of young technicians from similar backgrounds. One group was told that the text was the work of left-wing militants, while the other group was led to believe that the text had been produced by right-wing Giscardians. The members of each group were asked to read the text and to write a short summary, thus generating a 'right corpus' and a 'left corpus'. Pêcheux et al. then submit the two corpora to a series of analyses which comprise what they call *analyse automatique du discours*. These analyses break up each corpus into a plurality of 'semantic domains' and map out the relations between these domains. In this way the authors seek to uncover some of the contradictions at work in each corpus and the tensions between the two corpora, contradictions and tensions which reflect the ambiguous texture of the Mansholt Report. Here I shall not undertake to criticize the details of the method developed by Pêcheux et al., nor the way in which it was applied in the case concerned. I wish simply to call attention to the specific *limits* within which this method operates, limits which define the method as *one possible phase of a more comprehensive interpretative theory*. The method developed by Pêcheux et al. is one version – a very sophisticated version – of what I previously called 'discursive analysis'. It is a method which does not preclude but rather presupposes the other two phases of the depth-interpretative procedure, the phases of social analysis and of interpretation proper. It presupposes social analysis because it requires an account of the social-historical conditions under which the Mansholt Report was produced, as well as a specification of the circumstances under which the corpora were generated. It presupposes interpretation because, as Pêcheux et al. admit, the results of the method do not 'speak for themselves' but must be 'interpreted'. Thus, in the study of the Mansholt Report, we are told that the presence of terms like 'the government' and 'the state' in the right corpus (R), as contrasted with expressions like 'it is necessary' and 'one must' in the left corpus (L), indicates 'the *domination* of R over L, in so far as the same signifier ("radical reforms") *encompasses two referents which tend to be antagonistic*: on the one hand a bourgeois solution which "manages the crisis", on the other hand the possible beginnings of a revolutionary transformation'.[106] But what is this 'indication', if not an *interpretation* which goes well beyond the construction of patterns of substitution, which seeks to unfold the referential dimension of discourse, which aims to elucidate the ways in which meaning serves to sustain relations of domination? The method developed by Pêcheux et al., far from demonstrating the irrelevance of hermeneutics as these authors aggressively claim, attests to the centrality and unsurpassability of the hermeneutical process.

CRITIQUE AND JUSTIFICATION

I now want to turn to the third and final cluster of issues which arise in connection with the analysis of ideology. These issues are of an epistemological character: the analysis of ideology raises complex problems of justification and truth. That such problems cannot be adequately stated, let alone resolved, by simply opposing ideology to science is a view which I have expressed in the first part of this essay. The concept of ideology may have emerged in conjunction with the idea of a science of society, as Gouldner seeks to show; but ideology cannot be viewed as failed science, as the hapless half of an inseparable pair. For the concept of ideology also emerged in conjunction with the critique of domination, and it is *this* link – as I have argued throughout this essay – which must be taken as basic. It cannot be assumed, moreover, that there is some stable relation between ideology construed in terms of domination, on the one hand, and the alleged opposition between science and ideology, on the other. Whatever difficulties there may be in the writings of Marcuse and other authors of the Frankfurt School, these thinkers have rightly stressed that under certain historical circumstances *science may become ideological*. Hence the epistemological problems raised by the analysis of ideology cannot be resolved by a presumptuous appeal to science, including the 'science' of historical materialism. It is my view that one can progress with these problems only if one is prepared to engage in a reflection of a genuinely epistemological sort, a reflection which is attuned to the question of critique and guided by the concept of truth.

In undertaking an epistemological reflection on the problems raised by the analysis of ideology, I shall draw heavily upon the work of Jürgen Habermas.[107] While defending a version of historical materialism, Habermas has done more than any other contemporary thinker to free historical materialism from the dogmatism of received tradition and the moral bankruptcy of a doctrine which has been used to justify the most oppressive regimes. 'Both *revolutionary self-confidence* and *theoretical self-certainty* are gone',[108] so that practice must be stripped of false certitude and handed over to the deliberations of responsible subjects. To hand practice over to the deliberations of responsible subjects is not, moreover, an unfortunate option, imposed by the contingencies of historical circumstance. On the contrary, one of the most interesting features of Habermas's recent work is his attempt to demonstrate that the claims to truth and correctness which are implicitly raised in everyday speech demand to be 'made good' or 'redeemed' through argumentation among the subjects concerned under conditions freed from asymmetrical relations of power. Such conditions, counterfactually projected and reconstructible through an analysis of the competencies required for successful communication, define what Habermas calls an 'ideal speech situation'. His view is that *if* a consensus concerning problematic claims to truth or correctness *were* attained through argumentation under the conditions of ideal speech, then such a consensus *would* be rational and *would* resolve the problematic claim. I believe that there is much in this view which is commendable, but I do not want to suggest that it is free from difficulties. Habermas's analyses of truth and correctness, his argument for the presupposition of the ideal speech situation and his characterization of the latter: all of these aspects leave much to be desired.[109] In the following discussion I shall therefore diverge substantially from the account offered by Habermas, even if it is Habermas's account which provides the *pierre de touche* for my proposals.

Let me begin by returning to the link between ideology and the question of critique. To study ideology, I maintained, is to study the ways in which meaning serves to sustain relations of domination; and I sketched a methodological procedure which combines social analysis and discursive analysis in order to mediate a depth interpretation of ideological discourse. This complex methodological procedure raises epistemological problems on several levels. Here, for the sake of simplicity, I shall focus on the final phase of the procedure and ask: what is the link between depth interpretation and critique? It is important to distinguish between two forms of critique which are relevant in this regard. First, as a construction of meaning and a formulation of what is said in a discourse, an interpretation raises a claim to truth which calls for recognition. An interpretation is an intervention, risky and conflict-laden; it makes a claim about something which may diverge from other views and which, *if true*, may provide a standpoint for criticizing other views, including the views of the subjects whose discourse is the object of interpretation. Critique guided by the truth of an interpretation must be distinguished from a second form of critique, closely related to the first. An interpretation that explicates the ways in which meaning serves to sustain relations of domination may render possible a critique, not only of other views (interpretations), but also of the relations of domination which meaning serves to sustain. It is in this sense that *the analysis of ideology bears an internal connection to the critique of domination*. But this connection, while internal, is not immediate. To analyse a form of discourse as ideological, to explicate the ways in which meaning serves to sustain relations of domination, even to establish that a particular interpretation is true: all of these achievements would greatly facilitate and profoundly affect a critical reflection on relations of domination, but they would not *as such* demonstrate that those relations were *unjust*. However close the connection between truth and justice may be – and the connection is, I believe, a close one – it is important to recognize the difference between inquiring into the truth of a statement, on the one hand, and deliberating on the justice of a particular social arrangement, on the other.

To inquire into the truth of a statement presupposes that we have some operative idea of truth. It is a common tendency among philosophers to analyse this idea in terms of a relation of correspondence: simply put, to say that a sentence is true is to say that it corresponds to a fact. It seems to me, however, that this apparently plausible account is less than satisfactory, not only because it has proved exceedingly difficult to say anything interesting either about the relation of correspondence or about the nature of the facts to which true sentences are supposed to correspond, but also because it is hard to see how anything *could* be said about this relation which was itself *true*. In view of these difficulties, it seems to me advisable to set aside the correspondence theory and to search for an alternative analysis which would capture our intuitions about truth. When we say that a statement is true, we lay ourselves on the line; we make a claim which could, we suppose, be defended or *justified* in some way. It is clear that truth cannot be simply equated with justified assertion or 'warranted assertability', as Habermas, following Dewey, once maintained. For it is easy to imagine cases in which the assertion of a statement is justified and yet the statement itself is false. A prospective English holiday-maker may have good grounds for maintaining that it is sunny in

Spain, but the truth of this statement is dependent upon what is happening in Spain and not upon the grounds that the prospective holiday-maker has. What this observation shows, however, is not that truth bears no connection to justification, but rather, first, that the justification for the assertion of a statement is not necessarily identical with the justification for the assertion that a statement is true; and second, that the justification for the assertion that a statement is true must be regarded as a *limiting notion*: that is, it refers to the justification that *could* be obtained under idealized conditions. 'We speak as if there were such things as epistemically ideal conditions', remarks Putnam in a recent book, 'and we call a statement "true" if it would be justified under such conditions.'[110] How are we to characterize these epistemically ideal conditions which seem implicated in our notion of truth? It seems to me that these idealized conditions could be explicated – at least partially although perhaps not perennially – in terms of the suspension of asymmetrical relations of power. Such a suspension would specify some of the *formal conditions* under which the truth of a statement *could* be ascertained. But these formal conditions do not pre-empt the *specific criteria* which may be invoked in seeking to establish the truth of a statement. It is important to recognize that the criteria invoked may be of differing statuses and may vary from one epistemic field to another. While the 'pragmatic criterion' of prediction and control has been filtered out from the history of the natural sciences, it does not follow that the same criterion must be adopted in other disciplines.[111] On the contrary, the thesis that I want to maintain is that the crucial criterion which operates in conjunction with the depth-hermeneutical procedure is provided by a *principle of self-reflection*. For the interpretations generated by this procedure are about an object domain which consists, among other things, of subjects capable of reflection; and for such interpretations to be *true* they would have to be justified – by means of whatever evidence deemed to be necessary under the formal conditions of argumentation – in the eyes of the subjects about whom they are made. Such interpretations would provide subjects with a clarification of their conditions of action and would thus bear, in this specific sense, an internal relation to practice.

An inquiry into the truth of a statement may prepare the way for, but is not identical with, a deliberation on the justice of a particular social arrangement. It may prepare the way for such a deliberation in so far as it clarifies the conditions of action for the actors themselves, who alone can bear the responsibility of deciding whether the social arrangements in which they live, or for which they are prepared to struggle, are just. It is not identical with such a deliberation because the questions which are being pursued, and the considerations which are adduced as relevant, are different in the two cases. When deliberating on the justice of a particular social arrangement we are concerned, not with the adequacy of the evidence that can be adduced to support a claim to truth, but rather with the extent to which that social arrangement is capable of satisfying the legitimate needs and desires of the subjects affected by it. As with truth, so too with justice: it must be conceived in terms of the justification that could be provided under idealized conditions of argumentation; but the object of justification and the terms of argumentation are different in each case. The distinctiveness of a deliberation on justice is brought out well by that heuristic device which Habermas calls the 'model of the suppression of generalizable interests'. A critical theory can inquire into the institutionalized power relations of a society, he submits, by comparing the existing normative structures with a hypothetical system of norms that would be formed discursively. Such a 'counterfactually projected reconstruction' may be guided by the following question:

> how would the members of a social system, at a given stage in the development of productive forces, have collectively and bindingly interpreted their needs (and which norms would they have accepted as justified) if they could and would have decided on organization of social intercourse through discursive will-formation, with adequate knowledge of the limiting conditions and functional imperatives of their society?[112]

There are aspects of this suggestive passage which are problematic and obscure – *who*, for example, would 'the members' be if they were placed under the hypothetical conditions of rational discourse, and which needs and norms could ever be expected to elicit collective recognition and consent?[113] Yet however intractable these problems may be, it seems to me that Habermas is right to adopt an approach to the question of justice which endows the subject with a crucial role, while acknowledging that, given actual circumstances in which asymmetrical relations of power prevail, this role must be counterfactually conceived. The development of this idea is one of the most urgent and important tasks in social theory today.

In drawing this section to a close, I should like to consider an objection that may be raised against the type of analysis which I have offered. To regard truth and justice as limiting notions, it may be said, is simply to render them *irrelevant* to the study of actual societies and forms of discourse. For what is the use of a notion that depends upon conditions which do not obtain here and now, indeed which might never obtain so long as human beings are inclined to embroil themselves in relations of domination? I do not believe, however, that this attitude of renunciation is well founded. A limiting notion is not irrelevant for being a limit: it is a goal which can be approximated and which, in the process of approximation, can call our attention to certain factors at the expense of others. Thus, to analyse truth in terms of the evidence that *would* suffice to justify a particular claim, or to analyse justice in terms of the needs and desires which *would* be satisfied by a particular arrangement, underlines the importance of searching for evidence and seeking to articulate needs and desires, as well as striving to defend or defeat a claim through argumentation and debate. There are, in other words, *empirical indicators* that may be employed in argumentation and it simply will not do to suggest, *à la* Hindess and Hirst, that the only way in which a theoretical discourse can be assessed is in terms of its own internal consistency. But it must be stressed that these empirical indicators are *only* indicators and not conclusive grounds; they retain a hypothetical status which could only be confirmed or confuted by a rational argumentation and deliberation among the subjects concerned. And this epistemological gap is not, in my opinion, an undesirable result. For it attests to the deep and ineliminable link between theory and practice in that sphere of social inquiry where *subjects* capable of action and reflection are among the *objects* of investigation.

In this essay I have conducted a critical survey of some recent work in English on the theory of ideology and methods of discourse analysis. It is important to consider these two themes – ideology and discourse analysis – in conjunction with one another, precisely because the study of ideology must be seen, at least in part, as the analysis of language in the social world. Language is the principal medium of ideology, for it is primarily through language that meaning is mobilized in the social world. I have tried to show, however, that recent theorists of ideology and analysts of discourse have developed approaches which suffer from many faults. Theorists such as Seliger, Gouldner and Hirst have advocated conceptions of ideology which are stripped of any critical edge, so that the link between ideology and the critique of domination is attenuated or altogether destroyed. The analysts of discourse have devised methods for studying verbal interaction and texts of various kinds, methods which are sensitive to social context and applicable to supra-sentential linguistic units; but these analysts have tended to focus on structure at the expense of content and have provided a very inadequate account of the non-linguistic context of language use. Neither the theorists of ideology nor the analysts of discourse have made a sustained and satisfactory attempt to integrate the study of ideology with the analysis of language, failing to pursue (or failing to perceive) the fundamental continuity of these concerns.

The critical survey of some recent work in English provided the basis for a series of constructive remarks. These remarks – admittedly sketchy, tentative, incomplete – were offered with the aim of elaborating an alternative approach to the study of ideology which draws together theoretical and methodological considerations. Ideology must be conceptualized, I maintained, within the framework of a general social theory, one which explores the relation between action and structure and gives a central role to the concept of power. To study ideology, within such a framework, is to study the ways in which meaning (signification) serves to sustain relations of domination. An inquiry into the interrelation of meaning and power may be seen, I suggested, as a form of depth hermeneutics. Mediated by the discursive analysis of linguistic constructions and the social analysis of the conditions of discursive production, the depth interpretation of ideology issues in a projection of meaning that unfolds the referential dimension of discourse and connects it with the relations of domination which meaning serves to sustain. As such, the study of ideology bears a close connection to the critique of domination. It raises complex problems of justification which can only be resolved by engaging in an epistemological reflection, a reflection focused on the concepts of truth and justice and sensitive to the peculiar constitution of the social world.

4

The Theory of Structuration

An Assessment of the Contribution of
Anthony Giddens

The problem of the relation between the individual and society, or between action and social structure, lies at the heart of social theory and the philosophy of social science. In the writings of most major theorists, from Marx, Weber and Durkheim to a variety of contemporary authors, this problem is raised and allegedly resolved in one way or another. Such resolutions generally amount to the accentuation of one term at the expense of the other: either social structure is taken as the principal object of analysis and the agent is effectively eclipsed, as in the Marxism of Althusser, or individuals are regarded as the only constituents of the social world and their actions and reactions, their reasons, motives and beliefs, are the sole ingredients of social explanation. In both cases the problem is not so much resolved as dissolved, that is, disposed of beneath a philosophical and methodological platform that is already located in one of the camps. Few questions in social theory remain as refractory to cogent analysis as the question of how, and in precisely what ways, the action of individual agents is related to the structural features of the societies of which they are part. In recent years several authors have confronted directly the problem of the relation between action and social structure and have attempted to deal with it in a constructive and systematic way.[1] Essential to these attempts is the shift from a static to a dynamic perspective, from a theory of structure to a *theory of structuration*. What must be grasped is not how structure determines action or how a combination of actions make up structure, but rather how action is *structured* in everyday contexts and how the structured features of action are, by the very performance of an action, thereby *reproduced*. The theory of structuration is thus inseparable from an account of social reproduction, that is, from an account of the ways in which societies, or specific forms of social organization, are reproduced by the activities of individuals pursuing their everyday lives. The theory of structuration is also linked, in a fundamental way, to other aspects of social analysis. For an adequate characterization of the relation between action and social structure would provide a framework within which other concerns, such as the analysis of power and ideology, could be recast.

My aim in this essay is to examine some of the claims and the prospects of the theory of structuration.[2] I shall do so by focusing on the contribution of its leading exponent, Anthony Giddens. In a series of publications stretching over the better part of a decade,[3] Giddens has elaborated a highly original formulation of the theory of structuration, a formulation which is far more sophisticated in its detail and far more suggestive in its application than any of the other versions currently found in the literature. The first section of this essay will present a brief overview of the basic elements of Giddens's account. In order to offer a rigorous assessment of this account, however, it is necessary to retrace a particular development in Giddens's work. For while the conception of structure originally presented in *New Rules of Sociological Method* is preserved *in principle* in his most recent writings, this conception is supplemented *in practice* by a much more ramified account of the structural features of societies. I shall thus begin my critical assessment by focusing on the original formulation and arguing that it is deficient in certain key respects. I shall then introduce the more ramified account and try to show that it is only partly successful in overcoming the deficiencies of the original formulation. In the final section I shall focus on Giddens's analysis of action, suggesting that this analysis fails to do justice to the role of structural constraint. Amid these critical remarks I shall point to some of the ways in which the theory of structuration should, I believe, be developed and refined. For it is my view that, while the details of Giddens's account may be wanting, his overall aims are perfectly sound: the dualism of action and structure must give way to the systematic study of processes of structuration and social reproduction.

OUTLINE OF THE THEORY

Let me begin by outlining the central themes of Giddens's account. This account is formulated with a view towards building upon the strengths, while avoiding the weaknesses, of certain theoretical orientations in the social sciences. Functionalism has rightly emphasized the institutional features of the social world and has focused attention on the ways in which the unintended consequences of action serve to maintain existing social relations. Structuralism and 'post-structuralist' approaches have developeds novel conceptions of structure, of structuring processes and of the subject, conceptions which have been applied with particular efficacy to the analysis of texts and cultural objects. But what functionalism and structuralism lack, in spite of much discussion of the 'action frame of reference' and the 'theory of the subject', is an adequate account of action and agency. The latter have been principal concerns of 'analytical philosophy' during the last two decades, as well as of the 'interpretative sociologies' influenced by Husserl, Wittgenstein and others. In various ways these philosophers and sociologists have portrayed individuals as competent agents who know a great deal about the social world, who act purposively and reflectively and who can, if asked, provide reasons for what they have done. But where functionalism and structuralism are strong, analytical philosophy and interpretative sociology are weak, for they largely neglect problems of institutional and structural analysis.

Giddens seeks to move beyond these various orientations by rethinking the notions of, and the relations between, action and structure. Rather than seeing action and structure as the counteracting elements of a dualism, they should be regarded as the complementary terms of a duality, the 'duality of structure'. 'By the *duality of structure*', writes Giddens, 'I mean that social structures are both constituted *by* human agency, and yet at the same time are the very *medium* of this constitution.'[4] Every act of production is at the same time an act of reproduction: the structures that render an action possible are, in the performance of that action, reproduced. Even action which disrupts the social order, breaking conventions or challenging established hierarchies, is mediated by structural features which are reconstituted by the action, albeit in a modified form. This intimate connection between production and reproduction is what Giddens calls the 'recursive character' of social life. His theory of structuration is a sustained attempt to tease out the threads that are woven into this apparently unproblematic fact.

Action, according to Giddens, should be conceived as a continuous flow of interventions in the world which are initiated by autonomous agents. Action must be distinguished from 'acts', which are discrete segments of action that are cut out of the continuous flow by explicit processes of categorization and description. Not all action is 'purposeful', in the sense of being guided by clear purposes which the agent has in mind; but much action is 'purposive', in the sense that it is *monitored* by actors who continuously survey what they are doing, how others react to what they are doing, and the circumstances in which they are doing it. An important aspect of this reflexive monitoring of action is the ability of agents to explain, both to themselves and to others, why they act as they do by giving reasons for their action. Individuals are, Giddens repeatedly emphasizes, *knowledgeable agents* who are capable of accounting for their action: they are neither 'cultural dopes' nor mere 'supports' of social relations, but are skilful actors who know a great deal about the world in which they act. If the 'rationalization of action' refers to the reasons which agents offer to explain their action, the 'motivation of action' refers to the motives or wants which prompt it. Unconscious motivation is a crucial feature of human conduct and Giddens takes on board, primarily through a critical appraisal of the so-called 'ego-psychology' of Erikson and Sullivan, a cluster of psychoanalytic concepts. However, in place of the psychoanalytic triad of ego, super-ego and id, Giddens adheres to distinctions between the unconscious, practical consciousness and discursive consciousness. While the latter two are separated from the unconscious by the barrier of repression, the boundary between practical consciousness and discursive consciousness is a vague and fluctuating one. Much of what actors know about the world is part of their 'practical consciousness', in the sense that it is known without being articulated as such; but that such knowledge *could* be rendered explicit and incorporated into 'discursive consciousness' is a vital consideration which has important consequences for the status of social scientific research.

These various aspects of action and agency are part of what Giddens calls the 'stratification model of action'. The model could be represented as in figure 6.[5]

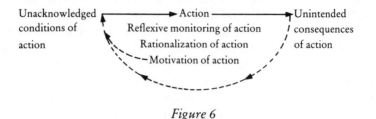

Figure 6

This model brings out the limitations of any attempt to analyse action by focusing on the individual agent. For the accounts which agents are able to give of their actions are 'bounded', both by unintended consequences of action and by unacknowledged conditions of action (including unconscious sources of motivation). The significance of the unintended consequences of action is stressed by Merton, who introduces the concept of 'latent function' in order to show that practices may serve to maintain institutions and organizations, regardless of whether this outcome is intended by the agents concerned. Giddens firmly rejects any suggestion that such a demonstration would *explain* the existence of the practice: 'there is *nothing*', he asserts, 'which can count as "functionalist explanation"'.[6] But he wishes to preserve the insight that action may have unintended consequences which become the unacknowledged conditions of further action. There are two principal ways, on Giddens's account, in which this feedback process can occur. Unintended consequences can become unacknowledged conditions by being incorporated in 'homeostatic causal loops', such as the so-called 'poverty cycle' of material deprivation→poor schooling→low-level employment→material deprivation. Unintended consequences can also become unacknowledged conditions in so far as the unintended consequence of action is the reproduction of the *structure* which renders further action possible. To clarify the latter process we must take up Giddens's discussion of the concept of structure.

In the sociological literature 'structure' is often conceived in a quasi-mechanical, quasi-visual way, like the girders of a building, the skeleton of a body or the 'patterning' of social relationships.

Giddens does not dismiss this connotation altogether; as we shall see, he preserves elements of it in his notion of 'social system'. To the concept of structure, however, he ascribes a different sense. Here I shall focus on the sense ascribed in *New Rules of Sociological Method*, reserving for later a consideration of certain modifications which are presented in subsequent works. In *New Rules of Sociological Method* Giddens approaches the concept of structure through a comparison of language and speech – 'not because society is like a language', he hastens to add, 'but on the contrary because language as a practical activity is so central to social life that in *some* basic respects it can be treated as exemplifying social processes in general'.[7] Thus, whereas speech is spatially and temporally situated, presupposing a subject as well as another to whom it is addressed, language is 'virtual and outside of time' and is 'subject-less', in the sense that it is neither the product of any one subject nor is it oriented towards any other. Giddens employs this comparison to draw a similar distinction between *interaction* and *structure* in social analysis. Whereas interaction is constituted in and through the activities of agents, structure has a 'virtual existence': it consists of 'rules and resources' which are implemented in interaction, which thereby structure interaction and which are, in that very process, reproduced. As Giddens explains, 'by the term "structure" I do not refer, as is conventional in functionalism, to the descriptive analysis of the relations of interaction which "compose" organizations or collectivities, but to systems of generative rules and resources'.[8]

Giddens analyses the rules and resources which comprise structure in terms of three dimensions or 'modalities'. These modalities are the lines of mediation between interaction and structure, as figure 7 indicates:[9]

INTERACTION	↑ communication	power	sanction
(MODALITY)	interpretative scheme	facility	norm
STRUCTURE	↓ signification	domination	legitimation

Figure 7

In the communication of meaning in interaction, agents draw upon interpretative schemes which, at the level of structure, can be

analysed as 'semantic rules'. When agents apply sanctions in interaction they draw upon norms which, at the level of structure, can
be analysed (in part)[10] as 'moral rules'. The use of power in
interaction involves the application of facilities which enable agents
to secure specific outcomes; at the structural level, these facilities
can be analysed as 'resources' which comprise structures of
domination. Giddens emphasizes that the distinction between
these three modalities is more analytical than it is substantive. 'In
any concrete situation of interaction, members of society draw
upon these [rules and resources] as modalities of production and
reproduction, although as an integrated set rather than three discrete components.'[11] Thus the communication of meaning cannot
be sharply separated from the use of power or the application of
sanctions. These different modalities are woven together in social
practices, so that even the most mundane action or interaction
expresses overlapping aspects of the structural whole.

The rules and resources which comprise structure may be
regarded as 'properties of social systems'. Social systems are
regularized patterns of interaction involving individuals and
groups; they are not structures in themselves, but rather they
'have' structures, in the sense that they are *structured by* rules and
resources. Structures do not 'exist' in time and space except as
moments in the constitution of social systems. When the regularized practices structured by rules and resources are 'deeply
layered' in time and space, stretching through many decades and
over large or fixed domains, Giddens speaks of 'institutions'. Institutions are clusterings of the practices that constitute social
systems; they can be classified according to the modality which is
most central in their structuration. In *Central Problems in Social
Theory* Giddens offers the classification found in figure 8.[12]

S-D-L	symbolic orders / modes of discourse
D(auth)-S-L	political institutions
D(alloc)-S-L	economic institutions
L-D-S	law / modes of sanction

Figure 8

The letters on the left refer to those aspects of structure which were
distinguished above (S = signification, D = domination,

L = legitimation); the first letter in each sequence indicates which aspect is primary in the structuration of the institutions. When we study legal institutions, for example, we focus primarily on the aspect of legitimation, although signification and domination are also involved. The differentiation between political institutions and economic institutions is based on an important distinction between two types of resources. 'Authorization' refers to capabilities which generate command over *persons*, while 'allocation' refers to capabilities which generate control over *objects*. This distinction gives Giddens a critical purchase on certain forms of social theory, especially on those forms of Marxism which tend to associate domination with the ownership or control of property and which give insufficient attention to problems of authority.

In his recent writings Giddens has been increasingly concerned to examine the ways in which the concepts of time and space enter into the theory of structuration. Social systems are not only structured by rules and resources, but they are also situated within time and space; hence 'social theory *must acknowledge, as it has not done previously, time-space intersections as essentially involved in all social existence*'.[13] Time and space should be thought of, Giddens argues, as boundaries to social analysis or as frameworks within which social life takes place. It is much more fruitful to think of time and space in the Heideggerian terms of 'presence' and 'absence' – or, more precisely, in terms of 'presencing' or 'being present'. Every interaction mixes together presence and absence in complicated ways. In face-to-face interaction the other is present both in space and in time. The interaction takes place in a definite setting or 'locale' and endures for a definite period; actors typically employ the spatial and temporal features of the interaction as a means of organizing their exchange. With the extension of social systems in space and time, however, the other may cease to be immediately present. Such time-space distancing (or 'distanciation', as Giddens calls it) was greatly facilitated by the development of writing, which renders possible communication with the past as well as with physically absent individuals. In more recent years, technological advances in transport and the media have rapidly transformed the time-space constitution of social systems, as 'time geographers' such as Hägerstrand have pointed out. With great imagination Giddens analyses the ways in which these transformations are connected with the *generation of power*. The development of writing, for example, greatly increased the capacity of societies to store information about their populations, and thereby to monitor and control their activities. If the power of nation-states and the threat of totalitarian political control are pervasive features of the modern world, their origins cannot be understood without examining the transformations in time–space relations which have rendered possible such terrifying power and control.

STRUCTURE AS 'RULES AND RESOURCES'

I want to begin my critical assessment of Giddens's account by returning to his conception of structure. Few concepts in the social sciences are more basic and essential, and yet more ambiguous and contested, than that of structure. It is to Giddens's credit that he tries to give this concept a clear sense and to integrate it within a systematic conceptual framework. In so doing he also gives the concept of structure a *novel* sense, one which diverges considerably from the ways in which this concept is commonly used in the literature of the social sciences. While I do not wish to dispute the importance of conceptual innovation, it is my view that Giddens's proposal to conceive of structure in terms of rules and resources is of questionable value, for it is a proposal which generates more confusion than it dispels and which tends to obscure some important issues. I shall try to substantiate this view by focusing first on the loose and abstract character of Giddens's conception. This character derives both from the ambiguities of the term 'rule' and from the very generality of Giddens's proposal, a generality which is apparent in his attempt to formulate a *general* notion of structure and in his tendency to neglect the *specific* features of *social* structure.

'Structure' is a vague and ambiguous term; the trouble with 'rule', as Austin might say, is that it does not stand in much better stead.[14] We use the expression 'rule' in a great variety of ways. We speak of moral rules, traffic rules, bureaucratic rules, rules of grammar, rules of etiquette, rules of football. We say of someone who regularly does something at a certain time that, 'as a rule', this is what he or she does. Workers who resist employers by sticking to the letter of their contracts are said to be 'working to rule'.

Giddens is fully aware of the diversity of senses encapsulated in the expression 'rule'. His way of narrowing down these senses and of attempting to give 'rule' a more rigorous application is to draw critically upon Wittgenstein's analysis of rule-following behaviour. To know the rules of a game is to know how to play it; to know a mathematical rule for the calculation of a series of numbers is to know how to continue the series, that is, 'how to go on'. To know a rule is not necessarily to be able to formulate it. As competent social actors we know countless rules which we would have difficulty stating in an explicit way: they form part, in Giddens's terms, of our practical consciousness. However, Giddens rightly warns against the tendency of Wittgenstein and Wittgensteinians to privilege the example of the rules of a game, such as chess. For these rules, Giddens remarks, are seldom *contested* in a chronic way. The rules which comprise structure are embroiled in struggles, are subject to rival interpretations and are continuously transformed in their very application. Rules, in other words, cannot be conceptualized in isolation from the resources which facilitate the exercise of power.

These cautionary remarks are certainly in order, but they still do not give us a clear idea of exactly what, on Giddens's account, are the rules which comprise *social* structure. In *New Rules of Sociological Method* Giddens suggests, as I indicated earlier, that structures of signification can be analysed as 'semantic rules' and structures of legitimation can be analysed as 'moral rules'. Elsewhere he modifies this account, placing less emphasis on two kinds of rules and stressing instead that all rules have two 'aspects': they relate both to the constitution of meaning and to the sanctioning of conduct. But what, we may justly ask, would be an example of such a rule? Would 'That's a "butterfly"', said to a child on its first excursion into the countryside, or 'Hold your toothbrush horizontally', uttered by a dentist to a patient whose dental hygiene was poor, be examples of the sort of rule that someone interested in social structure should be studying? In fact, until the recent publication of *The Constitution of Society*, Giddens has said virtually nothing about these matters. In *The Constitution of Society* he considers various candidates for the kind of rule which is most relevant to social structure – or, as he prefers to say, which is most relevant to the analysis of 'social life'. He puts aside the sense of 'rule' which pertains to games like chess ('the rule defining checkmate is . . .'); the sense of 'rule' which is roughly equivalent to habit or routine ('as a rule I get up every day at 6 o'clock'); the sense of 'rule' that is exemplified by regulations like 'all workers must clock in at 8:00 a.m.'. Giddens suggests that the sense of 'rule' most relevant to the analysis of social life is that expressed by formulae such as $a_n = n^2 + n - 1$. 'It is in the nature of formulae', he submits, 'that we can best discover what is the most analytically effective sense of "rule" in social theory.'[15] Analytically effective or not, this suggestion does little to clarify the precise character of the rules which could be said, on Giddens's account, to comprise social structure. Is he suggesting, most implausibly, that semantic rules and moral rules should be seen as quasi-mathematical formulae, as if ' "butterfly" = $moth^2$ + colour − cloth'? Or does he wish to maintain that such formulae convey the sense of rules *other than* the semantic rules and moral rules in terms of which structures of signification and legitimation can apparently be analysed, and if so *which* rules are these others? If Giddens expects readers to accept his proposal to conceive of structure in terms of rules and resources, then the onus is on him to provide clear and consistent examples of what would count as a relevant 'rule'.

So far I have been concerned to highlight the looseness of Giddens's conception of structure; I now want to offer some arguments against the view that it is useful and satisfactory to identify social structure with rules (and resources). In offering these arguments I shall focus on the study of rules, presuming, in the absence of a more precise account of 'rule' by Giddens himself, an intuitive understanding of this notion. I shall seek to establish the following point: while rules of various kinds are important features of social life, the study of rules (and resources) is not identical to, but rather distinct from and on a different level than, the analysis of social structure. There are four arguments which seem to me to substantiate this point.[16] The first argument bears upon the vagueness of the term 'rule' and Giddens's failure so far to render this term more precise. This failure is not mere oversight, for Giddens cannot clarify the sense of 'rule' and the kinds of rules which are relevant to social structure without presupposing a *criterion of importance*, and this criterion can never be derived from attending to rules alone. Thus, on the one hand, Giddens wants to regard rules as generalizable procedures implemented in every kind of social practice – shorthand summaries, as it were, of what actors know about their world and about how to act within it, about teaching and typing, speaking and shopping, voting, cooking and cracking jokes. On the other hand, Giddens is well aware that *some* rules, or some kinds or aspects of rules, are much more important than others for the analysis of, for example, the social structure of capitalist societies. But what justifies this implicit criterion of importance, if not an analysis of social structure which is separate from the study of those rules that are singled out in its name?

The second and third arguments give force to the first criticism by calling attention to what may be called *structural differentiation*. Consider first the case of a cluster of 'semantic rules', such as those governing the application of an adjective like 'bloody' or a noun like 'the Left' in contemporary Britain. To study these rules is to study part of the *semantic* structure of English. However, to study these rules is not *in itself* to analyse part of the *social* structure of Britain. The study of semantic rules may indeed be relevant to the analysis of social structure; and one way in which that relevance may be shown is by demonstrating that the rules are *differentiated* according to class, sex, region and so on. But to study their differentiation presupposes some framework, some structural points of reference which are not themselves *rules*, with regard to which these semantic rules are differentiated. Consider next the case of institutions, such as schools or universities, in which certain individuals, or certain groups and classes of individuals, have restricted opportunities for entry and participation. It seems evident that such restrictions cannot be adequately conceptualized in terms of 'moral rules' or 'sanctions', since such restrictions may operate independently of the rights and obligations of the agents concerned. It also seems inadequate to conceive of such restrictions as unintended consequences of action, like the homeostatic causal loops involved in the poverty cycle. For the issue is not so much whether the restrictions are intended or unintended consequences which may become the conditions of further action. Rather, what is at issue is the fact that the restrictions on opportunities operate *differentially*, affecting unevenly various groups of individuals whose categorization depends on certain assumptions about social structure; and it is this differential operation or effect which cannot be grasped by the analysis of rules alone.

If Giddens's conception tends to blur the question of differentiation, it also provides no way of grasping the features which a multiplicity of 'rules' may have in common. It provides no way, that is, of formulating the idea of *structural identity*: this is the fourth argument against his view. The importance of this idea can be demonstrated by considering two enterprises in different sectors of the British economy, such as the UK plants of the Ford Motor Company and the various establishments of the Macmillan Press. Each of these enterprises is a complex institution possessing vast resources of machinery, stock and capital. Each is an institution which is organized and operated with the aid of specific and detailed rules which stipulate how work is to be done, how decisions are to be made, how personnel are to be hired and dismissed, and so on. But beyond the particular rules and resources which characterize each of these institutions, there are certain features which Ford and Macmillan have in common, namely the features which define them as *capitalistic* enterprises. These features are not additional 'rules' which are 'drawn upon' by actors within these institutions, in the manner that a supervisor might 'draw upon' a rule in the contract in order to fire a worker who failed to turn up. The common features are of a different order altogether; they are better conceptualized, I believe, as a series of elements and their interrelations which together *limit* the kinds of rules which are possible and which thereby *delimit* the scope for institutional variation.[17] Whatever the merits of this alternative conception, these four arguments against Giddens's view will hopefully demonstrate that the proposal to conceive of structure in terms of rules (and resources) is deficient, for it presupposes but fails to address some of the most important concerns of structural analysis.

LEVELS OF STRUCTURAL ANALYSIS

I now want to return to Giddens's texts and to follow a line of thought which has become increasingly prominent in his recent work. Giddens would now accept, I think, that the account of structure presented in *New Rules of Sociological Method* is unsatisfactory in certain respects. It may be partially in response to considerations such as those adduced above that he has endeavoured to distinguish more clearly between different *levels of abstraction* in the analysis of the structural features of social systems. In *A Contemporary Critique of Historical Materialism* these levels are portrayed as in figure 9.[18]

LEVEL OF ABSTRACTION ↑ structural principles
structural sets (structures)
elements / axes of structuration

Figure 9

The study of 'structural principles' is the most abstract level of analysis. To study such principles is to examine the major alignments, the modes of articulation and differentiation, of the institutions which constitute a society. In Giddens's words, 'structural principles are principles of organisation implicated in those practices most "deeply" (in time) and "pervasively" (in space) sedimented in a society'.[19] The identification of structural principles provides the basis for Giddens's threefold classification of types of society. In 'tribal societies', including hunting–gathering bands and settled agricultural communities, the dominant structural principle 'operates along an axis', as Giddens says, between kinship and tradition; time-space distanciation is low, kinship networks are the *locus* of interaction and links with the past are maintained only through the actualization of tradition. The dominant structural principle of 'class-divided societies' (city-states, ancient empires and feudal societies) operates along an axis relating urban areas to rural hinterlands. The city – centred on temples and surrounded by walls – emerges as a special kind of 'storage container' for the generation of political and military power. In contrast to class-divided societies, the class societies of modern capitalism are organized along an axis relating state institutions and economic institutions. The rapid expansion of an economy based on the capital/wage-labour relation creates the conditions for the accumulation of political power in the hands of the nation-state. At the same time, the predominance of the city–countryside relation is destroyed by the incessant commodification of time and space, which produces the 'created environment' wherein most people live out their daily lives.

At a less abstract level of analysis, the structural features of social systems can be studied as 'structural sets'. By 'structural sets'

Giddens means 'sets of rules and resources, specified in terms of "clusterings" of transformation/mediation relations'.[20] It is at this level of analysis, argues Giddens, that we can understand Marx's account of the key structural relations involved in the capitalist system of production. Consider the relations involved in the following 'structural set':

private property : money : capital : labour contract : profit

The development of capitalism is characterized by the universalization of the commodity form. The condition of this universalization is the formation of a *money economy* in which money, as the medium of pure exchange value, enables private property to be converted into capital and allows labour power to be constituted as a commodity, to be bought and sold on the market like any other. Capital and wage labour can thus enter into a definite kind of relation, governed by the labour contract, in which labour power is exchanged for wages and in which profit is produced via the extraction of surplus value. By studying the various relations of convertibility between private property, money, capital and so on – a study which could be extended, Giddens suggests, to industrial authority, educational advantage and occupational position – one can identify some of the principal structural features of the institutions created by capitalism.

The most concrete level of analysis is concerned with 'elements' or 'axes' of structuration. This level is the most concrete because it bears most directly upon the relations of co-presence established between agents in social interaction. Giddens offers the example of the division of labour within the capitalist enterprise. The division of labour is one source of what Giddens calls, in *The Class Structure of the Advanced Societies*, 'proximate structuration':[21] it links the broader characteristics of capitalism with the more immediate organization of the industrial enterprise. In the early development of manufacturing industry, two forms of the division of labour prevailed. On the one hand, capitalists assembled workers with different craft skills and co-ordinated their activities into the production of a particular product; on the other hand, workers with the same skills were brought together and each worker was required to produce the same product. In both cases the productive process was broken down into detailed tasks, resulting, as Marx put it, in 'a productive mechanism whose parts are human beings'.[22]

The division of labour is vital to the organization of the capitalist enterprise, not only because it enhances the productivity and profitability of the enterprise, but also because it creates conditions for the direct surveillance of the work-force and for the consolidation of labour discipline. Technological developments are closely connected with the division of labour, profoundly altering both the nature of the tasks and the boundaries between them. These boundaries in turn have a significant effect on the formation and fragmentation of class consciousness in contemporary capitalist societies.

This attempt to distinguish several levels of structural analysis represents, I believe, a substantial improvement on the rather blurred account of structuration presented in *New Rules of Sociological Method*. Nevertheless, it seems to me that these distinctions raise serious difficulties for certain aspects of Giddens's approach. In discussing these difficulties I shall, for the most part, put aside the question of content, that is, the empirical and historical adequacy of Giddens's analyses. I shall focus instead on questions of form or conceptual consistency. The first difficulty concerns the implications of these distinctions for the conception of structure as rules and resources. Even in his most recent writings Giddens continues to adhere to this conception. Thus, in *The Constitution of Society*, he writes: 'I treat structure, in its most elemental meaning at least, as referring to ... rules (and resources)'.[23] But to adhere to this conception of structure, while at the same time acknowledging the need for the study of 'structural principles', 'structural sets' and 'axes of structuration', is simply a recipe for conceptual confusion. A structural principle, such as that which 'operates along an axis' relating urban areas to rural hinterlands, is not a 'rule' in any ordinary sense: it is neither a semantic rule nor a moral rule nor a 'formula' which expresses what actors know in knowing how to go on in social life. To insist that a structural principle *must* be some such rule, or must be capable of being analysed in terms of rules, is to force on to the material a mode of conceptualization which is not appropriate to it, and which stems less from a reflection upon the structural features of social life than from an implicit ontology of structure. Similarly it seems unhelpful and misleading to interpret Marx's account of the structural relations involved in the capitalist system of production in terms of 'sets of rules and resources'. The constitution of labour power as a commodity, the determination of its value as the labour time socially necessary for its production, its exchange on the market under conditions which guarantee that it exchanges at its value and yet simultaneously produces surplus value and profit: these features of the capitalist system cannot be treated as so many 'rules' that workers follow when they turn up at the factory gates, as if every worker who accepted a job had an implicit (albeit partial) knowledge of Marx's *Capital*.[24] The account offered by Marx would be better seen, I think, as an attempt to identify and explicate the differing kinds of conditions which render possible the processes of capitalist production and exchange. These conditions range from the circumstances which facilitate the formation of a 'free' labour force to the elements, the relations and the principles involved in the constitution of value and the generation of profit. I see no merit whatsoever in attempting to force these varied conditions into the conceptual mould of structure *qua* rules and resources. Moreover, I find it difficult to reconcile any such attempt with Marx's claim to be uncovering the essence of capitalist relations which is concealed beneath their phenomenal form, a form in terms of which the nature and value of commodities is *mis*understood by the very individuals involved in their production.[25] Giddens's account tends to equate social structure with practical knowledge and hence to elide the distinction between an analysis of the structural conditions of a certain kind of society, on the one hand, and a mere summary of what actors already know in knowing 'how to go on' in that society, on the other.[26] I believe that it is important to preserve this distinction, both for the purposes of social analysis and for the tasks of social science as *critique*. I believe, moreover, that this distinction can be preserved without succumbing to the 'derogation of the lay actor' which Giddens so rightly warns against.

The second difficulty I wish to raise concerns the consequences of Giddens's distinctions for the problem of social reproduction. Part of the attraction of conceiving of structure in terms of rules and resources is that it offers a simple and readily graspable picture of how individuals, in pursuing their everyday activities, reproduce social structure. For in pursuing their activities individuals 'draw upon' rules and resources which are thereby reproduced, just as in speaking English one 'draws upon' and reproduces the rules of English grammar. This picture lies at the heart of Giddens's account; it is the constant point of reference in his many discussions of the duality of structure and the recursive character of social life. But the picture is deceptively simple. It presupposes that all structural features of social systems can be conceived in terms of rules and resources, where by 'rules' we understand something similar to the rules of English grammar. I have argued that this presupposition cannot be sustained. I have also argued that Giddens's own distinctions between different levels of structural analysis cannot be easily reconciled with this presupposition. These arguments call into question, in turn, the adequacy of Giddens's account of reproduction. And indeed it makes no sense, I would say, to suppose that 'structural principles' are reproduced by being 'drawn upon' by individuals in social interaction.[27] Hence what may have appeared to be the main attraction of Giddens's approach is in fact one of its principal shortcomings: the problem of reproduction is at best only partially resolved. In order to deal more adequately with this issue, I believe that one must distinguish more sharply than Giddens does between the reproduction of institutions and the reproduction of social structure. Institutions are characterized by rules, regulations and conventions of various sorts, by differing kinds and quantities of resources and by hierarchical relations of power between the occupants of institutional positions. When agents act in accordance with these rules and regulations or exercise the power which is institutionally endowed upon them, they may be said to reproduce the institutions. If, in so doing, the institutions continue to satisfy certain structural conditions, both in the sense of conditions which delimit the scope for *institutional variation* and conditions which underlie the operation of *structural differentiation*, then the agents may be said to reproduce social structure. Thus individuals who, in their everyday productive activities, reproduce the institutions of the Ford Motor Company may also be said to reproduce the conditions in virtue of which those institutions are capitalistic. But it is not difficult to imagine circumstances in which individuals may effectively transform those institutions *without* transforming their structural conditions. Every act of production and reproduction may also be a potential act of transformation, as Giddens rightly insists; but the extent to which an action transforms an institution does *not* coincide with the extent to which social structure is thereby transformed.

As a third and final point, I want to forestall a possible objection to the criticisms made above. Surely I have overlooked, it may be said, Giddens's many references to the role of 'methodological bracketing'. According to Giddens, one may adopt one of two approaches to the study of the structural features of social systems. On the one hand, one can conduct an *institutional analysis* in which structural features are treated as chronically reproduced properties of social systems; on the other hand, one can pursue an *analysis of strategic conduct*, focusing on the ways in which actors draw upon structural features in the course of social interaction. Giddens stresses that this methodological distinction is merely a difference of emphasis: 'there is not a clear-cut line that can be drawn between these, and each – crucially – has to be in principle rounded out by a concentration upon the duality of structure'.[28] However, this is a distinction which must be treated with great care. For it can serve all too easily as a methodological blanket to cover over what are, I believe, deep conceptual difficulties in Giddens's account. Thus it will not suffice to object to my critic- isms by saying that the analysis of structural principles, structural sets and so on is *not supposed* to show how such features are invoked and thereby reproduced by agents in social interaction, since it places interactional analysis in methodological brackets. This will not suffice because the problem is not a methodological but a conceptual one: a structural principle governing the align- ment of institutions does not become a rule drawn upon in interac- tion by the mere removal of methodological brackets. I do not think that Giddens would wish to claim the contrary; but so far he has refused to acknowledge, as I think he must, that the recogni- tion of different levels of structural analysis places intolerable strain on his original conception of structure.

ACTION, STRUCTURE AND CONSTRAINT

To this point I have concentrated on the structural side of Giddens's attempt to overcome the dualism of action and struc- ture. I now want to turn my attention briefly to his analysis of action and its relation to structure and constraint. Action may be conceptualized, Giddens suggests, in terms of a stratification mod- el that takes account of the reflexive monitoring of action which agents routinely carry out, as well as the rationalization and motivation of action (including unconscious sources of motivation). Essential to the stratification model is the idea that, while much day-to-day life occurs as a continuous flow of intentional action, many acts have unintended consequences which may become the unacknowledged conditions of further acts. It is primarily in this way, according to Giddens, that action is linked to structure. For in pursuing some course of action the agent draws upon the rules and resources which comprise structure, thereby reproducing unintentionally the structural conditions of further acts. '*Structure thus is not to be conceptualised as a barrier to action, but as essentially involved in its production*':[29] structure is *enabling* as well as constraining and is implicated in even the most radical processes of social change.

There are many aspects of Giddens's stratification model which I find attractive. He offers a framework for the analysis of action which makes room for the insights of many authors – from Heidegger and Schutz to Garfinkel, Goffman and Freud – without neglecting the dimension of institutions and social structure. Nevertheless, I believe that there are certain problems with this approach. Some of these problems can be raised by asking whether, in stressing the *enabling* character of structure, Giddens does justice to the role of *structural constraint*.[30] Let me begin to examine this question by returning to *New Rules of Sociological Method*, where the rules constitutive of structure are characterized as semantic rules and moral rules. In what senses do these rules operate as constraints on possible courses of action? Semantic rules are constraining in the sense that they oblige a speaker, who wishes to be understood by another, to adopt certain linguistic and grammatical forms; a speaker who uttered an expression like 'purple politicians spell in their sleep' would simply not be understood by a competent speaker of English. Moral rules are constraining in the sense that they are associated with sanctions which may be 'internal', relying upon the moral commitment of the agent or upon fear or guilt, or 'external', relying upon the offer of rewards or the threat of force. These are important kinds of constraint and their significance in social life is not to be underestimated. It seems evident, however, that they are not the only kinds of constraint which are relevant to social analysis. When a school-leaver is faced with the choice of joining a youth training scheme or signing on the dole, the constraints which operate are not simply those of comprehensibility or sanctioning. For it is the *range of alternatives* which is restricted, and these restrictions do not stem from semantic and moral rules but from the structural conditions for the persistence (and decline) of productive institutions.

Giddens is aware of the importance of structural constraint and would no doubt accept that his earlier remarks on this theme are in need of elaboration. In *The Constitution of Society* he takes up the theme and seeks to show that his account can fully accommodate the role of constraint. There is no difficulty in showing, to begin with, that the theory of structuration is compatible with the recognition of limits imposed by the physical environment. Similarly it presents no problem to acknowledge that institutions, conceived of as regularized practices which are 'deeply layered' in time and space, both pre-exist and post-date the lives of the individuals who reproduce them, and thus may be resistant to manipulation or change by any particular agent. But what of structural constraint, that is, of constraint which derives neither from physical conditions nor from specific institutions but from social structure? 'As with the constraining qualities of sanctions', proposes Giddens, 'it is best described as *placing limits upon the feasible range of options open to an actor in a given circumstance or type of circumstance.*'[31] Consider the limits imposed by the 'contractual relations of modern industry'. For individuals who have been rendered propertyless and deprived of their means of subsistence, there is only one alternative: namely, to sell their labour power to those who own the means of production. To say that there is only one alternative is to say that there is only one 'feasible option' – one option, that is, that actors having certain patterns of motivation (in this case, the wish to survive) will regard as reasonable to pursue. While a worker may have a choice between several job possibilities, in the end these options reduce to one, for ultimately the worker has no choice but to accept a job, whichever one it may be.

This elaboration of Giddens's views concurs with some of the modifications discussed in the previous section and is, once again, to be welcomed. Nevertheless, it seems to me that this elaboration raises two major problems for Giddens's account. In the first place, what Giddens now describes as 'structural constraint' cannot be readily reconciled with his proposal to conceive of structure in terms of rules and resources. The constraints which reduce the options of propertyless individuals to one – and increasingly today to the 'option' of unemployment – are imposed in part by the conditions of capitalist production and exchange; and I have already argued that it is unhelpful and misleading to try to force these conditions into the conceptual mould of structure *qua* rules and resources. The second problem concerns the relation between structural constraint and agency. A central theme of Giddens's account is that the concept of agency implies that a person 'could have done otherwise': 'an agent who has no options whatsoever', he insists, 'is no longer an agent'.[32] In his discussion of structural constraint, however, Giddens acknowledges the possibility that such constraint may reduce the options of an individual to one. It is not difficult to see that an individual who has one option has no options, for there are no other courses of action which the individual could have pursued and hence it seems senseless to say that he or she 'could have done otherwise'. Structure and agency no longer appear to be the complementary terms of a duality but the antagonistic poles of a dualism, such that structural constraint may so limit the options of the individual that agency is effectively dissolved.

Giddens's response to this evident problem is to emphasize the distinction between 'option' and 'feasible option'. An individual who has only one option is not an agent, for there is no sense in which that individual 'could have done otherwise'. But an individual who has only one *feasible* option is an agent, for the option is limited to one only in the sense that, *given* the individual's wants and desires, there is only one option that the individual would regard as reasonable to pursue. This response does not resolve the problem, however; it merely *bypasses* the problem by reaffirming a concept of agency which is, for all *practical* purposes, irrelevant. There is simply no imaginable circumstance in which an individual could not have done otherwise if, by 'the individual', we understand some pure and rarefied self, abstracted from every want and desire and always able to choose.[33] Giddens admits this much; even a prisoner who is gagged and bound and placed in solitary confinement remains an agent, 'as hunger strikes, or "the ultimate refusal" – suicide – indicate'.[34] Giddens manages to preserve the complementarity between structure and agency only by *defining* agency in such a way that any individual in any situation could not *not* be an agent.

A more direct confrontation with these issues would require, I believe, a more satisfactory conception of structure and structural constraint as well as a more systematic analysis of the wants and desires that are relevant to individual action and choice. All options are 'feasible options' in the sense that they are conditional upon the wants and desires of the agents whose options they are: a possible course of action would not be an option for an agent if it had no relevance to anything that the agent wanted. But options vary greatly in their range, their nature and in the character of the wants and desires upon which they depend. One of the key tasks of social analysis is to explore this space of possibilities, both in terms of the differential distribution of options according to class, age, sex and so on, but also in terms of the kinds of wants and desires, the interests and needs, which are themselves differentially possessed.[35] The differential distribution of options and needs implies that certain individuals or groups of individuals have greater scope for action and choice than other individuals or groups of individuals: freedom, one could say, is enjoyed by different people in differing degrees. To explore the space between the differential distribution of options, on the one hand, and the wants and needs of different kinds and of different categories of individuals, on the other, is to examine the degrees of freedom and constraint which are entailed by social structure. Such an analysis would show that, while structure and agency are not antinomies, nevertheless they are not as complementary and mutually supporting as Giddens would like us to believe.

Let me conclude this essay by summarizing my main criticisms of Giddens's work. I began by sketching the central themes of his account and by showing how, in *New Rules of Sociological Method*, the concept of structure is approached through a comparison of language and speech. While Giddens carefully qualifies this approach, nevertheless it is the source, I believe, of many of the difficulties in his account. For it is through a reflection on language and its relation to speech that he initially formulates a general conception of structure as rules and resources. I have argued that the proposal to conceive of structure in this way is unsatisfactory for several reasons: (1) the notion of rule is terribly vague and Giddens fails to provide a clear and consistent explication; and (2) the study of rules (and resources) does not address

directly some of the key concerns in the analysis of social structure, such as the analysis of structural differentiation and the study
of structural identity. We do not need a general conception of
structure of which social structure, or the 'structures most relevant
to the analysis of social life', would be a specific instance; we need
a careful explication of what is involved in social structure and in
the various forms of structural analysis in social inquiry. In his
recent writings Giddens responds in more detail to the latter
demand and distinguishes more clearly between different levels of
structural analysis. While these distinctions are helpful, I believe
that they place intolerable strain on the conception of structure
qua rules and resources, a conception to which Giddens continues,
somewhat tenaciously, to adhere. Moreover, these distinctions
merely highlight the shortcomings of Giddens's approach to the
problem of reproduction, an approach which is based on the
over-simplified picture of an actor 'drawing upon' a rule. Finally,
turning my attention briefly to the analysis of action, I tried to
show that Giddens's emphasis on the enabling character of structure has led him to underplay the role of structural constraint. A
more adequate treatment of the latter would have to acknowledge,
I think, that action and social structure are neither contradictory
nor complementary terms, but rather two poles which stand in a
relation of tension with one another. For while social structure is
reproduced and transformed by action, it is also the case that the
range of options available to individuals and groups of individuals
are differentially distributed and structurally circumscribed.

In developing my criticisms I have focused primarily on the
conception of structure *qua* rules and resources and on the relation
between action and structural constraint. For the sake of concise-
ness I have not examined the many interesting and important
contributions which Giddens has made to the analysis of power,
the theory of ideology and the conceptualization of time and space,
let alone his more substantive work on class structure and the state.
I have put aside these contributions partly because I accept
Giddens's view that the relation between action and structure is in
a certain sense primary, for it is in terms of this relation that the
analysis of power, the theory of ideology and the conceptualization of time and space must be cast. It is my opinion that Giddens
has done more than any other contemporary thinker to advance
our understanding of the complex ways in which action and

structure intersect in the routine activities of everyday life. If my criticisms of Giddens's account are sound, then they will merely contribute to a task which he above all has set for social theory.

5

Action, Ideology and the Text

A Reformulation of Ricoeur's Theory of Interpretation

For authors influenced by the tradition of hermeneutics, the phenomenon of ideology is a challenge which lies at the heart of their concerns. From Dilthey onwards the tradition of hermeneutics has emphasized the symbolic constitution of the social-historical world. This world is composed of individuals who speak and act in meaningful ways, who create the very world which endows them with their identity and their being, and whose creations can be understood only by means of a process of interpretation. As a system of representations which pertain to politics, ideology, it might be said, is just another creation of this kind; but the phenomenon of ideology raises questions which cannot be dealt with so comfortably. For in so far as ideology is understood, not simply as a system of representations pertaining to politics, but as a form of signification which justifies social relations, it raises questions of power, of domination and of the critique of domination. When the phenomenon of ideology is dragged before one's eyes, the social-historical world can no longer be seen as a sphere of creativity and co-belonging. It must also be seen as a field of conflict and coercion, a realm in which 'meaning' may be a mask for repression and self-deception. By calling attention to the relations of force which bind individuals and underlie their utterances and acts, the phenomenon of ideology is a challenge to any author who wishes to sustain the hermeneutical emphasis on the symbolic constitution of the social-historical world.

It is to the credit of Paul Ricoeur that he has taken up this challenge in a direct and imaginative way. Against the backcloth of an illuminating analysis of meaning and creativity in language,

Ricoeur has formulated a concept of the text which provides the basis for a *theory of interpretation*. He argues that this theory can be extended beyond literary texts to the sphere of social action, by virtue of certain features which are shared by action and texts. To see action as a text is to view it as meaningfully constituted behaviour which can be interpreted in various ways; and to view action as meaningfully constituted behaviour is to identify the primary source of the phenomenon of ideology. For ideology, argues Ricoeur, is first and foremost a cluster of symbols and representations which facilitate the meaningful constitution and social integration of action. In its most fundamental sense ideology is a positive phenomenon, expressing the necessity for any group to give itself an image of itself, to fill the gap between its origin and its actuality, its founding project and its fading collective memory. Yet if ideology is fundamentally a positive phenomenon, it is also a phenomenon which lends itself to rationalization and distortion. The image of origins is a simplifying, schematizing, sedimented phenomenon; it lends itself to the justification of a system of domination and – as the Marxist concept of ideology underlines – to the maintenance of a system of class domination. The phenomenon of ideology thus calls for a moment of critique. It calls, that is, for an interpretative attitude which seeks to differentiate, without claiming to distinguish once and for all, between the 'pre-understandings' which link us to a culture and a tradition, on the one hand, and the 'prejudices' which merely perpetuate distortion and self-deception. If this critical moment is possible, it is because we *belong to* our history only by virtue of a *distance from* it, a distance which is inscribed, Ricoeur maintains, in the constitution of action and texts.

My aim in this essay is to explore this imaginative line of reflection and to unfold from it the elements of a theory for the critical interpretation of ideology. In the first part of the essay I offer a reconstruction of Ricoeur's views on language, textual interpretation, action and ideology. The second part of the essay is critical and constructive. I assess Ricoeur's arguments for the similarity of action and texts and I probe the limitations of his theory of interpretation. I try to show that, while Ricoeur's theory of interpretation is questionable in various respects, it can nevertheless be reformulated in a way which is of considerable value for the study of social phenomena in general, and for the analysis of ideology in particular. It should be stressed at the outset that this essay focuses on Ricoeur's contribution to a specific set of issues and makes no attempt to evaluate his work as a whole. Other volumes and other critics will introduce the reader to a rich and wide-ranging corpus which is still in a state of development.[1]

I

Language and discourse

Since the early 1960s Ricoeur has developed his views through a systematic reflection on language. The stage for this reflection was set by the structural linguistics of Ferdinand de Saussure and by the perspectives elaborated in the schools of Copenhagen and Prague. These contributions defined the conditions for a *science of language* which has had a profound impact not only on linguistics, but also on many spheres of social and cultural inquiry. Drawing upon the work of Saussure and that of the Danish linguist Louis Hjelmslev,[2] Ricoeur summarizes these conditions as follows. First, language must be treated as a homogeneous and strictly circumscribed object which can be investigated scientifically; hence Saussure's famous distinction between *langue* and *parole*, a distinction designed to put aside the individual and irregular instances of speech and to isolate a homogeneous object of inquiry. Second, in studying this system, one must distinguish between a science of the states of the system, or a 'synchronic linguistics', and a science of changes, or a 'diachronic linguistics'. These two approaches are not on a par; the synchronic has priority over the diachronic, for change can be understood only by reference to specific states of the system. Third, in any state of the system there are no absolute terms but only relations of mutual dependence. That is, the signs of the system have 'value', not by virtue of any intrinsic content they may possess or any object to which they may refer, but solely by virtue of their relations to one another. 'Language, thus relieved of its fixed contents, becomes a system of signs defined by their differences alone'.[3] The fourth condition follows directly from the preceding three: the collection of signs must be treated as a closed and autonomous system of internal dependencies. Language can thus be studied as if it had no exterior, for the relations which constitute value are internal to the system of signs.

The four conditions render possible a certain kind of structural linguistics, but at the same time they occlude some important features of language. Ricoeur highlights these features by elaborating Benveniste's distinction between a *semiotics of the sign* and a *semantics of the sentence*.[4] A semiotics may study signs of different kinds – phonological, lexical, even 'mythological'; and such an inquiry may, within the limits which render it possible, be a legitimate and illuminating inquiry. But there is a level of language which escapes the purview of semiotics, namely the level of the *sentence*. For a sentence is not a sign, nor a mere concatenation of signs. While a sentence is composed of signs, it has a character which distinguishes it from signs:

> the sign only has a function of discrimination: what is peculiar to each sign is what distinguishes it from other signs; for the sign, to be distinctive and to be significant are the same thing. The sentence, by contrast, has a function of synthesis. Its specific character is to be a predicate.[5]

The sentence is the basic unit of what Ricoeur, following Benveniste, calls 'discourse'. Unlike a system of signs which is considered synchronically and therefore a-temporally, discourse has an eventful, actual, evanescent character. A sentence is uttered in a specific here and now and, once uttered, is eclipsed by subsequent events. If the utterance of a sentence is an ephemeral phenomenon, nevertheless a sentence has a *meaning* which may be re-identified on future occasions. The meaning of a sentence is a product of the complex operation constituted by the *predicative act*. A sentence has a synthetic structure in which a quality, a relation or some other aspect is predicated of a subject. The predicative act endows the sentence with a specific meaning – what Benveniste calls the *intenté*, to distinguish it from the *signifié* which is the correlate of the *signifiant* at the level of the sign. It also endows the sentence with a specific relation to an extra-linguistic reality, that is, with a *reference*. At this point we reach the most fundamental feature of the distinction between semiotics and semantics. Whereas the sign is defined by difference, the sentence is endowed with reference. In uttering a sentence a speaker expresses the intention to say something *about* something *to* someone. The instance of discourse is thus the medium through which language transcends itself, taking hold of the world, of the self and of others and expressing their hold on language.

A semiotics of the sign and a semantics of the sentence are not, according to Ricoeur, two approaches of equal status; a semantics of the sentence has a certain priority, for it is only at the level of the sentence that one can account for the phenomena of *creativity* within language. The basic condition of creativity is the intrinsic polysemy of words, that is, the feature by which words in natural languages have more than one meaning. The boundaries of polysemy can be defined by a semiotics of the sign, since the potential uses of a word are accumulated and codified in the lexical system. Ricoeur maintains, however, that the phenomenon of polysemy can be fully grasped only at the level of the sentence. For a lexical entity is not yet a word, and a word has meaning only in the nexus of a sentence. By virtue of their polysemy, words provide sentences with a surplus of meaning which must be sifted through a process of interpretation. 'Interpretation', in this primordial sense, 'is the process by which, in the interplay of question and answer, the interlocutors collectively determine the contextual values which structure their conversation.'[6] Polysemy provides the basis, not only for the reduction of ambiguity through interpretation, but also for the creative extension of meaning through *metaphor*. The distinctive feature of metaphor, according to Ricoeur, is the semantic tension or 'impertinence' which gives rise to new meaning. This feature can be grasped only if we leave behind the traditional view of metaphor – in which metaphor was seen as the mere substitution of one word for another – and focus on the level of the sentence. The metaphor then appears as a semantic innovation which resolves a tension established by the deviant use of predicates in the sentence. The emergent meaning can be grasped only through a constructive interpretation which makes sense of the sentence as a whole. Such an interpretation is an act of *imagination*, of 'seeing as . . .', of seeing time as a beggar, old age as the evening of life. Meaning is created and reality is redescribed by means of the sentence which supports a metaphor, thus attesting to the importance of discourse as the dynamic and mediating dimension of language.

Concept of the text

Language can be studied, not only as systems of signs or as types of sentence, but also as extended sequences of written discourse, that is, as *texts*. To move from the sentence to the text is to move from the sphere of semantics to the domain of hermeneutics; new problems are raised in this transition and certain issues which appeared in the sphere of semantics are eclipsed or transformed. The text is a written work of discourse and hence, in the first instance, a *work*. There are, Ricoeur proposes, three principal features which are characteristic of a work. In the first place, a work is a structured totality which is irreducible to the sentences of which it is composed. The work thus gives rise to a new problem of understanding, a problem which cannot be resolved by the step-by-step comprehension of the constituent sentences. The second feature of the work is that it is produced in accordance with a series of rules or codes which define its literary genre, and which transform discourse into a novel, a poem, a play. The literary genre is less a means of classification than a means of production; it provides a generative framework which governs both the production of discourse as a work and its interpretation as a work of a certain kind. If a work is produced in accordance with a genre, it is also produced as a unique configuration which constitutes its *style*: this is the third feature of the work. The style of a work expresses its singularity, its eventful, idiosyncratic character as a personal response to a situation which suddenly appears undone, unresolved, open. To characterize a work as a structured totality of a certain genre and style is to exploit fully the ambiguity of 'work'. For these are categories of production and of labour; 'to impose a form upon material, to submit production to genres, to produce an individual: these are so many ways of treating language as a material to be worked upon and formed'.[7]

In addition to being a work of discourse, the text is a *written* work. The inscription of discourse in writing involves a series of transformations which Ricoeur encapsulates in the key concept of *distanciation*. The first and most obvious transformation concerns the fixation of discourse. Writing preserves the meaning of what is said, fixing it in a material medium such as papyrus or paper and thereby surpassing the fleeting character of the instance of discourse. This surpassing of the event of saying by the meaning of what is said is the first form of distanciation. It is rendered possible by what Ricoeur calls the 'intentional exteriorization' of the speech-act. The various components of the speech-act – the 'locutionary', 'illocutionary' and 'perlocutionary' acts in Austin's terminology[8] – are expressed in ways which, with the aid of grammatical and other devices, can be realized in writing. Thus the locutionary act (the act *of* saying something) is expressed in a sentence which, by virtue of its synthetic structure, may be re-identified as the same and thereby inscribed. The illocutionary act (the act performed *in* saying something) is expressed, at least in part, by certain grammatical features which convey the 'force' of the utterance – its force, that is, as a promise, a warning, a command. To the extent that the illocutionary act is so expressed, it can be preserved in writing. The perlocutionary act (the act performed *by* saying something) is the least inscribable aspect of discourse. But it is also 'the least discursive aspect of discourse: it is discourse *qua* stimulus'.[9] The perlocutionary act operates, as Ricoeur says, in an 'energetic mode'. It has an effect on someone, less by virtue of its character as discourse than by virtue of its occurrence as an act. So while the perlocutionary act belongs more to speech than to writing, this does not constitute an obstacle to the inscription of discourse in writing, for the perlocutionary act is largely non-discursive.

It would be quite misleading, however, to view the text solely in terms of inscription, as if speaking were the oral fount of every written work. For to write is to produce a text which acquires a certain *autonomy*; the remaining forms of distanciation pertain to this 'semantic autonomy of the text'. The second form of distanciation concerns the relation between the meaning of the text and the intention of the author. Whereas in spoken discourse the intention of the speaking subject and the meaning of what is said frequently overlap, there is no such coincidence in the case of writing. As Ricoeur remarks,

> the text's career escapes the finite horizon lived by its author. What the text says now matters more than what the author meant to say, and every exegesis unfolds its procedures within the circumference of a meaning that has broken its moorings to the psychology of its author.[10]

The third form of distanciation introduces a similar discrepancy between the text and its social conditions of production. In contrast to spoken discourse, where the hearer is determined by the dialogical situation, a text is addressed to an unknown audience and potentially to anyone who can read. The text 'decontextualizes' itself from its social and historical conditions of production, opening itself to an unlimited series of readings. The fourth and final form of distanciation marks the emancipation of the text from the limits of 'ostensive reference'. Spoken discourse always contains some reference to the shared situation of the interlocutors and always offers the possibility of clarifying, by pointing or some other gesture, the referential import of what is said. This link between discourse and ostensive reference is shattered by writing. A text does not refer to features of the situation in which it was produced, but opens up a world and projects a way of being. To unfold this referential dimension of the text, and to relate it to the subject who is 'metamorphized' by the text, is the task of the theory of interpretation.

Theory of interpretation

The concept of the text, as a written work which exhibits the four forms of distanciation, is the primary focus of Ricoeur's theory of interpretation. In this respect Ricoeur remains faithful to the tradition of hermeneutics; for this tradition has often treated texts, or documents with a status comparable to texts, as the principal medium of our relation to the past. However, Ricoeur's analysis of the text enables him to avoid the 'Romantic' and 'psychological' tendencies which have characterized some forms of hermeneutics. If the text may be seen as a written work endowed with a certain autonomy, then interpretation may be regarded as a kind of reading which responds to this autonomy, drawing together elements of 'understanding' and 'explanation' and integrating them into a complex interpretative process. One aspect of this process may be discerned by attending to the consequences of the first two forms of distanciation. The eclipse of the event of saying by the meaning of what is said, and the severance of the latter from the intentions of the authorial subject, imply that the objective meaning of a text is something other than the alleged intention of its author. The meaning of a text must be constructed or construed as a whole, acknowledging its character as a structured totality irreducible to the sentences of which it is composed. Such a construction is necessarily a guess, and one guess among others; a text contains an inherent plurivocity which enables it to be construed in more ways than one. This feature renders interpretation an open process but it does not hand it over to arbitrariness and caprice. For 'it is always possible to argue for or against an interpretation, to confront interpretations, to arbitrate between them and to seek agreement, even if this agreement remains beyond our immediate reach'.[11] To argue for or against an interpretation is to adduce evidence, reasons or examples which show that one interpretation is more or less plausible than some other. It is more a matter of validation than verification, of probability than proof. The interpretation of texts is an argumentative discipline which can avoid scepticism without aspiring to certainty.

The third and fourth forms of distanciation have equally important consequences for the theory of interpretation. The emancipation of written discourse from the interlocutors and circumstances of the dialogical situation engenders two possible attitudes towards the text. On the one hand, the reader may suspend any judgement 'concerning the referential dimension of the text, treating the latter as a worldless and self-enclosed entity. On the other hand, the reader may abandon this *epoché* and seek to unfold the non-ostensive references of the text. The first attitude is adopted by structuralist approaches to the study of literature and myth. Within limits, these approaches are perfectly legitimate and illuminating. They apply to texts a new type of *explanation*, a type which comes not from the natural sciences but from the field of language itself. Consider, for example, Lévi-Strauss's classic analysis of the Oedipus myth.[12] Assuming that myths are made up of constitutive units – 'mythemes' – which are analogous to the units constitutive of other levels of language, Lévi-Strauss proceeds to divide the sentences of the myth into four columns. The first column consists of sentences which overrate blood relations (for example, Oedipus marries his mother, Jocasta), while the second consists of sentences which underrate blood relations (e.g. Oedipus kills his father, Laios). The third column concerns monsters and their destruction (Cadmos kills the dragon, Oedipus kills the Sphinx); the fourth groups together proper names which suggest difficulties in walking straight and standing upright (lame, left-sided, swollen-foot). Lévi-Strauss then observes a series of relations between these columns. The first and second columns overrate and underrate blood relations, whereas the third and fourth columns deny and affirm the autochthonous origin of human beings. 'It follows', infers Lévi-Strauss, 'that the fourth column is related to the third column as the first is to the second . . .; the overrating of blood relations is to their underrating as the attempt to escape from autochthony is to the impossibility of succeeding in it.'[13] The myth thus appears as a kind of logical instrument which brings out contradictions and relates them through the 'structural law of the myth'.

Ricoeur is not unsympathetic to Lévi-Strauss's analysis, or to the somewhat similar analyses which can be found in the writings of Vladimir Propp, A. J. Greimas and Roland Barthes.[14] Ricoeur argues, however, that such analyses presuppose, without explicitly addressing, a form of understanding which cannot be reduced to structural explanation. The presupposed form of understanding is the concern of the second attitude that the reader may adopt towards the text. For the reader may seek to grasp, not a pattern or structure internal to the text, but a world projected by it, that is, a world *about which* it speaks. While a text is not bound by the conditions of ostensive reference, it nevertheless has a referential dimension; or more precisely, the referential dimension is 'divided' or 'split', in such a way that the suspension of ostensive reference is the condition for the realization of a second order reference:

> the literary work discloses a world only under the condition that the reference of descriptive discourse is suspended. Or in other words: in the literary work, discourse unfolds its denotation as a denotation of the second order, in virtue of the suspension of the first order denotation of discourse.[15]

And indeed, even Lévi-Strauss cannot fail to allude to the referential dimension of the mythical text which he dissects. In the background of the Oedipus myth there is a question which structures the whole of his analysis, a question about life and death, a question which expresses the anguish of origins: whence comes the human being? From earth or from humans, from like or from other? The structural analysis helps to highlight this function of the myth as a narrative of origins, but such an analysis does not and cannot explore this function. For that is the task of interpretation – not a naïve and superficial interpretation, but a *depth interpretation* which is mediated by the techniques of structural analysis. In undertaking a depth interpretation the reader enters the world of the text, following the movement from its sense to its reference, from its internal structure to the world which it projects. The reader thereby *appropriates* the world of the text, where by 'appropriation' Ricoeur understands, not an act of possession by an autonomous ego and even less a return to the intentions of the author, but rather an act of *dispossession* through which one may relinquish a prior self and deepen one's understanding of oneself and others by virtue of the meaning inscribed in the text. Explanation and understanding are thus two phases of a process of interpretation which, while avoiding subjectivism, does not dispense with the subject.

Action as a text

The theory of interpretation may be extended beyond the sphere of the text, in so far as other human phenomena share some of the features of the written work. One phenomenon which shares some of these features, Ricoeur suggests, is 'meaningful action' – the phenomenon which Weber regarded as the principal object of sociological study.[16] Meaningful action can become an object of sociological study only on condition that it undergo a kind of *objectification* which is similar to the forms of distanciation expressed in the text. Thus, just as the fixation of discourse involves the surpassing of the event of saying by the meaning of what is said, so too action may be objectified in such a way that the event of doing is eclipsed by the significance of what is done. This eclipse is rendered possible by certain traits of action which are analogous to the components of the speech-act. An action has the structure of a locutionary act in so far as it has a 'propositional content' that can be re-identified as the same. Actions also exhibit a variety of illocutionary traits which are similar to those of the speech-act: actions have the 'force' of warnings, threats, expressions of compassion or solidarity. Hence Ricoeur submits that, 'like the speech-act, the action-event (if we may coin this analogical expression) develops a similar dialectic between its temporal status as an appearing and disappearing event, and its logical status of having such-and-such identifiable meaning or "sense-content"'.[17] The meaning or 'sense-content' of action can acquire an autonomy which is comparable to the semantic autonomy of the text. Just as a text is divorced from its author, so too an action becomes detached from the actor and develops consequences of its own. The meaning of an action is thereby severed from the intentions of the agent, set loose to leave its mark on the course of events which constitute human history. Morever, just as the inscription of discourse shatters the narrowness of the dialogical situation, so too action is an 'open work': it is there to be interpreted and judged by anyone who can 'read', not only by the individuals who witnessed its performance. Finally, just as the written work is freed from the restrictions of ostensive reference, so too human action transcends the social conditions of its production. For the importance of an action may go beyond its relevance to the circumstances in which it occurs. Hence an action, like a text, may open up new worlds through the actualization of possibilities which it bears within itself.

To the extent that meaningful action may be regarded as a text, it falls within the scope of Ricoeur's theory of interpretation. The interpretation of action in accordance with this theory has distinct advantages. For it avoids the traditional opposition between 'explanation' (*erklären*) and 'understanding' (*verstehen*) which has been a feature of debates in the philosophy of social science since the nineteenth-century *Methodenstreit*; it offers a way of linking these two concerns in a coherent methodology for the interpretation of action. To render this methodology plausible, Ricoeur attempts to show that the various aspects of his interpretative theory are applicable to action. Just as a text is a structured totality which may be construed in various ways, so too human action has a specific plurivocity which makes it a limited field of possible interpretations. One understands an action when one can explain why the person acted as he or she did; and one can explain that when one can provide a reason or motive for the action, that is, when one can subsume the action under a particular category of wants or beliefs. Thus an agent can render his or her action intelligible by explaining that it was done out of jealousy, or that it was done to avenge another for something that was done in the past. However, there is nothing definitive about this process. To explain one's action in this way is to make a *claim* which could be defended or contested. 'Like legal utterances, all interpretations in the field of literary criticism and in the social sciences may be challenged, and the question "what can defeat a claim" is common to all argumentative situations.'[18] Yet whereas in the legal tribunal there is an accepted point at which the procedures of appeal are exhausted, in literary criticism and the social sciences there is no such point; or if there is, remarks Ricoeur, it is because the discussion has been terminated by violence.

The other aspects of the theory of interpretation are equally applicable to action. The structuralist mode of analysis can be extended beyond the linguistic sphere to all social phenomena which may be said to have a 'semiological character', that is, which may be characterized in terms of systems of interrelated signs. The extension of this mode of analysis confers upon the social sciences a type of explanation quite different from that implied by a Humean account of causality, for structuralist explanation posits relations that are correlative rather than consecutive or sequential. Ricoeur maintains, however, that the establishment of such correlations does not exhaust the task of interpretation: it is only a preliminary phase in the depth interpretation of social phenomena.

> [T]he search for correlations within and between social phenomena treated as semiotic entities would lose importance and interest if it did not yield *something like* a depth semantics. In the same way as language-games are forms of life, according to the famous aphorism of Wittgenstein, social structures are also attempts to cope with existential perplexities, human predicaments and deep-rooted conflicts. In this sense, these structures, too, have a referential dimension. They point towards the *aporias* of social existence, the same *aporias* around which mythical thought gravitates.[19]

The social phenomena constituted by objectified action have a 'reference' as well as a structure, for they point towards the *aporias* of human existence and thereby project a world in a way analogous to the non-ostensive referential function of the text. Moreover, the appropriation of the world disclosed by depth interpretation does not reduce the objectivity of the social sciences to the subjectivity of the individual. For such appropriation has nothing to do with the intuitive grasp of an agent's intentions or the emotional identification with another psychic life. To appropriate is to expand one's own horizons, to allow one's sphere of consciousness and understanding to be enlarged through the incorporation of worlds which hitherto were 'alien' and 'other'. That the interpretation of action culminates in an act of appropriation attests to the fact that, in the domain of inquiry where the objects of investigation are products of subjects like ourselves, whatever knowledge we acquire is knowledge of a being that we are or could be. Hence the ineliminable circle which characterizes knowledge in the social-historical sphere, a circle which is not a vicious trap but a positive condition of hermeneutical inquiry.

Ideology and the imaginary

The constitution of action as meaningful, as a text to be interpreted by actors and others, is the primordial ground of the phenomenon of ideology. In its most elementary sense, argues Ricoeur, ideology is linked to the image which a social group gives of itself, to its self-representation as a community with a history and an identity. Ideology thus avails itself of the sense inscribed in the action-events which lie at the origin of a group. 'Its role is not only to diffuse the conviction beyond the circle of founding fathers, so as to make it the creed of the entire group; its role is also to perpetu-ate the initial energy beyond the period of effervescence.'[20] The growing gap between the inaugural events of a group and its present life calls for images and symbols, for *ongoing interpreta-tions of action-events*, which mediate between present and past and integrate the members of a group. The primary function of ideo-logy, therefore, is to mediate and integrate, to consolidate and conserve. In this respect, ideology contrasts sharply with 'utopia' or with utopian forms of literature and thought, as Mannheim remarked in his classic study.[21] While ideology tends to integrate the social order by *closing* the gap between present and past, utopia tends to subvert the social order by *creating* a gap, by projecting a possible future of what present society could be. Ideology and utopia may thus be seen as two forms of imaginative practice, two expressions of what Ricoeur calls 'the social imaginary'.[22] By 'imagination' or 'the imaginary' one should not understand a mere reflection or illusory image of some pre-existing reality. Rather, the imaginary is the productive, creative dimension of language, action and social life; it is not a mere reflection of reality but a

medium for the projection of new realities and for the criticism of
what is accepted as 'real'. The interplay of ideology and utopia is
the interplay of two contrary tendencies of the social imaginary.
One of these tendencies reaches backwards, constructing a past by
means of images and representations which serve to integrate the
present. The other tendency reaches forwards, creating a possible
future which would stand in a critical relation to the present and
which would show us what we potentially are.

If ideology is primarily a positive phenomenon, constituting the
symbolic texture of the social bond, it nevertheless contains features which endow it with a negative character. The diffusion of
conviction beyond the founding members of a group readily gives
way to rationalization and justification. Ideology becomes an argumentative device, a simplifying schema, an 'ism', which persuades
the members of a group that they are right to think as they do.
Ideology acquires an inertia which is intolerant of novelty and
resistant to change. It is in order to bring out these negative
features that Ricoeur introduces two additional concepts of ideology. Each of these additional concepts may be seen as a further
specification of the first conception (that is, of ideology conceived
as a medium of social integration); each narrows down the scope of
the first conception by linking ideology to other mechanisms and
functions. Thus, according to the *second concept*, ideology is not
just a medium of integration but a 'code of interpretation which
secures integration by *justifying the system of authority as it is*'.[23]
Every system of authority seeks to legitimate itself in the eyes of
the individuals subjected to it. It *claims* a legitimacy for itself which
exceeds the *belief* accorded to it, and ideology is called upon to fill
this justificatory deficit. The second concept of ideology brings us
to the threshold of a *third concept*, the properly Marxist concept.
According to the latter, ideology is linked not to domination in
general, but to *class* domination; and it justifies class domination
by virtue of a *distortion* which inverts the order of reality and ideas
and conceals certain features of the social world. While Ricoeur is
cautious about some of the claims associated with the Marxist
concept, he nevertheless regards it as a valuable contribution to an
analysis of the form and function of ideology in modern societies.

The second and third concepts bring out features of the
phenomenon of ideology which call for critique. Such a critique is
an important undertaking; but it is legitimate, argues Ricoeur, only

in so far as it is seen to be limited by conditions of a hermeneutical kind. For all objectifying knowledge about our position in society and in history is preceded by a relation of *belonging* upon which we can never fully reflect. We belong to a group, a class, a tradition, before we can have any critical distance from it; and this belonging is sustained by ideology in the most elementary sense, by ideology as image and self-representation, as medium of social integration. Yet if all objectifying knowledge is preceded by a relation of belonging, it can nevertheless acquire a 'relative autonomy'. It can acquire this relative autonomy because we belong to history only by virtue of taking a *distance* from it. We understand ourselves as historical beings only when we rise above our own particularity, exposing our consciousness, as Gadamer would say, to the 'effects of history'.[24] This moment of distanciation should not be seen, Ricoeur contends, as some sort of loss, an unfortunate fall from historical grace; rather, it is the positive condition of historical understanding. Distanciation is implied, as we have seen, in the fixation of discourse by writing and in comparable processes of objectification. Interpreting texts and their analogues is therefore a way of understanding ourselves and our world through an *objectified* medium and in a *critical* way.

> Since distanciation is a moment of belonging, the critique of ideology can be incorporated, as an objective and explanatory segment, in the project of enlarging and restoring communication and self-understanding. The extension of understanding through textual exegesis and its constant rectification through the critique of ideology are properly part of the process of *Auslegung* [interpretation].[25]

If the critique of ideology is rendered possible by the objectification obtained through distanciation, it is limited by the relation of belonging which is the counterpart of distanciation. The critique of ideology is necessarily partial, fragmentary, incomplete. It can never be conducted from a position outside of the history and the society to which we belong. The critique of ideology is only a moment – albeit an important moment – in the endless hermeneutical task of renewing and appraising our social-historical heritage.

II

So far I have been concerned to present Ricoeur's views on language, action and ideology in a systematic and sympathetic way; and many of these views, especially those pertaining to the analysis of language, are contributions which deserve to be endorsed. While remaining open to the insights of other approaches, Ricoeur has elaborated a novel account of language which calls attention to features that have been neglected or suppressed by other approaches. His analysis of discourse, his conception of the text and his theory of interpretation are important and original contributions. Nevertheless, I believe that Ricoeur's writings contain numerous difficulties. Here I shall develop my criticisms with a specific aim in mind: the aim of formulating a framework for the interpretation of ideology. This is not an aim, it should be said, which Ricoeur himself pursues. He analyses the phenomenon of ideology (that is, he seeks to *conceptualize* ideology) and he offers a theory of interpretation (that is, he develops a theory for the *interpretation* of action and texts); but he does not bring these two concerns together as closely as he might. I shall attempt to fill this lacuna by sketching a *theory for the interpretation of the discourse in which ideology is expressed.* In so doing I shall be led to revise Ricoeur's analysis of ideology and to reformulate his theory of interpretation. It is on the basis of these revisions and reformulations that I shall endeavour to continue the dialogue, which he has nourished and sustained, between hermeneutics and the critique of ideology.

Analysis of action

Since the phenomenon of ideology is rooted in certain aspects of action and social life, I shall begin by reconsidering Ricoeur's analysis of action. I shall focus here on his proposal to conceive of action as a text, although other writings of Ricoeur suggest other ways of analysing action.[26] It is justified to focus on this proposal, not only because it is regarded by Ricoeur as a key to his contribution to the methodology of the social sciences,[27] but also because it is a proposal which has been cited with approval by influential authors such as Geertz.[28] So let us examine the arguments which underpin the analogical treatment of action and texts. The first argument concerns the 'intentional exteriorization' of action: like speech-acts, argues Ricoeur, actions exhibit a variety of 'locutionary' and 'illocutionary' traits by virtue of which the event of doing may be eclipsed by the significance of what is done. Ricoeur supports this argument by referring to Kenny's analysis of verbs of action.[29] Kenny examines some of the grammatical differences between verbs of action, understood as the main verb in the answer to a question of the form 'what did A do?', and relational expressions like '. . . is taller than . . .'. Kenny thereby shows, according to Ricoeur, that action has a 'propositional content' which can be re-identified as the same, which can be detached from the process of interaction, fixed in some medium and turned into an object of interpretation. In fact, Kenny does not show anything like that. The strongest conclusion that his analysis warrants is that sentences containing verbs of action exhibit features which distinguish them from relational sentences; and if anything may be said to have a 'propositional content' which can be re-identified as the same, then it is surely these sentences and not the actions which they describe. Ricoeur's argument is based on a conflation of 'action' and 'action-sentences', such that certain features of the latter are misleadingly ascribed to the former. The result is that 'the meaning of an action' is transformed into an ethereal essence, a 'sense-content' which is *there* and waiting, as it were, to be picked up and re-presented by the interpreter. Ricoeur thereby obscures the extent to which 'the meaning of an action' depends upon *the way in which it is described*; and it is these descriptions (or these creative interpretations) which are transmitted, transcribed and contested in the trace-ridden process of history.

The second series of arguments for the possibility of treating action as a text concern the emancipation of action from the circumstances and participants of the interactional situation. Just as a text is autonomous from its author, from its social conditions of production and from the limits of ostensive reference, so too action, argues Ricoeur, becomes detached from its agent, is open to anyone who can 'read' and has an importance which goes beyond its relevance to the situation in which it originally occurs. There are numerous difficulties with this series of arguments. The first difficulty is that it employs terms which are used in a very loose way and which hardly justify the claim that the properties of action are comparable to those of a text. For example, whatever plausibility may be given to the distinction between ostensive reference and the non-ostensive referential dimension of a text, the relation between this distinction and that between the 'relevance' and the 'importance' of an action seems little more than metaphorical (what, one would like to ask, is the non-ostensive referential dimension of an action?). Moreover, it seems implausible to maintain that an action, or 'the meaning of an action', can be emancipated from its context in this way, detached from its agent, abstracted from the circumstances and participants of interaction and rendered accessible to all. For if, as I have suggested, the meaning of an action depends upon how it is described, then it cannot be considered in isolation from social context, since how an action is described is deeply affected by contextual considerations. Later I shall examine some other implications of Ricoeur's tendency to abstract from social conditions; here it will suffice to conclude that Ricoeur's proposal to conceive of action as a text is based on arguments which are not wholly convincing.

In criticizing Ricoeur's proposal I do not wish to suggest that there is nothing commendable in his approach to action. On the contrary, I believe that he is right to try to formulate a framework for the interpretation of action and to do so in a way which would overcome the rigid oppositions between 'explanation' and 'understanding', between 'motive' and 'cause'. I also believe that he is right to emphasize the continuity of concerns between different disciplines in the humanities and social sciences, disciplines which have too often been held apart. My objection is that he is wrong to pursue these projects on the basis of the assumption that action may be treated as a text. This assumption exemplifies a tendency which can be discerned in much recent work in social theory and the philosophy of social science, namely the tendency to generalize from certain features of language to the form of action as such. Whether we consider Winch's thesis that meaningful action is rule-governed behaviour, or Habermas's preoccupation with action oriented to reaching an understanding, or Ricoeur's proposal to conceive of action as a text: in each case language is treated as a paradigmatic form of action, as if one could unfold, by attending to certain properties of language or speech, the essential or most important characteristics of human action. This is a tendency which has, I believe, resulted in misleading analyses of action and in unsatisfactory accounts of the relation between action and the language with which it is described.[30]

Integration, domination, ideology

It is in the transition from the level of action to the level of social relations and groups that, according to Ricoeur, the phenomenon of ideology appears. For a social group must integrate itself by means of images and representations which can be collectively shared and which can co-ordinate the actions and orientations of its members. Such images are provided by interpretations of founding actions and events; it is these ongoing interpretations, this 'hermeneutics of everyday life', which generates what Ricoeur sees as the fundamental form of ideology. In this form ideology is the fabric which integrates a group, tying together its members and preserving the traces of its past. Ideology *qua* integration is fundamental because only on the basis of this form can the more specific instances of ideology – ideology as domination and ideology as dissimulation – have any efficacy for the members of a social group. In a minute I shall return to the relation between these three forms of ideology; but first I want to examine the assumption which underlies Ricoeur's argument concerning the fundamental character of ideology *qua* integration. A social group must integrate itself, he contends, by providing itself with images of itself and of its past, images which can be shared by all members of the group. It is not clear just what Ricoeur understands by the scope of 'social group' – whether he supposes, for example, that a friendship between two individuals is 'integrated', and thus animated by 'ideology', in the same way as an ethnic minority or a nation-state. However, if we consider a very large social group, such as a nation-state like contemporary Britain, it seems questionable to assume that such a group is integrated, or must integrate itself, by means of images or representations which are collectively shared. On the contrary, there is evidence to suggest that very few values and beliefs are shared or accepted by all (or even most) members of a modern industrial society.[31] It seems likely that our societies are 'integrated' less by virtue of some underlying consensus among all of its members than by virtue of widespread dissensus and fragmentation, that is, by virtue of a proliferation of divisions which obstruct the development of oppositional movements. This does not mean that ongoing interpretations of past events have no social and political role in our societies; but it does mean that we should be wary of the suggestion that their role *as ideology* can be understood by assuming that they provide collectively shared images which integrate social life.

Ricoeur does not, however, leave the matter there. He is fully aware that, at least since Napoleon, the term 'ideology' has acquired a negative sense; and he seeks to examine the negative features of the phenomenon to which it refers, features which link ideology to the exercise of *power*. Ricoeur highlights these features by introducing two further concepts of ideology: ideology understood as a means of justifying the existing system of authority, and ideology understood as a distortion which serves to justify a system of class domination. I think that Ricoeur is right to call attention to these additional aspects of the phenomenon of ideology. It seems to me unsatisfactory, however, to analyse these aspects by simply introducing further concepts, with the suggestion that each subsequent concept is a specific instance of, and therefore presupposes, the preceding one. To conceive of ideology as a code of interpretation which serves to justify an existing system of authority is not necessarily to view it as a specific way of securing integration, if by 'securing integration' we understand the provision of collectively shared images and representations. A system of authority can be sustained by stirring up conflicts, by opening old wounds, by setting one faction of a community against another; divide and rule is a strategy well known to dominant individuals and elites. Moreover, to justify a system of class domination is not a specific instance of justifying a system of authority. For authority implies recognition; that is, it implies that the individuals subjected to authority recognize that the latter has power which can be exercised over them. Domination, on the other hand, carries no such implication. Individuals may be enmeshed in a system of domination without recognizing that they are, or without recognizing the extent to which they are, subjected to the power of others. It follows that a code of interpretation which serves to justify a system of domination – whether class domination or some other form – cannot be satisfactorily treated as a specific instance of a code which justifies a system of authority.

In view of the questionable character of the assumption which underlies Ricoeur's first conception of ideology, and in view of the complications which surround the relations between the first conception and the subsequent two, I propose to abandon Ricoeur's 'polymorphous' approach to the phenomenon of ideology. I wish instead to elaborate a unitary approach which takes into account both the ongoing interpretative activities of agents pursuing their everyday lives, and the ways in which asymmetrical relations of power are routinely and systematically sustained. To study ideology, I propose, is *to study the ways in which meaning (or signification) serves to sustain relations of domination*. This approach to the phenomenon of ideology captures the key features highlighted by Ricoeur's analysis while abandoning its questionable assumptions. It captures the idea that actions and events are constantly interpreted and re-interpreted by lay actors, while abandoning the assumption that such interpretations integrate a group or society by providing images which are shared by all. It incorporates the notion that ideology serves to sustain relations of domination, without trying to subsume this role to a general problematic of social integration. It leaves open the possibility that one of the ways in which relations of domination may be sustained is by being represented as legitimate; hence it can accommodate the features highlighted by Ricoeur's second concept, without isolating these features and treating them as the object of a distinct concept of ideology. To analyse ideology in terms of the relation between meaning and domination is, however, to give the concept an essentially negative sense. In so doing I do not wish to deny that social relations are symbolically constituted in some general way, nor do I wish to downplay the importance of the imaginary dimension of social life. But I do wish to claim that it is neither illuminating nor defensible to characterize the symbolic constitution of social relations as the fundamental form of ideology.

Texts and interpretation

So far I have been concerned to criticize Ricoeur's analyses of action and ideology, analyses which are closely connected in so far as ideology is linked to the ongoing interpretation of action-events. I now want to turn to another cluster of issues which are focused on the question of how ideology is to be interpreted. This is not, however, a question which Ricoeur directly addresses. Rather than beginning with this question we shall have to arrive at it, via an appraisal of his theory of interpretation and the concept of the text upon which it is based. The text may be conceived, according to Ricoeur, as a work of discourse submitted to the condition of inscription. By virtue of being realized in *writing* as distinct from speech, the text acquires an autonomy with regard to its author, with regard to the social-historical conditions of its production, and with regard to the limits of ostensive reference. This does not imply, Ricoeur hastens to add, that writing should be treated as the privileged medium of language, the medium through which language betrays its most essential properties, as some contemporary thinkers would have us believe.[32] Rather, we should treat speaking and writing as complementary modes for the realization of discourse, while recognizing that the realization of discourse in writing raises issues of a special kind. In an age of electronic communication, when speech can be recorded and transcribed and when 'inscription' can assume many different forms, one may have reservations about Ricoeur's sharp juxtaposition of speaking and writing. The issue which I want to consider here, however, is somewhat different. I want to consider the claim that the text, in contrast to spoken discourse, should be seen as an autonomous entity which is severed from the social and historical conditions of its production. Whereas spoken discourse is addressed to someone in a dialogical situation, the text, claims Ricoeur, is addressed to an unknown audience and potentially to anyone who can read. But surely this is overstating the contrast. A text, or a specific instance of written discourse such as an editorial in a newspaper or an article in a journal, is not addressed to 'anyone', nor does a spoken expression have an audience of 'one' (utterances can be overheard or, if media-ted in certain ways, heard by millions). A text is written *for* an audience and the anticipation of its reception by that audience is part of the conditions of production of the text itself.[33] Only by attending to this feature of texts can we take into consideration a phenomenon which Ricoeur neglects: texts are produced, not only as works to be read, but also as *objects to be consumed*. Texts are not only written works but also potential commodities. Their status *qua* commodities is evident in the case of less prestigious forms of writing, such as the 'leisure' magazines and romantic novelettes which fill the shelves of newsagents' shops. But 'higher' forms of literature are not altogether freed from the conditions of consumption, only appearing to be so by virtue of their very conformity to these conditions.

If the foregoing remarks indicate that the autonomy of the text is limited in certain respects, they also suggest that Ricoeur's theory of interpretation must be modified in various ways. For it is the alleged autonomy of the text from the circumstances of the dialogical situation which creates the space for Ricoeur's account of the relation between explanation and understanding. 'Explanation', on this account, is explanation *within* a text that is severed from the world in every way, *within* a text that is treated as a self-enclosed entity. I share Ricoeur's opinion that such an analysis may yield valuable insights concerning the internal constitution of a text; but just as our understanding of a text must go beyond such analytical insights and seek to grasp the world which the text unfolds, so too our understanding can be nourished by an inquiry into the social-historical conditions in which and for which the text was produced. Such an inquiry would also be an explanatory concern, but the sense of 'explanation' would be quite different from that involved in most forms of 'structuralism'. For what is being explained is not the internal constitution of the text, the ways in which its constituent elements relate to one another, but rather the social-historical production of the text, that is, the ways in which the elements of a text relate to the social institutions and historical circumstances in which the text was produced. Moreover, such an inquiry would not necessarily impugn the importance of the final moment in Ricoeur's theory of interpretation. To explain a text with reference to its social-historical conditions of production is not necessarily to *reduce* it to those conditions, any more than Lévi-Strauss's analysis of the Oedipus myth could be said to *exhaust* the content of the myth. Both forms of explanation may properly be seen as integral phases of an interpretative theory which leaves room for the creative appropriation of the worlds projected by a text.

The importance of taking social-historical conditions into account may be seen particularly clearly in the interpretation of action. Ricoeur's proposals for the interpretation of action are based on the assumption that action may be treated as a text, and hence may be interpreted in the same way that one interprets texts. I have already offered various reasons for rejecting the assumption which underlies this analogical extension of the theory of interpretation. I now want to show that, in discussing the interpretation of action, Ricoeur acknowledges the importance of social-historical conditions in a way which highlights the limitations of his own theory. The interpretation of action, suggests Ricoeur, is similar to the juridical process whereby actions are imputed to agents and such imputations are regarded as defeasible in the light of excuses and defences. But the defeat of an imputation may be based, and often is based, on an appeal to the *circumstances* in which the agent was acting, as is emphasized by Hart (an author to whom Ricoeur refers);[34] and if one can appeal to the circumstances in which the agent was acting, then one cannot pretend to be treating the action as a text which is severed from its social-historical conditions of production. The most questionable aspect of Ricoeur's proposals for the interpretation of action concern the application of the structuralist model. I have criticized this aspect elsewhere[35] and shall restrict myself here to pointing out what is presupposed by the application of this model. Ricoeur argues that action may be explained in a structuralist manner by being treated as an element of a semiological system, but that such an explanation can be no more than a preliminary phase of a depth interpretation which seeks to grasp the conflicts and predicaments to which actions and social structures are a response. But how are we to grasp actions and 'social structures' – a concept, it may be said in passing, which Ricoeur employs without precision – as *responses to* conflicts and predicaments, as 'attempts to cope with' such situations, if we believe that action should be treated as a text which is *severed from* the social-historical conditions of its production or performance? The interpretation of action cannot be isolated from a reconstruction of the conditions which 'generate' an action and which, by explaining an action with reference to its social-historical conditions, enable it to be understood.[36]

Interpretation of ideology

The detour through the theory of interpretation provides us with the resources to answer the question which Ricoeur does not address, the question of how ideology is to be interpreted.[37] Ricoeur rightly stresses the link between ideology and the ongoing interpretations of action-events; but he does not directly address the question of how the ideologies constituted by such interpretations are themselves to be interpreted. In pursuing this question I shall take for granted the approach to ideology which I proposed as an alternative to Ricoeur's account. To study ideology, I suggested, is to study the ways in which meaning (or signification) serves to sustain relations of domination. Hence one cannot study ideology without studying *the relations of domination which meaning serves to sustain*. In emphasizing this point I am echoing my criticism of Ricoeur's tendency to abstract from the social-historical conditions of the production of a work. I have cast doubt on the legitimacy of this abstraction in the interpretation of action and texts; I now wish to maintain that, in the interpretation of ideology, no such abstraction can be made. For an expression is ideological only in so far as it serves to sustain relations of domination. To analyse ideology, therefore, one must analyse the social-historical conditions in which ideological expressions are produced and received, conditions which include the relations of domination which these expressions serve to sustain.

If ideology must always be studied *in situ*, it is nevertheless expressed in *forms of discourse* which may be analysed in various ways. In speaking of 'forms of discourse' I want, for the purposes which concern me here, to put aside the distinction between spoken and written discourse. It seems to me, as I indicated earlier, that this contrast is overstated by Ricoeur and that it is overshadowed by modern media of communication. Moreover, while the emergence of writing may have had important consequences for the organization of social life, I do not believe that the distinction between speaking and writing is crucial for the characterization of ideology, since the latter may be expressed in discourse which is spoken or inscribed. To say that ideology is expressed in *discourse* is to say, among other things, that it is realized in *extended linguistic constructions which display an articulated structure*. Specific methods may be employed in order to analyse these constructions with a view towards explicating their ideological features. Linguistic constructions may be studied, for example, as *narratives* which display a certain logic or 'actantial structure', to borrow a term from Greimas.[38] Such an analysis may facilitate the explication of the ideological features of discourse because ideology, in so far as it seeks to sustain relations of domination by representing them as *legitimate*, tends to assume a narrative form. Stories are told which seek to justify the exercise of power by those who possess it and which serve to reconcile others to the fact that they do not. In the films which fill our cinemas and television screens we are constantly confronted with visions of world history and images of social life, visions and images which are woven into a narrative tissue that tells us how things are and how, by implication, they ought to be. In the stories and jokes which fill much of our everyday lives we are continuously engaged in recounting the way that the world appears and in reinforcing, through laughter which profits at another's expense, the apparent order of things. To analyse the structure of these stories within which we live, and by means of which so much of our social life is carried on, is one way in which the analyst may begin to unfold the ideological features of discourse.

The use of formal methods to study the structure of discourse can never be more than a *partial contribution* to the analysis of ideology. However elaborate such methods may be, they can never abolish the need for a creative construction of meaning, that is, for an interpretative explication of what is said. In putting forward this thesis I concur with Ricoeur's forceful criticism of Lévi-Strauss and of other 'structuralist' authors. I share Ricoeur's conviction that, while the analyses of such authors may be illuminating, they cannot be regarded as exhaustive, for they presuppose without addressing a cluster of issues concerning meaning, reference and interpretation. Hence the analyses of Lévi-Strauss and others may be seen as important but preliminary phases in a depth-hermeneutical approach. It is this idea of a depth-hermeneutical approach that I wish to elaborate for the analysis of ideology. To study the structure of the discourse in which ideology is expressed may mediate the process of *interpreting ideology*, which is the process of explicating the connection between the meaning (signification) of discourse and the relations of domination which that meaning serves to sustain. As a guiding idea for this process of interpretation, I should like to take up and transform the notion of *split reference* which is imaginatively employed by Ricoeur. For Ricoeur this notion is linked, it will be recalled, to the inscription of discourse in writing: the written work is freed from the limits of ostensive reference but it is not stripped of all referential features, since the suspension of ostensive reference is the condition for the realization of a second order reference to other aspects of experience or being. I want to remove this notion from the specific connection with writing and to suggest that it may be helpful in exploring the links between discourse, ideology and power. The mobilization of meaning in order to sustain relations of domination commonly involves, I want to suggest, a splitting of the referential domain. The terms of a discourse may carry out their ideological role by explicitly referring to one thing and implicitly referring to another, by entangling these multiple referents in a way which serves to sustain relations of domination. Hence the importance of metaphor, of metonymy, of ambiguity: of creative turns of phrase which slide from one object to another or condense several referents into one. To interpret discourse *qua* ideology is to construct a meaning which unfolds these multiple referents and which shows how relations of domination are sustained by their entanglement. The interpretation of discourse *qua* ideology may thus be linked to a moment of critique. It may be conceived as an interpretation which is animated by a *critical concern*, a concern which it shares with what Ricoeur describes as the utopian tendency of the social imaginary.

Towards a critical hermeneutics

To elaborate an interpretative and critical approach to the study of ideology is to contribute to the development of a 'critical hermeneutics'. The contours of such a project are sketched by Ricoeur in his probing and provocative analyses of contemporary thinkers. Ricoeur shows that, while hermeneutics and the critique of ideology may set themselves different tasks, nevertheless they presuppose one another in specific ways. Hermeneutics presupposes a critical instance because we belong to a culture and a tradition only on condition of a certain distance from ourselves and our past, a distance which is expressed above all in the distanciation undergone by texts. The condition of distanciation turns hermeneutics towards the critique of ideology. Freed from the limits of ostensive reference, the text is capable of projecting a world, or a mode of being in the world, which can subvert the social order and disrupt our sense of ourselves. The dispossession involved in the appropriation of texts implies a critique of the illusions of the subject; hence it implies, in a way that is insufficiently grasped by Heidegger and Gadamer, the interminable project of distinguishing between the 'pre-understandings' which make us what we are, enabling us to understand ourselves and others, and the 'prejudices which constitute our self-deception and which deserve to be unmasked. If hermeneutics thus presupposes a critical instance, so too, argues Ricoeur, the critique of ideology is limited by hermeneutical conditions. For there is no position outside of history and society from which we could survey the social-historical sphere. We are part of the very world which we seek to understand; and any attempt to step out of this world – whether by a presumptuous appeal to 'science' in the manner of Althusser, or by the postulation of a 'transcendental idea' in the manner of Habermas – is likely to go astray, striving for a kind of abstraction which overlooks our condition as social-historical beings. Hence any critique of the social world and of ourselves must always be partial, fragmentary, limited by the hermeneutical character of historical understanding.

There are many aspects of these arguments which are compelling. They offer a way of drawing upon the traditions of hermeneutics and the critique of ideology while avoiding some of the shortcomings of both, thereby opening a path for the development of a critical hermeneutics. However, the epistemological problems which are raised by such a project cannot be left in this abstract state. We must confront directly the question of how a critique of ideology, and how the interpretations which facilitate such a critique, are to be justified. In response to this question, Ricoeur's writings are less than satisfying. The world projected by a text may provide a basis for criticizing reality and consciousness, but it could also be said that the latter may provide a basis for criticizing the former; and it is not clear, in the light of Ricoeur's arguments, why the direction of criticism should be one way. Moreover, *which* world is projected by a text depends upon how the text is interpreted, and texts may be interpreted in various ways. Can we take it for granted that there are evident standards – 'criteria of relative superiority which may easily be derived from the logic of subjective probability',[39] as Ricoeur blandly announces at one point – by means of which conflicts of interpretation can be arbitrated and resolved? Finally, even if we accept that our knowledge of the social-historical world is 'conditioned' by the fact that we are part of this world, it remains to be shown what kinds of knowledge we can have of this world and how such knowledge can be related, precisely and justifiably, to the conduct of critique. For the critique of ideology pursues a critical project on the basis of a *claim to know*; it differs, in this respect, from many forms of utopian thought. If the critique of ideology is based on a claim to know, then the question is, what is the status of this claim to know when the objects of knowledge include subjects who are capable of knowing?

Let me take up this question, in a brief and very schematic way,[40] by returning to my proposals for the interpretation of ideology. To interpret ideology, I proposed, is to enter into a complex methodological process which seeks to show how meaning serves to sustain relations of domination. Restricting our attention to the final phase of this process, it may be noted that an interpretation, as a construction of meaning and a formulation of what is said in discourse, raises a claim to truth which calls for recognition. An interpretation raises a claim, that is, to be acceptable or *justifiable* in some way. It seems to me that we presuppose, moreover, that an interpretation could not be justified by being *imposed*. Hence we could say that the claim to truth *would* be sustained if the interpretation *could* be justified under conditions which included the suspension of asymmetrical relations of power.[41] Such a suspension would specify some of the formal conditions under which a claim to truth could be sustained, although it would not provide the specific criteria which would have to be invoked in seeking to sustain a particular claim. These criteria could be elucidated only by attending to the procedures which are operative in different epistemic fields. Nevertheless, in the case of interpreting ideology, I wish to maintain that the criteria are governed by an overriding principle, which may be called the *principle of self-reflection*. For the interpretations generated by the depth-hermeneutical procedure are about an object domain which consists, among other things, of subjects capable of reflection; and if their claim to truth is to be sustained, then these interpretations would have to be justified – by means of whatever evidence deemed to be necessary under the formal conditions of justification – in the eyes of the subjects about whom they are made. Such interpretations would thus provide a potential basis for the *self*-criticism of the subjects whose discourse is the object of interpretation, in so far as these interpretations diverged from the accounts offered by actors in everyday life. They would also facilitate a critique of the relations of domination which meaning serves to sustain, in so far as they would illuminate these relations and call into question the everyday accounts which sustain them. The interpretation of ideology may thus be linked – without presuming a privileged path to knowledge or proposing an impossible escape from the social-historical sphere – to self-criticism and social critique. And we may agree with Ricoeur that this criticism would remain an open process, interminable so long as we are enmeshed in relations of domination and in the discourse with which such relations are sustained.

I have tried, in the course of this essay, to bring out some of the distinctive contributions of Ricoeur. I have outlined his approach to language and have shown how, on the basis of this approach, he formulates a concept of the text and a theory of interpretation. In a provocative way Ricoeur extends this theory beyond the domain of textual interpretation, emphasizing the links between different domains of inquiry and seeking to overcome some of the methodological dualisms which have plagued the philosophy of social science. While I sympathize with these concerns, I nevertheless believe that the proposed extension of the theory of interpretation falters on a number of points. Action cannot be conceived as a text, for actions do not possess the properties of the sentences with which they are described. Neither texts nor actions can be satisfactorily conceptualized in isolation from the social-historical conditions in which they are produced or performed. Hence the theory of interpretation, whether applied to texts or to other social phenomena, must take into account, in a way that Ricoeur does not, the social-historical conditions in which we produce and receive, or perform and respond to, texts, utterances and actions.

I have developed these criticisms of Ricoeur with my attention focused on a specific problem, a problem which has troubled the tradition of hermeneutics: the problem of ideology. My aim was to show that, in developing his approach to language, action and interpretation, Ricoeur also offers a novel and illuminating analysis of the phenomenon of ideology. I nevertheless found reason to criticize his analysis and to propose an alternative account which incorporates many of the features highlighted by Ricoeur. This proposal provided the basis for the constructive task of the essay: the attempt to elaborate a depth-hermeneutical approach to the study of ideology. In pursuing this task I have modified Ricoeur's theory of interpretation while preserving its essential form. I have altered the structure of the theory so as to include a phase of social analysis, while preserving its form as a depth-hermeneutical procedure. I have also redirected the theory towards an analysis of ideology and have explored some of the ways in which the interpretation of ideology may be linked to a moment of critique. In so doing I have sought to contribute to the project of critical hermeneutics, a project for which Ricoeur, with great insight and imagination, has prepared the way.

6

Narratives of National Socialism

An Analysis of the Work of Jean Pierre Faye

'Narratives', observed the French historian Mably, 'were going to change the face of nations'. If this could be said of the Huns, recounting to their compatriots the wonders they had seen on the other side of the Rhine, so too it could be said of Mably's *Observations sur l'histoire de France*, which introduced words like *'patrie'* and *'citoyen'* into the French language and helped, in the opinion of Augustin Thierry, 'to make us what we are'.[1] The commentaries of Mably and Thierry point to the profound connections between the *history* that we make and recount, on the one hand, and the *stories* that are told by historians and individuals in everyday life, on the other. While these connections have often been discussed in the philosophical literature of the English-speaking world, such discussions have tended to remain abstract; philosophers have examined the logic and language of historical explanation, but they have paid insufficient attention to the fact that hi-stories are themselves part of the social world, that they belong to and help to produce the very world which they recount. Much of the philosophical discussion has thus bypassed the specifically *political* aspect of the relation between history and narrative. How the stories told by historians and others enter into the social world, how they construct the 'semantic space' within which agents pursue their aims, how they are used as weapons in the struggle for power and scarce resources – such questions have been left to the side of the philosophical debate.

It is therefore of great interest to consider the work of the French novelist, historian, critic, Jean Pierre Faye. In the course of a career which has been concerned as much with literary production as with philosophical and political issues, Faye has developed a distinctive approach to the theory of narrative and to the relations between language, history and politics. This approach has emerged out of, and has in turn guided, his rich and illuminating study of the narratives produced by right-wing political groups in Germany during the period which preceded and accompanied the rise to power of the Nazis. These narratives of the present and the past, these calls for revolution and pleas for conservation, were not mere reflections of events which transpired on some other, more 'material' plane; they were themselves interwoven with the flow of events and helped to make possible the accession of Hitler. Only by exploring this complex field of narratives can we understand how the Nazi Party – that 'small *völkische* sect', as Hermann Rauschning was to call it – could capture the imagination of the German people and lead them into the nightmare of mass destruction. To study the narratives of National Socialism is to immerse oneself in a field where the political dimension of the relation between history and narrative cannot be ignored.

My aim in this essay is to offer a critical analysis of Faye's contribution to the theme of history and narrative.[2] I shall not discuss those parts of Faye's substantial corpus which do not bear directly on this theme,[3] nor shall I examine in detail the extensive body of research which deals with the political, economic and cultural conditions of the Weimar Republic and the Third Reich.[4] Rather, my limited aim is to use Faye's work as a basis upon which to raise some questions concerning the analysis of narrative and its relation to history and politics. I shall begin by situating Faye's approach within the context of recent Anglo-American debates about history and narrative. In the second section I shall sketch the central contours of his detailed study of right-wing political literature in inter-war Germany. The final section will provide the occasion to engage in a critical reflection on Faye's work.

I

In recent years English-speaking philosophers have given considerable attention to the question of the extent to which historical knowledge assumes a narrative form.[5] The debate is part of a long controversy, stretching back through the nineteenth century, concerning the character of the knowledge that we can have of the social-historical world. Some participants in this controversy have maintained that there are important differences between the kinds of explanation that are appropriate to the natural and the social-historical spheres, while others have argued that there is an essential continuity of concerns. The so-called 'narrativists' stand in the first of these camps; they challenge the view, put forward most trenchantly by Carl Hempel,[6] that historical explanation is merely a form, albeit implicit and seldom complete, of an explanatory model derived from the natural sciences. 'History', contends a leading narrativist, W. B. Gallie, 'is a species of the genus Story'.[7] Writing history is like writing stories: one describes a sequence of actions and experiences of a number of people, presenting them in some typical human stituation which they are engaged in changing or reacting to. As these changes and reactions accumulate, they reveal hidden aspects of the original situation and give rise to new predicaments which call for thought and action on the part of one or more of the characters. If writing history is like writing stories, so historical understanding lies in the ability to follow a story. Following a story is not merely a matter of understanding the words and sentences that compose it, but also a matter of being drawn forward by the development of a plot. The 'conclusion' of the story is the pole towards which the reader is drawn; it is rarely something that the reader can predict or deduce, but rather something that, however surprising, is 'acceptable' in the circumstances. This does not mean that historians can dispense with evidence and explanations of various kinds. But such explanations should be seen, Gallie argues, in terms of their function of 'enabling one to follow further when one's vision was becoming blurred or one's credulity taxed beyond patience'.[8]

The provocative thesis of Gallie and other narrativists has elicited a lively response. Philosophers have questioned the precise scope of the thesis and have pressed for clarification of the criteria which allegedly distinguish historical narratives from stories of fiction and fantasy. However, by focusing on the character of historical *knowledge*, this debate has neglected an issue which is of comparable interest: namely, the extent to which historical *events* are themselves embedded in narratives. Here the ambiguity of the term 'history' is thrust into full view. 'History' refers both to the sequence of events which occurred at particular times and places, and to the study of those events; and narrative should be seen, not only as a form in which the study of events can be cast, but also as a medium through which such events are produced. This productive function of narrative is what Faye calls the 'narrative effect', the *effet de récit*. The narration which he offers of the Weimar Republic

> is not simply, or strictly, that of an 'historian': it recounts the narrations which rendered possible that unrecountable object called the Hitlerian Reich. For to narrate Hitler's ascent is impossible if one wants to restrict oneself to enumerating the sequence of facts: the series of actions (or events), the series of discourses which precede or follow them, the series of movements in the relations of production and exchange – for example, the Night of the Long Knives, the speech of 13 July, the 'economic miracle' – are not parallel series which would be more or less in correlation. The speech of July belongs as well to that which *produced* the night of June, in so far as it gathers together the narratives which, in advance, had sketched out the poles of sense and action, the field of possibility and of acceptability.[9]

There are evident similarities between the *effet de récit* and what, within English-speaking philosophy, has been discussed under the rubric of 'speech-acts'. However, it must be stressed, first, that the effectiveness of individual speech-acts depends upon their location within a complex network of narratives and social-historical conditions; and second, that in many cases it is not the speech-act itself which is effective, but rather the way in which it is recounted or reported in subsequent narratives. In 1923 Hitler could brandish a revolver in a Munich beer hall and declare that the National Revolution had begun, all to little avail. Yet it was in *recounting* that incident and numerous others – the First World War, the Treaty of Versailles, the German Revolution – that the 'National Movement'[10] in general, and Hitler in particular, were to grow enormously in power.

While historical events are embedded in narratives and produced by them, narratives are not, of course, the whole of what history is. There is another dimension of history *qua* sequence of events, the 'heavy' history (*histoire lourde*) of the production and circulation of commodities, of the struggle for power and the perpetration of violence. Faye has no wish to deny or occlude this heavy history, in the manner of those thinkers who tend to absolutize the text. The task which Faye sets himself is rather to explore some of the ways in which heavy history is caught up in narratives which react back on it, producing their effects on the level of production, circulation and power. What better field could one find for such an inquiry than the Germany which extends from the Treaty of Versailles to the outbreak of the Second World War, a field which trembles with economic earthquakes and which becomes the *lieu d'expérimentation* for an insidious and sanguinary programme of recovery? What, moreover, was Marx doing in *Capital* if not exploring the interconnections between the production and circulation of commodities, on the one hand, and the production and circulation of narratives, on the other? Interconnections at several levels: at the level of the narratives of political economy, through the critique of which one may discern the developmental tendencies of the capitalist mode of production; at the level of the reports (the ac-counts, re-counts) of factory inspectors, through the analysis of which one may grasp the conditions of work in the most advanced capitalist country. And 'if', adds Marx in the preface to the first German edition,

> the German reader shrugs his shoulders at the condition of the English industrial and agricultural labourers, or in optimist fashion comforts himself with the thought that in Germany things are not nearly so bad, I must plainly tell him, '*De te fabula narratur!*' ['Of you this story is told'].[11]

The study of the interrelations of narratives and of their effects in history requires the elaboration of specific *methods* of inquiry. Various forms of narrative analysis have been worked out in recent years, following Propp's classic investigations of Russian folklore.[12] Thus A. J. Greimas – one of the most eminent of Propp's successors – has sought to elaborate a basic matrix of roles and relations which defines the permutations of narrative plot.[13] While this approach may be useful for the analysis of political discourse,[14] it is not, from the viewpoint of Faye's research, sufficiently sensitive to the ways in which narratives circulate in a field of positions which are socially and historically specific, and upon which these narratives have an effect. The field of positions constitutes an underlying structure or 'topography', in the sense of a map which represents the relations of opposition between the principal narrators and circumscribes the space of their operation. The topography is not an abstract model imposed upon the historical terrain, but rather a structure implicit in the narratives produced therein, a structure in terms of which the narrators define themselves, their friends and their enemies. It is 'a whole continent, buried beneath the ice of great, well-known sentences, [which] appears when one follows the circulation of narratives'.[15] The topography is also 'generative' in Chomsky's sense, or, more precisely, in the sense of the 'generative poetics' of Jacques Roubaud and others.[16] The field of positions is a 'deep structure' which *generates* – that is, both limits and renders possible – the kinds of narratives which appear in the historical domain. It renders possible and renders *acceptable*: this *mise en acceptation* is the outcome of a process which underlies the production and circulation of narratives. It is by studying this process and by uncovering the political topography of the time that Faye hopes to shed light on the question of how Hitler and his 'small *völkische* sect' could be 'rendered acceptable' to the German people.

Faye distinguishes three levels at which such a study must be pursued. The first level is that of a *sociology of language*. This is an empirical discipline which is concerned to grasp the chains of narration and to relate them to the social groups or classes from which they emerge. In conjunction with this empirical inquiry one must constitute a theoretical domain, a *semantics of history*. Just as Chomsky sought to elaborate a linguistic theory which would show how surface forms could be derived, via rules of transformation, from underlying syntactic structures, so too Faye wishes to move beyond the surface form of narratives and to reconstruct the formal configurations which underlie them. While these configurations contribute to the determination of meaning (*sens*), they do not do so in a strict or mechanical way; there are many rhetorical devices, such as the alliteration involved in *Blut und Boden*, which enter into the alchemy of *sens* and which must be taken into account by a semantics of history. The third and final level is properly philosophical: the development of a sociology of language and a semantics of history opens up a new sphere of knowledge which calls for a 'critique' in the sense of Kant, a *critique of narrative reason/economy*. Such a critique would seek to articulate the conditions of possibility of the knowledge that we have of history, that is, would seek to show that

> this operation of knowledge is only possible on, and as an extension of, the *fundamental narrative process* of History making itself, and this fundamental narrative process is so closely linked to the very production of the commodity language that only a *generalized economics* could take account of the two-sided process of reality (the process pertaining both to commodities and to language).[17]

It is on the terrain of inter-war Germany, a terrain traversed by countless narratives and severely shaken by the Great Depression, that Faye undertakes this generalized economics of history.

II

Faye pursues his study of inter-war Germany under the title of 'totalitarian languages'. The latter expression has a specific sense which is determined by the genesis and circulation of the term 'totalitarian', a term which first appeared in the utterances of Mussolini and Gentile and which was transmitted into German through the writings of Carl Schmitt and his associates. Thus Faye distances himself from what he regards as the arbitrary redefinitions of 'totalitarianism' offered by Hannah Arendt or Nicos Poulantzas;[18] for Faye, by contrast,

> we designate as 'totalitarian languages' the chains of discourse where the Italian epithet 'totalitario' and the syntagm *Stato totalitario* are introduced (explicit criterion). In a correlative way, and by the effect of 'translation', we also include those chains in German which develop the 'formula' of the *totale Staat*.[19]

If the 'formula' of the *totale Staat* provides one of the guiding threads for Faye's study, an 'antithesis' provides the other: the antithesis, expressed in differing ways by Gentile and Rocco, of the *rivoluzione conservatrice*. The formula and the antithesis intersect in complex ways in the writings of Italian politicians, philosophers and jurists such as Guido Bortolotto, whose *Fascismo e Nazione* was translated into German and appeared in Germany in 1932, ten years after its initial publication. In the passage from Italian to German these key expressions undergo complex transformations. They are used to form new compounds and they are integrated into narratives which belong to a specific field of discourse. By attending to these transformations, to the circulation and multiple intersection of the formula and the antithesis, Faye hopes to bring out the polarities which underlie this field of discourse.

Whereas the formula *Stato totalitario* introduces us to the *centre* of the Italian political sphere, its German equivalent appears initially as the *periphery* of the German National Movement. That is, *Stato totalitario* is emitted by the Fascists *after* they are in a position of political power. It is on 22 June 1925, in a speech concerned to cover up the assassination of the Social-Democratic leader Matteotti, that Mussolini first employs the epithet '*totalitaria*': '*nostra feroce volontà totalitaria*', he warns, 'will be pursued with even greater strength'.[20] Five days after this speech, Gentile contrasted Mussolini's conception of the state to the fragmented character of the liberal state and the free trade unions. The German version of the formula, on the other hand, circulates for many years on the periphery of the political sphere, passing from one point to another and cutting across the path of the antithesis, before being emitted, in Hitler's speech at Leipzig on 2 October 1933, by the central power itself. Faye's initial task is to retrace the paths of the formula and the antithesis across the periphery of the political sphere and thereby to uncover the topography which underlies the narratives in which they appear. This topography, he endeavours to show, consists of two principal axes: a horizontal or 'real' axis which represents a polarity between the 'Young Conservatives' (*jungkonservativ Bewegung*) and the 'National Revolutionaries' (*nationalrevolutionär Bewegung*); and a vertical or 'imaginary' axis which juxtaposes the Youth Movement (*Bündische Jugend*) and the 'racist', or *völkische* sects. Between these basic polarities are a number of intermediate groups which occupy specific positions on the topography. The various relations and oppositions may be illustrated as in figure 10.

The *jungkonservativ Bewegung* comprises a whole network of clubs and organizations which flourished during the Weimar Republic. Its principal luminary was Moeller van den Bruck, author of *Das dritte Reich* and one of the founders, in 1919, of the *Juni-Klub*. Opposed to the signing of the Treaty of Versailles on

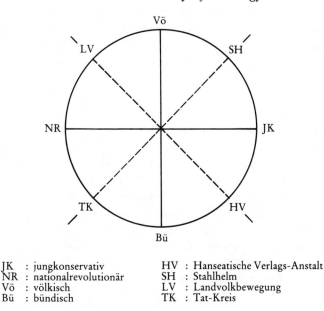

JK : jungkonservativ
NR : nationalrevolutionär
Vö : völkisch
Bü : bündisch

HV : Hanseatische Verlags-Anstalt
SH : Stahlhelm
LV : Landvolkbewegung
TK : Tat-Kreis

Figure 10: Topography of the National Movement[21]

28 June 1919, the members of the *Juni-Klub* met regularly at their headquarters in Berlin, discussing their ideas, entertaining guest speakers – including a relatively obscure Adolf Hitler, described by Moeller as a 'primitive proletarian' – and diffusing their opinions by means of a weekly journal, *Gewissen* ('Consciousness'). On 31 March 1920, following the abortive Kapp *Putsch* in Berlin led by a group of disgruntled officers, a special issue of *Gewissen* appeared with the title 'The Victory of the Revolution'. The issue opens with an article by Moeller in which he boldly declares, 'We want to win the Revolution'. Essays follow by well-known *porte-parole* of the right: Martin Spahn, Eduard Stadtler, Heinrich von Gleichen. But most remarkably, the issue contains an article by Fritz Weth, described by some as a 'Bolshevik', by others as the 'worker' of the *Juni-Klub*. Under the title of 'Object of Reflection for Radicals', Weth writes of the general strike which followed the Kapp *Putsch*. The workers, he explains, were unhappy with the results of the strike, for the simple reason that their Marxist leaders preached only *goals* and not *steps*. As for what these steps might be, the narrative of Weth passes via some interesting detours. The

events of March 1920 show us the necessity of finding a 'German form' for the idea of socialism, that is, a national economy free from foreign influence and a political system opposed to 'social democracy', which is but a western, reactionary doctrine. Thus the 'Counter-Revolution of 1920' had not been in vain, for it too had denounced social democracy; its lessons must be learned and pushed further until, concludes Weth, we have won the Revolution. Thus Weth ends up at the point from which Moeller departs, but via a path which is the reverse of Moeller's and which reflects their specific positions in the narrative field. For Weth the 'detour' is the Counter-Revolution of March 1920; for Moeller, on the other hand, the 'detour' is the Revolution of November 1918, in the wake of which it will be possible 'to tame the movement of the Revolution in a conservative way'. The article of Fritz Weth – this man of the 'far left' in this club of the 'far right' – thus serves to transform the Kapp *Putsch* and its collapse into a step on the way towards 'the Revolution'. Here we see, Faye remarks,

> that what is positive and what is negative, what is an aim and what is a detour, are rigorously permutated between the language of Moeller and that of Weth. In the middle of these permutations, however, one element remains identical: 'to win the revolution'. Which revolution? The revolution is defined precisely, in the sense that both understand, by this symmetrical inversion of 'detours', this splitting of the *Umweg*.[22]

The *jungkonservativ Bewegung* entered a period of crisis following the death of Moeller in 1925. The *Juni-Klub* was succeeded by the *Herrenklub*, founded by Heinrich von Gleichen, and by its 'youthful' affiliation, the *Jungkonservativ-Klub*. In 1928 a new weekly appeared, *Der Ring*, directed by von Gleichen. Between 1928 and 1932 the circle of *Der Ring* was reduced to one pole within the National Movement: in face of von Gleichen's group, which defines itself as *jungkonservativ*, one hears the voice of those who designate their movement as *nationalrevolutionär*.

In the topography of the Weimar Republic, the *nationalrevolutionär Bewegung* lies on the 'left' of the 'far right'. Its key figure is Ernst Jünger, director of a journal which emerged in 1926–7 under the title of *Der Vormarsch* ('March Ahead'). Whereas Moeller wanted to tame the Revolution in a conservative way, Jünger wants to discover within revolution a new content of tradition. Just how this content might differ from the ideas of the Young Conservatives is brought out well by the narrative of Hermann Ehrhardt in the collaborative volume, *Wir Klagen an!* ('We Accuse!'), published by *Vormarsch Verlag* in 1928. The famous Captain Ehrhardt, leader of the brigade that spearheaded the Kapp *Putsch*, recounts the course of his career, how he came to hate the 'cowardice and materialism' of the bourgeoisie who were prepared to betray their nation, how he was above all a nationalist but was convinced that the German people would go through new revolutionary times. At that point the Captain will not align himself with the class doomed to decline, for the future of Germany will be built on the shoulders of other classes, wherein there still subsists, observes Ehrhardt, 'the will to fight, racial health and the feeling of common belonging'.[23] Thus Captain Ehrhardt, who had resisted the 'red upheaval' of 1918–19 and colluded in the Kapp *Putsch*, now traverses the class struggle in declaring himself nationalist and revolutionary at once. This distinctive *mélange* of nationalism and revolutionary fervour is shared by a cluster of groups which lie on the left-hand fringe of the *nationalrevolutionär Bewegung*, the so-called 'National-Bolshevik' groups. Emerging from Hamburg in the aftermath of 1918–19, National Bolshevism was initially propelled along the trajectories of Karl Radek and Ernst Niekisch. Resigning from the Bavarian SPD in 1919, Niekisch moved to Berlin and founded a journal entitled *Widerstand* ('Resistance'). Its aim was to struggle against the reparations demanded by the victorious powers of the First World War, against *Weltkapitalismus*; it thus became a platform of opposition to all 'western-oriented' politics and expressed a turn to the East, an *Ostorientierung*. The influence of the *Widerstand-Kreis* spread in different directions, towards the Youth Movement and towards the *völkische* sects, as well as towards the *nationalrevolutionär Bewegung* of Jünger. The importance of National Bolshevism became particularly clear in the spring of 1930, when Otto Strasser split with Hitler and set up a National-Bolshevik group, while newspaper headlines dramatically announced that 'The Socialists leave the NSDAP'. Strasser thus abandoned to Hitler the very links with the workers' movement that he, Strasser, had spent so many years trying to forge.

The term '*völkisch*' can be found throughout the writings of Young Conservatives and National Revolutionaries, but it occurs with most frequency in a particular zone of the narrative field, a zone occupied by the *Deutsch-völkische Freiheitspartei*. '*Völkisch*' is a dangerously ambiguous term: it is not merely the adjectival form of *Volk* ('people'). Originally '*völkisch*' was used as a German translation for '*national*', but it gradually became a word of combat which accentuated racial opposition against Jews. It was thus integrated into a tradition of anti-Semitism which reached back into the nineteenth century. Wilhelm Marr and Theodor Fritz were among the most vociferous anti-Semites of the 1870s and 1880s, and by 1890 there were two established parties founded under the sign of anti-Semitism. While the strength of these parties declined at the turn of the century, by 1920 the anti-Semitic movement had picked up fresh momentum in the form of the *völkische* parties. The crucial transformation underlying these developments is that '*völkisch*' becomes the positive expression for the negative term 'anti-Semite'. As Liebermann von Sonnenberg declared with a chilling sense of foresight in 1881: it is no good being 'purely anti-Semitic' for one must struggle to unify all Germans in a genuine *Volksgemeinschaft* ('Community of people/race'). The underlying transformation is summed up well by Faye:

> Between the language of the Anti-Semitic Parties of the 1880s and that of the Nazi Party, a tissue of narrative discourse is interposed, beginning at the turn of the century, which prepares to render Nazi discourse acceptable by replacing the wholly 'negative' word *anti-semitisch* with the word which is 'positive' *par excellence* in the language of German nationalism: *völkisch*.[24]

This transformation was mediated by a number of key narrators and organizations, such as the notorious *Thule-Gesellschaft* of Munich. Among the associates of the latter was Dietrich Eckart, whose racist tract of 1918, *Auf gut' Deutsch* ('In good German'), was distributed in the streets of Munich by the thousands. Eckart and Hitler met on many occasions in the early 1920s, Eckart assuming a professorial role towards this untutored anti-Semite and introducing him to eminent exponents of the cause, such as Houston Stewart Chamberlain.

The transformation of the *völkisch* narration is closely linked to the language of the Youth Movement, with which it stands in a relation of tension. The German Youth Movement has an organizational beginning: on 4 November 1901, in a suburb of Berlin, Karl Fischer and nine friends founded an association called *Wandervogel, Ausschuss für Schülerfahrten* ('Migrating Birds, Association for Student Excursions'). This association crystallized a movement which had existed for several years and which, in the years that followed, underwent numerous divisions and reorientations. One such reorientation was stimulated by the translation into German of *The Confession of the Kibbo Kift*, a mystical treatise by the eccentric English scout chief John Hargrave. In his introductory remarks F. L. Habbel – a leading figure in that branch of the Youth Movement known as the *Pfadfinderbund* – stresses that Kibbo Kift is more than a scout group for boys: it is a *Bund* of men who have exchanged a dead civilization for the spirit of the woods and, fortified by that spirit, have grasped a sense of their own direction. This reorientation is pursued by Martin Voelkel, a young pastor from Berlin who, between 1922 and 1926, became the new sign of unity within the Youth Movement. He writes in the journal *Der Weisse Ritter* ('The White Knight') of how the old *Bünde* are going to give way to something new, to *Stammescharen* ('tribal troops') which correspond to the old Germanic tribes rooted in their soil, 'united under the banner of the one Reich'.[25] What Germany needs, opines Voelkel the minister, is no longer a profession of faith but a regime of authority and service. This new language is far from the early conceptions of the *Wandervogel*; the image of the itinerant schoolboy has been replaced by the rigorous hierarchy of a would-be knighthood. During the late 1920s a number of fringe groups split away from the unifying centre of the Youth Movement and accentuated their links with political parties and positions. Faye traces the processes by which some of these groups began to gravitate, both in ideas and in membership, towards the Nazi Party. *Hitler-Jugend* grew rapidly between 1931 and 1933, from 20,000 to 107,000 members; in early 1933 major segments of the Youth Movement openly aligned themselves with the Nazis. This imminent convergence was clearly seen in 1931 by a Dr Georg Holthausen, alias Ernst Forsthoff. Writing in the Young-Conservative journal *Der Ring* on the National-Revolutionary theme of *totale Mobilmachung* ('Total Mobilization'), Forsthoff identifies the National-Socialist Party as the natural outcome of the *bündische* movement. This text, remarks Faye, is a veritable palimpsest of the narrative field:

At the intersection of the paths which lead to these diverse poles, what, in Forsthoff's terms, emerges 'above all is the National-Socialist Party' – that which will realize both the *Dritte Reich* dreamed of by Moeller and his Young-Conservative followers and the *totale Mobilmachung* described by Jünger and expected by the National-Revolutionaries; both the model of the *völkische Staat* constituted in the name of the German 'Volkstum', and the final trumpet-call of the *bündische* movement and its *Volksgemeinschaft*.[26]

The two principal axes and four poles of the topography must be supplemented by a pair of oppositions relating groups which are situated in specific classes or institutions. One such group is the *Hanseatische Verlags-Anstalt* of Hamburg, a publishing company founded in 1920 by the National Union of Business Employees. The Hanseatic Press was the vehicle through which some of the canonical texts of Italian Fascism passed into German; it also published the work of Carl Schmitt, Ernst Forsthoff, Gerhard Günther and others, thus becoming the *lieu* where the language of the *totale Staat* was constituted. In opposition to the Hanseatic Press and its circle, confronting it in the way that the country confronts the city, was the *Landvolkbewegung*, the 'Peasant Movement'. Faye explores the contours of this Movement through the writings of Ernst von Salomon, editor of the journal *Das Landvolk* and author of the novel *Die Stadt*. The second supplementary opposition lies along a paramilitary axis: on the one hand, the *Stahlhelm* ('Steel Helmets'), founded soon after the armistice and numbering a million members by the late 1920s; on the other hand, a small group of individuals who published the journal *Die Tat* ('Action'), which greatly increased its circulation in the early 1930s and exercised a considerable influence by virtue of its association with General Kurt von Schleicher. In April 1934 – one year after the Nazis' final victory at the polls, three months before the Night of the Long Knives – *Die Tat* published an article by Ernst Rudolf Huber on *Die Totalität des völkischen Staates*. This text is the last explicit plea for a *totale Staat* which was pronounced in the Third Reich. It seeks to rescue the concept of *totale Staat* from its 'latin' origins and to defend it as an accurate designation of the National-Socialist State. Huber recounts the history of the relations between state and society, from the absolutist state of the Middle Ages through the 'neutral state' of liberalism to the *faschistische Totalität* and the *totale völkische Staat* of today. It is the distinction between the latter two forms that is important on Huber's account. Whereas the *faschistische Totalität* annihilates political parties to the advantage of a dictatorship from above, the *totale völkische Staat* draws on the vital forces of the people and discovers a political unity therein. So Huber seeks 'to "save" the austere ideological concept of *totale Staat* by the mythological magic of the word *"völkisch"*',[27] just as Forsthoff had tried to show, several years before, that the passage from *totale Mobilmachung* to the National-Socialist movement was mediated by the *bündische* theme. The imaginary axis thus plays a crucial role in transmitting the formula of the *totale Staat* into the narrative field in which it resonates, helping to create the conditions for Hitler's usurpation of total power.

Hitherto we have explored the topography of the National Movement without considering how this domain relates to the overall political space of the Weimar Republic. In the autumn of 1932, during an evening organized by the *Gesellschaft für deutsches Schrifttum* ('Society for German Literature'), a speaker proposed to abandon the bourgeois schema based on the distinction between 'right' and 'left' and to represent the political parties and currents in the form of a *Hufeisengestalt*, a 'horseshoe'. This proposal, embedded in the narrative of an observer, is taken up by Faye and used to extend his reconstruction of the topography (figure 11). The curved figure of the topography passes through all of the major parties of the Weimar Republic, from the far left KPD through the Catholic *Zentrum* to the NSDAP on the far right. However, the curved figure is bypassed by a strange mode of linguistic generation, a sort of 'semantic oscillator' – to alter the metaphor – which lies between the two poles without passing through the centre. This space 'in between' is the zone where 'National Bolshevism' and 'National Communism' confront one another, coming together and at the same time sustaining a relation of tension, constituting an 'ideological spark-gap' (*éclateur idéologique*) which disrupts the language of the established parties and redirects energy in unexpected ways. The narrative of Richard Scheringer offers a vivid illustration of this process. On 23 September 1930 Scheringer was accused of spreading National-Socialist

Figure 11: *Horseshoe of parties*[28]

KPD	: Kommunistische Partei Deutschlands
SPD	: Sozialdemokratische Partei Deutschlands
DDP	: Deutsche Demokratische Partei
Z	: Zentrum
DVP	: Deutsche Volkspartei
DNVP	: Deutschnationale Volkspartei
USPD	: Unabhängige Sozialdemokratische Partei Deutschlands (independent socialists: fusion with KPD)
EX	: Expressionismus
KPO	: Kommunistische Partei Opposition
AAK	: Aufbruch Arbeitskreis ('National Kommunismus')

vö, DVFP	: völkisch, Deutschvölkische Freiheitspartei
Bü	: bündisch, Bündische Jugend
JK	: jungkonservativ (Jungkonservative Klub)
NR	: nationalrevolutionär
NB	: nationalbolschewik
HV (DHV)	: Hanseatische Verlags-Anstalt (Deutschnationaler Handlungsgehilfen Verband)
SH	: Stahlhelm
LV	: Landvolkbewegung
TK	: Tat-Kreis
NSDAP	: Nationalsozialistische Deutsche Arbeiter-partei (Nazi Party)

propaganda in the army; on 18 March 1931 he announced his shift from the NSDAP to the KPD and formed a new group around the journal *Aufbruch* ('Break through'). What is important is the *way* that Scheringer announces his passage across the space between the two poles of the horseshoe. The aims of German revolutionary youth presuppose, he explains, the elimination of the capitalist system and the rejection of the terms dictated to Germany by foreign powers, whether in the form of the Treaty of Versailles or the Young Plan. That is why he had chosen to become an officer in

1924: for him, the *Reichswehr* was merely the core of the future army of liberation. Since then the KPD has declared itself to be committed to the revolutionary defence of the homeland. Hence Scheringer wants to distance himself definitively from 'Hitler and pacifism' in order to dedicate himself, alongside the 'proletariat in arms', to 'national and social liberation'.[29] In seeking to discredit the Nazis in favour of the far left, in declaring that Nazism is too 'pacifist' to realize the aim of national and social liberation, this remarkable tale works to the benefit of the very pole that Scheringer wishes to distance himself from. For not only does it affirm that the aim of national and social liberation is shared by the far left and the far right, but it also presents Hitler as a *moderate*, opposed to the excessive use of violence. 'Whence the double operation: on the one hand, the *enlargement of the field of acceptability*, on the other hand, the *return-effect* in favour of the focal point of the national-social field thus enlarged, that is, in favour of the National-Socialists properly speaking.'[30]

The extraordinary effect which presents Hitler as a 'moderate' in the political field is also produced by the narrative of Hermann Rauschning. Published in Switzerland in 1938, Rauschning's *Die Revolution des Nihilismus* describes the dynamic of the Third Reich from the viewpoint of a Young Conservative. From this viewpoint, National Socialism blurs into National Bolshevism, appearing to be more revolutionary than national. In order to counter this slide to the left, Rauschning urges a shift towards the conservative doctrines of Edgar Jung. For the great strength of the National-Socialist movement is that its leader always presented himself as the only *Faktor der Mässigung*, the only 'factor of moderation'. That is, Hitler's tactical skill stems above all from his *position* as an intermediate element capable of taking hold of the diametrically opposed languages of 'total Revolution' and 'consolidating Restoration'. So much was seen with exceptional perspicacity by Rauschning. But not only does Rauschning's narrative suffer from the optical illusion produced by its own location in the topography, it also underplays, according to Faye, the importance of the axis that provided the *mode d'entrée* of Hitler:

[Hitler's] privileged position in the space of the National Movement is not due – contrary to what Rauschning tirelessly repeats – to the fact that he appears as the man of the total Revolution proceeding under the mask of the Restoration, but rather to the fact that he intervened in the middle of this *konservativ-revolutionär* axis while his eyes were on a completely different axis of vision: that which could be called . . . *völkisch-bündisch*.[31]

It was because the imaginary axis provided the principal orientation for Hitler and his 'small *völkische* sect' that he was able to move so effortlessly on the conservative-revolutionary axis, appeasing the proponents of political views that were diametrically opposed. In this process the conservative-revolutionary axis was itself transformed, so that conservatism became identical with the *völkische* preservation of the primitive elements of race and revolution was presented as the insurrection of young people, many of whom were, in the early 1930s, unemployed. Thus Hitler could declare without paradox, before an assembly of youth leaders in 1936, that 'I am the most conservative revolutionary in the world'.[32] Without paradox, because the very signs of the political relation were displaced by the vertical axis and projected into the imaginary.

The unique position of the Nazi Party can also be discerned through the narratives of its own members. In *Mein Kampf* Hitler recounts his fervent anti-Semitism, nurtured by his days as a down and out in Vienna; his role in the formation of the *Nationalsozialistische Deutsche Arbeiterpartei*, which he succeeded in building around a fundamentally *völkische* interest; his commitment to nationalism and socialism, where the latter is understood in terms of a 'community of men which is linked by blood, united by one language, subsumed to a common destiny'.[33] While Hitler entered the political arena via the *völkische* pole and later addressed himself to the *bündische* youth, nevertheless the campaign on the National-Revolutionary left led by Goebbels, and the alliance with the Young-Conservative right and heavy industry, were vital stages in the growth of the National-Socialist movement. In *Kampf um Berlin* Goebbels recounts his struggle to turn the Nazi Party into a mass movement by means of a 'new language' which would appeal to the 'man in the street'. A language which disavows an explicitly *völkische* reference, and yet which succeeds in reconciling the revolutionary character of the movement with an apology for conservative authority only by invoking a 'poison' which has allegedly infected the masses, namely the poison of the 'Jewish press'. 'Nothing shows more clearly', remarks Faye in a similar context, 'how speech is inscribed in an oriented space of play. How ideo-logy is written on the surface of history by an ideo-*graphy*: an underlying *cartography*.'[34] Equally vital for the growth of the movement was the alliance, stimulated by the opposition to the Young Plan, with Alfred Hugenberg, who transmitted the language of the Nazis through his vast network of newspapers and who helped to secure much needed revenue from conservative industrialists and financiers. Following the Nazi successes in the polls of September 1930 and April 1932, Hitler entered into a complex political battle on a terrain dominated by the conflicting signs of TK (Schleicher and the *Tat-Kreis*) and JK (Papen, Jung and the *jungkonservativ Bewegung*). When the initial stages of this battle were over and Hitler was appointed Chancellor on 30 January 1933, it was as though these conflicting signs were eclipsed and the forces around the sign SH (*Stahlhelm*) emerged as victor. The key steps in Hitler's subsequent march to total power are well known: the burning of the *Reichstag* on 27 February 1933, followed by the suppression of civil liberties and the unleashing of brutal violence against left-wing organizations; the passage of the Enabling Act on 23 March which conferred substantial new powers on the government; the Night of the Long Knives on 30 June 1934 when remaining sources of opposition – including Schleicher and Jung – were purged. On 13 July Hitler explained this purge to the *Reichstag* with words that clearly echoed the *feroce volontà totalitaria* of Mussolini: 'at that moment recounted Hitler, 'I was responsible for the destiny of the German people, and so I became the supreme judge (*Oberster Gerichtsherr*)'.[35]

Occurring in the context of a severe economic depression, Hitler's rise to power was also conditioned by the narratives of economic 'experts' and their competing programmes of recovery. The topography of this narrative field overlaps to some extent with the topography explored so far. Thus the programmes of Günther Gereke and Wilhelm Lautenbach – 'German Keynesians' who advocated the creation of jobs through the use of work vouchers (*Arbeitswechsel*) – entered the political arena under the sign TK. However, it is illuminating to trace the displacements effected by one of the principal opponents of such programmes, Hjalmar Schacht. In his *Grundsätze deutscher Wirtschaftspolitik* ('Principles of German Political Economy'), published in 1932, Schacht attacked the policy of large public works which yield no immediate profit and immobilize capital; instead he urged, as a solution to the problem of unemployment, a return to the countryside and the home and a loosening of the relation between salary and labour time. Schacht was appointed President of the *Reichsbank* in March 1933 and began, two months later, to implement a programme which contravened his own principles. The programme sought to stimulate production by means of a new system of credit, the so-called 'Mefo-bills' (*Mefowechsel*) which were underwritten by the *Reichsbank* and repayable within five years. At the same time a secret society was established, the *Metallurgische Forschungsgesellschaft* ('Society for Metallurgical Research'), the principal function of which was to issue Mefo-bills to the four major armament firms. Yet while Schacht was under-*writing* this economy of armament and war, he continued to *speak* in accordance with his earlier principles and to urge the restriction of consumption by saving. 'The distinctive efficacy of the Schacht experiment', observes Faye,

> was achieved through this splitting of language and by means of the displacement effected, at the same time and in the inverse direction, of what was at stake. In a shrill voice it invokes suspicion towards the so-called creation of work – and it begins to underwrite the Mefo-bills. It calls for saving – and it initiates enormous expenditures without 'capital'.[36]

The economic programmes of Gereke, Lautenbach and others were thereby displaced, articulated on to other premises and related to quite different aims. The 'economic miracle' of Schacht was above all the result of this complex displacement of economic discourse, which enabled unemployment to be reduced while consumption was controlled, and which enabled rearmament to take place under the guise of social welfare. The narratives of economic experts were thus translated, via the 'Schacht experiment', into a heavy history of production which culminated in total war.

III

At this point I shall terminate my presentation of Faye's study – a presentation which, in view of the scope and detail of that study, is unavoidably superficial – in order to initiate a critical reflection on his work. My critical remarks will be primarily methodological and philosophical in character; while I shall occasionally make reference to other research on the Weimar Republic and the Third Reich, I shall do so only in so far as it sheds light on the theoretical issues raised by Faye. Three themes will form the focal points of my reflection: the method of analysis, the concept of acceptability, and the critique of narrative reason.

1   The method of analysis

I believe that Faye's work represents a very fruitful attempt to elaborate a method for analysing language as a socially and historically situated phenomenon. While this method bears some affinity to the 'structuralist' approaches worked out by other French authors in the 1960s and early 1970s, nevertheless Faye is sharply critical of the tendency of such authors to employ rigid categories of analysis and to study texts in isolation from the social conditions of their production. Faye regards his method, not so much as a form of 'structuralism', but as a kind of 'transformationism', closer to Chomsky than to Saussure. Like Chomsky, he seeks to discern a structure which underlies the surface form of discourse and which is related to the latter by rules of transformation. But this underlying structure is not a *syntactic* structure; rather, it is a series of *positions*, comparable to what Jacques Roubaud, developing an hypothesis of Halle and Keyser, regards as the figures of a prosody.[37] The series of positions is related to the surface form of discourse like a stressed metre is related to the poetic verse. Moreover, the series of positions is not fixed but is perpetually changing, perpetually undergoing displacements as if it were a *prosodie oscillante*. 'So in addition to the basic topological grammar which governs the *relations of position* of the messengers or *actants*', explains Faye, 'there is a transformational history in which the *changes of position* take place in effective time (and not merely in the abstract successions which characterise the transformations of syntax).'[38]

While the fruitfulness of these methodological proposals is amply demonstrated by Faye's study of 'totalitarian languages', nevertheless it seems to me that the proposals are limited and imprecise in several respects. In the first place, Faye's distance from the assumptions of 'structuralism' is more apparent than real, since his procedure for constructing the topography is based on the Saussurian idea that the value of a sign is determined by the system of which it is part and by the relations of opposition and proximity which obtain therein.[39] This procedure results in a set of oppositions which seems to be somewhat arbitrary, invoking criteria which are hardly justified by the texts alone. Precisely why, for example, is the sign 'HV' juxtaposed to 'LV' and situated so far from 'Vö', given that 'HV' and 'LV' are conjoined in the narrative of *Der Ring* and that *völkische* themes are central to the narratives marked by 'HV'? Why should the distinction between city and country be invoked as decisive in this case, when there are so many other respects in which 'HV' and 'LV' converge? I do not believe that Faye provides a satisfactory response to such questions, nor does he present a sustained defence of the oppositional procedure which he inherits from Saussure and which seems to force the material into a small number of over-simplified moulds. The second difficulty concerns the generative and transformational aspects of Faye's methodology. The series of positions which constitute the underlying structure are supposed to generate the surface forms of discourse and are themselves susceptible to transformation; the difficulty is that Faye says very little about just how these processes of generation and transformation occur and what form they assume. Sometimes he speaks abstractly of the 'mapping rules' which relate deep structure to surface, but seldom does he provide an explicit formulation of such a rule and a cogent demonstration of its use. It seems to me that Faye may be expecting too much from the theoretical approach of Chomsky, that he may be imposing on social-historical processes a series of concepts that have their proper application elsewhere.[40] The final methodological issue to which I want to call attention has to do with the topographical orientation of Faye's work. This orientation is both the major strength of his methodology and a major limitation: the major strength, because it displays the narrative field as an *oriented* domain in which relations of force underpin the texts and enter into the constitution of *sens*; a major limitation, because it overrides any concern with the *internal* structure of the particular texts that make up the narrative field. For Faye it is the series of positions discerned *through* the texts, rather than the relations constituted *within* the text, that provides the object of structural analysis. It is my opinion, however, that the latter relations, no less than the former positions, must be taken into account. A concern with the narrative field does not preclude an analysis of the permutations of narrative plot. It may be that Faye's reaction against the formalism of certain methods of textual analysis has blinded him to their possible achievements.[41]

2 The concept of acceptability

The whole of Faye's analysis is ultimately concerned with the question of how the language and action of Hitler and the Nazi Party were rendered *acceptable* to the German people: this, he repeatedly declares, is *la question primitive*. What were the processes which rendered 'acceptable' the language of this 'small *völkische* sect', which rendered 'acceptable' a certain solution to the economic crisis, which rendered 'acceptable' a final solution involving war and savage extermination? Without doubt these are questions of the utmost importance for any attempt to understand the interplay of language and history. It seems to me, however, that Faye's *way* of posing these questions, his use of an *undifferentiated* concept of 'acceptability', tends to obscure a number of crucial issues. Let me raise these issues by asking two further questions: (1) *to whom* was the language and action of Hitler and the Nazis rendered acceptable? (2) *why*, and in precisely *what sense*, was it accepted? As regards (1), it must be said that Faye is remarkably vague. He speaks loosely of 'the German nation', of 'the German people', of *'un très grand nombre'*; but nowhere does he analyse in detail the social composition and scope of those who adhered to the doctrines of Hitler and his associates. This *lacuna* is important, for it has been argued by some historians of the Weimar Republic that the right-wing political literature of that period did little more than preach to the converted.[42] Much of this literature had a small circulation and was read primarily by party activists. In the case of the NSDAP, these activists came almost exclusively from the bourgeoisie or the old *Mittlestand*, scarcely ever from the working class. Moreover, the electoral evidence suggests that, in spite of active propaganda campaigns and access to the popular press through Hitler's alliance with Hugenberg, the Nazis had only limited success in converting supporters of the SPD and KPD to their cause. The number of voters supporting the SPD and KPD *together* increased by 700,000 between 1928 and 1930 and then remained constant at just over 13 million until the last free elections in 1932.[43] Of the 13.4 million votes cast for Hitler in April 1932, and of the 13.7 million cast for the NSDAP in July 1932, several million probably came from wage-earners and members of their families; but among those who were actually employed, it seems likely that many were engaged in small businesses or agriculture, living in small towns or rural areas of the Protestant provinces. In view of such considerations, which indicate that support for Hitler and the NSDAP was selective in terms of class, creed and other factors, Faye would be well advised to exercise more caution when he speaks of those to whom Nazi discourse was 'rendered acceptable'.

The fact remains that over 13 million Germans did vote for Hitler and the NSDAP in 1932: why, and in precisely what sense, was the language and action of the Nazis 'accepted' by these people? Faye is aware, of course, that the factors which led to the victory of the Nazis are extremely complex. He has no pretension of offering a comprehensive explanation, but he is convinced that no such explanation would suffice without an examination of the ways in which key reference points, such as the Treaty of Versailles and the Great Depression, were recounted in the narratives of political groups and coupled with themes transmitted from the past. I have no doubt that Faye's conviction is sound and that his examination is highly illuminating. Nevertheless, one may justly wonder whether Faye has given sufficient attention to the institutional and structural conditions which accompanied the Nazis' rise to power and which concerned directly the latter's 'acceptability'. While the NSDAP drew votes from wage-earners and the unemployed, it was above all a party of property-owners and salary-earners, a consideration which suggests that the articulation of *class interests* may have been more important than Faye's analysis seems to assume.[44] Moreover, the extent to which the people who voted for Hitler and the NSDAP were committed to the more doctrinaire aspects of Nazi ideology, to the *bündische* and *völkische* themes, is very much open to question. The *membership* of the NSDAP lagged far behind the number of votes it received in the elections of 1930 and 1932, and it seems likely that many votes were cast as an expression of despair with regard to the existing system of political parties rather than as a sign of positive support for the NSDAP. The 'acceptability' of a political language, like the 'legitimacy' of a political system, admits of degrees; Faye's discussion of the former concept, which remains abstract and unrelated to social conditions, fails to take this into account.

3 The critique of narrative reason

Let me now move to a more philosophical level of reflection and address myself to the general project announced by Faye's work, the project of a critique of narrative reason/economy. Narrative must be seen, not only as a form in which historical knowledge is expressed, but also as a medium through which history *qua* sequence of events is produced: this basic insight is pursued by Faye in an original and exemplary way. The narratives of historians, political commentators, economic experts and others both recount the course of events and react back on it, and it is above all this *effet de récit* which must be grasped. In precisely what sense, however, are all of these varied forms of language to be regarded as so many species of the genus 'narrative'? What exactly is a narrative on Faye's account and why does he regard it, as he appears to do, as the fundamental form of language, history and knowledge? 'Narration', remarks Faye, 'is language itself, at least language *en acte* and reporting (*rapportant*) its object.'[45] The key term here is *rapporter*: to report, to refer, to relate. To narrate is to bring language in relation to an object or event which it reports or to which it refers. Narration is thus the condition of possibility of historical knowledge and of history *en acte*, of the history which recounts what occurred and of the history which is embedded in, and engendered by, its own narration. One could even say, it seems, that narration is the condition of possibility of knowledge as such, for human beings can know only that which they narrate. It is evident that this notion of narration is very broad indeed, that it is virtually co-extensive with language itself, in so far as the expressions of a language refer to something. This broad notion should be distinguished, I think, from a narrower sense of 'narration' and of the related concept of narrative. According to the latter sense, a narrative is at least a *story* involving characters and a *plot*, that is, a dynamic and structured sequence of actions or events; and narration is the act of producing such a story. It is in this sense that we speak of a novel or a fairy tale as a narrative of fiction; it is also in this sense that authors such as Gallie analyse historical knowledge as narrative in form. Faye does not, I believe, pay sufficient attention to these narrower, more specific senses of 'narrative' and 'narration'. It is therefore not surprising that Faye's method of analysis directs our attention away from the dynamic dimension of narrative plot. Once again I would suggest that the analysis of this dimension is not precluded, but simply occluded, by Faye's very broad and somewhat misleading notion of narration.

As the condition of possibility of history and even of knowledge, narration is a process which calls for a 'critique' in Kant's sense. Faye does not hesitate to place his project in the tradition of the great Critiques: just as Kant provided a critique of pure reason and Marx a critique of political economy, so too Faye proposes a critique of narrative reason/economy. Just as Marx's critique sought to relativize the categories of bourgeois political economy to the historical conditions of their emergence and application, so too Faye criticizes the universalistic pretensions of the 'generative semantics' of Postal and others and seeks to reconnect language to the social-historical conditions of its production and circulation, that is, to elaborate a 'semantics of history'. I do not want to question the latter aim of Faye's work – an aim which seems to me to be well directed, even if his general claims concerning the centrality of the 'Third Critique' seem hasty and overstated. Instead, I want to dwell for a moment on the ambiguity of the term 'critique' and on its role in the study of ideology. I think that one must distinguish, as Habermas did in the postscript to *Knowledge and Human Interests*, between critique in the sense of reconstructing the conditions which make possible a type of knowledge or inquiry, and critique in the sense of exposing and attacking the conditions which bind the action of individuals or groups.[46] This distinction helps to prepare the way for a reformulation of the project of a *critique of ideology*. To study ideology, I have argued elsewhere,[47] is to study the ways in which meaning (signification) serves to sustain relations of domination. Such a study may facilitate a critique of specific constructions or interpretations of meaning, as well as of the relations of domination which meaning serves to sustain. The study of ideology and the conduct of critique give rise to complex epistemological problems which may require, for their resolution, a reconstruction of the conditions of justification. Here I allude to the project of a critique of ideology, not in order to spell out the ways in which Faye's methodology could contribute to such a project, but only in order to identify some additional shortcomings in his work. While Faye frequently uses the term 'ideology', he does so in a loose and inconsistent way, sometimes using it as an equivalent for 'political language' while on other occasions linking it to the concealment of class interests. Moreover, Faye's concept of critique seems to merge the two senses distinguished above, accentuating the former sense at the expense of the latter. He therefore fails to examine, in a clear and systematic way, what would be involved in a critique of ideology and in the justification of such a critique.

While Faye's work may suffer from certain difficulties and limitations, nevertheless it is worth emphasizing, by way of conclusion, the very considerable achievements of his approach. It is of great interest to explore what I have called the 'political' aspect of the relation between history and narrative and to examine, as Faye has done, the ways in which narratives circulate in the social world and produce their *effets de récit*. Faye has developed a distinctive method which is chracterized above all by its *topographical orientation*: by its concern, that is, to reconstruct the field of positions which underlies the production and circulation of narratives. Texts do not drift aimlessly in history, but rather are transmitted along lines of force which affect their very *sens*. These methodological guidelines are pursued by Faye in an extremely fruitful way. His detailed analysis of the narratives which circulated on the political terrain of the Weimar Republic is illuminating in numerous respects: in its reconstruction of the lines of force which structured the language of the National Movement, in its portrayal of the political constellation of the Weimar Republic as a 'horseshoe' in which the extremes of left and right are brought together in a relation of dangerous and disruptive tension, in its examination of the ways in which Hitler emerged as the factor of moderation, appropriating the slogans of his rivals and playing upon the axis of the imaginary. While one may wish to criticize Faye's contribution on certain methodological and philosophical grounds, one must also acknowledge the extraordinary fruitfulness of his approach. He has raised a series of issues and carried out extensive studies which are of considerable value for any attempt to explore the nature and role of language in the social world.

7

Ideology and the Analysis of Discourse

A Critical Introduction to the Work of Michel Pêcheux

The study of ideology is one area, it seems, where the divide between theoretical reflection and practical analysis is particularly deep. There is no shortage of thinkers, from Marx and Engels to Mannheim, Habermas and Althusser, who have offered theoretical accounts of the formation and operation of ideology in modern societies. Such accounts are seldom linked, however, to detailed investigations of actual ideologies, that is, to the ways in which ideology is actually manifested in the conceptions and expressions of everyday life. In this essay I wish to consider a notable exception to this unfortunate rule. Working within a broadly 'structuralist' tradition of thought, Michel Pêcheux and his associates have attempted to integrate an Althusserian approach to ideology with a technical apparatus for the analysis of discourse. What is at stake in this attempt – beyond the particular form in which it is undertaken – is the very possibility of establishing links between the 'critical heritage' left by Marx, on the one hand, and the methods of analysis developed by modern linguistics and related disciplines, on the other. As a sustained interrogation of this possibility, the work of Pêcheux and his associates deserves more attention than it has so far received in the literature outside of France.[1]

I shall not attempt, in the pages which follow, to provide a thorough analysis of the work of Pêcheux and his associates; in the interests of brevity, I shall adopt a selective and simplifying procedure. I shall focus on the writings of Pêcheux in particular, referring only occasionally to the independent publications of his associates, such as Paul Henry and Françoise Gadet.[2] I shall begin by presenting the central theses of the theoretical approach elaborated by these authors. In the second part of the essay, I shall describe the technical apparatus which is connected with this approach, before proceeding, in the third part, to an illustration of how this apparatus may be employed. The fourth and final part is critical in character. I shall argue that, while Pêcheux and his associates raise issues which are important for the analysis of ideology, nevertheless their contributions contain serious difficulties. Some indication will be given of how, in my view, these difficulties could be overcome.

I   THEORY OF DISCOURSE

One of the principal concerns of the project of Pêcheux et al.[3] is to explore the interconnections between the analysis of language and the assumptions of historical materialism. The writings of Marx and Engels themselves contain occasional but provocative reflections on language; thus they observe, in *The German Ideology*, that

> language is as old as consciousness, language *is* practical consciousness that exists also for other men, and for that reason alone it really exists for me personally as well; language, like consciousness, only arises from the need, the necessity, of intercourse with other men.[4]

However, the reflections of Marx and Engels are vague and ambiguous, falling far short of a systematic analysis of language. The contributions of more linguistically-minded Marxists, such as Nicholas Marr, have gone some way towards filling this lacuna; but these contributions seem problematic in turn, resulting either in the reduction of language to social class or in its elevation beyond the realm of class and social conflict. It is with the aim of avoiding the latter two extremes, while at the same time pursuing the possibility of an historical-materialist approach to language, that Pêcheux et al. elaborate the concept of *discourse*.

The concept of discourse features prominently in the work of many contemporary French authors, marking one of the key respects in which the latter distance themselves from 'classical structuralism', that is, from the theoretical framework initially outlined by Saussure. As is well known, this framework is premised upon the distinction between *langue* and *parole*, where *langue* is language considered as a system of values defined in terms of their internal and oppositive relations, and *parole* is the individual and subjective realization of *langue*. One of Saussure's basic theses is that 'value', which pertains to *langue*, dominates and determines 'signification', by which he understands the relation between the acoustic image and the concept for which it stands.[5] Thus, while the French word *'mouton'* and the English word 'sheep' share a certain range of signification, they are not synonymous, for there is an opposition between 'sheep' and 'mutton' in English which does not exist in French. What this thesis fails to appreciate, according to Pêcheux et al., is that there exist such 'problems of translation' within one and the same *langue*:

> If one considers, for example, the domain of politics and that of scientific production, *one observes that words change their meaning (sens)* according to the positions held by those who employ them. Consequently, discourses delivered from different positions clearly pose problems of translation, equivalence and non-equivalence which cannot, in our view, be resolved by relating these discourses to various sub-systems of *langue*.[6]

By distinguishing between *langue* and *parole* and by subordinating signification to the value constituted in *langue*, Saussure elided the ways in which significations are determined by particular social-historical conditions. The concept of discourse is introduced by Pêcheux et al. in order to bring into focus these social-historical conditions and their effects.

In elaborating the concept of discourse, Pêcheux et al. are strongly influenced by Althusser's interpretation of historical materialism and his account of ideology.[7] According to Althusser, the reproduction of relations of production in capitalist societies is partially secured by the 'repressive state apparatus' (the government, the army, the police, etc.) and the 'ideological state apparatuses' (the educational system, the family, the mass media, etc.). The ideological state apparatuses are organized into 'ideological formations' which incorporate class positions. Pêcheux et al. propose that an ideological formation contains, as one of its components, one or several 'discursive formations' – formations, that is, which determine what can and must be said from a certain position within the social formation.[8] Expressions 'have meaning' in virtue of the discursive formations wherein they occur, for meaning (*sens*) is constituted by the relations between the linguistic elements of a given discursive formation. These relations of substitution, synonymy and paraphrase are called 'discursive processes'. It follows that the meaning of an expression is not stable and fixed, but is produced in a continuous process of 'slipping', of 'sliding', of 'metaphor'. It also follows that expressions may 'change their meaning' in passing from one discursive formation to another: that is what the Saussurian conception could not grasp. Pêcheux et al. emphasize that discursive processes, thus conceived, have nothing to do with *parole*; the latter notion, with its individualistic and psychological overtones, is dismissed as 'idealistic'. The authors also emphasize, however, that the operation of discursive processes does not entail the reduction of *langue* to relations of class, as some Marxists have maintained. On the contrary, Pêcheux et al. regard *langue* as a 'relatively autonomous system' which is governed by internal laws and which provides the common basis for differentiated discursive processes:

> the system of *langue* is indeed the same for the materialist and the idealist, for the revolutionary and the reactionary, for he who possesses a given knowledge of it and for he who does not. It does not follow, however, that these various characters will deliver the same *discourse: langue* thus appears as the common *basis* of differentiated discursive *processes*.[9]

It is thus *alongside* of the linguistics of *langue* that a 'discursive semantics' may be conceived, a semantics which would seek to investigate the interlinking of elements in a discursive formation by reference to the ideological complex of which that formation is part.

The theory of discourse and discursive processes provides a framework for analysing some of the characteristics of the human subject. The fact that every discursive formation is situated within a structured whole of discursive formations ('interdiscourse'), and the latter within a complex of ideological formations, remains excluded from the view of the subject, who always 'finds itself' within a particular discursive formation. Pêcheux et al. use the term 'forgetting' (*oubli no. 1*) to characterize this exclusion. *Oubli no. 1* is distinguished from another type of 'forgetting' (*oubli no. 2*), which refers to that which could have been said but which, in fact, was not; so whereas *oubli no. 1* concerns a discursive zone which is inaccessible to the subject, *oubli no. 2* pertains to a zone which lies within the subject's grasp. These specific senses of 'forgetting' are, of course, quite special. In the case of *oubli no. 1*, it is not a question of subject losing something which had previously been known, but rather a matter of covering over or occluding the 'cause' of the subject. There is thus a definite link between *oubli no. 1* and the mechanism of repression, in the psychoanalytic – more specifically the Lacanian – sense of the term. By covering over the process whereby a discursive sequence is produced, *oubli no. 1* creates the illusion that the subject precedes discourse and lies at the origin of meaning. Far from this being the case, it is the subject which is 'produced' or 'called forth' by a discursive sequence; or more precisely, the subject is 'always already produced' by that which is 'preconstructed' in the sequence.[10] Pêcheux thus takes up and reformulates Althusser's well-known thesis that 'Ideology interpellates individuals into subjects':

> the functioning of Ideology in general as interpellation of indi-
> viduals into subjects (and specifically into the subjects of their
> discourse) is realized through the complex of ideological formations
> (and specifically through the interdiscourse which is intricated
> therein) and provides 'each subject' with its 'reality', that is,
> with a system of self-evident truths and significations perceived-
> accepted-submitted to.[11]

The 'imaginary me' which is the 'subject of discourse' is constituted through the subject's identification with the discursive
formation which dominates it, with the 'Other' in the terminology
of Lacan.[12] Yet the subject cannot recognize this identification-
subordination, precisely because the latter occurs under the 'form'
of autonomy. The subject 'acts', takes a position 'in all liberty'; but
this *prise de position* is merely the 'effect' of the ideological and
discursive formations that are 'exterior' to the subject, an exterior
which remains excluded from view by the functioning of *oubli no. 1*.

While the subject is incapable of grasping the ideological and discursive formations of which it is the effect, there nevertheless is – submits Pêcheux rather brusquely – one standpoint from which these formations may be represented for what they are: the materialist standpoint of the Marxist science of history. The generation of scientific knowledge is an historical process which is interlaced with other aspects of a social formation, so that this process is necessarily linked to economic production and class struggle. This does not imply, however, that scientific knowledge is on a par with the ideologies that constitute the complex whole of ideological formations. There is an 'epistemological break' between science and ideology, in so far as the knowledge which precedes the break is sustained in the form of 'evident sense' for the subjects who are its historical supports. The break which inaugurates a science calls into question this 'evidence of sense' and, more generally, the relation of knowledge to the subject as such.

> In other words, the specificity of any break is, it seems to us, to inaugurate, in a particular epistemological field, a relation of 'the thought' to the real *so that what is thought is not as such supported by a subject*. In speaking of the founding concepts of a science, produced in the very work of the break which inaugurates the latter, we designate this 'paradox' (which . . . is only a paradox from the viewpoint of idealism) of *a thought which has no subject as such*; so the concepts of a science do not have, properly speaking, a meaning (*sens*), but rather a function in a process.[13]

Like every science, the science of historical materialism was inaugurated by a break which freed it, at least partially, from the hold of theoretical ideologies and their subjective supports. However, unlike the natural sciences, where the production of knowledge can be accomplished despite a misrecognition of history and the class struggle, historical materialism takes as its object the very process of class struggle. It follows, contends Pêcheux, that historical materialism bears a unique relation to the movement of the working class; for the laying bare of the historical process – a task to which the analysis of discursive processes contributes – is simultaneously a step forward in the transformation of class relations through political practice.

II   ANALYSIS OF DISCOURSE

As a programme of empirical research, the analysis of discursive processes dates back to the late 1960s. The programme may be seen as a reformulation and development of the distributional methods of Zellig Harris, whose influential essay on 'Discourse analysis' was translated into French in 1969.[14] One of Harris's principal concerns was to extend descriptive linguistics beyond the limits of the sentence. He therefore proposed to focus on a sequence of sentences or a *text* and to conduct a formal analysis in terms of repeating patterns among its constituent elements. All assumptions about the pre-given meanings of the elements, as well as all references to discursive sequences beyond the text in question, were to be excluded. However, in restricting the analysis to an individual text, the Harrisian method proved inapplicable to discursive sequences which were not intrinsically repetitive. Such is the central criticism levelled by Pêcheux et al., who propose to take, as an alternative object of analysis, a 'discursive corpus' comprising an ensemble of texts which pertain to conditions of production that may be regarded as stable:

> Harris accords a methodologically privileged importance to texts of propaganda or advertising: that corresponds to the necessity, within his perspective, of treating the text as *its own dictionary*, whereas in the perspective which we [adopt] . . ., it is the *corpus* which plays the role of *auto-dictionnaire*.[15]

On the basis of this shift from the text to the discursive corpus, Pêcheux et al. develop a method which they call the 'automatic analysis of discourse' (hereafter AAD). The main contours of this method were outlined by Pêcheux in 1969; but since then the method has undergone a number of modifications, in response both to theoretical criticisms and to problems encountered in ongoing empirical studies.[16] In 1975 Pêcheux and Fuchs provided a restatement and clarification of the method which will serve here as the basis for discussion. The authors divide the method into three principal stages. The first stage is the construction of the discursive corpus. This construction is guided by theoretical principles which are external to, and are to be justified independently of, the technical apparatus of the AAD. The corpus is constituted by a series of discourses or 'discursive sequences' which are assumed to be 'dominated' by stable and homogeneous conditions of production; that is, while different discourses may stem from different situations, it is assumed that the dominant conditions of production are the same. The corpus thus constituted is then subjected to two distinct types of analysis. 'Linguistic analysis' or 'desuperficialization' operates on the linguistic surface of a discourse; it seeks to specify the syntactic mechanisms at work in the discourse and thereby serves to counter the effect of *oubli no. 2.* 'Discursive analysis' or 'desyntagmatization' operates on the discursive object produced by linguistic analysis and begins to counter the effect of *oubli no. 1.* The two stages of the AAD may be represented as in figure 12.[17]

Langue
analysis of
syntactic
mechanisms, etc.

Discourse
analysis of a
corpus of
discursive objects
functioning as
auto-dictionnaire

linguistic
surface of a
discourse
belonging to a
corpus

$\longrightarrow$ discursive
object

$\longrightarrow$ discursive
process

= linguistic
desuperficializa-
tion, aiming to
eliminate the
effect of *oubli no. 2*

= discursive
desyntagmatiza-
tion, beginning to
eliminate the
effect of *oubli no. 1*

Figure 12

The task of *linguistic analysis* is to produce a syntactic representation of the linguistic surface of the discourse. The analysis results in the construction of a graph whose points are constituted by elementary assertions (*énoncés*) and whose lines represent the relations connecting the assertions. An elementary assertion is a sequence in which the elements fall into any of eight basic morpho-

syntactic categoires; its structure is (F D_1 N_1 V ADV P D_2 N_2),
where F = form of the assertion (mood, tense, etc.),
D = determinant of a substantive, N_1 = subject of the assertion,
V = verb of the assertion, ADV = adverb, P = preposition,
N_2 = second substantive, pronoun or adjective.[18] A sentence can
generally be analysed into several elementary assertions. For
example, consider the sentence 'It seems to me that the Church
remains in the clouds and that it forgets the difficulties and the
problems of life.' Pêcheux and Fuchs analyse this sentence into the
following elementary assertions:

1 It seems to me S (= something),
2 the Church remains in the clouds,
3 the Church forgets the difficulties,
4 the difficulties (are) of life,
5 the Church forgets the problems,
6 the problems (are) of life.

It is then observed that there are three connectors in the example:
THAT, AND and DT, where DT indicates a relation of determination between one assertion and the noun of another. Further,
it is noted that the connector 'THAT' is distributive, linking not
only assertions 1 and 2, but also 1 and 3 as well as 1 and 5. The
sample sentence may therefore be represented by the graph in
figure 13.

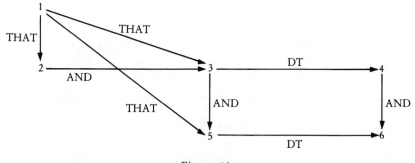

Figure 13

Linguistic analysis thus yields a 'discursive object' comprising:
(a) a list of elementary assertions, each analysed in terms of eight
morpho-syntactic categories; (b) a list of binary relations between
elementary assertions linked by connectors.

The *discursive analysis* of the material yielded by linguistic desuperficialization is conducted with the aid of a computer program. The first phase of discursive analysis involves a systematic comparison of the binary relations of each discourse with those of all the other discourses of the corpus. Here the decisive difference with the method of Harris is revealed, for it is the discursive corpus rather than the individual text which serves as the sphere of comparison. When two binary relations have the same connector, they are then submitted to a second phase of analysis. The computer program compares the two assertions of one relation with the two assertions of the other, using the eight morpho-syntactic categories as the basis of comparison. A system of 'weighting' is introduced in order to determine the relative proximity of the two relations. Suppose, for instance, that the initial phase had brought together two pairs of assertions, 'A and B', 'C and D', by virtue of the fact that they share the same connector. The second phase of analysis compares the contents of A and C, and of B and D, in terms of the morpho-syntactic categories they have in common. A numerical value is attributed to these common points and the summation of these values, S, is compared with fixed value, V; if $S \geq V$, then the assertions are said to belong to the same 'semantic domain'. The analysis results in the construction of a series of domains and in a specification of their interrelations (inclusion, exclusion, intersection), domains containing sequences which stand, by virtue of their proximity, in relations of inter-substitution.

Pêcheux et al. emphasize – here once again in criticism of Harris – that one must distinguish between two types of substitution. On the one hand, there are 'symmetrical' substitutions: given two substitutable elements P and Q, the path from P to Q is the same as that from Q to P ('synonymy'). On the other hand, there are 'oriented' substitutions, where one element implies the other but not vice-versa ('metonymy'). Consider, for example, the following result:

P = a catastrophe occurs	
	the use of the underground
Q = people avoid	

On the basis of this result, the analyst hypothesizes that the implicit relation between P and Q is an oriented substitution of the type '*It is because* a catastrophe occurs at x *that* people avoid x.'

The result is thus represented as follows:

$$\downarrow \begin{vmatrix} P \\ Q \end{vmatrix} \downarrow \quad \text{the use of the underground}$$

The hypothesis of an implicit relation which is not formulated in the corpus as such leads towards the investigation of the 'specific exterior' of the corpus, of that which imposes upon the substitutions and thereby orients them. The interpretation of the results of the AAD thus rejoins the central themes of the theory of discourse. For the specific exterior which imposes upon and orients the substitutions is the structured whole of discursive formations or 'interdiscourse', which remains inaccessible to the subject by virtue of the functioning of *oubli no. 1*. To fail to acknowledg this fundamental link between discursive processes and social-historical conditions – to suppose, for example, that 'semantics' is a branch of pure linguistics, that 'sense' is a derivative of syntactic structures – is to exclude from view the ways in which ideological and discursive formations enter into discourse and produce their *effets de sens*.

III   AN EXAMPLE: THE MANSHOLT REPORT

The method of the AAD has been fruitfully applied in a number of historical and empirical studies.[19] One of the most elaborate of these studies was conducted by Pêcheux et al. in the early 1970s, at a time when French political life was animated by the possibility of radical social change through an alliance between the Socialist and Communist Parties.[20] It was in this political climate that the social-ist Sicco Mansholt published a report defending the so-called 'zero growth theory', a theory which advocates rigorous economic plan-ning and a reorientation of economic goals in order to overcome the current crises in capitalist societies. The ambiguous political character of the Mansholt Report is evidenced by the reactions which it provoked in France: the ruling bourgeoisie regarded it as boldly realistic, the Communist Party denounced it as a reformist trick, and the socialists, while hesitating, expressed considerable interest. The aim of the study conducted by Pêcheux et al. is to examine this ambiguous character and to relate it to prevailing social-historical conditions. They propose to analyse, not the Mansholt Report itself, but rather two corpora which were generated in the following way. A one-page extract from the Report was presented to 50 young technicians from similar backgrounds (*petite bourgeoisie*) who were doing a retraining course at a university. The technicians were divided into two groups of equal size. They were not told that the text came from the Mansholt Report but were, instead, given different information concerning its origin. One group was informed that the text was the work of left-wing militants, while the other group was led to believe that the text had been produced by right-wing Giscardians. The members of each group were asked to read the text carefully. The text was then taken away and the participants were requested to write a short summary of the central themes. Two groups of summaries, hereafter referred to as the 'right corpus' and the 'left corpus', were thereby generated from the original text.

The material within the corpora was submitted to the two stages of analysis which comprise the AAD. The first series of results obtained concerns the semantic domains constructed by the computer program. Within each domain, symmetrical substitutions (indicated by vertical bars) are distinguished from oriented substitutions (indicated by vertical arrows), and these two types of

will to maximize the growth per capita

will to maximize the GNP per capita

idea to maximize the GNP per capita

reconsidering the maximization of GNP per capita

Figure 14

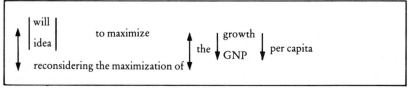

Figure 15

substitution are further distinguished from a contradictory relation between elements (indicated by vertical arrows pointing in both directions). The material in figure 14 is thus represented as in figure 15. The semantic domains within each corpus share features in common which enable them to be organized into four classes, dealing in turn with: (1) the causes of the crisis; (2) policy on economic reorganization; (3) policy concerning consumption; (4) policy on cultural development. The two corpora are then compared on the basis of these common classes or themes.

The comparison of the right and left corpora on the question of economic reorganization is particularly interesting. Key terms like production and consumption, planning and centralization, appear in both corpora; but whereas the right corpus emphasizes the need for the planning of consumption, the left corpus highlights the idea

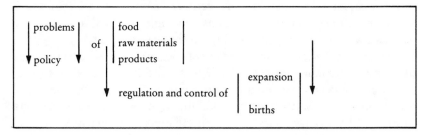

Figure 16: R41

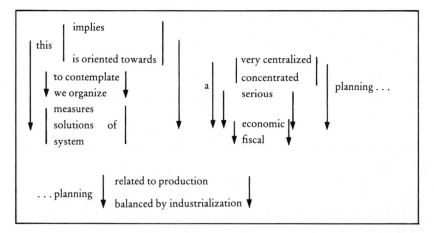

Figure 17: L33

of centralized planning concerning production. Compare, for example, the domain R41 (from the right corpus) with domain L33 (from the left corpus) in figures 16 and 17. The structures of these domains brings out the crucial difference between the rightist conception of planning, which involves the imposition of restrictions in the sphere of consumption, and the leftist conception of planning, which is concerned with the development of the economy and the reorganization of relations of production. However, the rightist conception is also present in some of the domains of the left corpus, a presence which indicates, according to Pêcheux et al., that the discourse of the left is 'dominated' by that of the right.

The 'domination' of the right discourse over the left is brought out by the second series of results. These results concern the relations between the domains within each corpus. Given two domains, the method enables one to determine which of the domains comes 'before' and which comes 'after' in the 'thread of the discourse'. By means of these relations, one can construct a graph which contains a 'point of departure' for the discourse and one or more 'points of arrival'. The points of departure and arrival are connected by paths which indicate the positions of the various domains in the discourse. The existence of several paths away from a single domain, or of several paths into another, reflects the fact that the linear appearance of the surface structures is broken up by the analysis; and this in turn, observe Pêcheux et al.,

> results from the fact that the corpus of these surfaces is treated as an *auto-dictionnaire*, and that the 'thread of the discourse' is broken up: disjoint, perhaps contradictory relations are thus brought out by the treatment of each of the two corpora, beneath the apparent unity and continuity of the surfaces constituting these corpora.[21]

Figure 18 is a summary of the relations which characterize the left corpus. Similar domains are grouped together and described with a short phrase. The structure of this graph, which is more complex than that of the right corpus, is characterized by a transverse connection between L32, L33 and L51, and by the branching from L53 towards L61 on the one hand and L52 on the other. Here one can see that a contradiction is at work. The paths L32–L33 and L53–L33 appear to express the necessity to plan production for the

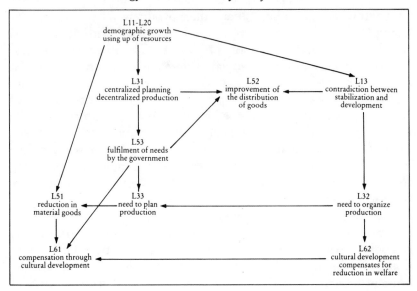

Figure 18

satisfaction of needs; but it nevertheless leads back to the pitfalls of an egalitarian redistribution of goods (L52) and a cultural compensation for economic recession (L61) – 'pitfalls' because no change is envisioned in the relations of production and hence such redistribution and compensation effectively coincide with the current objectives of bourgeois policy. The limits of the autonomy of the discourse of the left with regard to that of the right are apparent at this point. The fundamental 'blockage' is the notion, regarded as self-evident, that the (socialist) planning of production is inevitably accompanied by economic recession (L32–L33–L51). This notion is merely a version of the old idea that 'socialism' is not an achievement to be gained but a burden to be borne.

The study of the Mansholt Report illustrates, according to Pêcheux et al., some of the basic features of ideological struggle in contemporary capitalist society. This struggle never assumes the form of a confrontation between a purified discourse of the bourgeoisie and a purified discourse of the proletariat; rather, it always appears in complex, intermediate forms which, each in its own way, tend to one side or the other according to the class nature of the compromises realized therein: whence the central place of a notion like that of ambiguity for the study of the discursive processes in which such compromises are materially effected.[22]

The political situation in France at the time of this study was dominated by two antagonistic elements: on the one hand, the economic crisis and the consequent appearance of a 'hard line' among bourgeois politicians; on the other hand, the alliance between the Socialist and Communist Parties and the proposal to nationalize industry and plan production. These antagonistic elements polarized the ideological field, a polarization which is present in the ambiguous texture of the Mansholt Report. The opposing interests of the two principal classes in capitalist society are 'tendentially represented' across equivocal terms like 'planning', 'radical reform' and 'change'. The meanings of the terms slip and slide, shift from one sense to another depending on the positions held by those who employ them. It is for this reason that language has an essentially *political* character, a character which is effaced by every attempt to produce a universal and purified language, to produce, that is, *la langue introuvable*.[23]

IV   A CRITICAL DISCUSSION

I should like now to offer some critical reflections on the work of Pêcheux et al. Before undertaking this task, I want to emphasize my agreement with the overall project of conjoining a theoretical account of ideology with an empirical and historical analysis of its concrete forms. The importance of this project is particularly apparent if one compares the work of Pêcheux et al. with the results of what is called 'discourse analysis' in the English-speaking world; for the latter results tend to be meticulously descriptive and largely disregard the role of ideology.[24] While Pêcheux et al. have rightly attempted to link the theory of ideology with the analysis of discourse, I nevertheless believe that there are serious shortcomings and tensions in their work. Many of these difficulties stem, in my opinion, from the general orientations of 'structuralism', a tradition to which Pêcheux et al. continue to link themselves, albeit in a critical fashion. In the following paragraphs I cannot attempt to express all of my reservations, nor can I hope to elaborate my arguments in the detail which they demand. I shall, for the sake of clarity, focus my critical remarks on five issues which may be placed under the following headings: (1) *langue* and the autonomy of syntax; (2) discourse and the theory of meaning; (3) the limits of the AAD; (4) the nature of the subject; (5) science and the study of ideology.

1   Langue and the autonomy of syntax

Viewed against the backcloth of Saussurian linguistics, the theory of discourse may be seen as a way of calling into question *parole* while leaving *langue* intact. The latter remains, in the eyes of Pêcheux et al., the 'common basis' of differentiated discursive processes. The autonomous status of *langue* provides the justification for the stage of 'linguistic analysis' in the AAD and the grounds for rejecting all forms of 'sociologism' and 'psychologism' in linguistics. While the thesis of the autonomous status of *langue* is thus a central and constant theme in the work of Pêcheux et al., it is seldom stated in clear and unambiguous terms. In order to assess its plausibility, I shall propose the following formulation:[25] there exists a *syntactic* order which is independent of and logically prior to the social-historical conditions of linguistic realization, and which defines what is *impossible* in those conditions. Formulated in this way, the thesis seems very suspect. Much of the recent criticism of transformational grammar has been directed against the whole attempt to develop a theory of autonomous syntax, in which the distribution of forms could be predicted on purely syntactic grounds. Thus Robin Lakoff, focusing on auxiliary verbs, argues that the model proposed by Chomsky gives rise to problems that cannot be resolved without invoking semantic and pragmatic information.[26] Moreover, the work of sociolinguists, such as Labov's study of the deletion of the copula in black English vernacular, would seem to undermine the assumption of linguistic homogeneity at the level of syntax.[27] The results of such studies cannot be simply dismissed by raising the spectre of social-psychological reductionism, as Pêcheux et al. are inclined to do.[28] On a more general level, it is difficult to see why the *impossible* of language – that which defines what cannot be said – should be regarded as lying beyond the social-historical realm. For it would seem that the 'rules' of syntax are essentially social, and hence susceptible to the differentiation and variation which affects all social phenomena.[29] The thesis of the autonomous status of *langue* attests to the fidelity of Pêcheux et al. to the perspective opened up by Saussure; but by remaining faithful to this perspective, these authors appear to produce yet another example of a linguistic system sheltered from the effects of history, that is, of *la langue introuvable*.[30]

2   Discourse and the theory of meaning

If Pêcheux et al. have not been sufficiently critical of the Saussurian conception of *langue*, this could not be said of their attitude towards *parole*, which has been effectively replaced by the concept of discourse. It is in the sphere of discourse that social-historical formations and unconscious forces leave their traces in language. The task of 'discursive semantics' is to explore these *effets de sens* by reconstructing the discursive processes in which they are expressed. It seems to me that one of the major strengths of the work of Pêcheux et al. is this emphasis on the idea that 'semantics' cannot be divorced from a theory of the social-historical conditions in which meaning is produced, an idea which appears quite revolutionary in the context of recent French thought. Here I shall not pursue this idea and shall focus instead on what discursive semantics claims to provide but what, in my view, it clearly does not: a theory of meaning. What Pêcheux et al. call 'discursive processes' are in fact various forms of *substitution* between the elements of a discursive formation: 'meaning (*sens*) is always one word, expression or proposition *for* another word, expression or proposition'.[31] There is an evident proximity between this notion of *sens* and the Saussurian concept of *valeur*, a proximity which makes 'discourse' appear as little more than a contextualized version of *langue*. However, to regard meaning as exhausted by relations of substitution is to obliterate the question of what is *asserted* in spoken or written discourse, the question of the criteria which *justify* the assertion of a statement, the question of that *about which* one speaks or writes. A satisfactory theory of meaning, in my view, must seek to integrate the criterial and referential aspects of assertion, while at the same time recognizing that these

aspects are inseparable from the exercise of *power*. For if it is
supposed that the meaning of an expression may be analysed, at
least partially, in terms of the criteria of justified assertion, then it
must be added that such criteria are subject to systematic differentiation and manipulation, so that what counts as 'justified
assertion' is essentially open to dispute. Pêcheux et al. open the
way to this type of inquiry when they maintain, in opposition to
Saussure, that the meaning of expressions varies in accordance with
the positions held by those who employ them; but the way is
quickly foreclosed by the contention, this time derived from Saussure, that meaning is merely a pattern of substitution between the
pre-given elements of a discourse.

3   The limits of the AAD

The inadequacies of 'discursive semantics' may be further explored
by reconsidering the method of analysis developed by Pêcheux
et al. Drawing upon the work of Harris and others, the AAD
combines syntactic analysis and computer processing into a
method of considerable rigour and complexity. It will not be my
concern here to examine the details of this method and to pass
judgement on their soundness and suitability. The problem which
I shall pose is that of the *limits* of the AAD, the specific boundaries
within which it operates but beyond which it must be supplemented by assumptions and procedures which are different in
kind. These limits are defined by the construction of the corpus, on
the one hand, and the interpretation of the results, on the other.
The construction of the corpus precedes the implementation of the
AAD and is presumed to derive its justification independently of
the latter. Whether such justification is actually forthcoming is a
question which will be considered below; here I want only to
record the impression, difficult to dispel, that the results of the
AAD are deeply coloured by the hypotheses involved in the construction of the corpus. If the text of the Mansholt Report had
been ascribed to a group of ecologists and a group of industrialists,
or to a group from the 'developed world' and a group from the
'underdeveloped world', or to two groups of moderates with
slightly differing policies, then would one have established the
same 'semantic domains' within the two corpora? Would one have
organized the domains into the same classes for comparison?

Would one, in the end, have discovered the same 'discursive processes' at work in the original text? A similar impression of vagueness and arbitrariness is produced by the final specification of discursive processes, a specification which lies at the other limit of the AAD. This limit stems from the fact, recognized by Pêcheux et al., that the results of the AAD do not 'speak for themselves' but must be *interpreted*. It is precisely there, in the 'interpretation of the results', that the whole problem resides. For what is this process of interpretation, if not an act of elucidating meaning which goes well beyond the construction of patterns of substitution, which attempts to link what is asserted to the social conditions and referential objects of assertion, which seeks to unfold, in sum, the relation between language and the world? [32] The necessity of interpreting the results is a striking demonstration of the thesis that, however elaborate the formal methods of analysis in the social sciences may be, such methods could never be more than a limited and preliminary stage of a more comprehensive interpretative theory.[33]

4   The nature of the subject

The fourth issue, or cluster of issues, which I want to raise concerns the conceptualization of the subject. The project of Pêcheux et al. forms part of a general reaction, initiated in the 1960s by Lévi-Strauss, Althusser and others, against the subjective excesses of phenomenology and existentialism. No longer can the subject be treated as the origin of meaning or the locus of freedom, for the subject is constituted within a space that is defined in advance by the system of social relations, of language, of the unconscious. For my part, I do not wish to contest this displacement of the primacy of the subject; such a *critical move* seems to me to be a necessary part of any approach which does not succumb to the narcissistic illusions of the ego. Nor do I wish to examine here the details of the way in which Pêcheux et al. conceive of the constitution of the subject, details which could certainly be disputed in many respects.[34] My question is of a more general and thematic character. For it seems to me that in the writings of Pêcheux et al. the *displacement* of the primacy of the subject assumes the form of a *dissolution of the agent*, a dissolution which is difficult to reconcile with other aspects of their work. Gadet and

Pêcheux criticize what they see as the 'bio-psychological reductionism' of Chomsky on the grounds that 'one cannot see how, in such an organism, there could subsist any place for resistance and revolt, which presupposes that human language is something other than a pure mental organ'.[35] But surely the same criticism could be directed against the Althusserian conception of the subject developed by Pêcheux et al.: if the subject were simply an individual interpellated by a pre-existing ideological formation, then no room would be left for the emergence of resistance and revolt, for the revolutionary *creativity* which is an irrepressible feature of the historical process. Moreover, what would be the point of attempting to link an analysis of ideology to the presuppositions of historical materialism, if it were not assumed that the results of such an analysis could be appropriated by agents capable of acting knowledgeably and creatively in the social world?[36] A critical theory of ideology demands a conception of the subject which, while acknowledging that the latter is internally divided and dependent upon conditions which lie beyond its immediate grasp, nevertheless recognizes that the subject *qua* agent is capable of reflecting upon those conditions and acting creatively to alter them. Such a conception is one which the theoretical approach of Pêcheux et al. seems unlikely to provide.

5   Science and the study of ideology

My fifth and final series of critical remarks is concerned with the epistemological status of the project pursued by Pêcheux et al. That this project should give rise to intractable epistemological problems is not difficult to see. For the attempt to develop an analysis of discourse which would be necessarily aligned with the interests of the oppressed is obviously open to the charge of particularity and one-sidedness: is not such an attempt, one might well ask, itself ideological? The technical apparatus of the AAD, employed within the limits which are proper to it, largely bypasses this question. The points of most apparent arbitrariness – the construction of the corpus and the interpretation of the results – are presumed to derive their justification, at least in part, from the presuppositions of historical materialism. Yet why should historical materialism provide a position outside of ideology, from which ideology could be analysed in the interests of the oppressed? In *Les*

Vérités de la Palice Pêcheux's answer to this question was straight-forward and clear: historical materialism is a *science* which bears, by virtue of its object, a privileged relation to the aims of the proletariat, and there is an 'epistemological break' between science and ideology. Here I shall not undertake to criticize the undis-guised dogmatism of this account, a task which has been amply carried out with regard to Althusser, to whom Pêcheux owes this convenient response. Such a critique is all the less necessary since Pêcheux himself, like Althusser, has since rejected the opposition between science and ideology. The reference to the 'discourse of science' was, in the political context of the mid-seventies, a way of trying to free the workers' movement from the hold of bourgeois ideology; it was 'the French way of dreaming about an impossible "way out of ideology"'.[37] In the wake of this commendable self-critique, however, the original epistemological problem reappears. Having precluded the dogmatic appeal to *les vérités de la science*, it is by no means clear how Pêcheux et al. propose to conceive of an analysis of ideology which is in some sense 'objective' and which at the same time serves the interests of the dominated class. My view is that this problem must be approached *counterfactually*, through the specification of formal conditions free from domination under which a conflict of interpretations *could* be resolved by the agree-ment of anyone who entered the discussion.[38] It may be that these formal conditions would be rarely, if ever, realized in the actual conduct of interpretation and critique; but if this approach is sound, then it follows that any theoretical account which leaves no room for the self-reflection of human subjects, which relegates truth to the domain of scientific-technical expertise, must be renounced once and for all.

By way of conclusion, let me draw out some of the key ideas of the foregoing discussion. I have presented the work of Pêcheux et al. as a sustained attempt to integrate a theoretical account of ideology with an empirical analysis of its concrete forms. I sketched some central themes of their theory of discourse as well as the principal features of their method of discourse analysis, a method whose application was illustrated in detail. In addition to this admirable attempt to link theory and method, the writings of Pêcheux et al. raise problems which are of considerable importance for any attempt to develop a critical theory of ideology – problems, for example, of meaning and its relation to the social conditions of linguistic production, of the subject and its constitution within language, of the link between the analysis of ideology and the interests of the oppressed. I have argued, however, that on all of these points there are serious difficulties in their work. Many of my criticisms stem from the conviction that these authors remain too closely tied to the framework outlined by Saussure, failing to see that their own ideas tend to burst the bounds of the tradition to which they adhere.

If the criticisms which I have levelled against the work of Pêcheux et al. are sound, then it seems clear that the development of a critical theory of ideology would demand an alteration of approach. I have given some indication of how such an attempt might proceed. The notion of ideology must be situated within a theory of language that emphasizes the ways in which meaning is infused with forms of power. To study ideology is not to analyse a particular type of discourse, but rather to explore, by means of a general interpretative theory, the modes whereby meaningful expressions serve to sustain relations of domination. It is therefore misguided to search for a criterion of demarcation between science and ideology; the epistemological problems raised by the analysis of ideology demand a reflection of a quite different kind. From the perspective of Pêcheux et al., these suggestions might appear to be a step backwards, a regression to the era of 'philological-religious hermeneutics' which the rise of structuralism has long since destroyed. Yet if that era has passed, the problems with which it struggled persist. The problems of meaning and interpretation, of action and agency, of truth and justification: these are neither resolved nor dissolved by Pêcheux et al., but lurk beneath the surface of their work like so many memories of a forgotten dream, making their presence felt by their very absence. The writings of Pêcheux and his associates represent an important but limited contribution to a critical theory of ideology, whose formulation and elaboration are more urgent than ever.

8

Universal Pragmatics

*Habermas's Proposals for the Analysis
of Language and Truth*

In the course of uttering speech-acts we make presuppositions of various kinds. When I utter the expression 'Good morning' to a person passing in the street, I commonly presuppose that it is the early part of the day and that the person so addressed will understand my utterance as a greeting (and not, for example, as a description of the weather). When I recount an experience to a friend, I commonly presuppose that the experience is worth recounting, that the friend has some interest in hearing it and that he or she has not already heard it a thousand times before. When I promise to do something, I commonly presuppose that I am capable of doing it, that the person to whom I utter the promise would like me to do it and that, when the time comes to do it, I shall be under some obligation to keep my word. In these and many other ways, we presuppose specific things in speaking the way that we do. However, in addition to these *specific* presuppositions, do we not also make certain *general* presuppositions in the course of uttering speech-acts? Do we not generally presuppose, for example, that what we say is *true*, or at least true to the best of our knowledge? When we listen to others speak do we not generally presuppose that they are speaking *sincerely*, or at least that, if we were to discover that they were not speaking sincerely, this discovery would vitiate much of what they had said?

It is in pursuing questions such as these that Jürgen Habermas initiated, in the early 1970s, a programme of 'universal pragmatics'.[1] While the details of this programme remain sketchy and incomplete, the overall aim is clear: to investigate the general competencies required for the successful performance of speech-acts and thereby 'to reconstruct the universal validity basis of speech'.[2] The supposition is that such a reconstruction would provide a way of justifying a critique of ideology, in so far as ideology can be conceived as communication systematically distorted by the exercise of power. This attempt to provide a justification of critical theory through a reconstructive analysis of everyday speech may at first appear somewhat surprising. For even though communicative competence has been the object of analysis for many years, it is still a topic about which there is a great deal of disagreement and dispute. Nevertheless, Habermas has proposed a highly original and provocative programme which deserves more consideration that it has sometimes received in the Anglo-American literature.[3] In this essay I shall try to facilitate such consideration by offering an exposition and critique of Habermas's proposals for the analysis of language and truth. I shall begin by situating his writings on language within the context of his social theory as a whole, indicating a few of the respects in which his earlier views have been modified by his more recent work. The second part of the essay presents an exposition of some of the central themes of universal pragmatics. In the third part I select four of these themes and submit them to a critical examination. Finally, in the concluding part of the essay I consider some general issues and offer some constructive remarks, with the aim of indicating ways in which the obstacles encountered by Habermas's programme could be overcome.

I

The emphases and aims of universal pragmatics can be discerned throughout Habermas's earlier work. In common with other authors in the tradition of the Frankfurt School, Habermas has always opposed the reductionist tendencies which characterize the more orthodox versions of Marxism. He expresses this opposition by insisting that a society develops not only in the dimension of technological innovation and labour but also in the dimension of communicative interaction; and however close the connection between these dimensions may be, 'there is no automatic developmental relation between labor and interaction'.[4] Communicative interaction is an autonomous sphere in which cultural traditions are historically transmitted and social relations are institutionally organized. The concern with this sphere brings Habermas into contact with hermeneutics and ordinary language philosophy. He praises these approaches for stressing the way in which language is constitutive of social and historical phenomena, but criticizes their tendency to idealize this constitutive role. For language itself is dependent upon social processes which are not wholly linguistic in nature; it is, Habermas insists, '*also* a medium of domination and social force'.[5] So although the interpretation of symbolic formations may presuppose a 'deep common accord', as Gadamer maintains, one must not preclude the possibility that the latter is a consensus falsely induced by the unacknowledged exercise of power. In such cases the 'common accord' is not so much the prior condition of communication but rather the ultimate conclusion. Hence a critical theory must undertake to show both in what sense a common accord can be presupposed and operative in spite of the distorted conditions under which communication actually occurs, and in what way these distorted conditions can be explicated and criticized in the name of a consensus whose realization is perpetually postponed.

The importance of an inquiry into the foundations of language is similarly underlined by the arguments of *Knowledge and Human Interests*. In this study Habermas seeks to distinguish three categories of scientific disciplines in terms of their respective knowledge-constitutive interests, which in the case of the critical social sciences is called the 'interest in emancipation'. Thus in a discipline like psychoanalysis the reconstruction of developmental processes yields depth interpretations which can be corroborated if and only if patients willingly accept them as their own, thereby freeing themselves from dependence upon unrecognized constraints. Similarly, critical social science is concerned with identifying and dissolving relations of power and ideology in such a way that, in the end, 'knowledge coincides with the fulfilment of the interest in liberation through knowledge'.[6] Yet does not this alleged coincidence of knowledge and interest merely conceal the partisanship involved in the exercise of practical critique? What assurance have we that the interpretations offered by critical theory are any less ideological than the ideologies which they claim to expose? In short, how could it be established that the emancipatory interest, which Habermas places at the very heart of the critical enterprise, is anything other than pure fiction?[7] The outline of an answer to these and similar questions may be found in Habermas's 1965 Inaugural Lecture: 'The human interest in autonomy and responsibility is not mere fancy, for it can be apprehended *a priori*. What raises us out of nature is the only thing whose nature we can know: language.'[8] Habermas's subsequent work on the theory of language may be regarded as a sustained attempt to develop and defend this embryonic answer.

Despite the early anticipations of universal pragmatics, the latter programme is premised upon two distinctions which mark a significant modification of Habermas's original views. The first of these distinctions is concerned with the concept of self-reflection, which is perhaps the central concept of *Knowledge and Human Interests*. In the 1973 'Postscript' to the latter volume, Habermas observes that this concept encompasses and conflates two elements, an element of reconstruction and an element of critique.[9] Reflection in the sense of reconstruction refers to the quasi-Kantian exercise of elucidating the conditions which render possible a form of knowledge or a mode of action. In recent years this type of reflection has been rehabilitated on a linguistic basis, assuming the form of a rational reconstruction of systems of rules which are necessarily drawn upon in everyday speech. Since these reconstructions seek merely to represent what is always and already operative, they constitute a type of knowledge which 'has always claimed a special status: that of "pure" knowledge';[10] and hence they fall outside of the epistemological scheme presented in *Knowledge and Human Interests*. Reflection in the sense of critique, on the other hand, is concerned with subjectively produced illusions that objectively constrain the social actor. Unlike the anonymous systems of rules which are the object of rational reconstruction, these illusions appertain to the particular self-formative process of an individual or group; and the critical dissolution of such illusions leads to the emancipation of the subject from previously unconscious constraints. However, the explicit distinction between reconstruction and critique does not imply that these two types of self-reflection are unrelated. On the contrary, a discipline which aspires to a critical stance cannot avoid, in Habermas's view, the exercise of rational reconstruction. For if critique 'accepts as its task the explanation of a systematically distorted communication, then it must have the mastery of the idea of undistorted communication or reasonable discourse';[11] and unfolding the idea of undistorted communication is the reconstructive task of universal pragmatics.

The second distinction underlying universal pragmatics also marks a departure from Habermas's earlier views. A central theme of *Knowledge and Human Interests* is that the logical-methodological rules for the conduct of the various sciences are linked to an interest structure which is rooted in the self-formative process of the human species, and which prejudges both the possible objects of scientific analysis and the possible meaning of the validity of scientific statements. However, in the 1973 'Postscript', Habermas concedes the criticism that this thesis is too strong: it threatens to reduce the objectivity of the sciences to an anthropology of interests. Habermas proposes to avert this threat by introducing a distinction between action and discourse. 'Action' refers to everyday contexts of social interaction, in which information is acquired through sensory experience and exchanged through ordinary language. 'Discourse', on the other hand, designates a realm of communication which is abstracted from the contexts of everyday life. The participants of a discourse are concerned, not to perform actions or to share experiences, but rather to search for arguments and justifications; and the only motive allowed in this search is 'a cooperative readiness to arrive at an understanding'.[12] In the light of this distinction Habermas can maintain that, while the object domains of the sciences are differentially constituted by the interests which operate at the level of action, the validity-claims which these sciences raise are subject to the unitary conditions of discursive argumentation. For the objectivity attainable by science is based upon a suspension of action constraints, and this alone 'permits a discursive testing of *hypothetical* claims to validity and thus the generation of *rationally grounded* knowledge'.[13] Precisely how the validity-claims implicitly raised in action contexts can be rationally redeemed in discourse is a question which will be considered in due course.

II

Habermas introduces the programme of universal pragmatics by indicating the limitations of other approaches to language. In the dominant schools of linguistics and formal semantics, the object domain is constituted by an initial abstraction from the performative aspects of speech. Chomsky's focus on 'linguistic competence', and his tendency to treat 'performance' as an empirically limited outcome of the latter, is a case in point. Linguistic competence is conceptualized as a 'monological capability . . . founded in the species specific equipment of the solitary human organism'.[14] If this capability is to provide an adequate basis for the communicative process, then the latter in turn must be reconstructible in monological terms; and it is precisely this, Habermas contends, that cannot be done. For 'in order to participate in normal discourse, the speaker must have – in addition to his linguistic competence – basic qualifications of speech and of symbolic interaction (role-behavior) at his disposal, which we may call communicative competence'.[15] Accordingly, the analysis of language must be extended to include an investigation of the qualifications which enable a speaker, not simply to produce grammatically well-formed sentences, but to embed these sentences in successful speech-acts. Only then can the gulf be bridged between the generative competencies of speaking and acting subjects on the one hand, and the pragmatic features of concrete speech situations on the other.

The performative aspects of speech have been explored in considerable depth by the so-called 'ordinary language philosophers', such as Austin, Searle and the later Wittgenstein. Rejecting his earlier conception of language as a formal system of representation, the later Wittgenstein turns towards a detailed examination of the ways in which expressions are actually used in everyday language-games. This is a change of emphasis with which Habermas is wholly sympathetic; but his reservation is that 'in Wittgenstein and his disciples, the logical analysis of the use of language always remained particularistic; they failed to develop it into a *theory of language games*'.[16] The elements of a more general theory can be found, Habermas suggests, in the various writings concerned with the notion of speech-act. Austin introduces this notion in order to draw attention to the fact that in uttering a sentence a person may also be performing an action and not just reporting or describing an event. Indeed even in the case of reporting and describing, as Austin subsequently points out, saying something is also doing something. Hence the way is prepared for a theory of language which would take the speech-act as its basic unit and which would proceed to analyse and categorize its primary forms. Habermas thus regards the contributions of Austin, Searle, Strawson and others as a congenial starting-point for his programme. They are, however, only a starting-point, for they 'do not generalize radically enough and do not push through the level of accidental contexts to general and unavoidable presuppositions'.[17] Universal pragmatics therefore seeks to elucidate those performative aspects of speech which are presupposed by the ability to utter, not any particular speech-act, but speech-acts as such.

The general presuppositions of speech can be initially uncovered through an analysis of speech-acts in the 'standard form'. Such speech-acts exhibit the essential features of communicative action; and the latter, conceived dynamically as 'action oriented towards reaching an understanding' (*verständigungsorientierten Handelns*), is regarded by Habermas as the basis type of social action.[18] The standard form can be represented by the schema 'I . . . (verb) . . . you that . . . (sentence)', or by a simple variant thereof. A speech-act which satisfies this form thus possesses a distinctive double structure. It comprises, on the one hand, an illocutionary element specified by a performative sentence in the first person present indicative with a direct object in the second person and, on the other hand, a propositional component which contains referring and predicative expressions. The propositional component can remain invariant throughout changes in the illocutionary element, so that speech-acts in the standard form may be said to be 'propositionally differentiated out'. In Habermas's view, this internal differentiation of the standard speech-act reflects two levels upon which the speaker and hearer must move if they wish to communicate: '(a) the level of intersubjectivity, upon which the speaker/ hearer communicate *with one another*; and (b) the level of objects, *about* which they come to an understanding'.[19] The question then arises as to how the issuance of a speech-act can result in the establishment of an intersubjective relation. How is one to account for the specific *engagement* which the speaker enters into when uttering a speech-act, and which enables the hearer to rely upon the person who speaks? In the case of speech-acts which are closely connected with other social conventions, this engagement may be derivable from the validity of established norms; but what about 'institutionally unbound speech-acts', which in this respect must be regarded as the more fundamental case? In reply to such questions, Habermas submits that the relevant commitments can be accounted for only on the assumption that certain validity-claims are implicitly raised and reciprocally recognized with the utterance of every speech-act. 'In the final analysis, the speaker can illocutionarily influence the hearer and vice versa, because speech-act-typical commitments are connected with cognitively testable validity claims – that is, because the reciprocal bonds have a rational basis.'[20]

The rational basis which underlies the illocutionary force of a speech-act consists of four distinguishable validity-claims. In issuing an utterance, the speaker implicitly claims that what is said is intelligible (*verständlich*), that the propositional content is true (*wahr*), that the performative component is correct (*richtig*), and that intentions are being expressed sincerely (*wahrhaftig*). These four validity-claims, which 'competent speakers must reciprocally maintain with each of their speech-acts',[21] constitute the background consensus of normally functioning language-games. The consensus can be shaken by calling into question one or more of the claims, in which case the continuation of communicative action is dependent upon whether the relevant claim can be redeemed. The intelligibility of an utterance can be challenged by questions such as 'What does that mean?' or 'How should I understand that?' The answers to these questions are to be found in the structure of language itself; for intelligibility, in the sense of grammatical well-formedness, is a factual condition rather than a counterfactual claim of communication. The sincerity of the speaker can be impugned with questions like 'Is this person deceiving me?' or 'Is this person pretending?' These questions can only be answered by the subsequent course of interaction, for whether or not someone is expressing intentions sincerely will eventually show itself in actions. Finally, the truth of a propositional content or the correctness of a performatory component can be placed in doubt with questions such as 'Is it really as you say it is?' or 'Is it right to do what you have done?' Habermas maintains that these questions cannot be fully answered within the context of communicative action; rather, they raise 'claims of validity which can be proven only in discourse'.[22] The formal features of the discursive realm, and hence the conditions under which the claims to truth and correctness can be redeemed, are specifiable in terms of the pragmatic universals which every communicatively competent speaker must possess.

The ability to embed grammatically well-formed sentences in speech-acts presupposes, according to Habermas, that speakers have at their disposal a series of 'pragmatic' or 'dialogue-constitutive universals'. These universals are intersubjective, a priori linguistic elements which enable the speaker, in the course of producing a speech-act, to reproduce the general structures of the speech situation. The universals are not merely a linguistic articulation of pre-existing conditions, but rather are the very elements which establish these conditions. For 'without reference to these universals, we could not even define the recurrent components of possible speech: namely the expressions themselves, and then the interpersonal relations between speakers/hearers which are generated with the expressions, and finally the objects about which the speakers/hearers communicate with one another'.[23] Habermas proposes several categories of expressions which function as pragmatic universals.[24] First, the personal pronouns and their derivatives form a reference system between potential speakers, enabling each participant to assume the roles of 'I' and 'You' simultaneously and thereby securing the intersubjective validity of semantic rules. Second, the deictic expressions of space and time, as well as the articles and demonstrative pronouns, form a reference system of possible denotations, linking the plane of intersubjectivity upon which subjects interact with the plane of objects about which they converse. Third, the performative verbs, as well as non-performative intentional verbs and some modal adverbs, form a system of possible speech-acts which enables the subject to draw certain distinctions and express certain relations 'which are fundamental for any speech situation'.[25] Habermas's contention is that the ability to enter into a conversation presupposes that subjects could deploy these various types of expression, thereby displaying the mastery of pragmatic universals which defines their communicative competence.

In developing this proposal, Habermas concentrates on the performative verbs in the third category of pragmatic universals. He seeks to show that these verbs may be divided into four basic classes; and since every speech-act in the standard form exhibits such a verb, the demonstration may be expected to provide 'a systematic account for the classification of speech acts'.[26] The first class is the 'communicatives' (to say, to ask, etc.), which are directed at the process of communication as such, and which facilitate the distinction between meaning and the fluctuating signs wherein it is expressed. The second class, the 'constatives' (to assert, to describe, etc.), are concerned with the cognitive application of sentences, enabling a subject to differentiate between a public world of being and a private world of appearance. 'Representatives' (to admit, to conceal, etc.) constitute the third class; these verbs serve to express the intentions, attitudes and feelings of the speaker, thereby making possible the distinction between the individuated self and the expressions in which it appears. The fourth class is the 'regulatives' (to order, to prohibit, etc.), which refer to norms that can be followed or broken, and which thus mark a distinction between empirical regularities and valid rules. This fourfold classification can be combined with the typology of validity-claims to yield a general model of linguistic communication. Even though all four validity-claims are implicitly raised with every speech-act, nevertheless a speaker can explicitly thematize a particular claim by employing a speech-act from one of the above classes.[27] In so doing the subject expressly articulates one of the four regions of reality which 'must always simultaneously appear'[28] in the utterance of a successful speech-act: namely, the regions of external nature, society, internal nature, and language. The general model of communication which thus emerges from Habermas's work may be summarized as in Table 2.

The pragmatic universals which communicatively competent speakers have at their disposal provide the means for the construction of an ideal speech situation. The latter situation is characterized by 'pure intersubjectivity', that is, by the absence of any barriers which would obstruct the process of communication. In addition to contingent forces which impinge upon the situation from without, such barriers include the constraints which are produced by the structure of communication itself; and Habermas proceeds on the basis of the following assumption: 'the structure of communication itself produces no constraints if and only if, for all possible participants, there is a symmetrical distribution of chances to choose and to apply speech-acts'.[30] The assumption of symmetry forms the general framework of the ideal speech situation, allowing the latter to be specified further in terms of the four

TABLE 2: GENERAL MODEL OF COMMUNICATION[29]

Domains of reality	Modes of communication	Types of speech-act	Themes	Validity-claims	General functions of speech
'the' world of external nature	cognitive: objectivating attitude	constatives	propositional content	truth	representation of facts
'our' world of society	interactive: conformative attitude	regulatives	interpersonal relation	correctness	establishment of legitimate social relations
'my' world of internal nature	expressive: expressive attitude	representatives	speaker's intention	sincerity	disclosure of speaker's subjectivity
language	—	communicatives	—	intelligibility	—

classes of speech-acts. Equality in the opportunity to apply communicatives means that all potential participants have the same chance to initiate and sustain discussion through questions and answers, claims and counter-claims. A symmetrical distribution of chances to apply constatives implies that all potential participants have the same opportunity to proffer interpretations and explanations, so that no preconceptions remain excluded from view. An equal opportunity to apply representatives gives all potential participants the same chance to express intentions and attitudes, creating the circumstances in which subjects become transparent to themselves and others in what they say and do. Finally, symmetry in the distribution of chances to apply regulatives entails that all potential participants have the same opportunity to order and prohibit, to obey and refuse, thereby precluding the privileges that arise from one-sided norms. The situation thus portrayed is, of course, an ideal; the conditions of empirical speech are not generally identical with those of the ideal speech situation. 'Nevertheless it belongs to the structure of possible speech', writes Habermas, 'that in the execution of speech-acts (and actions) we contrafactually proceed as if the ideal speech situation . . . were not merely fictive but real – precisely what we call a presupposition.'[31]

The claims of truth and correctness implicitly raised in communicative action can be redeemed in discourses which have the structure of an ideal speech situation. For truth and correctness, in Habermas's view, are concepts that can be analysed in terms of the discursive justification of validity-claims. A statement is true when the validity-claim of the speech-act with which it is asserted is justified; and the validity-claim is justified, according to Habermas, if and only if the statement would command the consent of anyone who could enter into a discussion with the speaker. 'The condition for the truth of statements is the potential consent of all others. . . . Truth means the promise to attain a rational consensus.'[32] The circumstances under which a consensus holds as rational, and *ipso facto* as true, are precisely those of the ideal speech situation. Similarly, just as truth may be regarded as a validity-claim redeemable in an ideally structured theoretical discourse, so too correctness may be conceived as a claim which can be redeemed in a discourse of a practical nature. Hence Habermas rejects empiricist and decisionist approaches to ethics, approaches which share the assumption that moral controversies cannot, in the last analysis, be rationally resolved. The formal properties of the discursive situation establish the conditions under which a rational consensus can be attained concerning a problematicized value or norm. Moreover, to the extent that such a consensus marks a divergence from the institutional arrangements which exist in fact, it follows that the results of practical discourse stand in a critical relation to the social world. The exercise of this critique *must* be undertaken in so far as the ideal speech situation is necessarily anticipated in every act of speech; and it *can* be undertaken in so far as every competent speaker possesses the means to construct such a situation, however distorted the actual conditions of speech may be. 'On this unavoidable fiction', submits Habermas, 'rests the humanity of relations among men who are still men.'[33]

III

Having sketched the overall aims and initial results of universal pragmatics, I now wish to focus, in a more analytical and critical way, on some of the basic claims of this programme. Among other things, Habermas seeks to establish the following theses: (1) that the utterance of a speech-act implicitly raises four validity-claims; (2) that communicatively competent speakers have at their disposal a series of pragmatic universals; (3) that an ideal speech situation, which can be constructed in terms of pragmatic universals, is presupposed in everyday speech; and (4) that truth is a validity-claim that can be rationally redeemed in a discourse having the structure of an ideal speech situation. In the following paragraphs I shall examine each of these theses in turn, reconstructing and criticizing the arguments upon which they rest. I hope thereby to clarify a few of the issues which are raised by Habermas's programme and to show that some of his contributions are, at least, in need of further defence.

The *first thesis* rests upon an argument which may be summarized as follows:

1 Every speech-act in the standard form contains an illocutionary component, represented by a performative sentence, and a propositional content which is differentiated out.

2 The differentiation of the standard speech-act reflects two
  levels which are involved in communication: the level of intersubjectivity and the level of objects; a successful speech-act
  results in the establishment of a relation in which at least two
  subjects come to an understanding about a state of affairs.
3 The establishment of such a relation can be accounted for only
  on the assumption that four validity-claims are implicitly
  raised and reciprocally recognized with the utterance of every
  speech-act.

Habermas thus *begins* his analysis with speech-acts in the 'standard
form', but how this initial restriction of the analysis is to be
justified remains unclear. One possible justification may be found
in Habermas's interpretation of Searle's principle of expressibility.
According to Habermas, the principle can be reformulated as
follows: 'for every interpersonal relation that a speaker wants to
take up explicitly with another member of his language community, a suitable performative expression is either available or, if
necessary, can be introduced through a specification of available expressions'.[34] However, even supposing that every interpersonal relation could be articulated in terms of an appropriate
speech-act, it is by no means clear that the illocutionary force of
the speech-act could be represented by a 'suitable performative
expression'. The latter view is apparently indebted to the so-called
'performative hypothesis' of Ross, McCawley and others, a
hypothesis which has been thoroughly and justly criticized in the
linguistic and philosophical literature.[35] For it is not obvious what
performative expression could capture the illocutionary forces involved in many indirect speech-acts, such as the distinctive
mélange of question and request in 'Don't you think the rubbish is
beginning to smell?';[36] nor is it apparent how the performative
schema 'I . . . (verb) . . . you' is to deal with more complex cases of
personal pronominalization, as may be found, for example, with
reflexive verbs. Considerations such as these do not vitiate Habermas's positive programme, but they do cast some doubt upon his
grounds for restricting the analysis to speech-acts in the 'standard
form'.

The problematic nature of the restriction becomes increasingly
evident in the third stage of the argument. There is considerable
plausibility in the suggestion that when a speaker utters a speech-

act the audience is generally entitled to assume that the speaker is sincere, that he or she takes what is said to be true, and so on. There is also a clear continuity between the claims which Habermas identifies and the conditions which Searle proposes for the successful performance of a speech-act. However, it seems to me implausible and misleading to contend, as Habermas does, that all four validity-claims are necessarily raised with the utterance of *every* speech-act. In what sense does reading a poem, telling a joke or greeting a friend presuppose the truth of what is said? Is not sincerity characteristically suspended rather than presupposed by the participants in a process of collective bargaining, or by friends engaged in the light-hearted activity of 'taking the mickey'? In what sense, precisely, does the utterance of a sentence like 'The sky is blue this morning' raise a claim to correctness which is clearly distinguishable from its intelligibility or its truth? Habermas may be right to criticize Austin for working with an undifferentiated notion of 'objective assessment'; but Habermas in turn seems mistaken to maintain that the various claims which he discerns in this notion are necessarily raised with every speech-act, albeit in an implicit and unthematic form. No doubt Habermas would deny that the above instances constitute counter-examples to his thesis, insisting instead that they must be treated as subsidiary forms of communication, as mere 'derivatives' of action oriented towards reaching an understanding. Yet such a reply would simply assume what must be shown, namely that orientation towards understanding is the basic aim of communication. So long as this assumption remains unsubstantiated, hence so far as the justification for restricting the analysis to speech-acts in the 'standard form' remains problematic, then so too the extent to which Habermas's programme qualifies as a *universal* pragmatics must be held in doubt.

A *second thesis* which can be elicited from Habermas's writings is that communicatively competent speakers have a series of pragmatic universals at their disposal. The argument underlying this thesis may be roughly reconstructed as follows:

1 The ability to enter into a conversation implies that the speaker is able (a) to relate to a world of subjects, (b) to relate to a world of objects, and (c) to draw certain fundamental distinctions.

2 These abilities presuppose that the speaker has mastery of (a) personal pronouns and their derivatives, (b) deictic expressions and demonstrative pronouns, and (c) performative verbs and certain intentional expressions.

3 The mastery of specific types of performative verbs enables the speaker to draw the distinctions which are fundamental for the speech situation; this link, together with the differential thematization of validity-claims, provides a principle for the classification of speech-acts.

Habermas's thesis concerning pragmatic universals must be regarded as one of the more speculative aspects of his recent work. The volume of essays edited by Greenberg, to which Habermas sometimes refers in this context, is of a highly provisional and exploratory nature; and some of the inconsistencies which characterize the volume have been pointed out by subsequent authors.[37] Cases have often been made for the universality of deictic elements and personal pronouns, but there is considerably less support for the third category proposed by Habermas. Since it is the latter category which is particularly important for the construction of the ideal speech situation, it is worth investigating the relevant argument in more detail.

Habermas contends that there are certain distinctions which are fundamental for any speech situation, and that the ability to draw these distinctions presupposes that the subject has mastery of various kinds of speech-acts. This contention raises two questions: (1) Why are precisely these distinctions fundamental to any speech situation? (2) To what extent does the ability to draw these distinctions presuppose a mastery of the various kinds of speech-acts? As regards the second question, it is not entirely clear how strongly Habermas's claim is to be construed, nor what sort of evidence he would regard as supporting or refuting his view. However, recent research on the perceptual and communicative activities of infants seems to weigh against his view, suggesting that the child may be able to make some sort of distinction between appearance and reality well before it has mastered an established system of speech-acts.[38] As regards the first question, there is a similar lack of clarity about the nature of the distinctions cited by Habermas and the grounds for treating these distinctions as fundamental. Without a more precise specification, it is difficult to judge whether the proposed distinctions are genuinely universal or merely extrapolated from the tradition of Western philosophy. Moreover, it seems possible that there are other differentiations which are at least equally primordial, such as the differentiation, emphasized by the early Wittgenstein, between what can and what cannot be said, or the differentiation, developed by modal logic, between what is and what could be the case. Habermas appears to believe that the latter differentiation could be accommodated within his framework in terms of the intentional obfuscation of the distinctions which he regards as fundamental.[39] It may be doubted, however, whether such an account would do justice to the imaginative and creative character of language use. Language may be a medium of interrelating several worlds, but it is also, as Ricoeur insists, a medium whereby these worlds can be shattered and enlarged.[40] Habermas's proposals concerning pragmatic universals thus converge with his analysis of speech-acts in the 'standard form': poetry and humour, metaphor and word-play, are relegated to a secondary status in the functioning and comprehension of language.

The *third thesis* of Habermas's programme asserts that the ideal speech situation is a necessary presupposition of communication. The argument in support of this thesis may be reconstructed in six steps:

1 The process of communication implies that it is possible for at least two subjects to come to an agreement about a state of affairs.
2 To come to an agreement implies that it is possible to distinguish between a genuine and a deceptive agreement.
3 A genuine agreement is an agreement induced by the force of better argument alone.
4 The force of better argument prevails if and only if communication is not hindered through external and internal constraints.
5 Communication is not hindered through internal constraints if and only if for all potential participants there is a symmetrical distribution of chances to select and employ speech-acts.
6 A situation in which there is a symmetrical distribution

of chances to select and employ communicative, constative, representative and regulative speech-acts is an ideal speech situation.

The first step of the argument invokes the assumption of the privileged status of *verständigungsorientierten Handelns*, exploiting the ambiguity of understanding/agreement which is conveyed by the word *Verständigung*. Since it has already been suggested that this assumption is in need of further defence, no more will be said about it here. I shall pass instead to the third step of the argument, where further problems appear to arise. For although the concept of agreement may presuppose the possibility of distinguishing between genuine and illusory cases, it is difficult to see why subjects can be said genuinely to agree about something only when their agreement is induced by the force of better argument, as opposed, for example, to the feeling of compassion or the commitment to a common goal. Yet if there are, as there certainly seem to be, alternative ways in which a genuine agreement can be induced, then the momentum which allegedly leads to the presupposition of an ideal speech situation is dissipated at an early stage.

Let us suppose, none the less, that Habermas has identified a principal mode whereby genuine agreements can be distinguished from their illusory counterparts. The question then arises as to whether this mode is adequately explicated by the fourth and fifth steps of the argument. Habermas maintains that the force of better argument prevails if and only if communication is not hindered by external and internal constraints, and that internal constraints are excluded if and only if for all potential participants there is a symmetrical distribution of chances to select and employ speech-acts. What it means to speak of 'a symmetrical distribution of chances to select and employ speech-acts' is not altogether clear; and how one is to characterize the exclusion of external constraints, which seem to have been swept under the fifth step of the argument, remains uncertain. Moreover, it seems doubtful whether the elimination of internal constraints could be guaranteed by a symmetrical distribution of chances to select and employ speech-acts, however the latter stipulation may be construed. For one can imagine a debate in which all potential participants have an equal opportunity to deploy the various kinds of speech-acts; and yet in spite of this formal equality the final decision is merely an expression of the prevailing status quo, bearing little resemblance to the quality of the arguments adduced. What Habermas's assumption of symmetry seems to neglect, and what his occasional allusions to the model of 'pure communicative action' do nothing to mitigate,[41] is that the constraints which affect social life may operate in modes other than the restriction of access to speech-acts, for example by restricting access to weapons, wealth or esteem. The neglect of these issues is closely connected to the dubious distinction between labour and interaction, and it is heavy with consequences for the attempt to use psychoanalysis as a model for critical theory. These connections and consequences cannot be pursued here;[42] but I hope that enough has been said to suggest that Habermas's argument for the presupposition of an ideal speech situation, as well as his conceptualization of the latter, are in need of considerable attention.

The *fourth thesis* which I have drawn from Habermas's programme is concerned with the concept of truth. The argument underlying this thesis may be summarized in the following way:

1 It is statements, and not sentences or utterances, which are true or false.
2 Truth is a validity-claim which is connected with constative speech-acts: to say that a statement is true is to say that the assertion of the statement is justified.
3 The assertion of a statement is justified if and only if that statement would command a rational consensus among all who could enter into a discussion with the speaker.
4 A rational consensus is a consensus that is argumentatively attained under the conditions of an ideal speech situation.

The second step of the argument expresses the crucial point, which is at the same time the most problematic. For it is by no means clear that to say that a statement is true is to say that the assertion of the statement is justified. Habermas appears to treat this equation as analytic, defending it with the observation that 'truth means "warranted assertability"'.[43] If this were indeed what truth meant, then it would be meaningless to say that the assertion of a statement is justified when the statement itself is false. However, there seem to be many cases when this would not be meaningless, especially with respect to statements about events that may or may not transpire in the future. One may have very good grounds for maintaining that it will rain tomorrow, but the truth of this statement is dependent upon what happens tomorrow and not upon the grounds that one has today.[44] The third and fourth steps of the argument do not, it seems to me, alleviate this difficulty. For I have already suggested that the recourse to the conditions of ideal speech may be neither necessary nor sufficient for the attainment of a 'rational consensus'; and, as I shall now try to show, such an appeal fails to clarify an important aspect of the concept of truth.

The thesis that truth is a discursively redeemable validity-claim does not adequately elucidate what may be called the 'evidential dimension' of the concept of truth. Habermas concurs with Strawson's view that a fact is what a true statement asserts; and both of these authors justly criticize Austin and others for conceiving of facts on the model of things. However, it seems implausible to maintain, as Habermas does, that an existing state of affairs is merely the content of a proposition which has survived discursive argumentation. There are moments when Habermas relaxes this uncomfortable legislation, conceding that 'in the case of elementary empirical propositions such as "this ball is red" a close affinity exists between the objectivity of experience and the truth of a proposition as expressed in a corresponding statement'.[45] Yet Habermas does not explain why this special condition should hold for 'elementary empirical propositions' alone, nor does he clarify wherein this 'close affinity' between experience and 'corresponding statements' consists. Similar obscurities arise in the characterization of the role of experimental data in the redemption of scientific claims to truth. Although Habermas contends that in stating a fact one is not asserting that some experience exists, he nevertheless allows that one can 'draw upon structurally analogous experiences as data in an attempt to legitimate the truth claim embodied in [a] statement'.[46] Once again, however, Habermas does not specify what kind of 'structurally analogous experiences' would be relevant here, nor how they could be 'drawn upon' to legitimate a truth-claim. He suggests that such questions could be answered by a 'non-objectivistic philosophy of science', but it is by no means clear that the answers thus provided would be wholly consistent with Habermas's current approach. For if the participants of a discourse can adduce certain kinds of experience, 'structurally analogous' though it may be, and if the discursive realm includes certain kinds of action, even though it may be 'experimental' in nature, then it is quite uncertain what remains of the distinction between contexts of action-related experience and realms of discourse, a distinction which is fundamental to the whole of Habermas's recent work. Whether the collapse of this distinction would provide a way of recovering some of the more provocative themes of Habermas's earlier writings must here by left as an open issue.

IV

In the preceding paragraphs I have focused my critical remarks on specific themes in the programme of universal pragmatics. I have not raised any questions concerning the way in which Habermas wishes to employ universal pragmatics within the framework of critical theory, nor have I suggested any ways in which the difficulties encountered by his programme might be overcome. In this final part of the essay I shall briefly take up these two remaining issues. The first issue may be approached by noting that Habermas, in seeking to link the conduct of critique to a reflection on the general and unavoidable presuppositions that we make as competent speakers, is clearly at odds with some of his predecessors in the Frankfurt School as well as with many contemporary authors in other traditions of thought. At a time when some form of cultural relativism is accepted by many thinkers and when some form of Nietzschean cynicism is practised by others, the project pursued by Habermas may seem to be rather eccentric. Be that as it may, I think that Habermas is right to address directly the question of the justification of critique. He is right to relinquish the confident expectation that history will follow an inevitable course, eventually delivering us, with a necessity that bears the burden of responsibility, to the society of freedom and plenty. He is right to relinquish this expectation *without* abandoning the attempt to analyse, in a systematic and justifiable way, the processes which have produced the societies in which we live and which sustain these societies as unequal and unjust.

Whether the requisite justification could be provided through a reflection on the presuppositions of speech is, it must be admitted, much less clear. The claim that such reflection unfolds a model of idealized speech which can be used for the critique of ideology may appear somewhat vacuous, at least until one has specified precisely how it is to be used. Habermas has not, I believe, been altogether pellucid in this respect. Sometimes he suggests that the formal symmetries of the ideal speech situation provide an adequate tool for identifying and criticizing systematically distorted communication.[47] Just how this critical activity is to be carried out is not, however, explicated in any detail. Moreover, it is certainly questionable whether these formal symmetries would be sufficient to discriminate between alternative and competing views, without making some recourse to the contents of historical tradition. As Ricoeur aptly remarks, 'man can project his emancipation and anticipate an unlimited and unconstrained communication only on the basis of the creative reinterpretation of cultural heritage'.[48] The latter objection could to some extent be met by the model which Habermas presents in *Legitimation Crisis*.[49] For the 'counterfactually projected reconstruction' of a system of norms formulated discursively would appear to provide a critical standard which is not purely formal, but which acquires its content from the conclusions attained under conditions that are formally defined. Once again, however, the model is presented at a very abstract level and it remains to be seen whether it can be developed to avoid the obstacles that confront most formalistic approaches to practical issues.

If the criticisms which I have levelled at universal pragmatics are sound, then the spirit of Habermas's project could be sustained only on the basis of a more systematic reflection on the notions of truth and justice, of rationality, self-reflection and critique. In drawing this essay to a constructive close, I can do no more than indicate a direction of thought which seems to me to be promising, and which I have pursued at greater length elsewhere.[50] When we offer an interpretation of an action or of a form of discourse, we implicitly claim, as Habermas suggests, that our interpretation is in some sense 'true'. We implicitly claim, that is, that our interpretation is worthy of recognition and that, if called upon to defend it, we could muster some reasons in support. Such reasons might include various kinds of *evidence* which we regarded as relevant in formulating our interpretation; and in seeking thereby to defend the interpretation, we are engaging in a process of argumentation which is quite different from merely *imposing* our view. The latter distinction could be explicated, I think, in terms which are not dissimilar from Habermas's assumption of symmetry, provided we recognize that asymmetrical relations of power may operate in modalities other than the restriction of access to speech-acts.

This approach might provide a way of sustaining the spirit of Habermas's project while at the same time rehabilitating some of his earlier views. The assumption of symmetry may specify some of the formal conditions of discursive argumentation, but it would not provide the specific criteria which would have to be employed in attempting to sustain a particular interpretation. Such criteria may be of differing statuses and may vary from one epistemic field to another. While in the natural sciences these criteria may have been reduced to a 'pragmatic criterion' of prediction and control, as Hesse suggests,[51] there is no reason to assume that the same criterion must be accepted as the overriding value in all spheres of social inquiry. On the contrary, it could be maintained that the crucial criteria for the acceptance of interpretations of action or of forms of discourse are governed by a *principle of self-reflection*. For such interpretations are about an object domain which consists, among other things, of subjects capable of reflection; and if these interpretations are to be acceptable, then they would have to be justifiable – by means of whatever evidence deemed to be necessary under the formal conditions of argumentation – in the eyes of the subjects about whom they are made. The interpretation of action or of forms of discourse thus bears an internal connection to the clarification of the conditions of action, and to the critique of ideological forms of discourse, for and by the actors themselves. It is by virtue of this internal connection that we may speak, as Habermas did in his earlier writings, of a special relation between theory and practice in that sphere of inquiry where subjects capable of reflection are among the objects of investigation.

In conclusion, let me briefly summarize the main points of this essay. After situating universal pragmatics within the context of Habermas's social theory, I outlined some of the principal aims and provisional results of this programme. I then focused on four major theses, reconstructing and criticizing the arguments upon which they rest. I suggested that Habermas's conclusions concerning validity-claims are reached by an unsubstantiated restriction of

the analysis to speech-acts in the 'standard form'; that his proposals concerning pragmatic universals are in need of further
clarification and defence; that his argument for the presupposition
of an ideal speech situation is problematic at several points; and
that his analysis of truth is hard to sustain as it stands. In the final
part of the essay I raised some general questions about the role of
universal pragmatics and offered a few constructive remarks. It is
far from clear whether the obstacles which seem to confront
Habermas's programme can be overcome; but what is clear is that
the issues which he has raised, and the lines of inquiry which he has
encouraged, are urgently in need of being pursued.

9

Rationality and Social Rationalization

An Assessment of Habermas's Theory of Communicative Action

The ideas of reason and rationality are central to the tradition of Western philosophy, so much so that they seem definitive of philosophy itself. Yet with the rise of the positive sciences in the eighteenth and nineteenth centuries, philosophy lost its pretention to provide a rational explanation of the phenomena which constitute the world. The alleged autonomy and self-sufficiency of philosophy was destroyed; thenceforth, philosophy could continue to explore the theme of rationality only in conjunction with the sciences of nature, of language, of society. Among the social sciences it was above all sociology which was able to conjoin its concepts to the theme of rationality. For unlike politics and economics, sociology was interested in all forms of action and hence could not neglect the foundations of the theory of action and interpretation. Moreover, from the outset sociology was saddled with the task of explaining the rise of capitalism and the modern state from the traditional texture of old European societies. The co-existence of these two preoccupations – the meta-theoretical concern with the conditions of rational action, the historical concern with the conditions of social rationalization – is particularly evident in the work of Max Weber.

It is therefore not surprising that the work of Max Weber looms large in Habermas's recent two-volume treatise, *Theorie des kommunikativen Handelns*.[1] Like Weber, Habermas is concerned to explore the interrelations between the conditions of rational action and the conditions of social rationalization; but he wishes to take account of two theoretical shifts which have occurred in philosophy and social science since the time of Weber. The first shift is from a teleological concept of action – that is, from viewing action as the successful pursuit of an agent's aim or desires – to a *concept of communicative action*, which emphasizes the *inter*action in which two or more subjects seek to reach an understanding concerning their shared situation. This first shift presupposes the transition from a philosophy centred on the conscious subject to a philosophy focused on language and it prepares the way for the formulation of a notion of 'communicative rationality'. The second theoretical shift has to do with the historical or empirical preoccupation of sociology. Habermas is sensitive to the value of Weber's analysis of capitalist modernization in terms of social rationalization, as well as to the impact which this analysis has had on Marxist thinkers such as Lukács, Horkheimer and Adorno. Habermas maintains, however, that the critical appropriation of Weber's analysis requires, among other things, a shift from the critique of instrumental reason to a *critique of functionalist reason*; for it is in the writings of social theorists who have espoused some form of 'functionalism' or 'functionalist systems theory', such as Talcott Parsons and Niklas Luhmann, that one can find both a key to analysing the processes of rationalization and the limits of a purely 'objectivistic' approach to such processes. It is on the basis of these two theoretical shifts that Habermas defines his task: that of elaborating a theoretical account which demonstrates the interconnections of communicative action and social systems and which provides a framework for comprehending the tensions and tendencies, the conflicts and potentialities, that characterize the industrial societies of today.

In this essay I want to discuss some of the themes of Habermas's most recent and remarkable work.[2] I shall divide my discussion into three sections. In the first section I shall describe the main features of Habermas's theory of communicative action and the associated notion of communicative rationality. The second section will discuss the link between communicative action and systems theory and will present Habermas's reformulation of Weber's theory of rationalization. In the third and final section I shall offer some critical reflections on the arguments advanced in *Theorie des kommunikativen Handelns*.

I

The theory of communicative action is concerned to explore the consequences of the fact, as evident as it is profound, that language is a medium of social interaction. These consequences were largely neglected in previous forms of philosophy and social theory, for these forms were dominated, in Habermas's view, by a teleological concept of action and an orientation to the sphere of consciousness. Thus, while Weber distinguishes various types of action and links them to the establishment of social relationships, nevertheless the individualistic model of goal-directed action remains his point of reference: 'what counts as fundamental is not the interpersonal relation between at least two subjects capable of speech and action – a relation which refers back to reaching understanding within language – but the purposive activity of a solitary acting subject'.[3] The predominance of a teleological concept of action and a philosophy of consciousness can be traced through many currents of twentieth-century thought, from the phenomenology of Husserl and Schutz to the critical theory of Horkheimer and Adorno. However, the predominance of these models has not gone unchallenged. Within both the pragmatist writings of George Herbert Mead and the philosophy of language developed by Wittgenstein, Austin and others, one can find the beginnings of a 'paradigm shift' from the model of teleological action to that of linguistically mediated interaction. It is by drawing out the implications of this shift that Habermas formulates his concept of communicative action.

To speak a language is to perform an action: such is the basic insight underlying Austin's theory of speech-acts. But neither Austin nor his followers have pursued this insight far enough. They have tended to remain at the level of analysing the conditions necessary for the successful utterance of particular speech-acts, such as promising, requesting or referring; they have not paid sufficient attention to the *general presuppositions* that we make in uttering and responding to speech-acts. In uttering a speech-act, submits Habermas, the speaker makes an *offer* which the hearer can either accept or reject. Suppose a flight attendant says to a passenger, 'You must stop smoking now'. The attendant is making an offer – or, as Habermas prefers to say, raising a *validity-claim* –

which the passenger can accept by extinguishing the cigarette or reject by asking 'Why?'. In the latter case the attendant must give some reasons or grounds which would support the validity-claim raised with the original speech-act, for example by pointing out that the plane would soon be landing and that the safety regulations stipulated no smoking at such a time. The validity-claim raised with a speech-act is thus internally connected with reasons and grounds; and this internal connection indicates, according to Habermas, that there is a 'rationally motivating force' at work within the process of communication. 'A speaker can *rationally motivate* a hearer to accept his speech-act offer because . . . he can assume the *warrant (Gewähr)* for providing, if need be, convincing grounds which would stand up to the hearer's criticism of the validity-claim.'[4]

Habermas develops his account of the 'validity basis of speech' by distinguishing several types of validity-claim. Such a distinction has been hindered, argues Habermas, by the privilege accorded to the concept of truth, and therewith to the representative function of language, in the philosophical semantics stemming from Frege and the early Wittgenstein. We must radicalize Austin's critique of the 'descriptive fallacy': not only must we break with the representative bias, but we must isolate other modes of language use and identify their distinctive validity-claims. There are, Habermas maintains, at least three validity-claims which are raised with the utterance of speech-acts. A speaker may raise the claim (a) that the statement made is *true* (or the existential presuppositions are satisfied); (b) that the speech-act is *correct* in terms of the prevailing normative context (or the normative context itself is legitimate); (c) that the intention of the speaker is as it is expressed, that is, that the speaker is *sincere* in what he or she says. In raising these claims the speaker takes up relations to any of three object domains or 'worlds', with regard to which a claim can be contested by a hearer: (a) the *objective world* as the totality of entities about which true statements are possible; (b) the *social world* as the totality of legitimately regulated interpersonal relations; (c) the *subjective world* as the totality of experiences to which the speaker has privileged access. Each of these validity-claims and the corresponding world-relation is brought into play by a specific mode of language use. The *representative* function, performed with 'constative' speech-acts, accentuates the claim of truth and the relation to the objective world. 'Regulative' speech-acts, such as commands or requests, reflect what might be called the *appellative* or interactive mode of language use; this mode stresses the claim of correctness and the relation to the social world. Finally, there is a class of speech-acts which enable the speaker to disclose his or her subjectivity; in this case we are dealing with the *expressive* function, which highlights the claim of sincerity and the relation to the subjective world.

The threefold articulation of validity-claims, world-relations and modes of language use defines the complex concept of 'communicative action' or, more precisely, 'action oriented to reaching understanding' (*verständigungsorientiertes Handeln*). The distinction between 'action oriented to reaching understanding' and 'action oriented to success' is fundamental to Habermas's account. In drawing the distinction he employs three related criteria: the orientation of the actor, the mechanism of action co-ordination and the grounds on which the action may be assessed. When actors are oriented to the realization of their own ends, when their actions are co-ordinated through egocentric calculations and are appraised in terms of their efficacy, Habermas speaks of 'action oriented to success', a category which he further divides into 'instrumental action' and 'strategic action'. When, on the other hand, actors are oriented to reaching an understanding with other actors through a co-operative process of discussion, so that their actions are co-ordinated by, and assessed in terms of, a collective agreement which is the condition for pursuing their own plans, Habermas speaks of 'action oriented to reaching understanding'. These basic distinctions may be represented as in table 3.

TABLE 3: TYPES OF ACTION[5]

Action orientation / Action situation	Oriented to success	Oriented to reaching understanding
non-social	instrumental action	—
social	strategic action	communicative action

Action oriented to reaching understanding takes place within language, for it is through the process of raising and responding to validity-claims that the possibility of reaching understanding (*Verständigung*) on the basis of a rationally motivated agreement (*Einverständnis*) is secured. 'Reaching understanding is the inherent telos of human speech. . . The concepts of speech and reaching understanding reciprocally interpret one another.'[6]

The concept of communicative action, characterized in terms of the threefold articulation of validity-claims, world-relations and modes of language use and demarcated from action oriented to success, provides a framework for reconsidering the ideas of reason and rationality. When we use the term 'rational', observes Habermas, we assume that there is a close connection between rationality and knowledge. We assume, it seems, that actions or symbolic expressions are 'rational' in so far as they are based on knowledge which can be criticized. In calling an action 'rational' we may presume that the actor knows, or has good reason to believe, that the means employed will lead to success; in calling an expression 'rational' we may presume that it bears some relation to the world and hence is open to objective – that is, intersubjective – assessment. The former case, by linking the term 'rational' to the notion of action oriented to success, offers an intuitive basis for what Habermas calls 'cognitive-instrumental rationality'. The latter case links the term 'rational' to the notion of intersubjective assessment and thereby points towards a broader concept of *communicative rationality* 'in which various participants overcome their merely subjective views and, by virtue of the mutuality of rationally motivated conviction, assure themselves of both the unity of the objective world and the intersubjectivity of their life-relations'.[7] Habermas fills out the concept of communicative rationality with reference to each of the three validity-claims presupposed in speech. For an expression may be deemed 'rational', not only if it can be assessed in terms of its relation to the objective world, but also if it can be appraised with regard to a social world of legitimate norms or a subjective world of personal experiences. Expressions linked to the claims of correctness and sincerity, no less than those connected to truth, can satisfy the basic condition of communicative rationality: they can be criticized and, if need be, 'grounded'.

Since the concept of communicative rationality presupposes that expressions can be criticized and grounded, the nature of this concept can be fully explicated only by means of a *theory of argumentation*. The term 'argumentation' is used by Habermas to refer to a type of speech distinct from the communicative practice of everyday life, a type of speech in which individuals focus on specific validity-claims and try to criticize or support them through arguments. Habermas distinguishes several forms of 'argumentative speech' in terms of the types of validity-claim thematized within them. 'Theoretical discourse' is that form of argumentation in which claims to truth can be contested and supported with reasons, or in which unsuccessful experiences in the cognitive-instrumental sphere can be productively integrated into learning processes. 'Practical discourse' is the argumentative sphere in which claims to correctness can be hypothetically tested. Habermas takes a strongly cognitivist position on ethical issues: norms of action raise a claim to express the *common interest of those affected* and so 'must be capable in principle of meeting with the rationally motivated consent (*Zustimmung*) of all concerned under conditions that neutralize all motives other than that of co-operatively seeking the truth'.[8] There are two additional forms of argumentation which share some of the features of theoretical and practical discourses, but which must be qualified in certain respects. One can adopt a reflective attitude to 'value standards' about what is beautiful, for example, and one can offer reasons or grounds in support of such a standard; but this form of 'aesthetic criticism' remains bound to particular cultures and cannot pretend to yield conclusions which would elicit universal assent. Similar restrictions hold for the 'therapeutic critique' exemplified by psychoanalysis, in which the roles of participants are asymmetrically distributed and could be rendered symmetrical only if the analysis were successful. The various forms of argumentation which *explicitly* realize the rationality *implicit* in communicative practice can therefore be represented as in table 4.

In formulating the concept of communicative rationality through an analysis of the way in which the term 'rational' is used, Habermas relies on the modern occidental understanding of the world. He tries to elucidate some of the basic assumptions and kinds of reasoning which are taken for granted by members of contemporary societies in the West. Habermas is fully aware, of course, that these basic assumptions and kinds of reasoning may not be found everywhere and at all times. Indeed, if one examines the literature on archaic or tribal societies, one is struck by the

TABLE 4: FORMS OF ARGUMENTATION[9]

Forms of argumentation \\ Reference dimensions	Problematic expressions	Validity-claims
theoretical discourse	cognitive-instrumental	truth of propositions; efficacy of teleological actions
practical discourse	moral-practical	correctness of norms of action
aesthetic criticism	evaluative	adequacy of standards of value
therapeutic critique	expressive	sincerity of expressions

extent to which their views of the world appear to differ from ours. In the mythically interpreted world of such societies there seems to be no clear distinction between nature and culture, between the objective world of what is the case and the social world of legitimate norms; mythical world-views seem to be 'closed', in the sense of not allowing for the kind of criticism and argumentation that we associate with the term 'rational'. Does this imply that 'our' concept of rationality is merely one among many, a particularistic expression of one form of life which cannot be ascribed any universal significance, as authors such as Winch have maintained? It is Habermas's view that this implication does not follow from the evidence provided by anthropologists and others. He believes that 'the justified claim to universality on behalf of the rationality that gained expression in the modern understanding of the world'[10] can be sustained by a *theory of social evolution*, conceived as a complex research strategy which attempts to reconstruct the logic of development of world-views and to relate this to changes in the modes of production and forms of administration that characterize different societies. It is with the aim of elaborating this strategy that Habermas takes up Weber's theory of rationalization and the analyses of institutions and social systems worked out by Parsons.

II

Among the classical social theorists, Weber stands out as a thinker who sought to break away from the philosophy of history and nineteenth-century evolutionary theory while at the same time conceiving of the modernization of European societies in terms of a definite historical process of rationalization. In his studies of the great religions of the world, in his inquiries into the origins of capitalism and in his work on the sociology of law, Weber tried to identify some of the characteristics which are peculiar to the development of Western civilization. This enormous undertaking can be viewed, Habermas suggests, as a two-tiered theory of rationalization. On the one hand, Weber investigates the *rationalization of world-views*: he explores the structure and content of religious orientations and traces the course through which specific 'spheres of value', such as science, art and law, become differentiated from one another. On the other hand, in order to show how the rationalization of world-views leads to *social rationalization*, Weber examines the ways in which rationalized values are transposed into motivational and cognitive structures: such is the task of *The Protestant Ethic and the Spirit of Capitalism*.[11] While Habermas endorses this two-tiered approach to the process of rationalization, he is critical of each aspect of Weber's account. In investigating the rationalization of world-views Weber did not distinguish with sufficient sharpness between *form* and *content*. Only by drawing this distinction, argues Habermas, can we reconstruct the logic of development of world-views and thereby clarify the sense in which the rationality that gained expression in the West can lay claim to universality. Weber's account of social rationalization is equally problematic in so far as he does not consider the possibility that the modernization effected with the rise of capitalism may be merely a *selective* or *partial realization* of the structures of consciousness made available by the rationalization of world-views. 'A *narrowing*, heavy with consequences, of the concept of rationality becomes apparent in the transition from cultural to social rationalization. . . . For Weber takes up *directly* the factually given forms of occidental rationalism, without comparing these forms to the counterfactually projected possibilities of a rationalized life-world.'[12]

Habermas is not alone, of course, in wishing to draw out the implications of Weber's theory of rationalization without succumbing to its conclusions. Weber's theory has had a profound impact on authors within certain currents of Marxist thought, especially on Lukács, Horkheimer, Adorno and Marcuse. The phenomenon of reification analysed by Lukács, the dialectic of Enlightenment traced by Horkheimer and Adorno, the one-dimensionality of Western society denounced by Marcuse: all are so many attempts to come to terms with the world-historical processes of rationalization.[13] What these attempts lack, however, and what prevents them from providing a clear and defensible alternative to the pessimistic conclusions implied by Weber, are (1) an intelligible concept of rationality with regard to which one can assess the selective course of social rationalization; and (2) a sustained account of the relation between action and social systems which would enable one to analyse the different forms of social rationalization and to specify their contradictory consequences. Habermas undertakes to provide such an account by establishing a connection between the concept of communicative action and the notion of *Lebenswelt* or 'life-world', and by conjoining the notion of life-world to the theory of social systems elaborated by Parsons. Only in this way, he believes, can critical theory take account of the 'paradoxes' of social rationalization, paradoxes which stem 'less from an instrumental reason gone wild than from the fact that the functionalist reason of system-maintenance brushes aside the claim of reason embedded in communicative socialization and allows the rationalization of the life-world to run idle'.[14]

Habermas introduces the notion of life-world as a correlate of the concept of communicative action: it refers to collectively shared background convictions, to the diffuse, unproblematic horizon *within which* actors communicate with one another and seek to reach an understanding. The life-world of a society or social group preserves and transmits the interpretative work of preceding generations. It forms a symbolic space, as it were, within which cultural tradition, social integration and personal identity are sustained and reproduced. These processes of symbolic reproduction must be distinguished from the mechanisms which maintain the material substrata of society. Actions are not only embedded in the symbolic space of the life-world, but they are also organized into functional systems. Hence societies must be conceived *simultaneously* as system and life-world – or, as Habermas summarily states, 'as *systemically stabilized* action-contexts (*Handlungszusammenhänge*) of *socially integrated* groups'.[15] Functional systems can be conceptualized, following Parsons, as self-regulating action-contexts which co-ordinate actions around specific mechanisms or 'media', such as money or power. Habermas is critical, however, of Parsons's tendency to *over-generalize* the theory of media and thereby to misrepresent the distinctive character of the life-world. For the symbolic structures of the life-world are reproduced through the ongoing interpretative processes of communicative action; and the latter can neither be conceptualized as a medium like money, nor can they be replaced by such media *without pathological consequences*.

The concepts of system and life-world, which must be inter-related without being reduced to one another, specify the key dimensions of Habermas's theory of social evolution. 'I understand social evolution as a second-order process of differentiation: system and life-world not only differentiate themselves *as* system and life-world . . . but they also simultaneously differentiate themselves *from* one another.'[16] With the transition from clan societies through traditional or state-organized societies to modern forms of social organization, one can trace a progressive *uncoupling of system and life-world*. In the course of this uncoupling the life-world, which was initially co-extensive with society as a whole, is increasingly relegated to the status of one sub-system among others. New systemic mechanisms appear which are increasingly severed from the structures responsible for the reproduction of cultural tradition, social integration and personal identity. The most important of these systemic mechanisms are the *state apparatus*, which emerged with the separation of power from pre-existing patterns of kinship, and the *market economy*, which acquired a relatively autonomous and consequential role only with the rise of capitalism in Europe. While the new systemic mechanisms are thus differentiated from the structures of the life-world, they must nevertheless be anchored *in* the life-world by means of specific institutional complexes. These institutional complexes – for example, the status of descent groups within clan societies or bourgeois private law within capitalist societies – define the 'scope' (*Spielraum*) of system differentiation. Problems arise in the functional sub-systems of society which can only be solved through an evolutionary advance in the institutional core, an advance which renders possible the institutionalization of new levels of system differentiation.

The theory of social evolution provides a framework within which one can reformulate Weber's analysis of the process of rationalization. One must carefully distinguish, argues Habermas, between two forms of rationalization which pertain respectively to the dimensions of system and life-world. The rationalization of social systems can be characterized in terms of their *growth in complexity*. From this perspective one can analyse the formation and expansion of markets organized around the medium of money and the steady growth of political and administrative organizations. The rationalization of life-worlds, on the other hand, can be characterized in terms of both the *separation of spheres of value* and the *advancement of levels of learning*. While Weber's theory of rationalization takes account of the separation of spheres of value, it does not do justice, in Habermas's view, to those formal or structural shifts in world-views which 'devalue' the categorial framework of preceding modes of thought. 'These *devaluative shifts*', writes Habermas, 'appear to be connected with transitions to new levels of learning; in this way the conditions of learning in the dimensions of objectivating thought, moral-practical insight and aesthetic-practical expressivity are altered.'[17] In attempting to work out the logic of development of world-views, Habermas draws on Piaget's ontogenetic studies of cognitive development. These studies suggest that the development of world-views can be grasped as a progressive demarcation of the objective and social worlds from the subjective world of experience – that is, as a 'decentration' of an egocentric understanding of the world. Piaget's work also enables one to distinguish several stages of development *within* the dimension of moral-practical insight. Thus Habermas employs the distinction between pre-conventional, conventional and post-conventional structures of moral consciousness in order to reconstruct the logic of development of law and morality in the transition from clan societies to the modern day. Both the decentration of world-views and the appearance of post-conventional forms of law and morality render the background convictions of the life-world more vulnerable to criticism. The conservative weight of tradition is progressively offset by the risk of disagreement that arises with the possibility of criticizing specific validity-claims. Thus the rationalization of the life-world has to do, not with the growth of sub-systems of functionally co-ordinated action, but rather with the unleashing of the rationality potential which is implicit in communicative action.

The two paths of rationalization are not, however, unconnected; and it is in terms of their intersection that one can, Habermas contends, understand some of the traits and tensions of the modern era. While the rationalization of the life-world increases the *potential* for linking symbolic reproduction to the validity basis of speech, at the same time it allows for further growth in the complexity of systems which react back on the life-world and threaten to stifle that potential. This is what Habermas calls the 'inner colonization of the life-world'. He develops the thesis in the form of an 'argumentation-sketch' which he sums up as follows:

> The analysis of processes of modernization begins from the general assumption that a progressively rationalized life-world is both uncoupled from and made dependent on formally organized action domains, such as the economy and state administration, which are always becoming more complex. This dependence, stemming from the mediazation (*Mediatisierung*) of the life-world through system imperatives, assumes the social-pathological form of an *inner colonization* in so far as critical disequilibria in material reproduction (that is, steering crises accessible to system-theoretical analysis) can be avoided only at the cost of disturbances in the symbolic reproduction of the life-world (i.e., of 'subjectively' experienced, identity-threatening crises or pathologies).[18]

In order to specify the threshold at which the 'mediazation' of the life-world turns into an 'inner colonization', Habermas constructs a model of the exchange relations existing in modern societies between system and life-world. The formation of economic and administrative sub-systems in the rise of capitalism was accompanied by parallel developments in the life-world. The socially integrated action domains of the 'private sphere' and the 'public sphere' appeared, the former centred on familial institutions specializing in socialization, the latter constituted by institutions of mass communication which allowed for some degree of public participation in the reproduction of culture. Some of the relations arising between system and life-world are represented, from the system perspective, in table 5 (where P = medium of power, M = medium of money).

TABLE 5: RELATIONS BETWEEN SYSTEM
AND LIFE-WORLD[19]

Institutional orders of life-world	Exchange relations	Media-steered sub-systems
private sphere	P $\longrightarrow$ labour power M $\longleftarrow$ wages M $\longleftarrow$ goods and services M $\longrightarrow$ demand	economic system
public sphere	M $\longrightarrow$ taxes P $\longleftarrow$ organizational results P $\longleftarrow$ political decisions P $\longrightarrow$ mass loyalty	administrative system

Thus the economic system exchanges wages for labour, goods and services for demand, and so on. Habermas's thesis is that these exchange relations give way to an inner colonization of the life-world as soon as the monetarization and bureaucratization of the economic and administrative sub-systems step beyond their mediating roles and penetrate those spheres of the life-world which are responsible for cultural transmission, socialization and the formation of personal identity. The latter processes are internally connected to communicative action and any attempt to incorporate them into media-steered sub-systems will have secondary or 'pathological' effects and may be resisted by members of the life-world. Habermas finds support for this thesis in the tendency to increase the amount of legislation pertaining to education and the family and in the debates to which this tendency has given rise.

While Habermas has attempted to reconstruct the paradoxes of social rationalization in terms of the intrusion of systemic mechanisms into the life-world, he has not yet explained *why* the economic and administrative sub-systems tend to overshoot their limits, *why* they possess an irrepressible dynamic which impels them to overrun the action domains concerned with social integration. The beginnings of such an explanation can be found, Habermas maintains, in Marx's analysis of the processes of accumulation and valorization of capital, processes which underpin the intrinsic dynamic (*Eigendynamik*) of the capitalist economic system. However, Marx did not sufficiently appreciate the extent to which the economic system forms only *one* – albeit a very important one – of the sub-systems characteristic of capitalist societies. In opposition to the 'monism' of Marx's approach we must deal, argues Habermas, with two principal sub-systems and must consider how the dynamic of capital realization can be built into the model of exchange relations between system and life-world. In this way Habermas is able to take account of those features of *advanced* capitalist societies which are often neglected by more orthodox Marxist analyses: namely, state interventionism, mass democracy and the welfare state. As the state assumes an ever-increasing role in attempting to control the crises stemming from the economic system and to cushion their negative effects, it displaces the crisis tendencies into other domains and provokes conflicts which cannot be linked directly to class positions. 'To the extent that class conflict, which is built into societies with a private form of economic accumulation, can be dammed up and kept latent, problems press into the foreground which do not infringe *directly* upon class-specific interest positions.'[20] New conflicts arise along the channels of exchange between system and life-world, highlighting the roles of individuals as consumers of goods and clients of the welfare state. New movements appear which protest against the uncontrolled growth of system complexity:

such is the significance, in Habermas's view, of popular movements advocating ecology and peace, like the 'Greens' in Germany
or the CND in Britain. These movements seem to support the
thesis that the major problems facing advanced industrial societies
today have to do with the self-destructive consequences of system
growth – a growth which threatens to silence the potential for
reflection which, with the rationalization of the life-world, has
become accessible to us.

III

In the 1,200 pages that comprise *Theorie des kommunikativen
Handelns* Habermas develops his position with a philosophical
rigour and historical depth that can hardly be conveyed in the
space of an essay. Yet the preceding paragraphs provide sufficient
content for considering several objections that may be levelled
against Habermas's approach. I shall restrict my critical comments
to five themes which are, I believe, of particular importance.

1 The centrality of communicative action

In *Theorie des kommunikativen Handelns* and in several earlier
studies Habermas presents a theory of language, focused on the
analysis of speech-acts, which is of great interest and originality.
While drawing extensively on the work of English-speaking
philosophers such as Austin and Searle, Habermas's account
nevertheless differs from their work in two crucial respects: not
only does he attempt to elucidate the *general* presuppositions
involved in the exchange of speech-acts, but he also undertakes to
analyse the ways in which language contributes to the *reproduction*
of social life. It seems to me that, in these two respects, Habermas's
account marks a definite advance beyond much of the philosophical literature on language in the English-speaking world. None the
less there are many problematic points in the position put forward
by Habermas. One such point concerns the precise scope of
Habermas's analysis and the considerations which he adduces in
order to specify this scope. Habermas wishes to maintain that the
features brought out by his analysis of speech-acts – the presupposition of three validity-claims, three world-relations and

three modes of language use – define a model of language which is *fundamental* and which displays some of the *essential* conditions of speech; and yet Habermas is well aware that there are many forms of communication which do not readily concur with this model. In what sense, one might object, does reading a poem or telling a joke presuppose the truth of what is said? And is not sincerity characteristically suspended rather than presupposed by the participants in a process of collective bargaining or by friends engaged in the light-hearted activity of 'taking the mickey'? Habermas seldom confronts such objections directly; his strategy is rather to contend 'that the use of language with an orientation to reaching understanding is the *original mode* of language use, upon which indirect understanding, giving something to understand or letting something be understood, are parasitic'.[21]

Until now this contention has been little more than a promissory note. Criticism of the privilege accorded to 'action oriented to reaching understanding' – a notion which seemed to presuppose everything the analysis was supposed to uncover – was staved off with the suggestion that one could demonstrate, through a conceptual inquiry linked to an evolutionary account, the centrality of communicative action. In *Theorie des kommunikativen Handelns* Habermas initiates the conceptual inquiry through a reappraisal of Austin's distinction between illocutionary acts (the act performed *in* saying something) and perlocutionary acts (the act performed *by* saying something).[22] What this distinction shows, in Habermas's view, is that speech-acts can be *incorporated* into teleological actions oriented to success and thereby have perlocutionary effects, but that in such cases the speaker must *conceal* his or her aims, since otherwise the action would fail to have the desired effect. Hence perlocutionary acts are unsuitable for analysing the 'intersubjective binding effect' of speech-acts, that is, the commitments that speakers and hearers necessarily make and reciprocally recognize when they enter into communication. For the analysis of these commitments one is therefore justified, Habermas infers, in considering only 'those linguistically mediated interactions in which all participants pursue illocutionary aims, and *only* illocutionary aims, with their speech-acts'.[23] It seems to me misleading, however, to speak of illocutionary and perlocutionary 'aims' in this way, as if this distinction could yield a clear-cut criterion for singling out a privileged form of communication. When I tell a joke am I pursuing an 'illocutionary aim' (perhaps 'to make myself understood') or a 'perlocutionary aim' (such as 'entertaining my audience') or both simultaneously? And if I am pursuing the aim of entertainment, which can be openly declared and effective nonetheless, why should this serve to relegate this form of communication to a secondary status, as if it were a pale and somewhat distorted reflection of a form of communication which could be grasped in all its purity, untainted by the everyday aims and interests for which and with which we engage in communication? It is difficult to avoid the impression that Habermas's theory of communicative action is based upon a delimitation of the object domain which excludes, in an arbitrary or implausible way, every kind of communication that might provide a counter-example to his case.

2   *Rationality and the discourses of argumentation*

The link established between the analysis of speech-acts and the theme of rationality is one of the most provocative and innovatory aspects of *Theorie des kommunikativen Handelns*. In formulating the concept of communicative rationality Habermas develops a perspective which sheds light on some of the limitations of other theoretical approaches and which offers the possibility of sub-stantiating that appeal to reason – appearing all too often like a vague and utopian plea – which has animated critical theory from the outset. A great deal depends, of course, on just *how* Habermas proposes to fill out the idea of a discourse in which participants would be able to engage in argumentation free from the exercise of force; a great deal also turns on the claim that, with regard to certain sorts of controversy, the protagonists *cannot avoid* step-ping out of their contexts of interaction and entering the realm of argumentative discourse. These crucial issues bear upon Haber-mas's much discussed notion of an 'ideal speech situation' and his equally important, although less well-known, theories of truth and justice.[24] Given the importance of these issues it will come as something of a surprise to see what short shrift they get in *Theorie des kommunikativen Handelns*. There are scattered allusions to the notion of an ideal speech situation and interpretations of other authors which claim to show that such a notion is imminent in their work. But nowhere does Habermas systematically elaborate and defend his view of the conditions under which the rationality implicit in communicative practice could be explicitly realized.

Instead, what we are offered in *Theorie des kommunikativen Handelns* is an 'excursus in the theory of argumentation'. Habermas draws on the contributions of authors who, like Stephen Toulmin and W. Klein, have tried to work out a logic of argumentation, while taking them to task for their tendencies to slide into relativism or empiricism. The theory of argumentation must be formulated at a level of generality which acknowledges the *universality* of specific validity-claims and argumentative procedures without negating the evident *plurality* of cultural contents and values. Hence we are dealing with what Wellmer calls 'a *procedural* conception of rationality, i.e., a specific way of coming to grips with incoherences, contradictions and dissension'.[25] The problem is that Habermas says so little *about* these procedures that it is difficult to pin him down on just what he regards as universal and what he does not. Moreover, in the absence of a more detailed specification, it is hard to see precisely how his account would help to resolve the sorts of debates which centre on truth and justice. One may accept that the rationality of a cognitive or normative expression requires that it be based 'in the end' on reasons or grounds; but unless one can say more about what circumstances constitute 'the end', and unless one can provide a plausible case for assuming that actors placed in such circumstances will generally agree on which reasons are *good* reasons and hence have a 'rationally motivating force', then one can hardly be said to have transcended the struggle of devils and gods.[26] By pitching his proposed theory at a level of generality which purports to take account of 'relativism' without falling into it, Habermas runs the risk of elaborating an account which simply bypasses the most pressing problems.

3 The theory of social evolution

The full implications of communicative action and the full form of communicative rationality are not manifest everywhere and at all times: they come to light, Habermas argues, only in the course of social evolution. The theory of social evolution developed by Habermas is a reformulation and integration of Marx's historical materialism and Weber's views on rationalization. Habermas accepts much of Marx's account of the changing conditions which must be fulfilled for the reproduction of the material substrata of societies, while criticizing Marx for neglecting the dimension of symbolic reproduction and the transformation of world-views. Habermas largely concurs with Weber's analysis of the 'disenchantment' of traditional world-views in the transition to the modern era, but believes that Weber gave insufficient attention to the formal features of this process. By attending to such features Habermas hopes to reconstruct the logic of development of world-views and to show how this logic is related to the processes of differentiation which characterize social evolution. In fact Habermas's 'reconstruction' of the developmental logic of world-views looks very much like a mere projection of Piaget's ontogenetic stages on to the phylogenetic scale; many readers will no doubt baulk at what appears to be a continuation of Hegelian ambitions with cognitive-developmental means. One is bound to wonder, moreover, just how Habermas's theory of social evolution can be applied to the developmental courses of societies outside of Europe, just how it can avoid the ethnocentrism and oversimplification which characterize so many evolutionary schemes.

This is not the place to pursue such issues, which would demand a volume in itself. To Habermas's credit it must be said, however, that he is aware of the objections that can be made against his theory and has made some attempt to counter them. Thus he distinguishes assiduously between the *logic* of development and the *dynamics* of historical processes, emphasizing that the latter 'cannot be handled without recourse to contingent boundary conditions, without analysis of the relations of dependence between socio-cultural changes and transformations of material reproduction'.[27] Habermas does not provide as much analysis of the dynamics of historical processes – especially of those outside of Europe – as one might like, but nevertheless he stresses its importance and makes no pretension to unfold the complexity of historical phenomena from a handful of abstract concepts. The attention of Habermas is focused primarily on the *logic* of development, on its main parameters and theoretical status. We can speak of a 'developmental logic', he notes, only when the structures of the life-world vary in a way which is not accidental but *directed*, that is, in a way which is dependent on learning processes that can be systematically reconstructed. Such reconstructions have a hypothetical status; they cannot be proved directly but can be supported by being incorporated into theories which are used to explain other phenomena, like the ontogenesis of language or the development of legal systems. Piaget's theory is of interest to Habermas not only as a guide to the reconstruction of learning processes but also as an illustration of this co-operative division of labour. It is precisely because Habermas advocates this division of labour that those critics who accuse him of renewing some form of 'philosophical foundationalism' by and large miss the mark. It is for the same reason, however, that Habermas should be pressed to provide a more detailed account of the nature and status of the logic of development and a more precise statement of what would count *against* it.

4 Ideology and the inner colonization of the life-world

The critical force of Habermas's analysis of developmental processes is expressed in the thesis of the inner colonization of the life-world. This thesis attempts to capture the contemporary sense of what Weber referred to as the 'paradoxes' of rationalization; it tries to *explain* these paradoxes by means of a considerably revised version of Marx's analysis of the dynamics of capitalism and Parsons's account of social systems. The thesis thus reflects – to modify a phrase of Habermas – 'the reception of Weber and Parsons within the tradition of Western Marxism'. In formulating the thesis Habermas puts forward a number of contentions which must be distinguished and carefully assessed. Among these contentions are the following: first, that the symbolic reproduction of the life-world bears an internal connection to communicative action; second, that communicative action cannot be conceptualized 'functionally', that is, in terms of systems of action organized around media like money or power; third, that any attempt to replace communicative action *qua* dimension of symbolic reproduction by such media-steered systems will produce secondary or pathological effects; and fourth, that these pathological effects will find expression in protest movements, disturbances in processes of socialization, withdrawals of motivation and legitimation – that is, in reactions to processes which are experienced as 'threatening'. There are many aspects of these contentions that could be questioned. For example, while it seems plausible to argue that the reproduction of cultural tradition, social integration and personal identity takes place in and through language, it is quite another matter to maintain that symbolic reproduction bears an internal connection to *communicative action*, with everything that entails concerning the presupposition and rational redemption of validity-claims. And yet it seems clear that Habermas requires the stronger thesis if he is to justify his use of the term 'pathology' and to defend his view that 'under conditions of a rationalized life-world with highly individuated members, norms that are becoming abstract . . . and traditions whose claims to authority have been reflexively and communicatively broken through, only democratic processes of political will-formation can in principle produce legitimacy'.[28]

The issue on which I want to focus my critical remarks, however, is not the thesis of the inner colonization of the life-world *per se*, but rather the question of why, supposing this thesis is accurate, it is not more widely acknowledged by members of the life-world themselves. Why do members of the life-world *not* perceive that what they are threatened by is the uncontrolled growth of system complexity, rooted ultimately in the dynamics of capital accumulation and valorization? Why do they not resist this growth directly and demand, in an open and widespread way, the transformation of the economic system which underlies it? Such questions are, of course, the traditional fare of the theory of ideology. However, it is Habermas's view in *Theorie des kommunikativen Handelns* that the notion of ideology makes sense only with regard to the totalizing conceptions of eighteenth-century bourgeois culture and subsequent reactions to it, such as anarchism, communism and fascism. In the developed industrial societies of today, with their differentiated structures of communication and comprehension, no room is left for the power of ideology. If the contradictions of these societies are not evident to their members it is not because new forms of ideology have appeared but because these societies have developed a 'functional equivalent' *for* ideology. This functional equivalent is the fragmentation and dispersion of everyday consciousness, which prevents subjects from seeing through the imperatives of sub-systems and demanding the discursive redemption of validity-claims. 'In place of false consciousness steps *fragmented* consciousness, which precludes enlightenment about the mechanism of reification.'[29] The emphasis on the fragmentation of consciousness is a welcome shift in Habermas's position and one which certainly deserves to be pursued.[30] But it seems to me quite mistaken to maintain that fragmentation is an equivalent, 'functional' or otherwise, for ideology and that these two equivalents operate *in exclusion* of one another. By restricting the notion of ideology to the totalizing conceptions of past decades and centuries, Habermas leaves us without the theoretical and methodological means to examine critically the forms of language which serve *today* to sustain relations of domination. That such forms of language often operate by fragmenting consciousness in various ways, that they can be conceived as ideology and analysed with the help of specific methods – these are claims which I have defended elsewhere.[31] Suffice it to say here that few tasks seem more urgent than the continuation of that project of a *critique of ideology* which appears to have faded into the background of Habermas's work.

5   On the analysis of the present day

As the thesis of the inner colonization of the life-world makes clear, *Theorie des kommunikativen Handelns* is concerned above all with offering an analysis of the present day, a *Gegenwartsdiagnose*. The concepts of communicative action and rationality, as well as the theories of rationalization and social evolution, are not presented in abstraction: they provide the theoretical signposts for analysing the tensions and tendencies of the modern era. *Theorie des kommunikativen Handelns* is both a theoretical treatise and a practical intervention, a systematic riposte to the neo-conservative apologetic which would like to cope with the disintegrating consequences of growth by 'seeking refuge in the uprooted but rhetorically laden traditions of a cosy domestic culture (*biedermeierliche Kultur*)'.[32] Habermas's capacity to tie together theoretical and practical considerations, his ability to pursue complex philosophical issues without losing sight of substantial sociological and political concerns, is altogether astonishing. No one can read *Theorie des kommunikativen Handelns* without sensing the profound *commitment* that animates his work.

Nevertheless, for those who live in the industrial societies of today, the analysis offered by Habermas may seem somewhat narrow and out of date. With unemployment at unprecedented levels and still climbing, with fluctuating rates of interest and exchange and low demand pushing more and more businesses to the wall, the idea that crises stemming from the productive process can be contained by state intervention may seem a little implausible; in any case, the notion that such crises are displaced into other domains, manifesting themselves as withdrawals of motivation or losses of meaning, appears to require more qualifications than it may have needed in the Federal Republic a decade ago. While class conflict is not the only form of struggle that characterizes advanced capitalist societies, it would seem imprudent to maintain, as Habermas is inclined to do, that such conflict has been 'dammed up'. Moreover it is striking – although perhaps not surprising in view of its evolutionary emphasis[33] – that 'a' society or 'a' nation-state remains the *pierre de touche* of Habermas's account. Nowhere does he examine in detail the international *system* of nation-states, the multinational alliances which greatly affect economic development and threaten one another's survival with the accumulated means of waging war. It is at best incomplete to interpret the conflicts and protest movements of our societies from within a framework that filters out the confrontation of nation-states and the politics of mass destruction.

Whatever weaknesses and shortcomings there may be in Habermas's account, there can be no doubt that *Theorie des kommunikativen Handelns* represents a major contribution to contemporary social theory. Not only does it offer a compelling critique of some of the main perspectives in twentieth-century philosophy and social science, but it also provides a systematic synthesis of many of the themes that have preoccupied Habermas for thirty years. In its scrupulous analysis of other views, in its spirited defence of old themes and new ideas, in its unshirking response to lines of criticism, *Theorie des kommunikativen Handelns* is a testimony to the integrity of an author who has consistently and courageously defended the value of open argumentation and debate.

Notes

1 IDEOLOGY AND THE SOCIAL IMAGINARY

1. The research for this essay was supported by the Wolfson Foundation and the British Academy, to the trustees and fellows of which I express my gratitude. I also wish to thank Cornelius Castoriadis and Claude Lefort for their extensive comments on an earlier draft of the essay.
2. It may be helpful at this point to add a brief biographical and bibliographical note. Cornelius Castoriadis studied law, economics and philosophy in Athens, before arriving in France in 1945. Claude Lefort studied philosophy and politics under the guidance of Merleau-Ponty. In 1946 Castoriadis and Lefort founded a movement within the French Trotskyist party, the *Parti Communiste Internationale* (PCI), opposing in particular Trotsky's analysis of Russia and Stalinism. In 1948 they broke with the PCI, formed an independent group and published, in March 1949, the first issue of *Socialisme ou Barbarie*; the final issue of the journal appeared in June 1965.

   Most of Castoriadis's writings have been collected together and republished in eight volumes in the series 10/18 (Paris: Union générale d'éditions, 1973-9); among his other publications are *L'Institution imaginaire de la société* (Paris: Seuil, 1975); *Les Carrefours du labyrinth* (Paris: Seuil, 1978); and *Devant la guerre, vol. 1: les réalités* (Paris: Fayard, 1981). Most of the essays written by Lefort between 1950 and 1980 have been collected together in four volumes: *Eléments d'une critique de la bureaucratie* (Genève: Droz, 1971; an abridged version was published in Paris by Gallimard in 1979); *Les Formes de l'histoire: essais d'anthropologie politique* (Paris: Gallimard, 1978); *Sur une colonne absente: écrits autour de Merleau-Ponty* (Paris: Gallimard, 1978); *L'Invention démocratique: les limites de la domination totalitaire* (Paris: Fayard, 1981). Among Lefort's other publications are *Le Travail de l'oeuvre: Machiavel* (Paris: Gallimard, 1972); and *Un homme en trop: réflexions sur l'Archipel du Goulag* (Paris: Seuil, 1975). In June 1968 Castoriadis and Lefort published, together with Edgar Morin, a study of the events of May: *Mai 1968: la brèche* (Paris: Fayard).

An overview of Castoriadis's work may be found in his Introduction to *La Société bureaucratique*, vol. 1 (Paris: Union générale d'éditions, 1973), pp. 11–61. Lefort offers a reflection on the development of his work in his Preface to the 1979 edition of *Eléments d'une critique de la bureaucratie*, pp 7–28. English-speaking readers may wish to consult Dick Howard's general introductions to the writings of Castoriadis and Lefort: 'Introduction to Castoriadis', *Telos*, 23 (1975), pp. 117–31; 'Introduction to Lefort', *Telos*, 22 (1974–5), pp. 2–30; versions of these essays appear as chapters 9 and 10 of Howard's book, *The Marxian Legacy* (London: Macmillan, 1977). A valuable discussion of Castoriadis's work may be found in a two-part study by Brian Singer: 'The early Castoriadis: socialism, barbarism and the bureaucratic thread', *Canadian Journal of Political and Social Theory*, vol. 3, no. 3 (1979), pp. 35–56; 'The later Castoriadis: institution under interrogation', *Canadian Journal of Political and Social Theory*, vol. 4, no. 1 (1980), pp. 75–101.

Translations of essays by Castoriadis and Lefort have appeared in various issues of *Solidarity*, *Telos* and other journals. Castoriadis's *Les Carrefours du labyrinthe* has been translated under the title of *Crossroads in the Labyrinth*, tr. Kate Soper and Martin Ryle (Brighton, Sussex: Harvester, 1984). An English edition of Castoriadis's *L'Institution imaginaire de la société* is forthcoming with Polity Press and M. I. T. Press. A collection of Lefort's essays on bureaucracy, ideology and totalitarianism will also be published by Polity Press and M. I. T. under the title, *The Political Forms of Modern Society*. In this essay all quotations from Castoriadis and Lefort are my own translation.

3. Some of these differences are expressed in two very interesting interviews with Castoriadis and Lefort; see 'An interview with C. Castoriadis', tr. Bart Grahl and David Pugh, *Telos*, 23 (1975), pp. 131–55; and 'An interview with Claude Lefort', tr. Dorothy Gehrke and Brian Singer, *Telos*, 30 (1976–7), pp. 173–92.

4. Reprinted as Part One of *L'Institution imaginaire de la société*, pp. 11–157.

5. Cornelius Castoriadis, *L'Institution imaginaire de la société*, p. 26.

6. Ibid., p. 20.

7. Ibid., p. 106.
8. Ibid., p. 130.
9. Ibid., p. 256.
10. Ibid., p. 293.
11. There is also a specifically psychic level of the imaginary, which Castoriadis calls the 'radical imagination'. For Castoriadis's discussion of this level, and for his views on the psyche and on psychoanalysis more generally, see *L'Institution imaginaire de la société*, ch. VI; and *Les Carrefours du labyrinthe*, part one.
12. Cornelius Castoriadis, *L'Institution imaginaire de la société*, p. 203.
13. Ibid., p. 465.
14. Originally published in 1973–4, 'Esquisse d'une genèse de l'idéologie dans les sociétés modernes' was reprinted in *Les Formes de l'histoire*, pp. 278–329.
15. Claude Lefort, *Les Formes de l'histoire*, p. 287.
16. Ibid., p. 296. For a discussion of the distinction between 'historical societies' and 'societies without history', see 'Société "sans histoire" et historicité', in *Les Formes de l'histoire*, pp. 30–48.
17. Claude Lefort, *Les Formes de l'histoire*, p. 302.
18. Ibid., p. 308.
19. Ibid., p. 314.
20. Ibid., p. 315. For more extensive analyses of the characteristics and contradictions of totalitarianism, see *Eléments d'une critique de la bureaucratie*, part two, and the essays brought together in *L'Invention démocratique*.
21. Claude Lefort, *Les Formes de l'histoire*, p. 319.
22. The allusion here is to William H. Whyte, *The Organization Man* (Garden City, N. Y.: Doubleday, 1956).
23. Claude Lefort, *Les Formes de l'histoire*, p. 327.
24. See especially Jean Baudrillard, *La Société de la consommation: ses mythes, ses structures* (Paris: E. P. Denoël, 1970); and *Le Système des objets* (Paris: Gallimard, 1968).
25. Cf. Herbert Marcuse, *One Dimensional Man* (London: Routledge & Kegan Paul, 1964).
26. See especially Jürgen Habermas, *Legitimation Crisis*, tr. Thomas McCarthy (London: Heinemann, 1976); Claus Offe, *Contradictions of the Welfare State*, ed. John Keane (London: Hutchinson, 1984).
27. For an excellent exposition and critique of Habermas's theory of legitimation crisis, see David Held, 'Crisis tendencies, legitimation and the state', in *Habermas: Critical Debates*, ed. John B. Thompson and David Held (London: Macmillan, 1982), pp. 181–95.
28. This standpoint is developed in: Michael Mann, 'The social cohesion

of liberal democracy', *American Sociological Review*, 35 (1970), pp. 423–39; and *Consciousness and Action Among the Western Working Class* (London: Macmillan, 1973); Anthony Giddens, *The Class Structure of the Advanced Societies* (London: Hutchinson, 1973); and David Held, *Power and Legitimacy in Contemporary Britain*, prepared for Open University course D209 on the state (Milton Keynes: The Open University Press, 1984).

29. I do not want to suggest that Lefort is unaware of processes of fragmentation and differentiation in contemporary capitalist societies (see, for example, his Preface to *Eléments d'une critique de la bureaucratie*, especially pp. 10–11). My point is rather that Lefort does not grasp the full implications of these processes for the operation of ideology. Such processes imply that the maintenance of a system of domination may depend more on internal dissensus within subordinate groups and pragmatic acceptance of institutional arrangements than on a positive commitment to collective values. It cannot be assumed, therefore, that ideology in contemporary capitalist societies operates via a *unification* of the social field.

30. See Lefort's essay, 'La naissance de l'idéologie et l'humanisme', in *Les Formes de l'histoire*, pp. 234–77.

31. See especially Pierre Bourdieu, *Outline of a Theory of Practice*, tr. Richard Nice (Cambridge: Cambridge University Press, 1977); and *Le Sens pratique* (Paris: Minuit, 1980); Maurice Godelier, *Perspectives in Marxist Anthropology*, tr. Robert Brain (Cambridge: Cambridge University Press, 1977); and 'Pouvoir et langage', *Communications*, 28 (1978), pp. 21–7.

32. This point is forcefully made by Nicholas Abercrombie, Stephen Hill and Bryan S. Turner, *The Dominant Ideology Thesis* (London: George Allen & Unwin, 1980).

33. Some suggestive remarks in support of this view may be found in Theo Nichols and Peter Armstrong, *Workers Divided* (London: Fontana/Collins, 1976), pp. 142–7. It is tempting to interpret in a similar way the role of the Royal Wedding in the context of widespread strife in Britain's cities during the summer of 1981; for a brief discussion, see Helen Chappell, 'The wedding and the people', *New Society*, 57 (30 July 1981), pp. 175–7.

34. In proposing this view I am indebted to the work of Anthony Giddens; see especially his *Central Problems in Social Theory: Action, Structure and Contradiction in Social Analysis* (London: Macmillan, 1979).

35. Karl Marx, *The Eighteenth Brumaire of Louis Bonaparte*, in Karl Marx and Frederick Engels, *Selected Works in One Volume* (London:

Lawrence & Wishart, 1968), p. 96. Lefort offers a provocative analysis of this work in 'Marx: d'une vision de l'histoire à l'autre', in *Les Formes de l'histoire*, pp. 195–233. See also the remarkable study by Paul-Laurent Assoun, *Marx et la répétition historique* (Paris: Presses Universitaires de France, 1978).

36. One may also question, in this regard, Lefort's contention that in spite of Marx's allusions to religion in his analysis of the fetishism of commodities, 'he comes to conceive of a mechanism of illusion which no longer makes room (except accidentally) for evasion into another world' (*Les Formes de l'histoire*, p. 254). For a different view of the role of religion in Marx's analysis, see Sarah Kofman, *Camera Obscura. De l'idéologie* (Paris: Galilée, 1973).

37. The notion of split reference and its connection to the process of interpretation is developed by Paul Ricoeur in *The Rule of Metaphor: Multi-Disciplinary Studies of the Creation of Meaning in Language*, tr. Robert Czerny (London: Routledge & Kegan Paul, 1978); and *Hermeneutics and the Human Sciences: Essays on Language, Action and Interpretation*, ed. and tr. John B. Thompson (Cambridge: Cambridge University Press, 1981). I have examined some of Ricoeur's contributions in my book, *Critical Hermeneutics: A Study in the Thought of Paul Ricoeur and Jürgen Habermas* (Cambridge: Cambridge University Press, 1981).

38. See, for example, the work of George Duby in history, of Jacques Lacan in psychoanalysis, and of Paul Ricoeur in philosophy and literary theory.

39. Castoriadis generally describes the dissimulation of the creative core of a society as 'alienation' or 'heteronomy'; see *L'Institution imaginaire de la société*, pp. 148 ff.

40. I do not believe, moreover, that 'the real' can be defined as that which refuses to be covered over, as Lefort appears to maintain (see *Les Formes de l'histoire*, p. 292). For this definition seems hopelessly circular, merely shifting the demand for clarification on to the notion of 'covering over'; and the definition seems to leave no way for approaching cases of more 'successful' dissimulation.

41. It may be noted that the question of revolution is one of the key issues on which the views of Castoriadis and Lefort diverge. In the eyes of Lefort, to affirm the idea of an overthrow which would make possible the explicit self-institution of society is to reintroduce 'the myth, inherited from Marx, of a society able to master its own development and to communicate with all its parts, a society able in a way *to see itself*' ('An interview with Claude Lefort', p. 185). Lefort's rejection of the idea of revolution may be more consistent with the

overall attack on 'rationalism'; but it is because I wish to mitigate this attack, to draw out some of the themes which cut across it, that I have chosen to focus here on Castoriadis.

42. Cornelius Castoriadis, *L'Institution imaginaire de la société*, p. 137.
43. Ibid., p. 473.
44. In expressing this view I indicate my debt to the work of Jürgen Habermas, whose contributions I have discussed in my book, *Critical Hermeneutics*, and in my essays, 'Universal pragmatics: Habermas's proposals for the analysis of language and truth', and 'Rationality and social rationalization: an assessment of Habermas's theory of communicative action', both in this volume.
45. There are passages in which Castoriadis appears to allow for a more generous conception of the rational; for example: 'As for the enormous problem, at the most radical philosophical level, of the relation between the imaginary and the rational, of the question of whether the rational is only a moment of the imaginary or whether it expresses man's encounter with a transcendent order, here we can only leave it open, doubting moreover whether we could ever do otherwise' (*L'Institution imaginaire de la société*, p. 227, n. 55). See also the interesting remarks in 'L'exigence révolutionnaire', an interview with Castoriadis which was originally published in *Esprit* (1977) and reprinted in Castoriadis's *Le Contenu du socialisme* (Paris: Union générale d'éditions, 1979), pp. 323–66.

2 SYMBOLIC VIOLENCE

1. I wish to thank Pierre Bourdieu for his detailed comments on an earlier draft of this essay.
2. Bourdieu develops his approach to language in his recent book, *Ce que parler veut dire: l'économie des échanges linguistiques* (Paris: Fayard, 1981); the first part of this book is a new contribution, while parts II and III contain essays which were published elsewhere. Other essays of particular interest are the following: Pierre Bourdieu, 'L'économie des échanges linguistiques', *Langue Française*, 34 (mai 1977), pp. 17–34 [English translation: 'The economics of linguistic exchanges', tr. Richard Nice, *Social Science Information*, 16 (1977), pp. 645–68]; Pierre Bourdieu and Luc Boltanski, 'Le fétichisme de la langue', *Actes de la recherche en sciences sociales*, 4 (juillet 1975), pp. 2–32; and Pierre Bourdieu, 'Sur le pouvoir symbolique', *Annales*, 32 (1977), pp. 405–11 [English translation: 'Symbolic power', tr. Colin Wringe, in *Identity and Structure: Issues in the Sociology of*

Education, ed. Denis Gleeson (Nafferton, Driffield, England: Nafferton Books, 1977), pp. 112–19]. See also some of the essays in Bourdieu's *Questions de sociologie* (Paris: Minuit, 1980). A selection of Bourdieu's writings on language will appear in English under the title, *Language and Symbolic Power* (Cambridge: Polity Press, forthcoming).

Since 1960 Bourdieu has published some twenty books, many of which have been, or are being, translated into English. The following are among the most important for the issues discussed in this essay: Pierre Bourdieu and Jean-Claude Passeron, *La Reproduction: éléments pour une théorie du système d'enseignement* (Paris: Minuit, 1970) [English translation: *Reproduction: In Education, Society and Culture*, tr. Richard Nice (London and Beverly Hills: Sage, 1977)]; Pierre Bourdieu, *Esquisse d'une théorie de la pratique, précédé de trois études d'ethnologie Kabyle* (Genève: Droz, 1972) [English translation: *Outline of a Theory of Practice*, tr. Richard Nice (Cambridge: Cambridge University Press, 1977); the text of this translation differs from the original French edition]; Pierre Bourdieu, *La Distinction: critique sociale du jugement* (Paris: Minuit, 1979); and Pierre Bourdieu, *Le Sens pratique* (Paris: Minuit, 1980). For fuller bibliographies of Bourdieu's writings, see *Reproduction: In Education, Society and Culture*, pp. 237–41; and 'Pierre Bourdieu: a bibliography', *Media, Culture and Society*, 2 (1980), pp. 295–6.

Throughout this essay all quotations are my own translation and all references are to the original French editions; references to English translations are given in square brackets.
3. See Pierre Bourdieu, *Esquisse d'une théorie de la pratique* [*Outline of a Theory of Practice*].
4. Bourdieu offers an illuminating reflection on the development of his thought in the preface to *Le Sens pratique*, pp. 7–41. For a helpful survey of Bourdieu's contribution to the sociology of culture, see Nicholas Garnham and Raymond Williams, 'Pierre Bourdieu and the sociology of culture: an introduction', *Media, Culture and Society*, 2 (1980), pp. 209–23.
5. Pierre Bourdieu, *Ce que parler veut dire*, p. 27.
6. Cf. Ferdinand Brunot, *Histoire de la langue française des origines à nos jours* (Paris: Armand Colin, 1905–53). For a similar but more extended reflection on some of the implications of Brunot's work, see Renée Balibar and Dominique Laporte, *Le Français national: politique et pratique de la langue nationale sous la Révolution* (Paris: Hachette, 1974).
7. Pierre Bourdieu, *Ce que parler veut dire*, p. 34.

8. Pierre Bourdieu and Luc Boltanski, 'Le fétichisme de la langue', p. 8.

9. Cf. William Labov, *Sociolinguistic Patterns* (Philadelphia: University of Pennsylvania Press, 1972), pp. 128–32.

10. Cf. Noam Chomsky, *Aspects of the Theory of Syntax* (Cambridge, Mass.: M. I. T. Press, 1965), pp. 3–4.

11. Pierre Bourdieu, 'L'économie des échanges linguistiques', p. 20.

12. Cf. J. L. Austin, *How to do Things with Words* (Oxford: Oxford University Press, 1976), lecture II.

13. Pierre Bourdieu, *Ce que parler veut dire*, p. 73.

14. Ibid., pp. 107–9.

15. Pierre Bourdieu, *Questions de sociologie*, p. 114.

16. For extended discussions of such 'strategies of reconversion', see Pierre Bourdieu and Luc Boltanski, 'Le titre et le poste: rapports entre le système de production et le système de reproduction', *Actes de la recherche en sciences sociales*, 2 (mars 1975), pp. 95–107 [English translation: 'Formal qualifications and occupational hierarchies: the relationship between the production system and the reproduction system', tr. Richard Nice, in *Reorganizing Education: Management and Participation for Change*, ed. Edmund J. King (London and Beverly Hills: Sage, 1977), pp. 61–9]; and Pierre Bourdieu, *La Distinction*, pp. 145–85.

17. Adapted from Pierre Bourdieu, *Outline of a Theory of Practice*, p. 168.

18. Pierre Bourdieu and Luc Boltanski, 'Le fétichisme de la langue', p. 14.

19. See *La République des Pyrénées* (9 septembre 1974); relevant parts of the text are reproduced by Bourdieu and Boltanski in 'Le fétichisme de la langue', p. 13.

20. Pierre Bourdieu, *Ce que parler veut dire*, p. 63.

21. Pierre Bourdieu, *Esquisse d'une théorie de la pratique*, p. 175 [*Outline of a Theory of Practice*, p. 72].

22. For a discussion of the relation between habitus and life-styles, see Pierre Bourdieu, *La Distinction*, pp. 189–97.

23. Pierre Bourdieu, *Ce que parler veut dire*, pp. 83–4.

24. Mechanisms of self-elimination from the educational system are examined by Bourdieu and Passeron in *La Reproduction*, pp. 185–202 [*Reproduction: In Education, Society and Culture*, pp. 152–64].

25. Pierre Bourdieu, *Ce que parler veut dire*, p. 90.

26. Cf. Pierre Guiraud, *Le Français populaire* (Paris: Presses Universitaires de France, 1965).

27. It is difficult to convey in English the distinction, here exploited by

Bourdieu, between *bouche* and *gueule*; the latter term, while meaning literally 'mouth' or 'face', also conveys a sense of roughness or aggression (as with the English expressions 'gob' or 'trap').

28. Cf. William Labov, *Sociolinguistic Patterns*, pp. 301–4.

29. Pierre Bourdieu, *Le Sens pratique*, p. 219 [see *Outline of a Theory of Practice*, p. 192].

30. Pierre Bourdieu and Jean-Claude Passeron, *La Reproduction*, p. 238 [*Reproduction: In Education, Society and Culture*, p. 200].

31. Pierre Bourdieu, *Ce que parler veut dire*, p. 38.

32. This argument is developed by Michael Mann, 'The social cohesion of liberal democracy', *American Sociological Review*, 35 (1970), pp. 423–39; and *Consciousness and Action Among the Western Working Class* (London: Macmillan, 1973); Anthony Giddens, *The Class Structure of the Advanced Societies* (London: Hutchinson, 1973); and David Held, *Power and Legitimacy in Contemporary Britain*, prepared for Open University course D209 on the state (Milton Keynes: The Open University Press, 1984).

33. See Paul E. Willis, *Learning to Labour: How Working Class Kids Get Working Class Jobs* (Westmead, Farnborough, Hants.: Saxon House, 1977); see also the various contributions in *Resistance through Rituals: Youth Subcultures in Post-war Britain*, ed. Stuart Hall and Tony Jefferson (London: Hutchinson, 1976). I do not wish to suggest that Bourdieu is unaware of these strategies of conflict and resistance (see, for example, Pierre Bourdieu, 'Vous avez dit "populaire"?', *Actes de la recherche en sciences sociales*, 46 (mars 1983), pp. 98–105). But he tends to interpret these strategies as *implicit affirmations* of the dominant social forms rather than as so many ways of rejecting those forms, ways which, partially because of their diverse and fragmented character, nevertheless leave the hierarchies intact.

34. The results of such studies are summarized by David Held in *Power and Legitimacy in Contemporary Britain*.

35. My remarks on the concept of legitimacy are indebted to the work of Habermas; see especially Jürgen Habermas, *Legitimation Crisis*, tr. Thomas McCarthy (London: Heinemann, 1976). I shall return to the question of justification, in connection with the notion of truth, at the end of this essay.

36. For a critique of this assumption, see Nicholas Abercrombie, Stephen Hill and Bryan S. Turner, *The Dominant Ideology Thesis* (London: George Allen & Unwin, 1980).

37. I have discussed some issues relevant to this task in my essays, 'Theories of ideology and methods of discourse analysis: towards a

framework for the analysis of ideology', and 'Ideology and the analysis of discourse: a critical introduction to the work of Michel Pêcheux', both in this volume.

38. For numerous illustrations of the use of this concept in the analysis of culture, see Pierre Bourdieu (with Yvette Delsaut), 'Le couturier et sa griffe: contribution à une théorie de la magie', *Actes de la recherche en sciences sociales*, 1 (janvier 1975), pp. 7–36; Pierre Bourdieu, 'La production de la croyance: contribution à une économie des biens symboliques', *Actes de la recherche en sciences sociales*, 13 (février 1977), pp. 3–43 [English translation: 'The production of belief: contribution to an economy of symbolic goods', tr. Richard Nice, *Media, Culture and Society*, 2 (1980), pp. 261–93]; and *La Distinction, passim*. See also Luc Boltanski, 'La constitution du champ de la bande dessinée', *Actes de la recherche en sciences sociales*, 1 (janvier 1975), pp. 37–59.

39. Pierre Bourdieu, *Ce que parler veut dire*, p. 41.

40. Bourdieu practises this method of analysis in the essays reprinted in part III of *Ce que parler veut dire*. See also Pierre Bourdieu, 'L'ontologie politique de Martin Heidegger', *Actes de la recherche en sciences sociales*, 5–6 (novembre 1975), pp. 109–56.

41. Pierre Bourdieu, *Ce que parler veut dire*, p. 15.

42. Ibid., p. 105.

43. Elias Canetti, *Crowds and Power*, tr. Carol Stewart (Harmondsworth, Middlesex: Penguin, 1973, p. 331.

44. See my *Critical Hermeneutics: A Study in the Thought of Paul Ricoeur and Jürgen Habermas* (Cambridge: Cambridge University Press, 1981), ch. 4; and part III of my essay 'Theories of ideology and methods of discourse analysis: towards a framework for the analysis of ideology', in this volume.

45. Pierre Bourdieu, *Ce que parler veut dire*, p. 105.

46. For a more detailed and balanced analysis of some aspects of Austin's work, see P. F. Strawson, 'Intention and convention in speech acts', *Philosophical Review*, 63 (1964), pp. 439–60.

47. Bourdieu criticizes Habermas for leaning too heavily on the theory of speech-acts, a tendency which leads Habermas, in Bourdieu's view, 'to place the force of words in words – and not in the institutional conditions of their use' (*Ce que parler veut dire*, p. 25). It will be clear from my argument in the text why I think that this criticism is unsound.

48. See my *Critical Hermeneutics*, ch. 6; see also 'Universal pragmatics: Habermas's proposals for the analysis of language and truth', and 'Rationality and social rationalization: an assessment of Habermas's theory of communicative action', both in this volume.

3 THEORIES OF IDEOLOGY AND METHODS OF DISCOURSE ANALYSIS

1. I wish to thank Roger Fowler, David Good, John Keane and Gunther Kress for their helpful comments on earlier drafts of the essay.
2. For concise histories of the concept of ideology, see Hans Barth, *Truth and Ideology*, tr. Frederic Lilge (Berkeley: University of California Press, 1976); and George Lichtheim, 'The concept of ideology', in his *The Concept of Ideology and Other Essays* (New York: Random House, 1967), pp. 3–46. More extended discussions are provided by Jorge Larrain in his two useful books: *The Concept of Ideology* (London: Hutchinson, 1979); and *Marxism and Ideology* (London: Macmillan, 1983).
3. Cf. Clifford Geertz, 'Ideology as a cultural system', reprinted in his *The Interpretation of Cultures* (London: Hutchinson, 1975), pp. 192–233.
4. I have made some preliminary contributions to such a discussion in various essays; see especially chapter 7 in this volume, 'Ideology and the analysis of discourse: A critical introduction to the work of Michel Pêcheux'.
5. Cf. Martin Seliger, *Ideology and Politics* (London: George Allen & Unwin, 1976).
6. Martin Seliger, *The Marxist Conception of Ideology: A Critical Essay* (Cambridge: Cambridge University Press, 1977), p. 76.
7. Cf. *The End of Ideology Debate*, ed. Chaim Waxman (New York: Simon and Schuster, 1968).
8. Martin Seliger, *Ideology and Politics*, pp. 91–2.
9. Ibid., pp. 119–20.
10. Ibid., p. 109.
11. Ibid., p. 243.
12. See the pertinent discussion of Marx's conception and of Seliger's critique in Joe McCarney, *The Real World of Ideology* (Brighton, Sussex: Harvester, 1980).
13. Alvin W. Gouldner, *The Dialectic of Ideology and Technology: The Origins, Grammar and Future of Ideology* (London: Macmillan, 1976), p. 9.
14. Ibid., p. 30.
15. Ibid., p. 81.
16. See especially Basil Bernstein, 'Social class, language and socialization', in his *Class, Codes and Control, vol. 1: Theoretical Studies*

towards a Sociology of Language (London: Routledge & Kegan Paul, 1971), pp. 170–89.

17. Alvin W. Gouldner, *The Dialectic of Ideology and Technology*, p. 80.

18. Cf. Jürgen Habermas, *Strukturwandel der Öffentlichkeit. Untersuchungen zu einer Kategorie der bürgerlichen Gesellschaft* (Neuwied: Luchterhand, 1963).

19. Alvin W. Gouldner, *The Dialectic of Ideology and Technology*, p. 105.

20. Ibid., p. 231.

21. Ibid., p. 176.

22. Ibid., pp. 9, 277; cf. also pp. 54–5, 81, 105, 206 and 276.

23. Ibid., p. 276.

24. Cf. Jürgen Habermas, 'Technology and science as "ideology"', in his *Toward a Rational Society: Student Protest, Science, and Politics*, tr. Jeremy J. Shapiro (London: Heinemann, 1971), pp. 81–122. Gouldner offers some critical remarks on Habermas in chapters 11 and 12 of *The Dialectic of Ideology and Technology*.

25. For example, by Habermas in 'Technology and science as "ideology"'; and by Claude Lefort in 'Esquisse d'une genèse de l'idéologie dans les sociétés modernes', in his *Les Formes de l'histoire: essais d'anthropologie politique* (Paris: Gallimard, 1978), pp. 278–329.

26. Louis Althusser, *For Marx*, tr. Ben Brewster (Harmondsworth, Middlesex: Penguin, 1969), p. 232.

27. Cf. Louis Althusser, 'Ideology and ideological state apparatuses (Notes towards an investigation)', in his *Lenin and Philosophy and Other Essays*, tr. Ben Brewster (London: New Left Books, 1971), pp. 121–73.

28. Cf. Paul Hirst, *On Law and Ideology* (London: Macmillan, 1979).

29. For other studies influenced by Althusser, see Rosalind Coward and John Ellis, *Language and Materialism: Developments in Semiology and the Theory of the Subject* (London: Routledge & Kegan Paul, 1977); Ernesto Laclau, *Politics and Ideology in Marxist Theory: Capitalism, Fascism, Populism* (London: New Left Books, 1977); Colin Sumner, *Reading Ideologies: An Investigation into the Marxist Theory of Ideology and Law* (London: Academic Press, 1979); and Göran Therborn, *The Ideology of Power and the Power of Ideology* (London: New Left Books, 1980).

30. Paul Hirst, *On Law and Ideology*, p. 53.

31. Ibid., pp. 59–60.

32. For Althusser's original statement of this distinction, see *For Marx*, especially pp. 167 ff. The distinction was subsequently criticized and modified by Althusser himself in *Essays in Self-Criticism*, tr. Grahame Lock (London: New Left Books, 1976), pp. 119–25.

33. Paul Hirst, *On Law and Ideology*, p. 8.
34. Ibid., pp. 1, 22.
35. Ibid., pp. 7, 54.
36. Ibid., p. 73.
37. Ibid., p. 88. See also the recent book by Paul Hirst and Penny Woolley, *Social Relations and Human Attributes* (London: Tavistock, 1982), in which it is argued that 'human attributes' are the constructs of definite and historically variable social relations, so that 'the "person" is an effect and support of the repertoires of conduct employed in definite sets of social relations' (p. 43).
38. Barry Hindess and Paul Hirst, *Mode of Production and Social Formation: An Auto-Critique of 'Pre-Capitalist Modes of Production'* (London: Macmillan, 1977), p. 59. See also Barry Hindess, *Philosophy and Methodology in the Social Sciences* (Brighton, Sussex: Harvester, 1977).
39. Barry Hindess and Paul Hirst, *Mode of Production and Social Formation*, pp. 13–14.
40. For further reflections on this theme, see Paul Hirst and Penny Woolley, *Social Relations and Human Attributes*, where Winch's views on 'the inescapable relativity of distinct theoretical schemes and belief systems' (p. 269) are endorsed in opposition to Evans-Pritchard and to critics such as MacIntyre. This relativistic position is combined in a somewhat paradoxical way with a critique of 'sociological relativism' for its refusal 'to situate itself *in* definite social relations, ... to take questions of policy, reform, and genuinely available alternatives seriously' (p. 97).
41. Paul Hirst, *On Law and Ideology*, pp. 133–4.
42. For general introductions, from within the discipline of linguistics, to recent work in English on discourse analysis, see Malcolm Coulthard, *An Introduction to Discourse Analysis* (Harlow, Essex: Longman, 1977); Michael Stubbs, *Discourse Analysis: The Sociolinguistic Analysis of Natural Language* (Oxford: Basil Blackwell, 1983); and Gillian Brown and George Yule, *Discourse Analysis* (Cambridge: Cambridge University Press, 1983).
43. A sharp distinction is sometimes drawn between 'discourse analysis' and 'conversation analysis', where the former is regarded as an extension of the theoretical principles of linguistics and the latter is seen as an empirical and inductive approach (see Stephen C. Levinson, *Pragmatics* (Cambridge: Cambridge University Press, 1983), pp. 286 ff.). Here I shall use 'discourse analysis' in a more general way, following authors such as Stubbs (see *Discourse Analysis*, ch. 1); and I shall characterize different approaches in terms of clusters of concepts and assumptions which comprise fairly coherent research programmes.

44. For an example of a text in which the influence of recent French thought is evident if not wholly salutary, see Frank Burton and Pat Carlen, *Official Discourse: On Discourse Analysis, Government Publications, Ideology and the State* (London: Routledge & Kegan Paul, 1979).

45. An account of the aims and results of the original project is given in J. McH. Sinclair and R. M. Coulthard, *Towards an Analysis of Discourse: The English used by Teachers and Pupils* (Oxford: Oxford University Press, 1975). The project gave rise to a great deal of ongoing research, some of which is discussed in *Studies in Discourse Analysis*, ed. Malcolm Coulthard and Martin Montgomery (London: Routledge & Kegan Paul, 1981). For an overview of the literature and its relation to other forms of discourse analysis, see Malcolm Coulthard, *An Introduction to Discourse Analysis*.

46. I shall use abbreviations such as 'Sinclair et al.' when referring to joint publications or to views held by more than one author.

47. J. McH. Sinclair and R. M. Coulthard, *Towards an Analysis of Discourse*, p. 6.

48. Cf. M. A. K. Halliday, 'Categories of the theory of grammar', in *Halliday: System and Function in Language*, ed. Gunther Kress (Oxford: Oxford University Press, 1976), pp. 52–72.

49. J. McH. Sinclair and R. M. Coulthard, *Towards an Analysis of Discourse*, p. 24.

50. Ibid., p. 28.

51. Malcolm Coulthard, *An Introduction to Discourse Analysis*, p. 104.

52. Malcolm Coulthard et al., 'Developing a description of spoken discourse', in *Studies in Discourse Analysis*, p. 14.

53. Cf. David Brazil, 'Intonation', in *Studies in Discourse Analysis*, pp. 39–50; and 'The place of intonation in a discourse model', in *Studies in Discourse Analysis*, pp. 146–57.

54. Malcolm Coulthard et al., 'Developing a description of spoken discourse', p. 29.

55. Ibid., p. 33.

56. Kay Richardson, 'Sentences in discourse', in *Studies in Discourse Analysis*, p. 53.

57. J. McH. Sinclair and R. M. Coulthard, *Towards an Analysis of Discourse*, p. 130. On pp. 130–1 Sinclair and Coulthard speak, not only of 'the domination of the teacher's language', but also of 'a power struggle' in committee language. While the authors do not broach the problem of ideology as such, they observe that 'the teacher's orientation is rarely challenged. The process of education is seen as the pupils accepting the teacher's conceptual world, since he

is the mouthpiece of the culture' (p. 130). The key terms in these passages – 'domination', 'power struggle', 'challenge' and 'acceptance' of a 'conceptual world' – are left unanalysed.

58. Cf. Michelle Stanworth, *Gender and Schooling: A Study of Sexual Divisions in the Classroom* (London: Women's Research and Resources Centre, 1981).
59. Cf. Harold Garfinkel, *Studies in Ethnomethodology* (Englewood Cliffs, New Jersey: Prentice-Hall, 1967).
60. Emanuel A. Schegloff and Harvey Sacks, 'Opening up closings', *Semiotica*, 8 (1973), p. 290.
61. See especially Harvey Sacks, Emanuel A. Schegloff and Gail Jefferson, 'A simplest systematics for the organization of turn-taking for conversation', *Language*, 50 (1974), pp. 696–735. For helpful overviews of the work of Sacks et al., see Stephen C. Levinson, *Pragmatics*, pp. 294–370; and John C. Heritage, 'Recent developments in conversation analysis', *Sociolinguistics Newsletter* (forthcoming).
62. Harvey Sacks, Emanual A. Schegloff and Gail Jefferson, 'A simplest systematics for the organization of turn-taking for conversation', pp. 725–6.
63. Emanuel A. Schegloff and Harvey Sacks, 'Opening up closings', p. 298.
64. See especially Emanuel A. Schegloff, 'Sequencing in conversational openings', in *Directions in Sociolinguistics: The Ethnography of Communication*, ed. John J. Gumperz and Dell Hymes (New York: Holt, Rinehart and Winston, 1972), pp. 349–80; Emanuel A. Schegloff, 'Identification and recognition in telephone conversation openings', in *Everyday Language: Studies in Ethnomethodology*, ed. George Psathas (New York: Irvington Publishers, 1979), pp. 23–78; and Emanuel A. Schegloff and Harvey Sacks, 'Opening up closings', *Semiotica*, 8 (1973), pp. 289–327.
65. Emanuel A. Schegloff, Gail Jefferson and Harvey Sacks, 'The preference for self-correction in the organization of repair in conversation', *Language*, 53 (1977), p. 381.
66. See especially Harvey Sacks, 'Some technical considerations of a dirty joke', in *Studies in the Organization of Conversational Interaction*, ed. Jim Schenkein (New York: Academic Press, 1978), pp. 249–69. See also Harvey Sacks, 'An analysis of the course of a joke's telling in conversation', in *Explorations in the Ethnography of Speaking*, ed. Richard Bauman and Joel Sherzer (Cambridge: Cambridge University Press, 1974), pp. 337–53; Harvey Sacks, 'On the analyzability of stories by children', in *Directions in Sociolinguistics*, pp. 325–45; and Gail Jefferson, 'Sequential aspects of storytelling in conversa-

tion', in *Studies in the Organization of Conversational Interaction*, pp. 219–48.
67. Cf. William Labov, *Sociolinguistic Patterns* (Philadelphia: University of Pennsylvania Press, 1972). For a provocative interpretation of Labov's results, see Pierre Bourdieu, *Ce que parler veut dire: l'économie des échanges linguistiques* (Paris: Fayard, 1982).
68. Harvey Sacks, 'Some technical considerations of a dirty joke', p. 263.
69. The two major publications in which this approach is presented are: Roger Fowler, Bob Hodge, Gunther Kress and Tony Trew, *Language and Control* (London: Routledge & Kegan Paul, 1979); and Gunther Kress and Robert Hodge, *Language as Ideology* (London: Routledge & Kegan Paul, 1979).
70. Cf. M. A. K. Halliday, 'Language structure and language function', in *New Horizons in Linguistics*, ed. John Lyons (Harmondsworth, Middlesex: Penguin, 1970).
71. Roger Fowler and Gunther Kress, 'Critical linguistics', in *Language and Control*, p. 186.
72. Gunther Kress and Robert Hodge, *Language as Ideology*, p. 59.
73. Ibid., p. 22.
74. Ibid., p. 64.
75. Cf. G. R. Kress and A. A. Trew, 'Ideological transformation of discourse: or how the *Sunday Times* got *its* message across', *Sociological Review*, 26 (1978), pp. 755–76.
76. Gunther Kress and Robert Hodge, *Language as Ideology*, p. 127.
77. Cf. Gunther Kress and Roger Fowler, 'Interviews', in *Language and Control*, pp. 63–80.
78. Cf. M. A. K. Halliday, *Language as Social Semiotic: The Social Interpretation of Language and Meaning* (London: Edward Arnold, 1978).
79. Roger Fowler and Gunther Kress, 'Critical linguistics', p. 197.
80. For example, see Robin Lakoff, 'Linguistic theory and the real world', *Language Learning*, 25 (1975), pp. 309–38.
81. Cf. Bob Hodge, Gunther Kress and Gareth Jones, 'The ideology of middle management', in *Language and Control*, especially pp. 88–9.
82. Gunther Kress and Robert Hodge, *Language as Ideology*, p. 16; Bob Hodge, Gunther Kress and Gareth Jones, 'The ideology of middle management', p. 81.
83. See especially Anthony Giddens, *New Rules of Sociological Method: A Positive Critique of Interpretative Sociologies* (London: Hutchinson, 1976); *Central Problems in Social Theory: Action, Structure and Contradiction in Social Analysis* (London: Macmillan, 1979); and

The Constitution of Society: Outline of the Theory of Structuration (Cambridge: Polity Press, 1984).

84. See, for example, the analyses offered by Giddens in *A Contemporary Critique of Historical Materialism, vol. 1: Power, Property and the State* (London: Macmillan, 1981). I have developed these and other criticisms of Giddens's work in my essays, 'Rethinking history: for and against Marx', *Philosophy of the Social Sciences* (forthcoming); and 'The theory of structuration: an assessment of the contribution of Anthony Giddens', in this volume.

85. For a more detailed discussion of this and other issues raised in the third part of this essay, see my *Critical Hermeneutics: A Study in the Thought of Paul Ricoeur and Jürgen Habermas* (Cambridge: Cambridge University Press, 1981).

86. This point is forcefully stated by Anthony Giddens in *A Contemporary Critique of Historical Materialism*, ch. 10.

87. Cf. Max Weber, *Economy and Society: An Outline of Interpretive Sociology*, ed. Guenther Roth and Claus Wittich (Berkeley: University of California Press, 1978), vol. 1, chs. 1 and 3.

88. For an insightful discussion of the ways in which understanding may be 'blocked' or 'limited' see Paul E. Willis, *Learning to Labour: How Working Class Kids Get Working Class Jobs* (Westmead, Farnborough, Hants.: Saxon House, 1977).

89. Claude Lefort, 'Esquisse d'une genèse de l'idéologie dans les sociétés modernes', p. 296.

90. Pierre bourdieu, 'L'économie des échanges linguistiques', *Langue Française* (mai 1977), p. 20.

91. Cornelius Castoriadis, *L'Institution imaginaire de la société* (Paris: Seuil, 1975), p. 469.

92. Menachem Begin, in an interview on American television which is reported in the *Guardian* (22 June 1982). According to Begin, 'you invade a land when you want to conquer it, or annex it, or at least conquer part of it. We don't covet even one inch.' This convenient account may be compared with the OED definition of 'invasion': 'an entrance or incursion with armed force; a hostile inroad'.

93. Editorial comment in the *Sun* (30 June 1982), p. 6.

94. Martin Heidegger, *Being and Time*, tr. John Macquarrie and Edward Robinson (Oxford: Basil Blackwell, 1978), p. 195.

95. See especially Paul Ricoeur, *Hermeneutics and the Human Sciences: Essays on Language, Action and Interpretation*, ed. and tr. John B. Thompson (Cambridge: Cambridge University Press, 1981); see also Ricoeur's critical essays on structuralism in *The Conflict of Interpretations: Essays in Hermeneutics*, ed. Don Ihde (Evanston:

Northwestern University Press, 1974); and his brilliant study of psychoanalysis, *Freud and Philosophy: An Essay on Interpretation*, tr. Denis Savage (New Haven: Yale University Press, 1970).

96. Paul Ricoeur, 'What is a text? Explanation and understanding', in *Hermeneutics and the Human Sciences*, p. 161.

97. I have expressed these and other reservations in my *Critical Hermeneutics*, ch. 5; and in my essay, 'Action, ideology and the text: a reformulation of Ricoeur's theory of interpretation', in this volume.

98. Cf. Erving Goffman, *The Presentation of Self in Everyday Life* (Harmondsworth, Middlesex: Penguin, 1959); and Pierre Bourdieu, *Outline of a Theory of Practice*, tr. Richard Nice (Cambridge: Cambridge University Press, 1977).

99. 'Media studies' is a subject in its own right; among the recent publications of particular interest are the two volumes by the Glasgow University Media Group, *Bad News* (London: Routledge & Kegan Paul, 1976); and *More Bad News* (London: Routledge & Kegan Paul, 1980).

100. The main elements of Greimas's method are presented in A. J. Greimas, *Sémantique structurale: recherche de methode* (Paris: Larousse, 1966); and *Du sens: essais sémiotiques* (Paris: Seuil, 1970). The method has been applied to political discourse by Yves Delahaye in *La Frontière et le texte: pour une Sémiotique des rélations internationales* (Paris: Payot, 1977) and *L'Europe sous les mots: le texte et la déchirure* (Paris: Payot, 1979). See also the monumental study by Jean Pierre Faye, *Langages totalitaires: critique de la raison/l'economie narrative* (Paris: Hermann, 1973).

101. Cf. Roland Barthes, *Mythologies*, tr. Annette Lavers (St. Albans, Herts.: Paladin, 1973).

102. For an example of the analysis of argumentative structure, see Pierre Lascoumes, Ghislaine Moreau-Capdevielle and Georges Vignaux, 'Il y a parmi nous des monstres', *Communications*, 28 (1978), p 127–63. For a more theoretical discussion, see Georges Vignaux, *L'Argumentation* (Genève: Droz, 1977).

103. See especially Paul Ricoeur, *The Rule of Metaphor: Multi-Disciplinary Studies of the Creation of Meaning in Language*, tr. Robert Czerny (London: Routledge & Kegan Paul, 1978), chs. 7 and 8.

104. Cf. Roland Barthes, *Mythologies*, p. 116.

105. This study, conducted by Michel Pêcheux, Paul Henry, Jean-Pierre Poitou and Claudine Haroche, was published under the title 'Un exemple d'ambiguité idéologique: le rapport Mansholt', *Technologies, Idéologies et Pratiques*, vol. 1, no. 2 (avril–juin 1979), pp. 3–83.

For a detailed discussion of this example and of the method employed, see my essay, 'Ideology and the analysis of discourse: a critical introduction to the work of Michel Pêcheux', in this volume.

106. Michel Pêcheux et al., 'Un exemple d'ambiguïté idéologique', p. 69.
107. See especially Jürgen Habermas, *Theory and Practice*, tr. J. Viertel (London: Heinemann, 1974); 'Wahrheitstheorien', in *Wirklichkeit und Reflexion: Walter Schulz zum 60. Geburtstag*, ed. H. Fahrenbach (Pfüllingen: Neske, 1973), pp. 211–65; and *Legitimation Crisis*, tr. Thomas McCarthy (London: Heinemann, 1976).
108. Jürgen Habermas, 'A reply to my critics', in *Habermas: Critical Debates*, ed. John B. Thompson and David Held (London: Macmillan, 1982), p. 222.
109. I have discussed some of these difficulties in my essays, 'Universal pragmatics: Habermas's proposals for the analysis of language and truth', and 'Rationality and social rationalization: an assessment of Habermas's theory of communicative action', both in this volume.
110. Hilary Putnam, *Reason, Truth and History* (Cambridge: Cambridge University Press, 1981), p. 55.
111. See the important essay by Mary Hesse, 'Theory and value in the social sciences', in *Action and Interpretation: Studies in the Philosophy of the Social Sciences*, ed. Christopher Hookway and Philip Pettit (Cambridge: Cambridge University Press, 1978), pp. 1–16.
112. Jürgen Habermas, *Legitimation Crisis*, p. 113.
113. For an examination of these and other issues, see Steven Lukes, 'Of gods and demons: Habermas and practical reason', in *Habermas: Critical Debates*, pp. 134–48; and my *Critical Hermeneutics*, ch. 5.

4 THE THEORY OF STRUCTURATION

1. In addition to the writings of Anthony Giddens (cited in note 3), see Pierre Bourdieu, *Outline of a Theory of Practice*, tr. Richard Nice (Cambridge: Cambridge University Press, 1977) and *Le Sens pratique* (Paris: Minuit, 1980); and Roy Bhaskar, *The Possibility of Naturalism: A Philosophical Critique of the Contemporary Human Sciences* (Brighton, Sussex: Harvester, 1979).
2. This essay develops remarks initially made in my *Critical Hermeneutics: A Study in the Thought of Paul Ricoeur and Jürgen Habermas* (Cambridge: Cambridge University Press, 1981), pp. 143–9 and 173–8; and in my review essay, 'Rethinking history: for and against Marx', *Philosophy of the Social Sciences* (forthcoming). I am grateful

to Michelle Stanworth for her helpful comments on an earlier draft of this essay.

3. The publications of Anthony Giddens most relevant to this essay are as follows: *New Rules of Sociological Method: A Positive Critique of Interpretative Sociologies* (London: Hutchinson, 1976); *Studies in Social and Political Theory* (London: Hutchinson, 1977); *Central Problems in Social Theory: Action, Structure and Contradiction in Social Analysis* (London: Macmillan, 1979); *A Contemporary Critique of Historical Materialism, vol. 1: Power, Property and the State* (London: Macmillan, 1981); *The Constitution of Society: Outline of the Theory of Structuration* (Cambridge: Polity Press, 1984).

4. Anthony Giddens, *New Rules of Sociological Method*, p. 121.

5. Adapted from *Central Problems in Social Theory*, p. 56.

6. Anthony Giddens, *A Contemporary Critique of Historical Materialism*, p. 17.

7. Anthony Giddens, *New Rules of Sociological Method*, p. 127.

8. Ibid.

9. From *New Rules of Sociological Method*, p. 122; modified in accordance with the diagram in *Central Problems in Social Theory*, p. 82.

10. In *New Rules of Sociological Method* Giddens writes: 'the moral constitution of interaction involves the application of norms which draw from a legitimate order. . . . Structures of . . . legitimation [can be analysed] as systems of *moral rules*' (pp. 122–4). In subsequent writings the notion of moral rule is subsumed under the more general category of 'normative sanction' (see *Central Problems in Social Theory*, pp. 270–1, n. 63).

11. Anthony Giddens, *New Rules of Sociological Method*, p. 124.

12. From *Central Problems in Social Theory*, p. 107.

13. Anthony Giddens, *Central Problems in Social Theory*, p. 54.

14. Alluding to philosophers who have urged us to stop talking about *meaning* and to study instead how expressions are *used* in everyday life, Austin complains that '"use" is a hopelessly ambiguous or wide word, just as is the word "meaning", which it has become customary to deride. But "use", its supplanter, is not in much better case' (J. L. Austin, *How to do Things with Words*, ed. J. O. Urmson and Marina Sbisà (Oxford: Oxford University Press, 1976), p. 100).

15. Anthony Giddens, *The Constitution of Society*, p. 20.

16. See my *Critical Hermeneutics*, p. 144.

17. This proposal is developed in my *Critical Hermeneutics*, pp 145 ff.; and in part III of my essay, 'Theories of ideology and methods of discourse analysis: towards a framework for the analysis of ideology', in this volume.

18. From *A Contemporary Critique of Historical Materialism*, p. 54.
19. Anthony Giddens, *A Contemporary Critique of Historical Material-ism*, pp. 54–5.
20. Ibid., p. 55.
21. See Anthony Giddens, *The Class Structure of the Advanced Societies* (London: Hutchinson, 1973), pp. 107–8.
22. Karl Marx, *Capital: A Critical Analysis of Capitalist Production*, vol. 1, tr. Samuel Moore and Edward Aveling (London: Lawrence and Wishart, 1970), p. 320. For Giddens's discussion of Marx's account, see *The Constitution of Society*, pp. 189–90.
23. Anthony Giddens, *The Constitution of Society*, p. 17.
24. I do not wish to deny that people know a great deal about the conditions under which they work. In a remarkable study, illumina-tingly discussed by Giddens in *The Constitution of Society* (pp. 289–304), Willis argues that certain aspects of the behaviour of working-class youths can be interpreted as 'cultural penetrations' of the structural conditions of capitalist production; their evasion of au-thority in the workplace, for example, can be interpreted as a penetra-tion of the fact that labour power is a variable resource in capitalist society (see Paul E. Willis, *Learning to Labour: How Working Class Kids get Working Class Jobs* (Westmead, Farnborough, Hants.: Sax-on House, 1977). But Willis also argues that these penetrations are *partial*, that they bear on only certain aspects of the capitalist system and that even then they are 'repressed, disorganised and prevented from reaching their full potential or a political articulation by deep, basic and disorienting divisions' (p. 145). The interpretation of penetrations as *partial* presupposes an analysis of the structure of capitalist production which is independent of the *limited* knowledge possessed by the youths.
25. See especially Marx's discussion of the 'fetishism of commodities' in *Capital*, vol. 1, pp. 76–87; see also his analysis of the 'mystified form' in which profit is understood by capitalists and economists in *Capit-al*, vol. 3, pp. 25–40.
26. Bourdieu criticizes, rightly in my view, the tendency to project on to the object (or subject) of investigation the very models that one constructs in order to understand (or explain) it. This tendency is exacerbated by the notion of rule, which facilitates the 'sliding from the model of reality to the reality of the model' (Pierre Bourdieu, *Le Sens pratique*, p. 67).
27. Giddens appears to acknowledge this point in his somewhat cryptic discussion of 'circuits of reproduction' in *The Constitution of Society*, pp. 190–2; for 'structural principles' are here situated *outside* of the

'duality of structure' which connects 'structural properties' to the 'reflexive monitoring of action'.

28. Anthony Giddens, *The Constitution of Society*, p. 288.
29. Anthony Giddens, *Central Problems in Social Theory*, p. 70.
30. For other discussions of Giddens's treatment of structural constraint, see Tommy Carlstein, 'The sociology of structuration in time and space: a time-geographic assessment of Giddens's theory', *Svensk Geografisk Årsbok*, 57 (1981); Margaret S. Archer, 'Morphogenesis versus structuration: on combining structure and action', *British Journal of Sociology*, 33 (1982), pp 455–83; and H. F. Dickie-Clark, 'Anthony Giddens's theory of structuration', *Canadian Journal of Political and Social Theory*, 8 (1984), pp. 92–110.
31. Anthony Giddens, *The Constitution of Society*, pp. 176–7.
32. Anthony Giddens, *A Contemporary Critique of Historical Materialism*, p. 63.
33. As Lukes observes, 'the way in which we answer the question "Could the agent have acted otherwise?" depends crucially on how the agent is conceptualised' (Steven Lukes, *Essays in Social Theory* (London: Macmillan, 1977), p. 25).
34. Anthony Giddens, *A Contemporary Critique of Historical Materialism*, p. 63.
35. Bourdieu's suggestive concept of *habitus* represents one attempt to explore the role of durable and differentially distributed wants and needs. See especially his *Outline of a Theory of Practice*, ch. 2.

5 ACTION, IDEOLOGY AND THE TEXT

1. I have offered a thematic exposition of Ricoeur's philosophy in my *Critical Hermeneutics: A Study in the Thought of Paul Ricoeur and Jürgen Habermas* (Cambridge: Cambridge University Press, 1981), ch. 2. For a detailed analysis of Ricoeur's work in the 1950s and 1960s, see Don Ihde, *Hermeneutic Phenomenology: The Philosophy of Paul Ricoeur* (Evanston: Northwestern University Press, 1971). Critical discussions of some aspects of Ricoeur's work may be found in two collections of essays: *Sens et existence: en hommage à Paul Ricoeur*, ed. Gary B. Madison (Paris: Seuil, 1975); and *Studies in the Philosophy of Paul Ricoeur*, ed. Charles E. Reagan (Athens, Ohio: Ohio University Press, 1979).

A full bibliography of Ricoeur's work up to 1972 has been compiled by Dirk F. Vansina and is published in three instalments in the

Revue philosophique de Louvain: 60 (1962), pp. 394–413; 66 (1968), pp. 85–101; and 72 (1974), pp 156–81. An abridged and updated version of this bibliography may be found in *Studies in the Philosophy of Paul Ricoeur*, pp. 180–94.

2. Cf. Ferdinand de Saussure, *Course in General Linguistics*, tr. Wade Baskin (London: Fontana/Collins, 1974); and Louis Hjelmslev, *Prolegomena to a Theory of Language*, tr. Francis J. Whitfield (Madison, Wisconsin: University of Wisconsin Press, 1966).

3. Paul Ricoeur, 'The question of the subject', tr. Kathleen McLaughlin, in Paul Ricoeur, *The Conflict of Interpretations: Essays in Hermeneutics*, ed. Don Ihde (Evanston: Northwestern University Press, 1974), p. 250.

4. Cf. Emile Benveniste, *Problems in General Linguistics*, tr. Mary Elizabeth Meek (Florida: University of Miami Press, 1971); and 'La forme et le sens dans le langage', in *Le Langage, II: actes du XIIIe congrès des sociétés de philosophie de langue française* (Neuchâtel: Editions de la Baconnière, 1967), pp. 29–40.

5. Paul Ricoeur, 'Philosophie et langage', *Revue philosophique de la France et de l'Etranger*, 4 (1978), p. 455 (my translation).

6. Paul Ricoeur, 'Phenomenology and hermeneutics', in Paul Ricoeur, *Hermeneutics and the Human Sciences: Essays on Language, Action and Interpretation*, ed. and tr. John B. Thompson (Cambridge: Cambridge University Press, 1981), p. 107.

7. Paul Ricoeur, 'The hermeneutic function of distanciation', in *Hermeneutics and the Human Sciences*, p. 136.

8. Cf. J. L. Austin, *How to do Things with Words*, ed. J. O. Urmson and Marina Sbisà (Oxford: Oxford University Press, 1976).

9. Paul Ricoeur, 'The hermeneutical function of distanciation', p. 135.

10. Paul Ricoeur, 'The model of the text: meaningful action considered as a text', in *Hermeneutics and the Human Sciences*, p. 201.

11. Paul Ricoeur, *Interpretation Theory: Discourse and the Surplus of Meaning* (Fort Worth, Texas: Texas Christian University Press, 1976), p. 79.

12. Cf. Claude Lévi-Strauss, 'The structural study of myth', in *Structural Anthropology*, tr. Claire Jacobson and Brooke Grundfest Schoepf (Harmondsworth, Middlesex: Penguin, 1968), pp. 206–31. Ricoeur discusses Lévi-Strauss's work in various essays; see especially 'What is a text? Explanation and understanding', in *Hermeneutics and the Human Sciences*, pp. 145–64; and 'Structure and hermeneutics', tr. Kathleen McLaughlin, in *The Conflict of Interpretations*, pp. 27–61.

13. Claude Lévi-Strauss, 'The structural study of myth', p. 216 (translation modified).

14. See, for example, A. J. Greimas, *Sémantique structurale: recherche de méthode* (Paris: Larousse, 1966); and *Du sens: essais sémiotiques* (Paris: Seuil, 1970). For a critical appraisal of Greimas's work, see Paul Ricoeur, 'The narrative function', in *Hermeneutics and the Human Sciences*, pp. 274–96.

15. Paul Ricoeur, *The Rule of Metaphor: Multi-Disciplinary Studies of the Creation of Meaning in Language*, tr. Robert Czerny (London: Routledge & Kegan Paul, 1978), p. 221 (translation modified).

16. Cf. Max Weber, *Economy and Society: An Outline of Interpretive Sociology*, vol. 1, ed. Guenther Roth and Claus Wittich (Berkeley: University of California Press, 1978).

17. Paul Ricoeur, 'The model of the text', p. 205.

18. Ibid., p. 215.

19. Ibid., pp. 219–20.

20. Paul Ricoeur, 'Science and ideology', in *Hermeneutics and the Human Sciences*, p. 225.

21. Cf. Karl Mannheim, *Ideology and Utopia: An Introduction to the Sociology of Knowledge* (London: Routledge & Kegan Paul, 1936).

22. Ricoeur explores the relation between ideology and the social imaginary in two essays: 'L'imagination dans le discours et dans l'action', in *Savoir, faire, espérer: les limites de la raison* (Bruxelles: Publications des Facultés Universitaires Saint-Louis, 1976), pp. 207–28; and 'Ideology and utopia as cultural imagination', *Philosophic Exchange*, 2 (summer 1976), pp. 17–28. For a rich and extended discussion of the concept of the social imaginary, see Cornelius Castoriadis, *L'Institution imaginaire de la société* (Paris: Seuil, 1976).

23. Paul Ricoeur, 'Can there be a scientific concept of ideology?', in *Phenomenology and the Social Sciences: A Dialogue*, ed. Joseph Bien (The Hague: Martinus Nijhoff, 1978), p. 48.

24. Cf. Hans-Georg Gadamer, *Truth and Method* (London: Sheed & Ward, 1975).

25. Paul Ricoeur, 'Phenomenology and hermeneutics', p. 111.

26. See especially Paul Ricoeur, *Freedom and Nature: The Voluntary and the Involuntary*, tr. Erazim V. Kohák (Evanston: Northwestern University Press, 1966); and 'Le discours de l'action', in Paul Ricoeur et al., *La Sémantique de l'action* (Paris: Editions du Centre National de la Recherche Scientifique, 1977), pp. 1–137. For an exposition and criticism of Ricoeur's writings on action, see my *Critical Hermeneutics*, pp. 60–4 and 123–30.

27. See Ricoeur's response to my introduction in *Hermeneutics and the Human Sciences*, pp. 32–40.

28. Cf. Clifford Geertz, *The Interpretation of Cultures* (New York: Basic Books, 1973), ch. 1.
29. Cf. Anthony Kenny, *Action, Emotion and Will* (London: Routledge & Kegan Paul, 1963).
30. These arguments are developed in my *Critical Hermeneutics*, ch. 4.
31. See especially Michael Mann, 'The social cohesion of liberal democracy', *American Sociological Review*, 35 (1970), pp. 423–39; and *Consciousness and Action Among the Western Working Class* (London: Macmillan, 1973). Some of the issues discussed by Mann are developed in interesting ways by Anthony Giddens, *The Class Structure of the Advanced Societies* (London: Hutchinson, 1973); and David Held, *Power and Legitimacy in Contemporary Britain*, prepared for Open University course D209 on the state (Milton Keynes: The Open University Press, 1984).
32. See especially Jacques Derrida, *Of Grammatology*, tr. Gayatri Chakravorty Spivak (Baltimore: The Johns Hopkins University Press, 1974).
33. This point is brought out well by Pierre Bourdieu in numerous studies; see, for example, 'Intellectual field and creative project', tr. Sian France, in *Knowledge and Control: New Directions for the Sociology of Education*, ed. Michael F. D. Young (London: Collier-Macmillan, 1971), pp. 161–88.
34. Cf. H. L. A. Hart, 'The ascription of responsibility and rights', *Proceedings of the Aristotelian Society*, 49 (1948–9), pp. 171–94.
35. See my *Critical Hermeneutics*, pp. 162–3.
36. I have elaborated this approach to the interpretation of action in my *Critical Hermeneutics*, pp. 173 ff.
37. For a more extended discussion of this question, see my essay, 'Theories of ideology and methods of discourse analysis: towards a framework for the analysis of ideology', in this volume.
38. Cf. A. J. Greimas, *Sémantique structurale*, pp. 172–91.
39. Paul Ricoeur, 'The model of the text', p. 213.
40. These epistemological issues are discussed at greater length in my *Critical Hermeneutics*, ch. 6; and in part III of my essay, 'Theories of ideology and methods of discourse analysis: towards a framework for the analysis of ideology', in this volume.
41. I owe this idea to Habermas. For an evaluation of his views, see my essays, 'Universal pragmatics: Habermas's proposals for the analysis of language and truth', and 'Rationality and social rationalization: an assessment of Habermas's theory of communicative action', both in this volume.

6 NARRATIVES OF NATIONAL SOCIALISM

1. See L'Abbé de Mably, *Observations sur l'histoire de France*, vol. 1 (Paris: J. L. J. Brière, 1823); and Augustin Thierry, *Récits des temps mérovingiens, précédés de considerations sur l'histoire de France*, vol. 1 (Paris: Just Tessier, 1840).

2. I wish to thank Jean Pierre Faye for his sympathetic and supportive response to an earlier draft of this essay.

3. It may be helpful to provide the reader with a brief biographical and bibliographical note. Faye's career itself falls into a 'double narration': on the one hand, he has written more than a dozen novels and collections of poetry; on the other hand, he has produced (or contributed to) numerous volumes on the theory of language and on particular forms of political discourse. His interest in 'totalitarian languages' began in the late 1950s, after he had spent several months in the United States studying the Great Depression. During the 1960s he was associated with the journal *Tel Quel*; in 1967 he broke with this journal and became, together with Jacques Roubaud, Mitsou Ronat and others, a founder of the journal *Change*. In 1972 he published *Théorie du récit* (Paris: Hermann) and *Langages totalitaires: Critique de la raison/l'économie narrative* (Paris: Hermann); in 1973 these two books were combined in a single volume of over 900 pages. Also in 1973 a collection of essays and interviews was published under the title of *La Critique du langage et son économie* (Paris: Galilée); the first essay in this collection was translated into English by Elizabeth Kingdom and published in *Economy and Society*, 5 (1976), pp. 52–73. Faye has recently offered a reflection on his own *parcours* in the form of a discussion with Philippe Boyer, published as *Commencement d'une figure en mouvement* (Paris: Stock, 1980).

4. For two recent and helpful overviews of some of this research, see Jeffrey Herf, 'Reactionary modernism: some ideological origins of the primacy of politics in the Third Reich', *Theory and Society*, 10 (1981), pp. 805–32; and Jane Caplan, 'Theories of fascism: Nicos Poulantzas as historian', *History Workshop*, 3 (1977), pp. 83–100.

5. Among the principal proponents of some version of the narrativist thesis are: W. B. Gallie, *Philosophy and the Historical Understanding* (London: Chatto & Windus, 1964); Arthur C. Danto, *Analytical Philosophy of History* (Cambridge: Cambridge University Press, 1965); and Morton White, *Foundations of Historical Knowledge* (New

York: Harper & Row, 1965). For a useful synopsis of the debates, see
W. H. Dray, 'On the nature and role of narrative in historiography',
History and Theory, 10 (1971), pp. 153–71.

6. Cf. Carl G. Hempel, 'The function of general laws in history',
Journal of Philosophy, 39 (1942), pp. 35–48.

7. W. B. Gallie, *Philosophy and the Historical Understanding*, p. 66.

8. Ibid., p. 105.

9. Jean Pierre Faye, *Théorie du récit*, pp. 3–4. This and all subsequent
translations are my own.

10. 'National Movement' (*Nationale Bewegung*) is a term which refers to
the *ensemble* of groups on the far right of the political spectrum in
Germany between 1920 and 1933.

11. Karl Marx, 'Preface to the first German edition', in *Capital: A
Critical Analysis of Capitalist Production*, vol. 1, tr. Samuel Moore
and Edward Aveling (London: Lawrence & Wishart, 1974), p. 19.

12. Cf. V. Y. Propp, *Morphology of the Folktale*, tr. L. Scott (Austin:
University of Texas Press, 1969).

13. Cf. A. J. Greimas, *Sémantique structurale: recherche de méthode*
(Paris: Larousse, 1966); and *Du sens: essais sémiotiques* (Paris: Seuil,
1970).

14. See, for example, Yves Delahaye, *La Frontière et le texte: pour une
sémiotique des relations internationales* (Paris: Payot, 1977); and
L'Europe sous les mots: le texte et la déchirure (Paris: Payot, 1979).

15. Jean Pierre Faye, interviewed by André Gisselbrecht and Louis
Guespin, 'Le nazisme: langages et idéologies', *La Nouvelle critique*,
83 (avril 1975), p. 29.

16. See the discussions of linguistics and methodology in the three collaborative volumes, *Hypothèses sur la linguistique et la poétique*
(Paris: Seghers/Laffont, 1972); *Changement de forme, révolution,
langage* (Paris: Union générale d'éditions, 1975); and *Langue:
Théorie générative étendue* (Paris: Hermann, 1977). I shall return to
the question of method in the third section of the essay.

17. Jean Pierre Faye, *La Critique du langage et son économie*, p. 179.

18. Cf. Hannah Arendt, *The Origins of Totalitarianism* (New York:
Harcourt and Brace, 1951); and Nicos Poulantzas, *Fascism and Dictatorship: The Third International and the Problem of Fascism*, tr. J.
White (London: New Left Books, 1974). Faye criticizes this aspect of
the work of Arendt and Poulantzas in an essay entitled 'Langage
totalitaire et "totalitarisme"', in *La Critique du langage et son économie*, pp. 63–71.

19. Jean Pierre Faye, *Langages totalitaires*, p. 5.

20. See Faye's discussion of Mussolini's speech in *Théorie du récit*,

pp. 52–3. For further analyses of the language of Italian Fascism and its relation to the languages of National Socialism, see Jean Pierre Faye, 'Langages totalitaires: Fascistes et nazis', *Cahiers internationaux de sociologie*, 36 (1964), pp 75–100; and 'Critique des langages et analyse de classe', in *Eléments pour une analyse du fascisme*, vol. 1, séminaire de Maria-A. Macciocchi (Paris: Union générale d'éditions, 1976), pp. 279–339.

21. Adapted from *Langages totalitaires*, p. 268.
22. Jean Pierre Faye, *Langages totalitaires*, p. 34.
23. Hermann Ehrhardt, quoted in *Langages totalitaires*, p. 71.
24. Jean Pierre Faye, *Langages totalitaires*, pp. 198–9.
25. Martin Voelkel, quoted in *Langages totalitaires*, p. 226.
26. Jean Pierre Faye, *Langages totalitaires*, pp. 263–4.
27. Ibid., p. 388.
28. Adapted from *Langages totalitaires*, p. 407.
29. Richard Scheringer, quoted in *Langages totalitaires*, p. 418.
30. Jean Pierre Faye, *La Critique du langage et son économie*, p. 162.
31. Jean Pierre Faye, *Langages totalitaires*, p. 472.
32. Adolf Hitler, Speech of 6 June 1936, quoted in *Langages totalitaires*, p. 397.
33. Adolf Hitler, *Hitlers Zweites Buch*, quoted in *Langages totalitaires*, p. 538.
34. Jean Pierre Faye, *Langages totalitaires*, p. 553.
35. Adolf Hitler, Speech of 13 July 1934, quoted in *Langages totalitaires*, p. 632.
36. Jean Pierre Faye, *Langages totalitaires*, p. 669.
37. See Morris Halle and S. J. Keyser, 'Chaucer and the study of prosody', *College English*, 28 (1966), pp. 187–219; and *English Stress: Its Form, Its Growth, and Its Role in Verse* (New York: Harper & Row, 1971). See also Jacques Roubaud, 'Quelques thèses sur la poétique', *Change*, 6 (septembre 1970); and the various contributions to *Hypothèses sur la linguistique et la poétique* and *Changement de forme, révolution, langage*.
38. Jean Pierre Faye, 'Esquisse d'une voie pour le transformationnisme. Sociologie des langages et sémantique de l'histoire', in *Langue: Théorie générative étendue*, p. 201.
39. See especially Jean Pierre Faye, *La Critique du langage et son économie*, p. 77.
40. In 'Esquisse d'une voie pour le transformationnisme' Faye reformulates some of the analyses of *Langages totalitaires* with the aim of showing how they can be formalized in terms of 'rules of transformation'. Thus the narrative of Fritz Weth in the special issue of *Gewis-*

sen can be seen as a realization, by application of certain grammatical operations, of an underlying structure represented by the proposition of Moeller van den Bruck. What seems missing from this reformulation, however, is a consideration of the specific *position* of Weth – this 'Bolshevik' in the *Juni-Klub*– in virtue of which his narrative was so effective.

41. See Faye's discussion of 'structuralism' and of Chomsky in *Commencement d'une figure en mouvement*, pp. 139 ff. For a more sympathetic appraisal of formalistic methods for the analysis of narrative and myth, see Paul Ricoeur, *Hermeneutics and the Human Sciences: Essays on Language, Action and Interpretation*, ed. and tr. John B. Thompson (Cambridge: Cambridge University Press, 1981), especially chs. 5 and 11.

42. See especially Richard Bessel, 'The rise of the NSDAP and the myth of Nazi propaganda', *Wiener Library Bulletin*, vol. 33, no. 51/52 (1980), pp. 20–9. See also Z. A. B. Zeman, *Nazi Propaganda* (London: Oxford University Press, 1964), ch. 1; Zeman emphasizes the role of mass meetings, emotive speeches and other propaganda techniques used by the Nazis, while maintaining that the various right-wing periodicals had 'little influence and a small readership' (p. 24). For figures on the circulation of some of these periodicals, see Kurt Sontheimer, *Anti-demokratisches Denken in der Weimarer Republik. Die politischen Ideen des deutschen Nationalismus zwischen 1918 und 1933* (München: Nymphenburger, 1962), p. 35.

43. Cf. Tim Mason, 'National Socialism and the working class, 1925– May, 1933', tr. Sarah Lennox, *New German Critique*, 11 (1977), pp. 49–93.

44. This point is stressed by Mason: 'The promise that the NSDAP would sustain the economic, social and political prerogatives of the bourgeoisie with all means at its disposal seems to have been the decisive element in encouraging its growth, especially at the local level' (ibid., p. 76). To raise this point here is not to reiterate the objection, expressed somewhat crudely by Poulantzas in his review of *Langages totalitaires*, that Faye ignores the class struggle and presents history as a matter of words (see Nicos Poulantzas, 'Note à propos du totalitarisme', *Tel Quel*, 53 (1973), pp 74–81). Rather, it is to suggest that Faye's neglect of the social composition of those who supported the NSDAP may have resulted in a misrepresentation of the very features of Nazi language which rendered it most 'acceptable'.

45. Jean Pierre Faye, *Théorie du récit*, p. 98.

46. Cf. Jürgen Habermas, 'A postscript to *Knowledge and Human In-*

terests', tr. Christian Lenhardt, *Philosophy of the Social Sciences*, 3 (1973), pp. 157–89. I have discussed this distinction in *Critical Hermeneutics: A Study in the Thought of Paul Ricoeur and Jürgen Habermas* (Cambridge: Cambridge University Press, 1981), chs. 3 and 5.

47. See my essay, 'Theories of ideology and methods of discourse analysis: towards a framework for the analysis of ideology', in this volume.

7 IDEOLOGY AND THE ANALYSIS OF DISCOURSE

1. The research for this essay was supported by the Wolfson Foundation and the British Academy, to the trustees and fellows of which I express my gratitude. I have benefited from numerous conversations with Michel Pêcheux, Paul Henry and Françoise Gadet; I also wish to thank Susanne Kappeler for her helpful comments on an earlier draft of the essay.

2. A brief biographical and bibliographical note may be helpful at this point. After studying philosophy at the *Ecole normale supérieure*, where Althusser was his *directeur d'études*, Pêcheux obtained a graduate degree in social psychology and entered the *Centre national de la recherche scientifique* (CNRS) in 1966. He directed various research groups in the CNRS until his tragic death in January 1984.

A version of Pêcheux's thesis was published in 1969 under the title of *Analyse automatique du discours* (Paris: Dunod). Two subsequent publications which are particularly important for this essay are: Michel Pêcheux and Catherine Fuchs, 'Mises au point et perspectives à propos de l'analyse automatique du discours', *Langages*, 37 (mars 1975), pp. 7–80; and Michel Pêcheux, *Les Vérités de la Palice: linguistique, sémantique, philosophie* (Paris: Maspero, 1975). An English edition of the latter volume has appeared as *Language, Semantics and Ideology: Stating the Obvious*, tr. Harbans Nagpal (London: Macmillan, 1982); I have quoted from the French volume but have given references to the English edition in square brackets.

The work of Pêcheux and his associates has had considerable impact in France, where it has been extensively discussed in the linguistics literature. Such discussions may be found in: Régine Robin, *Histoire et linguistique* (Paris: Colin, 1973); J.-B. Marcellesi and B. Gardin, *Introduction à la sociolinguistique: la linguistique sociale* (Paris: Larousse, 1974); and Dominique Maingueneau, *Initiation aux méthodes de l'analyse du discours: problèmes et perspectives* (Paris: Hachette, 1976). Other relevant literature is cited in the bibliographies in *Langages*, 37 (mars 1975), p. 125; and *Langages*, 62 (juin 1981), pp. 124–8. For discussions in English of Pêcheux's work, see Roger Wood 'Discourse analysis: the work of Michel Pêcheux', *Ideology and Consciousness*, 2 (1977), pp. 57–79; and Colin Mac-Cabe, 'On discourse', *Economy and Society*, 8 (1979), pp. 279–307.

3. I shall often use the abbreviation 'Pêcheux et al.' when referring to joint publications or to views shared by several authors.

4. Karl Marx and Frederick Engels, *The German Ideology*, ed. C. J. Arthur (London: Lawrence & Wishart, 1970), p. 51.

5. Cf. Ferdinand de Saussure, *Course in General Linguistics*, tr. Wade Baskin (London: Fontana/Collins, 1974), pp. 114–17.

6. Claudine Haroche, Paul Henry and Michel Pêcheux, 'La sémantique et la coupure saussurienne: langue, langage, discours', *Langages*, 24 (1971), p. 97. This and all subsequent translations are my own.

7. See especially Louis Althusser, 'Ideology and ideological state apparatuses (notes towards an investigation)', in his *Lenin and Philosophy and Other Essays*, tr. Ben Brewster (London: New Left Books, 1971), pp. 121–73.

8. The term 'discursive formation' is borrowed from Michel Foucault; see *The Archaeology of Knowledge*, tr. A. M. Sheridan Smith (London: Tavistock, 1972).

9. Michel Pêcheux, *Les Vérités de la Palice*, p. 81 [p. 58].

10. The notion of *préconstruit* is elaborated by Paul Henry in 'Constructions relatives et articulations discursives', *Langages*, 37 (mars 1975), pp. 81–98; and *Le Mauvais outil: langue, sujet et discours* (Paris: Klincksieck, 1977).

11. Michel Pêcheux, *Les Vérités de la Palice*, p. 147 [p. 113].

12. Cf. Jacques Lacan, *The Four Fundamental Concepts of Psychoanalysis* tr. Alan Sheridan (Harmondsworth, Middlesex: Penguin, 1977).

13. Michel Pêcheux, *Les Vérités de la Palice*, pp. 173–4 [pp. 136–7]. Pêcheux's views on the history and philosophy of science are influenced by the work of Bachelard and Canguilhem, which Pêcheux discusses in his essay on 'Idéologie et histoire des sciences', in Michel Fichant and Michel Pêcheux, *Sur l'historie des sciences* (Paris: Maspero, 1969), pp. 13–47.

14. Cf. Zellig S. Harris, 'Discourse analysis', *Language*, 28 (1952), pp. 1–30; French translation in *Langages*, 13 (1969), pp. 8–44.

15. Michel Pêcheux and Catherine Fuchs, 'Mises au point et perspectives', pp. 56–7.

16. The major publications which deal with technical aspects of the AAD are as follows: Michel Pêcheux, *Analyse automatique du discours*; Claudine Haroche and Michel Pêcheux, 'Manuel pour l'utilisation de la méthode de l'analyse automatique du discours (AAD)', *T. A.*

Informations, 13/1 (1972), pp. 13–55; Michel Pêcheux and Catherine Fuchs, 'Mises au point et perspectives'. For a brief discussion in English, see Michel Pêcheux, 'A method of discourse analysis applied to recall of utterances', in *Social Contexts of Messages*, ed. E. A. Carswell and R. Rommetveit (London: Academic Press, 1971), pp. 67–75.

17. The diagram is adapted from Michel Pêcheux and Catherine Fuchs, 'Mises au point et perspectives', p. 24.

18. For a detailed discussion of these categories and the principles behind their formulation, see Michel Pêcheux, *Analyse automatique du discours*, pp. 39–77; certain modifications are proposed in Michel Pêcheux and Catherine Fuchs, 'Mises au point et perspectives', pp. 45–6.

19. Some of these studies are cited in the bibliography of *Langages*, 27 (mars 1975), p. 125. For a more recent investigation which makes use of the AAD, see Jean-Jacques Courtine, 'Quelques problèmes théoriques et méthodologiques en analyse du discours, à propos du discours communiste adressé aux chrétiens', *Langages*, 62 (juin 1981), pp. 9–128.

20. This study, conducted by Michel Pêcheux, Paul Henry, Jean-Pierre Poitou and Claudine Haroche, was published under the title of 'Un exemple d'ambiguité idéologique: le rapport Mansholt', *Technologies, idéologies et pratiques*, vol. 1, no. 2 (avril-juin 1979), pp. 1–83. A much reduced version appeared in English as 'Are the masses an inanimate object?', in *Linguistic Variation*, ed. D. Sankoff (New York: Academic Press, 1978), pp. 251–66.

21. Michel Pêcheux et al., 'Un exemple d'ambiguité idéologique', p. 72.

22. Ibid., p. 81.

23. *La Langue introuvable* is the title of the most recent book by Françoise Gadet and Michel Pêcheux (Paris: Maspero, 1981). One of the central theses of this book is that linguistics, in so far as it aims to produce a 'universal semantics' which would be a sort of 'common language' for all humankind, effectively eliminates the historical and political dimension of language. Such a language would be emptied of the *memory* which haunts living languages, staining them with the struggles and insurrections of the past. While this thesis is certainly interesting, I shall not discuss it or other details from *La Langue introuvable*, since here I am primarily concerned with what the authors call 'discourse'.

24. For a discussion of some of the methods of discourse analysis which are practised in the English-speaking world, see my essay, 'Theories of ideology and methods of discourse analysis: towards a framework for the analysis of ideology', in this volume.

25. This formulation is based on an unpublished paper by Françoise Gadet entitled 'Le discursif est-il au bord de la langue?' See also *La Langue introuvable*, pp. 162–73.

26. Cf. Robin Lakoff, 'Linguistic theory and the real world', *Language Learning*, 25 (1975), pp. 209–38.

27. Cf. William Labov, *Sociolinguistic Patterns* (Philadelphia: University of Pennsylvania Press, 1972), especially ch. 8.

28. See, for example, Françoise Gadet, 'La sociolinguistique n'existe pas: je l'ai rencontrée', *Dialectiques*, 20 (1977), pp. 99–118.

29. It may be objected that, in the writings of Pêcheux et al., *langue* is regarded as a *relatively* autonomous system which is open to the 'return-effect' of discursive processes (for example, see *Les Vérités de la Palice*, p. 163 [p. 126]). However, to call this autonomy 'relative' is merely to identify the problem and not to solve it.

30. The expression '*la langue introuvable*' is ambiguous, denoting both the project of constructing an ideal language which is outside of history, and the specific reality of *langue* which, according to Gadet and Pêcheux, has been missed or misconstrued by most linguists. The problem, at least in part, is to know by virtue of what features the second sense escapes from the first, by virtue of what features, in other words, this ambiguity is not fatal.

31. Michel Pêcheux, *Les Vérités de la Palice*, pp. 241–2 [p. 188].

32. It seems to me that in their practical studies Pêcheux et al. constantly engage in a process of interpretation which impugns their limited conception of *sens*. Thus, in the study of the Mansholt Report, we are told that the presence of terms like 'the government' and 'the state' in discourse R, as contrasted with expressions like 'it is necessary' and 'one must' in discourse L, indicates 'the *domination* of R over L, in so far as the same signifier ("radical reforms") *encompasses two referents which tend to be antagonistic*: on the one hand a bourgeois solution which "manages the crisis", on the other hand the possible beginnings of a revolutionary transformation' (Michel Pêcheux et al., 'Un exemple d'ambiguité idéologique', p. 69).

33. The contours of a comprehensive interpretative theory are sketched by Paul Ricoeur in *Hermeneutics and the Human Sciences: Essays on Language, Action and Interpretation*, ed. and tr. John B. Thompson (Cambridge: Cambridge University Press, 1981). I have tried to draw out some of the implications of Ricoeur's work for the social sciences in my book, *Critical Hermeneutics: A Study in the Thought of Paul Ricoeur and Jürgen Habermas* (Cambridge: Cambridge University Press, 1981), and in my essay, 'Action, ideology and the text: a reformulation of Ricoeur's theory of interpretation', in this volume.

34. For a pertinent criticism of Pêcheux's unhappy *mélange* of Lacan and

Althusser, see Jean-Louis Houdebine's review of *Les Vérités de la Palice* in *Tel Quel*, 67 (automne 1976), pp. 87–97.

35. Françoise Gadet and Michel Pêcheux, *La Langue introuvable*, p. 232.

36. This problem is broached in the final chapter of *Les Vérités de la Palice*. In order to allow for the subjective appropriation of knowledge in proletarian politics, Pêcheux introduces the notion of *désidentification*, which is a form of interpellation in which ideology functions, as it were, 'in reverse'. This paradoxical notion is subsequently denounced in the third appendix to the English edition (see 'The French political winter: beginning of a rectification', in *Language, Semantics and Ideology*, pp. 211–20). Yet this denunciation leaves the original problem unsolved.

37. Michel Pêcheux, 'Idéologie et discursivité', unpublished paper presented at a conference in London (29 May 1981), p. 5.

38. I owe this approach to Jürgen Habermas, whose views I have examined in my book, *Critical Hermeneutics*, and in my essays, 'Universal pragmatics: Habermas's proposals for the analysis of language and truth', and 'Rationality and social rationalization: an assessment of Habermas's theory of communicative action', both in this volume.

8 UNIVERSAL PRAGMATICS

1. The major essays of Habermas which discuss various aspects of universal pragmatics are, in order of publication, as follows: 'Toward a theory of communicative competence', in *Recent Sociology*, no. 2, ed. Hans Peter Dreitzel (New York: Macmillan, 1970), pp. 114–48; 'Vorbereitende Bemerkungen zu einer Theorie der kommunikativen Kompetenz', in Jürgen Habermas and Niklas Luhmann, *Theorie der Gesellschaft oder Sozialtechnologie – Was leistet die Systemforschung?* (Frankfurt: Suhrkamp, 1971), pp. 101–41; 'Wahrheitstheorien', in *Wirklichkeit und Reflexion: Walter Schulz zum 60. Geburtstag*, ed. Helmut Fahrenbach (Pfullingen: Neske, 1973), pp. 211–65; 'Was heisst Universalpragmatik?', in *Sprachpragmatik und Philosophie*, ed. Karl-Otto Apel (Frankfurt: Suhrkamp, 1976), pp. 174–272; 'Some distinctions in universal pragmatics', *Theory and Society*, 3 (1976), pp. 155–67. A slightly revised version of 'Was heisst Universalpragmatik?' has appeared in English as 'What is universal pragmatics?', in Jürgen Habermas, *Communication and the Evolution of Society*, tr. Thomas McCarthy (London: Heinemann, 1979), pp. 1–68. It should be noted that, although I shall be concerned only with Habermas's work, he is not the only author who has sought to develop the programme of universal pragmatics. Other contributions, such as

those of Karl-Otto Apel, may be found in *Sprachpragmatik und Philosophie*.

2. Jürgen Habermas, 'What is universal pragmatics?', p. 5 (translation modified).

3. For an unsympathetic and largely uncomprehending critique, see Y. Bar-Hillel, 'On Habermas' hermeneutic philosophy of language', *Synthese*, 26 (1973), pp. 1–12. Critical discussions which are far more perceptive, and to which I am greatly indebted, may be found in Thomas McCarthy, 'A theory of communicative competence', *Philosophy of the Social Sciences*, 3 (1973), pp. 135–56; and Anthony Giddens, 'Habermas's critique of hermeneutics', in his *Studies in Social and Political Theory* (London: Hutchinson, 1977), pp. 135–64.

4. Jürgen Habermas, *Theory and Practice*, tr. J. Viertel (London: Heinemann, 1974), p. 169.

5. Jürgen Habermas, *Zur Logik der Sozialwissenschaften* (Frankfurt: Suhrkamp, 1970), p. 287. This and all subsequent quotations from German texts are my own translation.

6. Jürgen Habermas, *Theory and Practice*, p. 9.

7. These and similar questions are confronted by Habermas in the 1971 'Introduction' to *Theory and Practice*.

8. Jürgen Habermas, *Knowledge and Human Interests*, tr. J. J. Shapiro (London: Heinemann, 1972), p. 314.

9. Cf. Jürgen Habermas, 'A postscript to *Knowledge and Human Interests*', tr. C. Lenhardt, *Philosophy of the Social Sciences*, 3 (1973), pp. 157–89. Many of the revisions which Habermas makes in 'A postscript' can also be found in the 1971 'Introduction' to *Theory and Practice*.

10. Jürgen Habermas, 'A postscript', p. 184.

11. Jürgen Habermas, 'Summation and response', tr. M. Matesich, *Continuum*, 8 (1970), pp. 128–9.

12. Jürgen Habermas, *Theory and Practice*, p. 18.

13. Ibid., p. 20.

14. Jürgen Habermas, 'Toward a theory of communicative competence', p. 131.

15. Ibid., p. 138.

16. Jürgen Habermas, 'A postscript', p. 160.

17. Jürgen Habermas, 'What is universal pragmatics?', p. 8.

18. For an illustration and explication of the relations between Habermas's many categories of action, see *Communication and the Evolution of Society*, pp. 208–10 (see also pp. 40–1).

19. Jürgen Habermas, 'Vorbereitende Bemerkungen', p. 105.

20. Jürgen Habermas, 'What is universal pragmatics?', p. 63 (italics removed).

21. Jürgen Habermas, 'Wahrheitstheorien', p. 220.
22. Jürgen Habermas, *Theory and Practice*, p. 18.
23. Jürgen Habermas, 'Vorbereitende Bemerkungen', p. 110.
24. The following categorization is a modification and simplification of Habermas's account, which varies somewhat from one publication to the next.
25. Jürgen Habermas, 'Toward a theory of communicative competence', p. 142.
26. Ibid., p. 148.
27. The exception is the claim of intelligibility, which must be fulfilled by every speech-act in the same way. See 'What is universal pragmatics?', p. 57.
28. Jürgen Habermas, 'What is universal pragmatics?', p. 66.
29. Jürgen Habermas, 'What is universal pragmatics?', pp. 58, 68.
30. Jürgen Habermas, 'Vorbereitende Bemerkungen', p. 137.
31. Ibid, p. 140.
32. Jürgen Habermas, 'Wahrheitstheorien', p. 219.
33. Jürgen Habermas, 'Vorbereitende Bemerkungen', p. 120.
34. Jürgen Habermas, 'What is universal pragmatics?', p. 40.
35. The publications in which the performative hypothesis is expounded and defended include the following: J. R. Ross, 'On declarative sentences', in *Readings in English Transformational Grammar*, ed. R. A. Jacobs and P. S. Rosenbaum (Waltham, Mass.: Ginn, 1970), pp. 222–72; J. D. McCawley, 'The role of semantics in a grammar', in *Universals of Language*, ed. Emmon Bach and R. T. Harms (New York: Holt, Rinehart & Winston, 1968), pp. 125–70; J. M. Sadock, *Toward a Linguistic Theory of Speech Acts* (New York: Academic Press, 1974). For a summary of the critical literature, see Gerald Gazdar, *Pragmatics: Implicature, Presupposition, and Logical Form* (New York: Academic Press, 1979), ch. 2. The performative hypothesis is also criticized by John Searle in his review of *Toward a Linguistic Theory of Speech Acts* (See *Language*, 52 (1976), pp. 966–71). Searle dismisses the hypothesis as 'a breath-taking and prima facie implausible claim', a dismissal which places considerable strain on Habermas's interpretation of the principle of expressibility.
36. For discussions of the complexities involved in analysing indirect speech-acts, see some of the essays in *Syntax and Semantics, Volume 3: Speech Acts*, ed. Peter Cole and Jerry L. Morgen (New York: Academic Press, 1975); and *Proceedings of the Texas Conference on Performatives, Presuppositions, and Implicatures*, ed. Andy Rogers, Bob Wall and John P. Murphy (Arlington, Virginia: Center for Applied Linguistics, 1977).
37. Cf. *Universals of Language*, ed. Joseph H. Greenberg (Cambridge,

Mass.: M. I. T. Press, 1963). Critical discussions of this volume may be found in Hans-Heinrich Lieb, 'Universals of language: quandaries and prospects', *Foundations of Language*, 12 (1975), pp. 471–511; and Hansjakob Seiler, 'Universals of language', in *Proceedings of the Eleventh International Congress of Linguists*, vol. 1, ed. Luigi Heilmann (Bologna: Società editrice il Mulino, 1974), pp. 75–99.

38. A summary of some of the evidence is provided by T. G. R. Bower, 'The visual world of infants', *Scientific American*, 215 (December 1966), pp. 80–92. See also Michael A. K. Halliday, 'Early language learning: a sociolinguistic approach', in *Language and Man: Anthropological Issues*, ed. William G. McCormack and Stephen A. Wurm (The Hague: Mouton, 1976), pp. 97–124.

39. Cf. 'Some distinctions in universal pragmatics', pp. 365–7.

40. See especially Paul Ricoeur, 'Creativity in language', trans. D. Pellauer, *Philosophy Today*, 17 (1973), pp. 97–111. For a discussion of Ricoeur's views on language and other issues, see my *Critical Hermeneutics: A Study in the Thought of Paul Ricoeur and Jürgen Habermas* (Cambridge: Cambridge University Press, 1981), and my essay, 'Action, ideology and the text: a reformulation of Ricoeur's theory of interpretation', in this volume.

41. Habermas emphasizes that the application of the thesis of symmetry to representative and regulative speech-acts presupposes a reference to the organization of action contexts, and hence 'the emancipation of discourse from the constraints of action is possible only in the context of pure communicative action' ('Wahrheitstheorien', pp. 255–6). This does not mitigate the problem because communicative action is defined so as to exclude considerations of interest and strategy, of power and persuasion; thus the latter are not thematized and suspended by the model of pure communicative action, but are simply ignored.

42. For a pertinent discussion, see Anthony Giddens, 'Habermas's critique of hermeneutics', especially p. 152.

43. Jürgen Habermas, 'Wahrheitstheorien', p. 240; the allusions is to Dewey. Weaker versions of Habermas's thesis are suggested by Thomas McCarthy in 'A theory of communicative competence', pp. 149–50. However, if my interpretation of Habermas is correct, then such attenuations do not seem to obviate the present difficulty, which is that the truth of a statement is not settled when its assertion has been justified, irrespective of whether that justification is characterized as the 'meaning', 'condition' or 'criterion' of truth. It may be possible to overcome this difficulty by distinguishing, more sharply than Habermas does, between the justified assertion of a statement and the justified assertion that a statement is true.

44. Similar arguments against a straightforward justificatory analysis of truth are offered by Michael Dummett, 'What is a theory of meaning? (II)', in *Truth and Meaning: Essays in Semantics*, ed. Gareth Evans and John McDowell (Oxford: Clarendon Press, 1976), pp. 67–137; and Hilary Putnam, 'Reference and understanding', in his *Meaning and the Moral Sciences* (London: Routledge & Kegan Paul, 1978), pp. 97–119.

45. Jürgen Habermas, 'A postscript', p. 170.

46. Ibid., p. 169.

47. Cf. 'Toward a theory of communicative competence', pp. 144–6.

48. Paul Ricoeur, *Hermeneutics and the Human Sciences: Essays on Language, Action and Interpretation*, ed. and tr. John B. Thompson (Cambridge: Cambridge University Press, 1981), p. 97. For a similar reservation expressed in more Anglo-Saxon terms, see Steven Lukes, 'The critical theory trip', *Political Studies*, 25 (1977), pp. 408–12.

49. Cf. Jürgen Habermas, *Legitimation Crisis*, tr. Thomas McCarthy (London: Heinemann, 1976), pp. 111–17.

50. See my *Critical Hermeneutics* and my essay, 'Theories of ideology and methods of discourse analysis: towards a framework for the analysis of ideology', in this volume.

51. Cf. Mary Hesse, 'Theory and value in the social sciences', in *Action and Interpretation: Studies in the Philosophy of the Social Sciences*, ed. Christopher Hookway and Philip Pettit (Cambridge: Cambridge University Press, 1978), pp. 1–16.

9 RATIONALITY AND SOCIAL RATIONALIZATION

1. See Jürgen Habermas, *Theorie des kommunikativen Handelns*, Band I: *Handlungsrationalität und gesellschaftliche Rationalisierung*; Band II: *Zur Kritik der funktionalistischen Vernunft* (Frankfurt: Suhrkamp, 1981).

2. I am grateful to Thomas McCarthy for his willingness to provide translations of several sections in Volume One of *Theorie des kommunikativen Handelns*. In this essay all quotations are my own translation.

3. Jürgen Habermas, *Theorie des kommunikativen Handelns*, Band I, p. 378.

4. Ibid., p. 406.

5. From *Theorie des kommunikativen Handelns*, Band I, p. 384.

6. Jürgen Habermas, *Theorie des kommunikativen Handelns*, Band I, p. 387.

7. Ibid., p. 28.

8. Ibid., pp. 39–40.
9. Adapted from *Theorie des kommunikativen Handelns*, Band I, p. 45. Habermas mentions a fifth form of argumentation, 'explicative discourse', in which the comprehensibility or well-formedness of symbolic expressions *as such* is contested (see ibid., pp. 43–4).
10. Jürgen Habermas, *Theorie des kommunikativen Handelns*, Band I, p. 102.
11. Cf. Max Weber, *The Protestant Ethic and the Spirit of Capitalism*, tr. Talcott Parsons (London: George Allen & Unwin, 1930).
12. Jürgen Habermas, *Theorie des kommunikativen Handelns*, Band I, p. 306.
13. See especially Georg Lukács, *History and Class Consciousness: Studies in Marxist Dialectics*, tr. Rodney Livingstone (London: Merlin, 1971); Max Horkheimer and Theodor W. Adorno, *Dialectic of Enlightenment*, tr. John Cumming (New York: Seabury, 1972); and Herbert Marcuse, *One Dimensional Man* (London: Routledge & Kegan Paul, 1964).
14. Jürgen Habermas, *Theorie des kommunikativen Handelns*, Band I, p. 533.
15. Ibid., Band II, p. 228.
16. Ibid., p. 230.
17. Ibid., Band I, pp. 104–5.
18. Ibid., Band II, p. 452.
19. Adapted from *Theorie des kommunikativen Handelns*, Band II, p. 473.
20. Jürgen Habermas, *Theorie des kommunikativen Handelns*, Band II, p. 513.
21. Ibid., Band I, p. 388.
22. Cf. J. L. Austin, *How to do Things with Words*, ed. J. O. Urmson and Marina Sbisà (Oxford: Oxford University Press, 1976).
23. Jürgen Habermas, *Theorie des kommunikativen Handelns*, Band I, p. 396.
24. I have examined some of the difficulties in Habermas's notion of an ideal speech situation and his theory of truth in my *Critical Hermeneutics: A Study in the Thought of Paul Ricoeur and Jürgen Habermas* (Cambridge: Cambridge University Press, 1981), and in my essay, 'Universal pragmatics: Habermas's proposals for the analysis of language and truth', in this volume.
25. Albrecht Wellmer, quoted in *Theorie des kommunikativen Handelns*, Band I, p. 110.
26. For an illuminating analysis of some of the difficulties involved in trying to apply Habermas's account to practical issues, see Steven Lukes, 'Of gods and demons: Habermas and practical reason', in

Habermas: Critical Debates, ed. John B. Thompson and David Held (London: Macmillan, 1982), pp. 134–48.

27. Jürgen Habermas, *Theorie des kommunikativen Handelns*, Band II, p. 218.
28. Ibid., p. 507.
29. Ibid., p. 522.
30. That Habermas did not give sufficient attention to the fragmentation of consciousness in his early work is well argued by David Held in 'Crisis tendencies, legitimation and the state', in *Habermas: Critical Debates*, pp. 181–95.
31. See my essay, 'Theories of ideology and methods of discourse analysis: towards a framework for the analysis of ideology', in this volume.
32. Jürgen Habermas, *Theorie des kommunikativen Handelns*, Band I, p. 10.
33. See Anthony Giddens, *A Contemporary Critique of Historical Materialism, vol. 1: Power, Property and the State* (London: Macmillan, 1981).

Index